EDMUND HUSSERL'S
PHENOMENOLOGY

**Purdue University Press Series
in the History of Philosophy**

General Editors
Arion Kelkel
Joseph J. Kockelmans
Adriaan Peperzak
Calvin O. Schrag
Thomas Seebohm

EDMUND HUSSERL'S PHENOMENOLOGY

Joseph J. Kockelmans

Purdue University Press
West Lafayette, Indiana

98   97   96   95   5   4   3   2

The paper used in this book meets the minimum requirements of
American National Standard for Information Sciences—Permanence of
Paper Printed Library Materials, ANSI Z39.48-1984.

Printed in the United States of America

Interior design by Anita Noble

Library of Congress Cataloging-in-Publication Data
Kockelmans, Joseph J., 1923–
        Edmund Husserl's phenomenology / Joseph J. Kockelmans.
            p.   cm. — (Purdue University Press series in the history of
    philosophy)
        Includes the original and translation of Der Encyclopedia
    Britannica Artikel from Edmund Husserl's Phänomenologische
    Psychologie, originally published, in translation, in the
    Encyclopaedia Britannica in 1928.
        Includes bibliographical references.
        ISBN 1-55753-049-1 (cloth : alk. paper) — ISBN 1-55753-050-5
    (pbk. : alk. paper)
        1. Phenomenology. 2. Husserl, Edmund, 1859–1938.
    Encyclopedia Britannica Artikel. I. Husserl, Edmund, 1859–1938.
    Encyclopedia Britannica Artikel. English & German. 1994. II. Title.
    III. Series.
    B3279.H94K594 1994
    193—dc20   93-46224
                                                            CIP

CONTENTS

In this book I shall present a detailed account of what Husserl understood phenomenology to be, in what philosophical tradition it is to be understood, what phenomenology tries to accomplish, and what methods it uses in doing so. In harmony with the editors' goals for the volumes of this series in the history of philosophy, the book consists of text and commentary.

The text by Husserl chosen as the basis for the commentary is the fourth and final version of his article on phenomenology written for the *Encyclopaedia Britannica* in 1928. Husserl had been invited by the editors of the *Encyclopaedia* to write an essay on phenomenology for the fourteenth edition of this important work. He was very pleased by the invitation and worked hard to produce an essay that would effectively communicate to the readers of the *Encyclopaedia* what his new phenomenology was about. At first he had hoped that this article could have been written in close cooperation with Heidegger. Yet when it appeared that Heidegger's idea of phenomenology was substantially different from that originally developed by himself, Husserl decided to write the article alone.

During his long career, Husserl often made an effort to explain what he thought phenomenology ought to be. Thus I could have selected other essays to comment on. The reason for choosing the *Encyclopaedia* article as the basis for my commentary is that this essay was written at the high point of Husserl's career, when his conception of phenomenology had already been fully developed. Furthermore, this text was written with the greatest care; Husserl prepared four different versions, of which the one selected here is the last. It is true that shortly after the completion of this text, Husserl prepared a slightly different and a more elaborate text, which was published posthumously under the title "Amsterdam Lectures."

Although this latter text in some sense is superior to the one used here, I have nonetheless decided to use the final version of the *Encyclopaedia* article, since the "Amsterdam Lectures" are incomplete; the third part, on transcendental phenomenology, is missing there altogether. I am convinced that of the various texts that could have been selected as the basis for my commentary, the final version of the *Encyclopaedia* article is the best. Yet I have carefully compared the *Encyclopaedia* version with the text of the three earlier versions and that of the "Amsterdam Lectures"; in some instances, I have complemented the former with the help of the latter.

The reader will see that in this particular article, Husserl appears to be talking about phenomenological psychology more than about transcendental phenomenology proper. One might think that a description of the meaning and function of phenomenology from that particular point of view would be misleading. While Husserl has explained his position in regard to philosophy in ways other than the one selected here—such as the "Cartesian approach," or the approach from the perspective of the "life-world"—it should be noted that in all approaches to phenomenology, Husserl always discussed the intimate relationship between descriptive and transcendental phenomenology, that is, between phenomenological psychology and transcendental phenomenology. This is true for the first volume of *Ideas* but also for *Formal and Transcendental Logic, Cartesian Meditations,* and *Crisis.*[1] Particularly in the period between 1916 and 1938, Husserl was convinced that an introduction to transcendental phenomenology should be presented from the perspective of phenomenological psychology. As we shall see in the text of 1928, which will be used here, Husserl gives several reasons for why this is so.

Following Husserl himself, I, too, have divided the text into sixteen sections; in each case, I have placed a brief synopsis of the text between text and commentary to clarify Husserl's text. In these synopses, I have often used paraphrases of passages of the "Amsterdam Lectures." Husserl's essay was meant to become an entry in an encyclopedia, which had set strict limits for the length of each entry. Husserl thus attempted to produce a text that would give a good idea of the whole of phenomenology in as short an essay as possible. This explains why Husserl's text is dense and often difficult to read. In my synopses, I have sometimes proposed a somewhat simpler paraphrase of the text to clarify how some cryptic passages are to be understood. The synopses are also helpful in locating the issues to be commented on in each case.

In referring to works by Husserl, I have decided not to follow the custom of citing the volumes of the *Husserliana* edition in view of the fact that the reader may not immediately know what work by Husserl is meant. Thus instead of using *Hu,* III, 249, I use *Ideas,* 1:249, to make clear that the reference is to the first volume of *Ideas* and that the passage is to be found in the translation on page 249. The page numbers of the German editions listed in the Bibliography are added in square brackets.

The present book consists of two major parts, a general introduction on the one hand, and text and commentary on the other. In view of the fact that Husserl in his text does not refer to some aspects of his philosophy that in my view are important for a proper understanding of his thought, I have added a few sections in which some of these issues are discussed. These sections are placed where they appeared to be most appropriate from the perspective of my commentary.

As for the nature of my commentaries, I have made an effort to use Husserl himself as his own interpreter, thus following for Husserl the advice Friedrich Adolph Trendelenburg once gave for the interpretation of Aristotle.[2] I thus have tried to clarify the claims made in the *Encyclopaedia* article with paraphrases of, and commentaries on, other texts by Husserl where the same issues often are treated in a more comprehensive and systematic manner. I have made use in these cases particularly of the following major works: *The Idea of Phenomenology,* the first volume of *Ideas, Erste Philosophie, Phenomenological Psychology, Formal and Transcendental Logic, Cartesian Meditations, Experience and Judgment,* and *Crisis.* Obviously, in preparing my own commentary, I have also used the works of the leading commentators whose works have been quoted regularly.

My commentaries not only contain commentaries in the common sense of the term but also brief essays on specific topics hinted at by Husserl. It seemed to me that this procedure is the best way to make certain that the reader gradually will become acquainted with all the essential components of Husserl's phenomenology, taken both as a method and as a transcendental type of philosophy. Although my commentaries are meant mainly to explain important thematic issues of Husserl's phenomenology, I nonetheless have sometimes added some historical information pertaining to the genesis and development of Husserl's phenomenology between 1891 and 1938.

Finally it should be noted that several important aspects of Husserl's philosophy will be mentioned only in passing. This is true mainly for his work in mathematics and logic, his detailed analysis of passive synthesis, his analyses of inner time and immanent temporality, and his analyses on thing and space, just to mention a few.

The limitations placed on this book by the text selected as a basis for the commentary made hard choices often unavoidable. A second volume on Husserl's philosophy is being projected in which some of the more important topics mentioned will be discussed.

I have added a select bibliography in which I have listed only the publications cited in the commentary and some publications that may be helpful to the reader for further study.

I NOTES

1. To avoid needless duplication, I shall not provide bibliographic information in the footnotes as far as Husserl's own texts are concerned. This information can be found in the bibliography at the end of this book.

2. Friedrich Adolph Trendelenburg, *Aristoteles, De Anima Libri Tres* (Jena: Walzius, 1833), xx, 103. See also *Geschichte der Kategorienlehre* (Leipzig: Bethge, 1876), 2.

ACKNOWLEDGMENTS

The German text of Husserl's essay on phenomenology written for the fourteenth edition of the *Encyclopaedia Britannica* is taken from Edmund Husserl, *Phänomenologische Psychologie,* edited by Walter Biemel, Husserliana, vol. 9 (The Hague: Nijhoff, 1962), 277–301. Copyright © 1962 by Kluwer Academic Publishers. Reprinted by permission of Kluwer Academic Publishers. No part of the material protected by this copyright notice may be reproduced or utilized in any form or by any means, electronic or mechanical, including photocopying, recording or by any information storage and retrieval system, without written permission from the copyright owner.

The English translation of Husserl's article, by Richard E. Palmer, was taken from Peter McCormick and Frederick Elliston, eds., *Husserl: Shorter Works* (Notre Dame, Ind.: University of Notre Dame Press, 1981), 21–35. This text is a revised version of an earlier translation by Richard E. Palmer, which appeared in the *Journal of the British Society for Phenomenology* 2 (1971): 77–90. Copyright © 1981 by the University of Notre Dame Press. Reprinted by permission of the publisher and the editor of the *Journal of the British Society for Phenomenology.*

I am particularly grateful to the editors of Kluwer Academic Publishers, the *Journal of the British Society for Phenomenology,* and the University of Notre Dame Press for granting me permission to include these texts.

Several sections of this book have been taken from parts of my earlier publications on Husserl's phenomenology. In most instances, the text has been changed to provide new ideas or to correct errors; in other cases, minor and sometimes merely stylistic changes have been made. Yet generally speaking, the basic ideas presented in these sections have been maintained as they were formulated in my

earlier publications. I am very grateful to the publishers and editors
of these sources for allowing me to reprint this material.

Edmund Husserl's Phenomenological Psychology. Copyright ©
1967 by Duquesne University Press. Reprinted by permission of the
publisher.

A First Introduction to Husserl's Phenomenology. Copyright ©
1967 by Duquesne University Press. Reprinted by permission of the
publisher.

"The Founders of Phenomenology and Personalism," in *Reading Philosophy for the XXIst Century,* edited by George F. McLean.
Copyright © 1989 by the Council for Research in Values and Philosophy and the University Press of America, Inc. Reprinted by permission of the Council for Research in Values and Philosophy and the
publisher.

"Husserl's Original View on Phenomenological Psychology," in
my *Phenomenology: The Philosophy of Edmund Husserl and Its Interpretation.* Copyright © 1967 by Doubleday, a division of Bantam,
Doubleday, Dell Publishing Group, Inc. Reprinted by permission of
the publisher.

"On the Meaning and Function of Experience in Husserl's Phenomenology," in *Der Idealismus und seine Gegenwart,* edited by Ute
Guzzoni et al. Copyright © 1973 by Felix Meiner Verlag. Reprinted
by permission of the publisher.

"On the Meaning of the Transcendental Dimension of Philosophy," in *Perspektiven transzendentaler Reflexion,* edited by Gisela
Müller and Thomas Seebohm. Copyright © 1989 Bouvier Verlag
GmbH. Reprinted by permission of the publisher.

"Phenomenologico-Psychological and Transcendental Reductions in Husserl's *Crisis,*" *Analecta Husserliana* 2 (1972): 78–89. Reprinted by permission of Kluwer Academic Publishers.

"World-Constitution: Reflections on Husserl's Transcendental
Idealism," *Analecta Husserliana* 1 (1971): 11–35. Reprinted by permission of Kluwer Academic Publishers.

It has been a source of great confidence and comfort to know
that the manuscript of this book was in the caring and capable
hands of Dr. Margaret Hunt and her staff. Her contribution was invaluable and impeccable. Fortunate the authors whose forthcoming
books for this series come into Dr. Hunt's hands and under her editorial guidance. I cannot thank her enough for all that she did.

LIST OF ABBREVIATIONS

References to Husserl's publications are all to the English translations of his works as indicated in this list. However, where no English translations are available, the references are to the German original works as indicated below.

Cart. Med.	*Cartesian Meditations*
Crisis	*Crisis of European Sciences*
E. Phil.	*Erste Philosophie*
Exp. J.	*Experience and Judgment*
F. tr. L.	*Formal and Transcendental Logic*
The Idea	*The Idea of Phenomenology*
Ideas	*Ideas Pertaining to a Pure Phenomenology*
Die Idee	*Die Idee der Phänomenologie*
Ideen	*Ideen zu einer reinen Phänomenologie und phänomenologischen Philosophie*
Krisis	*Die Krisis der europäischen Wissenschaften*
L.I.	*Logical Investigations*
L.U.	*Logische Untersuchungen* (second edition [1913–21] unless otherwise specified)
Par. Lect.	*Paris Lectures*
Phän. Psych.	*Phänomenologische Psychologie*
Phen. Int. T. C.	*Lectures on the Phenomenology of Internal Time Consciousness*
Phen. Psych.	*Phenomenological Psychology*

Phil. d. Arithm.	*Philosophie der Arithmetik*
"Phil. Rig. Sc."	"Philosophy as Rigorous Science"
"Phil. str. W."	"Philosophie als strenge Wissenschaft"

| Edmund Husserl:
| A Biographical Sketch

Edmund Gustav Albrecht Husserl was born in Prossnitz (Prostejov) in Mähren (Moravia) on 8 April 1859 as the second of four children.[1] His father was Adolf Abraham Husserl, and his mother Julie Selinger, both of Jewish descent. Although Moravia later became part of Czechoslovakia, at the time of Husserl's birth it was still part of the Austro-Hungarian Empire, so that Husserl was an Austrian by birth.

Husserl finished his elementary education at the age of ten and then was sent to Vienna to enter secondary school. For several years, he attended the *Realgymnasium* in that city, but he completed his secondary education at the *Staatsgymnasium* in Olmütz (Mähren). In 1876 he went to the University of Leipzig with the intention of becoming an astronomer. When he arrived at the university, he did not yet show much promise, as his scholastic record at Olmütz had not been outstanding. With the exception of mathematics and physics, for which he had considerable enthusiasm, he had shown little interest in his courses.

At the University of Leipzig, Husserl first studied astronomy for three semesters (1876–78), along with mathematics and physics. During this time, he also attended lectures in philosophy given by Wilhelm Wundt; yet this leading scholar was unable to stimulate Husserl's interest in the study of philosophy. In 1878 Husserl left Leipzig and went to the Friedrich Wilhelm University of Berlin. There he met three of the leading mathematicians of the time, Leopold Kronecker, Ernst Kummer, and Carl Weierstrass, who introduced Husserl to a rigorous and disciplined way of thinking.

| 1

Under the influence of these stimulating mathematicians, Husserl developed a keen interest in the philosophy of mathematics, and his personal research in the field soon led him to broaden his interest in philosophy and to turn to other important philosophical issues as well. The lectures of Friedrich Paulsen contributed greatly to this growing interest. Paulsen recognized Husserl's capacity for reflection and tried to channel his thinking in ways that would later produce revolutionary insights.

After having been in Berlin for six semesters, Husserl transferred to the University of Vienna in 1881 with the intention of completing his education under the direction of the mathematician Leo Königsberger, even though Husserl had become more and more interested in philosophy. He received his doctoral degree in 1883; his dissertation, written under the supervision of Königsberger, was entitled *Beiträge zur Theorie der Variationsrechnung* (*Contributions to the Theory of the Calculus of Variations*).

In 1883 Husserl was called back to Berlin by Weierstrass, who had invited him to work with him as his assistant. Husserl accepted this invitation, although he would have preferred to stay in Vienna to study philosophy. When Weierstrass shortly thereafter became ill and thus was unable to lecture, Husserl decided to return to Vienna and to continue his study of philosophy. By that time, he had decided definitively to devote his entire life to philosophy. For the next two years, he attended the lectures of Franz Brentano. While he was in Vienna, his father died on 24 April 1884.

Husserl was deeply impressed by the way in which Brentano presented the philosophies of Hume and Mill and by his lectures on psychology, ethics, and logic. It was also Brentano who introduced him to the notion of intentionality, which later, rethought in a completely new and original manner, would receive a central place in Husserl's own phenomenology. During the same period, Brentano also directed Husserl in the study of the *Wissenschaftslehre* of Bernhard Bolzano, the importance of which had become clear to Husserl after he had made a careful study of Rudolf Hermann Lotze's *Logik*.

In addition to being impressed by Bolzano as introduced to him by Brentano, Husserl was particularly struck by the way in which Brentano himself tried to relate philosophy and science to each other. Brentano had always strongly stressed that philosophy, too, had to be truly "scientific." Husserl understood this to mean that all philosophers must recognize the necessity of employing rigorous methods of investigation. Whereas Paulsen and Wundt in this connection had emphasized the biological sciences when dealing with the relationship between philosophy and science, Brentano stressed psychology and logic. Given the fact that Husserl, under the influence of Mill, more or less began to identify philosophy with psychology, it is understandable why he became interested in investigations into the function of "philosophy," taken as a "strict and rigorous science," in regard to the realm of logic.

In October 1886, Brentano advised Husserl to go to the University of Halle to become Carl Stumpf's assistant in order to obtain a thorough training in psychology. One year later, after successfully completing his *Habilitationsschrift* (probationary thesis)*, Über den Begriff der Zahl: Psychologische Analysen (On the Concept of Number: Psychological Analyses)*, Husserl was made a *Privatdozent* under Stumpf and thus became a member of the philosophy faculty at Halle. On 24 October 1887, he presented his inaugural lecture on the aims and tasks of metaphysics, "Die Ziele und Aufgaben der Metaphysik."

On 8 April 1886, Husserl converted to Christianity and affiliated himself with the Evangelical Lutheran Church; he was baptized on 1 August 1886. On 6 August of the same year, Husserl married Malvina Steinschneider, who was also of Jewish descent but shortly before their marriage had also converted to Christianity; she, too, had become a member of the Evangelical Lutheran Church.

Between 1887 and 1891, Husserl gave lectures on the theory of knowledge, metaphysics, logic, ethics, philosophy of mathematics, and psychology. In 1891 he published his third book, *Philosophie der Arithmetik: Psychologische und logische Untersuchungen (Philosophy of Arithmetic: Psychological and Logical Investigations)*. Influenced by Gottlob Frege's criticism of this book as well as by several other factors that will be mentioned later, Husserl soon abandoned the psychologism of his earlier writings. As a matter of fact, in part 1 of *Logical Investigations: Prolegomena to Pure Logic,* Husserl explicitly rejected *every* form of psychologism in logic. This work was very well received by many of the greatest scholars of the time and definitely established Husserl as an important philosopher. In 1901, after long and difficult deliberations, the faculty of Göttingen invited Husserl to accept the position of "professor extraordinarius" in philosophy. Husserl accepted this invitation and remained in Göttingen until 1916. In 1905 the faculty refused to make him a "professor ordinarius" on the ground that he lacked "scientific distinction." But in 1906 he was made a regular university professor anyway because the Prussian minister of education had overruled the decision of the faculty. During the years in Göttingen, Husserl worked very hard: he substantially increased his knowledge of our philosophical heritage, wrote extensively, and taught a great number of courses. In addition to the kinds of courses he had taught in Halle, Husserl also gave lectures on the philosophies of Locke, Hume, Leibniz, Kant, Fichte, Bolzano, Ernst Mach, and others. It was also in Göttingen that Husserl began to lecture on phenomenology. During this fruitful period, Husserl wrote many important treatises, most of which remained unpublished, such as his investigations on time and space and *The Idea of Phenomenology.* The only writings that Husserl published during this period were the important article in the newly established journal *Logos* entitled "Philosophy as Rigorous Science" (1911) and the first volume of his magnum opus, *Ideas* (1913).

In 1916 Husserl was called to Freiburg to succeed Heinrich Rickert, who had retired that year. Husserl remained in Freiburg as a full professor until 1928, when he reached retirement age. The twelve years in Freiburg belong to the most productive and happy years of his life, even though a number of tragic events marked this period as well. In the spring of 1916, Husserl learned that his son Wolfgang had died at Verdun on 8 March of the same year. In April 1917, his son Gerhart was badly wounded, and in July of the same year his mother died.

On 3 May 1917, Husserl presented his inaugural lecture, "Die reine Phänomenologie, ihr Forschungsgebiet und ihre Methode" ("Pure Phenomenology: Its Domain of Research and Its Method"). In the same year, he gave three lectures on Fichte's ideal conception of humanity. In 1918 he presented lectures in London on phenomenological method and phenomenological philosophy. In December of the same year, he was elected as a corresponding member of the Aristotelian Society. In 1923 and 1924, he contributed essays to the Japanese journal *Kaizo.* Between 1919 and 1923, Heidegger was Husserl's assistant. In 1926 Heidegger presented Husserl with a copy of *Sein und Zeit,* and Husserl invited Heidegger to cooperate with him on the article for the *Encyclopaedia Britannica;* this effort to come to a close cooperation on a joint project failed because Heidegger's conception of phenomenology appeared to be substantially different from that developed by Husserl. In 1928 Husserl's *Vorlesungen zur Phänomenologie des inneren Zeitbewusstseins (Lectures on the Phenomenology of Internal Time Consciousness),* which Heidegger had edited, appeared in print. Husserl finally retired from the university on 31 March 1928. During these years, Husserl remained incredibly productive. He wrote a number of important treatises originally meant to be used as texts for lectures but later published in book form, including *First Philosophy, Formal and Transcendental Logic,* and *Phenomenological Psychology.*

After his retirement, Husserl still remained active. In 1928 he gave a series of lectures in Amsterdam. In 1929 he presented lectures on phenomenology in Paris at the three-hundredth anniversary of the publication of Descartes's *Meditations on First Philosophy*. Shortly thereafter Husserl developed these lectures into a book that later would be published under the title *Cartesian Meditations*. In 1930 he published his "Postscript" to *Ideas*. In 1931 he presented lectures in Frankfurt, Berlin, and Halle sponsored by the Kant Society.

Particularly after 1933, life became very difficult for Husserl and his wife. Although neither Husserl nor his wife ended up in a concentration camp, both nonetheless suffered enormously under the humiliation brought upon them and all other Jews they knew. In 1933 Husserl had received an invitation to join the philosophy faculty of the University of Southern California; Husserl deliberated about the implications of a possible move to the United States but finally declined the offer. In 1934 he addressed a letter to the Congress of Philosophers in Prague and expressed his ideas about the task of philosophy in the contemporary world. In the same year, plans were made to bring Husserl's manuscripts to Prague, but these plans never materialized. In 1935 Husserl presented a lecture in Vienna on "Philosophy in the Crisis of European Humanity." The next year, in November, he gave a lecture in Prague on "The Crisis of the European Sciences and Psychology." At the end of 1935, Husserl was forbidden by the National Socialist Party to teach. In 1936, however, he was able to send part 1 of his new book, *Crisis,* to Prague, where it was scheduled to appear in the journal *Philosophia*. In 1937 the German Ministry of Education refused Husserl's request to be allowed to participate in the Ninth International Congress of Philosophy in Paris.

Husserl died of pneumonia on 27 April 1939 at the age of seventy-nine.

∎ The Husserl Archives

In 1938 Herman L. Van Breda went to Freiburg im Breisgau to prepare his doctoral dissertation on the phenomenology of Husserl. There he learned that the Nazis were intending to destroy Husserl's manuscripts. After consultation with Husserl's widow, he began immediately to take the necessary measures to safeguard the extremely valuable collection. After many difficulties and various detours via Berlin and Brussels, the manuscripts finally arrived in Louvain, Belgium.

Presently the Husserl Archives contain not only Husserl's manuscripts but also his philosophical library, his letters, and numerous rewritings in longhand of manuscripts previously written in shorthand.[2] Among some eight thousand works kept at Louvain, there are many reprints dedicated to Husserl by several renowned philosophers. One can find Husserl's own annotations in the margins of many of these books and essays. One of the most remarkable items in this philosophical collection is a copy of the first edition of *Sein und Zeit* containing Heidegger's lengthy hand-written dedication to his master. This copy, too, is full of marginal philosophical remarks by Husserl; they gradually reveal his disappointment in noticing how his beloved pupil grew further and further away from him. After having read the book, he wrote on the title page: "Amicus Plato, magis amica veritas."

Almost all of the unpublished manuscripts that Husserl left behind at his death have been stored at Louvain; they comprise about forty thousand pages in octavo, practically all of which were written in the Gabelsberger shorthand system. These manuscripts have proven to be of inestimable value for the understanding of Husserl's philosophical evolution, for they contain the result of his philosophical explorations in his later and still fruitful years. Study of his latest manuscripts has brought to light the fact that his unpublished works are probably in a sense even more important than the books published during his lifetime.[3]

In addition to an extensive collection of letters and diaries, the archives contain also about seven thousand pages of longhand transcriptions of original shorthand Husserl texts; his assistants, Edith Stein, Ludwig Landgrebe, and Eugen Fink, are responsible for this work. Most of these pages have been scrutinized, annotated, and sometimes even reworked by Husserl. As early as 1916, Stein had started a systematic transcription that was later continued by Fink and Landgrebe. Multiple transcriptions exist for some of the lecture series and books, which make it possible to decipher Husserl's handwriting with greater ease and to test the accuracy of the copyists. In 1939 the most difficult job in this regard was still to be done.

In 1935 at Freiburg, Fink and Landgrebe undertook a first classification of the shorthand manuscripts following a system that Husserl had checked and endorsed. This system was made still more complete at Louvain. Subsequently all manuscripts were grouped in packages of approximately eighty pages each.

Since 1939 various scholars have been engaged in the systematic transcription of Husserl's writings with the intention of preparing the most important texts for publication. In 1939 Fink and Landgrebe came to Louvain to start the transcription of still-unstudied manuscripts. From 1942 until 1947, Stephen Strasser continued this labor of patience and endurance; from 1945 on Walter and Marly Biemel cooperated in this work for more than ten years, and after 1951 Rudolf Boehm carried the lion's share of this work.

After Boehm left for the University of Ghent, a number of scholars have prepared various manuscripts for publication, among them Margot Fleischer, Lothar Eley, Iso Kern, Ulrich Claesges, Paul Jansen, Eduard Marbach, and Ingeborg Stromeyer. At first this work was done exclusively in Louvain. Later, after research centers were established where copies of the manuscripts could be located and consulted, the work has been done also elsewhere, mainly in Cologne and Freiburg. In the United States, the manuscripts and other material can be consulted in New York City at the New School for Social Research as well as at Duquesne University in Pittsburgh. Van Breda died in 1974; he was succeeded as director of the archives at Louvain by Samuel IJsseling. Today the archives at Louvain are under the direction of Samuel IJsseling and Rudolf Bernet, the archives at Cologne are directed by Elisabeth Ströker, and those at Freiburg by Werner Marx.

Today more than twenty-five volumes have been published in the Husserliana series with the purpose of providing a systematically ordered whole of the complete philosophical oeuvre that Husserl left behind at his death. A supplement to these publications has existed since 1950. It is called *Phaenomenologica* and consists of philosophical and historical studies by scholars who think along phenomenological lines. Within the span of some forty years, more than one hundred volumes have been published in this series.

In connection with the Husserl movement and stimulated by the active directors of the Husserl Archives at Louvain, Van Breda and IJsseling, international congresses on Husserl's phenomenology have been held at Brussels, Krefeld, Royaumont, and Schwäbisch Hall. The proceedings of these congresses have been published each time in book form. In this work as well as in the work for the two series of books mentioned above, Jacques Taminiaux has been deeply involved together with the directors of the archives and other members of the staff.

| Periodizations of | Husserl's Development

A number of suggestions have been proposed in connection with the periodization of Husserl's philosophical development. Eugen Fink, Husserl's assistant in Freiburg, is responsible for the most familiar of these. He divides the development of Husserl's phenomenology into three stages that correspond to his years in Halle, Göttingen, and Freiburg. These phases comprise the periods of psychologism, descriptive phenomenology, and transcendental phenomenology. Husserl's *Logical Investigations* and *Ideas* mark the passing from periods one and two to the final phase. The first two periods, from the viewpoint of the later transcendental phenomenology, are to be seen as stages on the road to a philosophy accessible only through the transcendental reduction. Accordingly, it is also possible to speak of two major periods in Husserl's development, pretranscendental and transcendental philosophy.[4]

The above classification is useful in that it directs attention in each successive period to the trend toward a deeper and more general level of analysis. Herbert Spiegelberg, however, seems to distinguish the phases in a more comprehensive and more appropriate way.[5] He also divides Husserl's philosophical development into three periods: (1) the prephenomenological period, covering most of the Halle years and corresponding to his thinking expressed in the first volume of *Logical Investigations* (1894–1900); (2) the stage of phenomenology as a limited epistemological enterprise, corresponding to Husserl's first years in Göttingen (1901–6) and including the second volume of *Logical Investigations;* and (3) the period of pure phenomenology as the universal foundation of philosophy and science, which began in 1906 and led to a new transcendentalism as well as a characteristic phenomenological idealism whose increasing radicalization provides the theme for Husserl's Freiburg period (1916–38).

Spiegelberg holds that this developmental schema is analogous to a spiral. The prephenomenological period begins with the attempt to interpret mathematics via a psychology starting in the subject. When this appeared to be a partial failure, Husserl was led to the formulation of an "objectivistic" pure logic devoid of psychologism. Then the initial stages of phenomenology began to show equal stress on both the subjective and objective aspects of experience in their necessary correlation. In the further development of phenomenology, once again the subjective was stressed as the source of all objectivities, but now conceived as on a higher, transcendental level, beyond descriptive psychology. It is proposed that the course of this curvilinear development could account for the alternate attraction and repulsion that Husserl's philosophy exerted on the minds of those whose development might be characterized as more rectilinear.[6]

Although I agree with these authors that it is necessary to distinguish three major periods in Husserl's development, I nonetheless see the second period, the one between 1900 and 1916, more as a period of transition in which Husserl *gradually* moved from a pure, descriptive type of phenomenology to a fully transcendental phenomenology. One should not forget that in his later years Husserl continuously made changes in his earlier publications, notably in the first volume of *Ideas*. Anyone who studies Walter Biemel's critical apparatus to the first volume of *Ideas* will see that the distinction between the phenomenological and transcendental dimensions in 1911–12 was by no means as clear as it later will appear in Husserl's last writings. The first volume of *Ideas,* as we now have it, certainly belongs to Husserl's final period. Yet in the form in which it was published in 1913, it still seems to belong to the period of transition. The issue is not of great importance for the present study, since we shall be concerned with Husserl's final views only, those presented in the Freiburg period.

∎ Outline of Husserl's Phenomenology

In this section, I shall describe what Husserl himself understood by phenomenology, taken both as a method and as a set of philosophical disciplines to be developed with the help of this method. It seems to me that such a summary of some of the issues that in Husserl's own view constitute the core of his philosophy as a whole will be very helpful to understand the content of the *Encyclopaedia Britannica* article which will be discussed in the remainder of this book.

As far as phenomenology as a method is concerned, special attention will be given to the following questions: (1) What aim is one to achieve in philosophy by applying the phenomenological method? (2) What is the difference between the natural and the philosophical attitudes? (3) What conception of evidence is typical for the phenomenological approach? (4) Why is reduction an essential component of the phenomenological method? (5) What does Husserl understand by intentionality and intentional analysis? (6) Why is an eidetic reduction necessary in addition to the phenomenological and the transcendental reductions? (7) How does phenomenology define synthesis and constitution?

But more importantly, in addition to giving a brief description of the phenomenological method, I shall also attempt to justify why phenomenology proceeds in this way and what it hopes to achieve in doing so. In my effort to explain all of this, I shall follow Husserl himself as closely as possible by making use of the following "minor" publications and essays: *The Idea of Phenomenology* (1907), "Philosophy as a Rigorous Science" (1911), *Ideas,* vol. 3 (1912), the "Amsterdam Lectures" (1928), the *Paris Lectures* (1929), and the "Vienna Lecture" (1935). To the general outline that can be developed by employing these sources, some ideas will be added from the first volume of *Ideas* (1913), *Cartesian Meditations* (1913), and *Crisis* (1935).[7]

Origin and Development of Husserl's Phenomenological Method — The phenomenological method that Husserl gradually discovered between 1894 and 1900 in his research on the foundations of mathematics and logic was originally described as a pure, descriptive psychology. By this Husserl at that time understood a descriptive theory of knowledge that he believed would be able to avoid the errors and weaknesses of psychologism, which was dominant in the latter part of the nineteenth century. At that time, Husserl used the term "psychologism" in a rather narrow sense for the attempt on the part of certain philosophers to derive the basic laws of logic from psychological laws. Later Husserl would use the term in a broader sense, as we shall see later in this book. Husserl was convinced that his new descriptive psychology would be capable of solving the epistemological problems connected with the foundations of mathematics and logic. But as early as 1903, Husserl realized mistakes in his first characterization of phenomenology. It had gradually become clear to him that a new and a priori type of phenomenology was to be developed alongside the descriptive psychology used in the second volume of *Logical Investigations* (1901). The first systematic development of this new idea of phenomenology was presented in a series of lectures delivered at the University of Göttingen in 1907. After discussing the basic ideas of this new type of phenomenology with his students for several years and applying the method to various pertinent topics, such as internal time-consciousness, thing, space, material nature, animal nature, and the spiritual world, Husserl finally for the first time gave a clear, systematic, and adequate account of the new phenomenology in the first volume of *Ideas* in 1913. Yet since he was not fully satisfied with this presentation of the basic ideas of his philosophy either, he continued to improve on it in each publication that was to follow upon *Ideas*. In the later works, Husserl presented his transcendental phenomenology as the necessary method to be used in every authentically philosophical investigation concerning meaning and being (*Sein*). In his view, a systematic application of this method would necessarily lead to transcendental phenomenology as the philosophical theory of the universal constitution of all meaning and being by the transcendental ego. Although Husserl's transcendental phenomenology comes very close to the transcendental position defended by Kant insofar as its basic ideas are concerned, it nevertheless differs radically from Kant's philosophy because of the completely different method through which this basic conception is arrived at.[8]

In the sections to follow, only Husserl's "final" view will be explained in greater detail.

The Aim of Phenomenology — Husserl did not always describe the aim that phenomenology is to achieve in the same way. At first, the phenomenological method was meant to make a contribution to the foundations of the formal sciences. In a second phase, Husserl described the aim of phenomenology to pertain to every science and every form of knowledge. In 1907 Husserl defined phenomenology as the critical part of philosophy that has to provide metaphysics with its proper foundations. In the limited sense, phenomenology is characterized there as a *critique of knowledge (Erkenntniskritik)* that focuses both on the various kinds of knowledge as well as on their objects. In a broader sense, the term refers to a *science* developed with the phenomenological method. In a still broader sense, phenomenology refers to a *number of eidetic disciplines* that somehow constitute a unity because of their foundation in phenomenology. Since phenomenology is meant to make a contribution to the foundations of scientific knowledge, it itself cannot belong to the domain of the natural attitude; phenomenology is a new science with a new object domain, a new starting point, and a new method.

Toward the end of his life, Husserl began to add to this the foundational task of phenomenological philosophy in regard to *all* forms of human life. In the works which he himself published during his lifetime, this new conception of the aim of philosophy is found both in *Cartesian Meditations* and in *Crisis*.[9] By then it is clear that phenomenology is not just a critique of pure reason but equally a critique of practical and valuing or evaluating reason. In *Crisis* Husserl thus formulated the aim of phenomenology in the following terms: the aim of philosophy is to prepare humanity for a genuinely philosophical form of life, in and through which each human being gives him- or herself a rule through reason (*Crisis,* 15 [13]). By means of his new phenomenology and its completely novel method, Husserl hoped gradually to materialize the great ideas of Descartes, Leibniz, and Kant.

Philosophy as a Rigorous Science — The program that inspired all of Husserl's philosophical investigations from his *Philosophie der Arithmetik* (1891) to *Crisis* (1936) is the question of foundations. Husserl began by questioning the foundations of mathematics, from which he was led to the foundations of logic, epistemology, metaphysics, and finally to the philosophy of history. During many changes in his thinking throughout these forty-five years, Husserl always maintained that philosophy has to give the "absolute" foundation to all other sciences. Obviously, philosophy will never be able to reach this goal unless it itself is absolutely radical and as rigorous a science as possible.

Before attempting to explain Husserl's conception of phenomenology in greater detail, we must first point to a seemingly contradictory tendency that, in my view, is at the root of Husserl's whole philosophy. On the one hand, Husserl vigorously objects to any form of naturalism and scientism, claiming repeatedly that there is an essential difference between philosophy and science. On the other hand, he argues over and over again that a philosophy which is not a rigorous science will never be able to fulfill its vital task. Explaining his view in "Philosophie als strenge Wissenschaft" (1911), Husserl stresses that in his opinion philosophy, since its very beginning in Greece, always aspired to be an all-encompassing and intellectually completely justified knowledge of all that is ("Phil. Rig. Sc.," 71 [289]). As he sees it, philosophy cannot be a matter of feeling or of building more or less fanciful or subjective systems. It must try to get to "the things themselves" (*Ideas,* 1:35 [35]) and attempt to stay away from all free-floating constructions, accidental findings, unexamined preconceptions, and arbitrary prejudices. In this sense, philosophy must be as rigorous a science as possible.

Though every cultural period and every philosophical "system" has tried to realize in its own way this essential aim, Husserl is convinced that none of these attempts has ever completely succeeded. For him the most important reason why the attempts of modern philosophy to achieve this aim have failed can be found in its scientism, whether this be found in the form of naturalism, as in Descartes (1596–1650) and Kant (1724–1804); the form of psychologism, as in Hume (1711–76) and Mill (1806–73); or the form of historicism, as in Dilthey (1833–1911). Finally, Husserl was convinced that his new method of phenomenology, together with the set of philosophical disciplines that can be developed by employing it, will be able to realize the essential goal of philosophy without danger of again falling into the pitfalls of modern scientism.[10]

Two Fundamental Attitudes: The Natural and the Philosophical — It is thus understandable that when Husserl attempts to clarify what he understands by "transcendental phenomenology," he often takes his starting point in what he considered to be a far-reaching difference between the "natural sciences," which originate in the "natural attitude," and the philosophical sciences, which take their point of departure from the "philosophical attitude."[11]

In the natural attitude, our perception and thinking are wholly turned toward things, which are given to us as unquestionably and obviously existing and, depending on our standpoint, appear now in this way and now in that. Among all the acts which we can perform and which are concerned with the things in the world, perception is the <u>most original.</u> What perception offers to us we express in judgments, first in singular judgments and then in universal judgments. From these judgments we proceed through induction and deduction to new knowledge. In this way, natural knowledge makes progress. Constantly more encompassing, it lays hold of a reality that at first is taken to exist as a matter of course and whose content, elements, relationships, and laws are to be investigated more and more. In this way, the various sciences of the natural attitude have arisen. Because of the success they have attained in the course of the centuries, those who assume the natural attitude feel no need to ask any question concerning their proper meaning.

Moreover, in the natural attitude one tacitly assumes that we are in a world through which our mind can roam at will and in which we can consider any part we want, without changing the objective nature of what we consider. According to this view, the object pole of our knowing is an objectively existing, fully explainable world that can be expressed in exact, objective laws. This "objective" world exists wholly in itself and possesses a rationality that can be fully understood. The subject, on the other hand, is pure consciousness; it is fully transparent to itself and faces that rational world, which it can know objectively as it is in itself.

This idea of a single, objective, absolute, autonomous, and real world implies also that each of the different sciences has to occupy itself with a part of reality. Otherwise it would not be possible to explain the differences between these sciences because, in this view, there is no reason at all to defend a difference in method. Hence it stands to reason that all sciences together have to constitute a single objective synthesis. An essential difference between philosophy and the other sciences is not possible in this way of looking at things.

Husserl protests against such views. Philosophy, he says, lies in an entirely different dimension. It needs an entirely new starting point and an entirely new method, which in principle is different from those of any "natural science." A philosophy cannot naively begin straightforwardly, as the positive sciences do, which base themselves on the presupposed foundation of our experience of the world as something that is pregiven as obviously existing. Its aim as philosophy implies a form of radicalism of foundation, a reduction to some form of absolute presuppositionlessness, a fundamental method through which the philosopher at the beginning secures an absolute foundation for himself.

The Principle of All Principles — Husserl seeks the ultimate foundation of all our rational assertions in an immediate vision or an original intuition of the things themselves concerning which he wishes to make a statement. His maxim, "back to the things them-selves," means that we must return to the immediately given and original data of our consciousness. What manifests itself there in bodily presence is apodictically evident and needs no further foun-dation or justification (*Ideas,* 1:35–37 [34–37]).

Accordingly, Husserl sees the ultimate root or the radical and absolute starting point of philosophy as lying not in any single basic concept, principle, or *cogito* but rather in the entire field of original experiences (*Cart. Med.,* 31 [69–70]). His philosophy is a phenome-nology precisely because it has as its starting point a field of primor-dial phenomena. Within this realm of original phenomena, Husserl permits neither induction nor deduction but only intuition on the basis of precise analysis and exact description ("Phil. Rig. Sc.," 147 [341]). None of the methods used by the other sciences can be of any value here. Whereas they have to presuppose something in addition to the actually given, in the field of primordial phenomena charac-teristic of phenomenology, presuppositions are simply inconceiv-able. In the field of original phenomena, the fundamental principle is that every primordial, giving intuition is a legitimate source of knowledge, that everything which presents itself to us primordially in "intuition"—in its bodily reality, so to speak—is to be taken sim-ply as what it presents itself to be, but only within the limits in which it presents itself (*Ideas,* 1:44 [43–44]).

Reductions — Intuition implies that both subject and object are present to each other on the same level. Hence the intuition of the "first origins and beginnings" demands that one first try to arrive at the "most basic field of work" ("Phil. Rig. Sc.," 146 [341]) in which these foundations are immediately present to our knowing ego. Husserl believes that his theory of reductions can lead us to this pri-mordial field (*Ideas,* 1:57–62 [53–57]).

In general, Husserl means by reduction the methodic step by means of which one returns to the origin of our knowledge, of which our superficial everyday thinking has lost sight. By this procedure, one places oneself in the sphere of "absolute clear beginnings" ("Phil. Rig. Sc.," 146 [340]), in which one can perceive the things themselves as they are in themselves and independently of any prejudice. In other words, reduction means a change in attitude by virtue of which one learns to see things in a more original and radical way, to penetrate into things and see there the more profound layers of meaning behind those which first appeared (*Ideas,* 1:65–66 [59]).

Husserl distinguishes different types of reductions. The reduc-tive process that Husserl calls *philosophical reduction* consists in the adoption of a neutral position toward past philosophy. This procedure requires that philosophers must free themselves of the philosophical solutions that, over the course of philosophy's history, have been proposed for the various philosophical questions. They must take the original phenomena exactly as they present themselves, without any admixture of hypotheses or interpretation and without reading into them anything suggested by theories handed down from ancient to modern times. Only positions taken up in this way can be real "beginnings" (*Ideas*, 1:33–36 [33–37]).

A second reduction which must be mentioned here is the *eidetic reduction.* This reduction leads us from the realm of facts to that of their "essences." Eidetic reduction, therefore, is the procedure through which we raise our knowledge from the level of facts to the sphere of "ideas." Here "essences" or "ideas" mean not the "empirical generalities" that provide us with types encountered in experience but rather "pure generalities" that place before our minds pure possibilities whose validity is completely independent of factual experiences (*Ideas*, 1:8–11 [10–12]).

In order to understand the necessity of such a procedure, we must realize again that in Husserl's view philosophy must be an absolutely radical science. It can be so only if it is an eidetic science with immediate access to the realm of essence. Philosophy is not primarily interested in concrete real things, because as real they are mere contingent facts. Philosophy's attention must go out primarily to the invariable structures of the things as meant and intended.

In eidetic reduction, one proceeds as follows. As a rule one starts with an arbitrarily perceived or imagined, individual thing. With the aid of memory, modifications in perception, and especially acts of phantasy, one carefully investigates what changes can be made in the example without making it cease to be the thing it is. By making the most arbitrary changes that wholly disregard reality as it is and therefore are best made in our phantasy, the immutable and necessary complex of characteristics without which the thing cannot be conceived is made manifest. All variations have concrete similarities with the same prototype, and the manifold of new instances produced in phantasy is permeated by an invariant and identical content. In terms of this content, all the arbitrarily performed variations come to congruence, whereas their individual differences remain irrelevant. This invariant element prescribes a limit to all possible variations of the same prototype, for without this element an object of this kind can neither be thought of nor intuitively imagined.

The intuition of the *eidos* itself is *founded upon* the manifold of the variants produced in the process of arbitrary variation. The intuition, however, *consists in* an active apprehension of that which was passively preconstituted in phantasy. In other words, in the process of free variation, the "invariant" arises automatically and passively because the objects of the different acts overlap. This preconstituted and still-imperfect, identical content must still be seized in an active intuitive grasp, and it is through this active grasp that the absolutely immutable and unique *eidos* that governs all individuals of this species stands before our mind (*Exp. J.,* 340–48 [410–20]).

The Phenomenological and the Transcendental Reductions — We have seen that for Husserl all work in phenomenology will be in vain if one is not able to start with absolutely unquestionable "first beginnings." This means that in phenomenology nothing can be accepted as scientifically relevant if it cannot be fully justified by the principle of evidence. It is obvious that a purely descriptive method together with the eidetic reduction is unable to lead us immediately to the absolute foundation of all our knowledge.

The first question that we therefore must try to answer is where one can find evidences that are both primordial and apodictic, that is, evidences that as "first beginnings" precede all other evidences and are absolutely unquestionable. We have already seen that for Husserl the experiential evidence concerning the existence of the world is neither primordial nor apodictic (*Cart. Med.,* 14–18 [55–58]). But where else can we find evidences that are both immediate and apodictic? At this point, Husserl turns to Descartes's method of doubt, but he changes the act of doubt into an act of "bracketing," into a mere suspension of judgment, a mere *epoche.*

Between 1905 and 1916, Husserl seems to have used the expressions "transcendental" and "phenomenological" interchangeably where he speaks about reduction. What before 1916 was called either the phenomenological or the transcendental reduction had really a double task, first to bring about the bracketing of the natural world and thus the transition from what-is to its meaning; secondly, it was meant to bring about the transition from what-is-given to its ultimate condition and presupposition, that is, to the transcendental subject as source of all meaning.

When Husserl began to concern himself extensively with phenomenological psychology, it became clear that a distinction is to be made between the phenomenological reduction characteristic of phenomenological psychology, and the transcendental reduction typical for transcendental phenomenology. The phenomenological reduction employed in phenomenological psychology brings about the universal *epoche* of the world and thus leads us from the world of real things, as we take them in our natural attitude, to a world of pure, intentional phenomena. The (transcendental reduction) used in phenomenological philosophy consists in the bracketing of everything that phenomenological psychology can bring to light, including the psychological ego, and thus leads from phenomena in the phenomenological sense of the term to transcendental phenomena. Briefly formulated, the transcendental reduction leads from all-that-is-given and can be given to its ultimate condition and presupposition, the transcendental subject. By means of this reduction, I thus reduce my natural human ego and my natural psychic life, which was not yet affected by the phenomenological reduction, to my transcendental-phenomenological ego and the realm of transcendental-phenomenological self-experience. The objective world with all its objects, which is the only world that ever can exist for me, derives the entire meaning and existential status it has for me *from me as this transcendental ego.* This ego comes to the fore only in and through the transcendental reduction (*Par. Lect.,* 6–12 [6–13]).

Once Husserl had come to full clarity on this matter, he tried to sharpen the terminology used in the earlier works, particularly in *Ideas.* He often made the necessary corrections in the copies of his earlier works that he himself used. Some of these corrections have later been incorporated in new editions of the earlier works, but this has not always been done consistently. We do not have to be concerned about the details of the confusing situation that has been created in this way, since in the article for the *Encyclopaedia Britannica* Husserl will explicitly deal with the distinction between the two reductions mentioned, so that all confusion will eventually be eliminated.[12]

Intentionality and Constitution — We have seen that the transcendental reduction leads us from the things in the world to the transcendental ego, which epistemologically precedes all objective reality. Though, in a certain sense, this ego is even the source from which all objective knowledge originates, it is not an epistemological *ground* of our objective knowledge in the ordinary sense of the term. It does not make sense to use the "I think" (*cogito*) merely as an apodictically evident premise for deductive arguments; on the contrary, the phenomenological reduction opens an infinite realm of being of a new kind, the sphere of "transcendental experience." Where there is a new kind of experience, there must arise a new science, in this case, transcendental phenomenology (*Par. Lect.,* 11 [11–12]).

The phenomenologist must first describe faithfully the endless field of the ego's transcendental experience. In so doing, it is of the greatest importance to realize that the transcendental reduction in no way changes the fact that experiences are experiences of something, that all consciousness is and remains consciousness of something. In other words, the transcendental expression "I think" (*ego cogito*) is to be broadened by adding to it one more member: "I think what is thought" (*ego cogito cogitatum*), that is, all conscious awarenesses are intentional awarenesses (*Par. Lect.*, 11–13 [12–14]).

"Intentionality" signifies that all consciousness is consciousness of something. For Husserl, this means not only that all consciousness has an object or a content. The term also expresses, on the one hand, that the notion of "reality in itself" becomes incomprehensible and, on the other hand, that the Cartesian conception of a consciousness hermetically closed in on itself is equally excluded, for such a consciousness would not experience the world itself and thus would first have to make certain that it nonetheless is in genuine contact with "reality in the original." Therefore, the task of philosophy can no longer consist in installing itself between the subject and the object in a "critical" attitude in order to try to find out whether and in what sense the subject attains the world as it is in itself. All such problems are excluded by the concept of intentionality as conceived by phenomenology.

All that manifests itself in transcendental experience is to be described just as it manifests itself according to the principle of pure evidence. If we follow this methodical principle faithfully and remember that every "I think" (*cogito*) is an "I think what is thought" (*cogito cogitatum*), it will be clear that each description must include both the intentional object as such (*noematic description*) and the modes of the *cogito* itself that are related to this object (*noetic description*). Though these aspects can be clearly distinguished, it is obviously impossible to separate them in any description faithful to the phenomena (*Ideas*, 1:199–216 [167–83]).

Furthermore, the phenomenologist must realize that intentionality of consciousness has two other essential aspects, one *static* and the other *dynamic,* that call for two different but related forms of description. The static description of intentionality must try to determine all that is found in every lived experience in a concrete way, that is, its real components as distinguished from the intentional correlate to which they point. The dynamic description attempts to describe intentionality in its genesis and evolution. It is the latter of these that is phenomenologically more important, and its greatest problems are those involved in the constitution of the objects of consciousness. This needs some further explanation (*Cart. Med.*, 77–81 [111–14]).

We have seen that phenomenology wants to found all knowledge on apodictic evidence immediately rooted in intuition. Transcendental reduction discloses a field of transcendental experiences that are given with this type of evidence. What this realm is concretely, becomes more manifest as soon as one realizes that every act of thinking (*cogito*) necessarily implies that which is thought (*cogitatum*). If, however, consciousness essentially is consciousness of something, then the apodictic evidence extends not only to the act of thinking (*cogito*) but also to that which is thought (*cogitatum*), provided one maintains the reduction and considers that which is thought exclusively insofar as it is immediately given in this act of thinking.

Upon first consideration, it may seem that the intended things are immediately found in the evidence of every act of thinking, so that all we have to do is simply intuit and grasp them. Upon closer investigation, however, it becomes obvious that in the transcendental sphere, the different objects are not found in the thoughts as are matches in a box but rather are constituted in different types of syntheses. One of the major tasks of phenomenology consists precisely in analyzing and describing these different forms of syntheses from a noematic as well as a noetic point of view (*Cart. Med.*, 39–46 [77–83]).

A cube, for instance, is given continuously in perception as an objective unity (this cube) in a multiplicity of modes of appearing (noemata), which modes are the correlates of a multiplicity of individual acts of perception (noeses) performed from different perspectives. How can we explain and describe that we experience a multiplicity of aspects, given in a multiplicity of individually different acts, as one and the same perception of one single cube? Once we have started the phenomenological task of describing consciousness concretely, an endless horizon of facts discloses itself, all of which can be characterized as synthetic structures that give noetico-noematic unity to the individual thoughts and to their contents (*cogitata*). Only the elucidation of the peculiar operation in which the synthesis is brought about, the act of constitution, can render fruitful the disclosure of the *cogito* as consciousness-of. This elucidation takes place in the so-called intentional or constitutive analyses (*Cart. Med.*, 46–53 [83–89]).

Because all of this is of great importance for a correct understanding of the method of phenomenology, it is necessary to dwell on it a little longer. But for the sake of clarity, I shall no longer speak about acts of consciousness in a general and abstract way but shall focus instead on the most original of these acts, the act of perception.

Intentional Analysis of an Act of Perception — When one analyzes a particular act of perception,[13] it becomes at once evident that each act of perception seizes the perceived object only in a certain respect. Expressed in a correlative way, one could say that any perceptible thing is always perceived from a well-defined point of view. Standing in front of a house, I effectively perceive only the facade. The sides and the rear are still hidden from me. I can, of course, change my standpoint and place myself in a different position with respect to the house. If I do so, I still perceive the same house, but now only in a different respect. No matter how I place myself, I always perceive this house in a determined respect. The perceived gives itself in and through the act of perception only by means of profiles (*Abschattungen*) that are correlated to a determined attitude and standpoint of the perceiver (*Ideas,* 1:86–89 [73–76]).

Let us assume now that I perceive this particular house from the street in front of it, so that I can effectively see only its facade. If, subsequently, I want to learn more about this house's exterior appearance, then the only possibility is to have recourse to ever-new "partial perceptions," each of which will manifest separately a certain aspect of this house. What is typical here is the fact that in any such case we will always experience the manifold of profiles as profiles of this particular house. And in a correlate way, we experience the manifold of partial perceptions as perceptions of a single thing.

Thus, the perceived thing clearly does not exhaust itself in any one of its individual profiles; rather, that which is intended in each of the concrete acts—without, however, being effectively and as such perceived in any particular act whatsoever—remains the same in all cases. In this particular act of perception or *noesis,* this house effectively manifests itself always in this particular profile when this particular standpoint is assumed; but, nonetheless, each concrete act intends more than this particular profile and aims at the house as a whole. This intended total meaning, which is clearly constituted as the perceptional meaning in every particular act of perception of this house, taken precisely insofar as it manifests itself in this act, is called *noema.* This noema explains why every individual act of perception refers to other, possible perceptions of this same house. These perceptions are destined to complement and strengthen the first perception; and by virtue of them, this first perception is able to appear as a phase of a possible total process (*Cart. Med.,* 39–41 [77–79]). Let us clarify this point somewhat more extensively.

When different acts of perception are concerned with the same house, we experience all these acts as referring to one and the same thing, and therefore these distinct acts are in harmony and agreement, although that which is effectively perceived as such differs in all these cases. Despite the fact, however, that the profiles of the separate acts are different, it is clear that these acts cannot be in agreement if the profiles in question do not harmonize in one way or another. Consequently, the fusion of the different individual acts of perception concerning one and the same thing into a total process of perception presupposes, of necessity, that the corresponding profiles fit into a connected whole. Because the corresponding profiles organize themselves into a single, connected whole, the acts of perception can appear as phases of a total process (*Ideas,* 1:86–89 [73–76], 236–43 [201–8]).

Thus, the unification of the individual acts does not depend on the temporal relationships existing between them. It does not even appear necessary that the acts succeed one another without interruption. In other words, the unification in question does not refer to the acts themselves as psychical events occurring in a phenomenal time but only to their intentional correlates, that is, the noemata corresponding to them. Consequently, because the different partial perceptive presentations of one and the same material thing constitute a single noematic system, we can explain that the one-sidedness of each individual act is at the same time both experienced and overcome.

The one-sidedness of each particular act of perception of one and the same thing is overcome in the total process of perception only if the different profiles contained in the noematic system successively actualize themselves in and through the corresponding acts in such a way that the thing appears in a manifold of different but harmonious, explicit aspects. For in this way each particular perceptive act in which the thing manifests itself only in a particular aspect implies references to other partial acts in which the thing manifests itself in constantly different but harmonious aspects. Viewed *noematically,* these references are essential features of the perceptive noema in question; and *noetically* considered, they appear as the anticipation of new acts destined to complement this particular actual perception. Thus, it is not the temporal succession of the acts that overcomes the one-sidedness of each particular act but the fact that they confirm, complement, and perfect one another. Accordingly, the process of perception, noematically viewed, is a process of fulfillment (*Erfüllung*) (*Ideas,* 1:326–29 [282–85]).

Above we said that in the perceptive noema, that is, in the thing as it manifests itself to us in and through a given act of perception, a distinction has to be made between that which effectively manifests itself now and is given as such on the one hand and, on the other hand, the "rest." When we perceive a house, we effectively see only one side of it. Nevertheless, our actual perception has a greater content than what is effectively seen, for aspects that are not effectively perceived always play a role in the noema. Without such factors, we would merely see a not-too-sharply defined surface having a certain color but not the facade of a house. In other words, that which is effectively perceived always appears in the light of data that are not effectively perceived. The complex of the effectively and noneffectively perceived aspects constitutes the perceptive meaning in question.

To express the matter differently, every perceptive noema contains a rigidly defined core that is immediately given in experience and that, moreover, refers to not-immediately given aspects. Husserl calls the whole of the not-immediately given factors the "internal horizon" of the perceptive noema. We may add that the noematic core refers to the structures of the internal horizon, to a greater or a lesser extent, in proportion to the familiarity we already have with the perceived object. For this reason, the internal horizon can be unfolded on the basis of what is here and now effectively perceived, provided this explication adheres rigidly to the limits set by that which is effectively perceived (*Exp. J.,* 31–39 [26–36]).

Finally, we should keep in mind that whatever appears to a human being in his or her various acts of perception always manifests itself within a certain context. Every perceived thing or noema, Husserl says, has not only an internal horizon but also an *external horizon,* for every perceptible object appears to us as a certain figure against a certain background. The house, which I experience as a unit through a quasi-infinite series of profiles, appears really as a house only against the horizon of the street, the park, the square, or the garden in which it stands. A house that is not found in surroundings of which it is a part could never be a real house and could never be perceived as a house. When I direct my attention to this particular house on this street, then this house detaches itself from the background of meaning, but this horizon remains constitutive of the perceived real thing. If I direct my gaze to another house or to the car in front of it, the first house enters again into the horizon and cedes its privileged position to the other object of perception (*Ideas,* 1:51–55 [48–51]).

After these brief explanations, it should no longer be too difficult to understand the importance of the intentional analyses. The original function and importance of this method lies in its unveiling the implicit aspects contained in the actual states of our consciousness. Generally speaking, it is the method of bringing forward and explicating the constituent elements that are implicitly contained in certain actually given meanings. Its application to perception is based on an accurate analysis of that which is here and now given immediately but only implicitly in concrete perception.

If, then, we want to disclose the meaning of a perception, we must try to explicate the internal horizon together with the external horizon. This process has both a noetic and a noematic aspect. Noetically considered, this method demands that the inner and outer horizons be described as a deciphering of the anticipations of possible new and still-potential perceptions. This particular perception, therefore, must be considered in relation to the whole system of acts that in one way or another are connected with this concrete perception and could actuate its virtual content. Noematically considered, the intentional analysis endeavors to make explicit in consciousness all meanings that were only implicitly indicated in the effectively given datum. In fulfilling this function, it takes into account all the essential influences exercised by the internal and external horizons (*Cart. Med.,* 46–49 [83–87]).

Intentional Analysis of Other Forms of Synthesis — What has just been indicated by a concrete example is only one form of synthesis. Many others could be distinguished, analyzed, and described here. The first would be the relatively simple but basic form of phenomenological temporality, followed by a synthesis of the whole of conscious life into an all-embracing cogitation (*cogito*) that would synthetically comprise all particular conscious processes and intend the world as the horizon of every particular thought object (*cogitatum*) (*Cart. Med.,* 39–43 [77–81]).

We must realize further that the multiplicity of the intentionality belonging to every act of thought (*cogito*) that relates to the world is not exhausted with a consideration of that *cogito* as actually lived experience. On the contrary, every actuality involves its potentialities as possibilities that are actualizable by the ego. In other words, every lived experience has its inner or intentional horizon of references to potentialities of consciousness possessed by that experience itself (*Cart. Med.,* 44–46 [81–83]).

Whatever in the preceding reflection on perception was said about inner and outer horizons, the process of fulfillment, expectation, potentialities, and gradually increasing degrees of evidence is thus also applicable to any other intentional act, even though in many instances these acts will show characteristics not found in an act of perception.

Transcendental Idealism — Since we have reduced the problems of phenomenology to the constitution of objects in consciousness, phenomenology seems to be properly characterized as a transcendental theory of knowledge. This transcendental theory of knowledge must be contrasted with traditional epistemology (*Cart. Med.,*

83–88 [116–21]), whose main problem is the problem of transcendence. Traditional epistemology attempts to formulate and solve this problem within the realm of the natural attitude. There the problem must be stated as follows: How can my knowledge, abiding wholly within the immanence of my own conscious life, acquire objective significance for a world that is out there? Since obviously no answer to this question can be found within the realm of consciousness, Descartes tried to force a solution by appealing to God's veracity.

According to phenomenology, this whole problem became inconsistent the moment it was formulated within the realm of the natural attitude. For how could I, as a natural human being in the world, seriously and transcendentally ask either how I can get outside my island of consciousness, or how what presents itself in my consciousness can acquire objective significance for the world out there? Obviously, in formulating the question this way, I would perceive myself as a natural human being in the world and, in so doing, I would already have presupposed the outside world, which now is being put into question.

In Husserl's view, this inconsistency can be avoided only by the phenomenological reduction, which alone brings to light that conscious life by which transcendental questions about the possibility of transcendental knowledge can be asked. As soon as one performs such a reduction, the problem immediately dissolves, for it then becomes clear that all that exists for the pure ego is constituted in and by consciousness itself. Transcendence itself is nothing but an immanent existential characteristic constituted within the ego. Every conceivable thing, whether immanent or transcendent, falls within the realm of transcendental subjectivity, which constitutes its meaning and being. World and consciousness belong together essentially; concretely they are one in the absolute concretion of transcendental subjectivity.

Phenomenology, thus, is necessarily transcendental idealism. Yet it is an idealism in a fundamentally new sense. It is neither psychological idealism, which attempts to derive a meaningful world from meaningless sense-data, nor a Kantian idealism, which leaves open the possibility for a world of "things in themselves." Transcendental idealism is nothing other than a self-interpretation of my own ego as the subject of all possible knowledge, consistently carried out in the form of a systematic egological science (*Par. Lect.*, 33–34 [33–34]).

Solipsism or Intersubjectivity? — At this point, Husserl poses a very important question: If I, the meditating ego, reduce myself to my absolute ego and to what constitutes itself in that ego, do I not necessarily become isolated, a *solus ipse,* with the result that this whole philosophy of self-examination turns out to be a pure solipsism? Husserl claims that a phenomenologist does not have to answer these questions in the affirmative. First of all, within the realm of phenomenology there is a genuine possibility of exploring how in the ego an alter ego manifests itself or is constituted. Such an exploration must take its point of departure in the following facts: I experience other egos as real, that is, as united into one whole with "nature." Furthermore, I experience them as experiencing me in the same way that I experience them. Then I experience the world as being not my own private world but an intersubjective world in which others exist both as others as well as for each other (*Par. Lect.,* 34 [34–35]).

The act of empathy plays an important role in the explanation of the constitution of the other as alter ego. In order to be able to employ this basic act in a phenomenological analysis, one must first perform a new type of reduction that brackets all other minds and all those experiential levels of meaning in my world that originate from the explicit belief in the existence of other egos. In this way, a division is brought about in both my transcendental ego and the universe that is constituted therein. On the one hand, there is the sphere of my ownness and the coherent stratum of meaning consisting in my own experience of a world reduced to what is included in my ownness. On the other hand, there is the sphere of what is "other."

Once this division is brought about, it is phenomenologically possible to explain the constitution of the meaning of the "objective world valid for everybody." This constitution involves a number of phases, the first of which is the constitutional level of the other egos themselves. It is on this level that the act of empathy enters the picture. Once the constitution of the other egos is explained, one must focus attention on the universal superaddition of meaning to the world of my primordial ownness. By this addition, this world is able to manifest itself as an objective world, that is, as the identical world for everyone, myself included. Thus, the other ego makes it constitutionally possible for an infinite new realm of what is "other" to begin to appear as an objective world within the sphere of my ownness. In the constitution of this objective world, the others and I do not remain isolated. On the contrary, an ego community as a community of monads is constituted in the sphere of my ownness, which in its communalized intentionality constitutes the one identical world for everybody. In other words, my transcendental subjectivity is gradually expanded into a transcendental intersubjectivity or community, which in turn is the transcendental ground for the intersubjective value of nature and the world in general (*Par. Lect.,* 35 [35]).

∎ NOTES

1. For this biographical sketch, see Andrew D. Osborn, *The Philosophy of Edmund Husserl in Its Development from His Mathematical Interests to His First Conception of Phenomenology in "Logical Investigations"* (New York: International Press, 1934); Marvin Farber, *The Foundation of Phenomenology: Edmund Husserl and the Quest for a Rigorous Science of Philosophy* (Cambridge, Mass.: Harvard University Press, 1940); E. Parl Welch, *The Philosophy of Edmund Husserl: The Origin and Development of His Phenomenology* (New York: Octagon Books, 1965); Herbert Spiegelberg, *The Phenomenological Movement: A Historical Introduction,* 2 vols. (The Hague: Nijhoff, 1960), 1:73–163; H. L. Van Breda and J. Taminiaux, eds., *Edmund Husserl: 1859–1959: Recueil commémoratif publié à l'occasion du centenaire de la naissance du Philosophe* (The Hague: Nijhoff, 1959); Hans Rainer Sepp, ed., *Edmund Husserl und die phänomenologische Bewegung: Zeugnisse in Text und Bild* (Freiburg: Alber, 1988); Arion Lothar Kelkel and René Schérer, *Husserl: Sa vie, son œuvre, avec un exposé de sa philosophie* (Paris: Presses Universitaires de France, 1964); Rudolf Bernet et al., *Edmund Husserl: Darstellung seines Denkens* (Hamburg: Meiner, 1989).

2. See for the following H. L. Van Breda, "Le sauvetage de l'héritage husserlien et la fondation des Archives-Husserl," in *Husserl et la pensée moderne: Actes du deuxième colloque international de phénoménologie,* Krefeld, 1–3 novembre, 1956, ed. H. L. Van Breda and J. Taminiaux (The Hague: Nijhoff, 1959), 1–77; Bernet et al., *Edmund Husserl,* 225–28.

3. In the archives, Husserl's manuscripts have been ordered in the following way:

A. Mundane phenomenology
B. The reduction
C. Constitution of time as formal constitution
E. Intersubjective constitution
F. Lectures and addresses
K. Autographs
L. Manuscripts written in Bernau
M. Transcripts of manuscripts made in Freiburg before 1938
N. Postscripts and copies
P. Manuscripts from other authors
Q. Notes made by Husserl in lectures of his teachers
R. Letters

In each group of manuscripts, there are a number of bundles. One refers to the manuscripts by indicating the group, the bundle, and the page number, for example MS. F I 32. In this book, I shall refer to manuscripts only by means of secondary sources in which manuscripts have been quoted.

4. Spiegelberg, *The Phenomenological Movement,* 1:74.
5. Ibid.
6. Ibid., 74–75.

7. As was mentioned before, the "Amsterdam Lectures" can be found in *Phän. Psych.*, 302–49; Richard Palmer is preparing an English translation to appear in Husserliana. The "Vienna Lecture" can be found in *Crisis*, 269–99 [314–48]. For the other works and lectures mentioned, see the Bibliography at the end of this book.

8. Cf. Iso Kern, *Husserl und Kant: Eine Untersuchung über Husserls Verhältnis zu Kant und zum Neukantianismus* (The Hague: Nijhoff, 1964).

9. *Cart. Med.*, 152–57 [178–83]; *Crisis*, 3–18 [1–17].

10. Cf. "Phil. Rig. Sc.," 71–122 [289–322] passim; *Ideen*, 3:159–62.

11. For what follows, see *The Idea*, lecture 1, 13–21 [15–26].

12. Cf. Husserl, *Phän. Psych.*, 600–602 (letter from Heidegger to Husserl). For Husserl's conception of the transcendental reduction in general and its relationship to the phenomenological-psychological reduction, see "Amsterdamer Vorträge," ibid., 312–13 and 328–46. For the description of the distinction between the phenomenological and the transcendental reductions, see *Cart. Med.*, 65–75 [99–108], 83–88 [116–21] and *Crisis*, 235–65 [238–76]. See also chapters Four and Eight below.

13. For the intentional analysis of an act of perception, see Husserl, *Ideas*, 1:73–104 [64–87]; *Exp. J.*, 71–148 [73–171]. See also Aron Gurwitsch, *The Field of Consciousness* (Pittsburgh, Pa.: Duquesne University Press, 1964), 202–305.

Introduction to the *Encyclopaedia* Article

Text

Der Encyclopaedia Britannica Artikel (Vierte, letzte Fassung)

[Einleitung]

[277] "Phänomenologie" bezeichnet eine an der Jahrhundertwende in der Philosophie zum Durchbruch gekommene neuartige deskriptive Methode und eine aus ihr hervorgegangene apriorische Wissenschaft, welche dazu bestimmt ist, das prinzipielle Organon für eine streng wissenschaftliche Philosophie zu liefern und in konsequenter Auswirkung eine methodische Reform aller Wissenschaften zu ermöglichen. Zugleich mit dieser philosophischen Phänomenologie, aber zunächst von ihr nicht geschieden, erwuchs eine neue, methodisch und inhaltlich ihr parallele psychologische Disziplin, die apriorisch reine oder "phänomenologische [278] Psychologie", die den reformatorischen Anspruch erhebt, das prinzipielle methodische Fundament zu sein, auf dem allein eine wissenschaftlich strenge empirische Psychologie zu begründen ist. Die Umschreibung dieser dem natürlichen Denken näher stehenden psychologischen Phänomenologie ist als propädeutische Vorstufe wohl geeignet, um zum Verständnis der philosophischen Phänomenologie emporzuleiten.

"Phenomenology," Edmund Husserl's
Article for the *Encyclopaedia Britannica*
(1927)

Introduction

The term "phenomenology" designates two things: a new kind of descriptive method which made a breakthrough in philosophy at the
turn of the century, and an a priori science derived from it; a science
which is intended to supply the basic instrument (*Organon*) for a
rigorously scientific philosophy and, in its consequent application, to
make possible a methodical reform of all the sciences. Together with
this philosophical phenomenology, but not yet separated from it,
however, there also came into being a new psychological discipline
parallel to it in method and content: the a priori pure or "phenomenological" psychology, which raises the reformational claim to being
the basic methodological foundation on which alone a scientifically
rigorous empirical psychology can be established. An outline of this
psychological phenomenology, standing nearer to our natural thinking, is well suited to serve as a preliminary step that will lead up to
an understanding of philosophical phenomenology.

Reprinted with permission from *Journal of the British Society for Phenomenology* 2 (1971): 77–90. Revised translation by E. Palmer. The translator
gratefully acknowledges the help he received from Professor Herbert
Spiegelberg (Washington University, St. Louis, Missouri) and Professor
Gisela Hess (MacMurray College, Jacksonville, Illinois) in the preparation
of the original translation for *JBSP*. For the present edition, the translator
has revised his earlier effort in accordance with corrections received from
various sources. Principally, the translator wishes to thank Herbert
Spiegelberg for his continued help, as well as Karl Schuhmann, who for-
warded a marked-up copy of the translation, which he had used as the text
for a seminar in parallel with the German original. Under the impetus of
the criticisms of Professor Schuhmann, the translator has reviewed the
entire text and devised many new renderings (not always those suggested
by Professor Schuhmann) which he hopes have improved the present
translation. [The text in brackets is Palmer's, that in curly braces is mine.]

❚ Synopsis

In the introduction to his article for the *Encyclopaedia Britannica,* Husserl mentions the following ideas:

1. At the turn of the century, a new kind of descriptive method was developed; this method was then tentatively called the phenomenological method.
2. With the help of this method, a new science can be developed; this science is an a priori discipline, that is, a science that is to be developed methodically independent from experience; this science is a *philosophical* discipline.
3. This new science is intended to supply the basic instrument, or *organon,* for a rigorously scientific philosophy. It is to provide a new kind of foundation to all other sciences, particularly to the eidetic and the empirical sciences and thus bring about a methodical reform in all these disciplines.
4. Parallel to this philosophical science, a new psychological science that makes use of the same method also came into being. The psychological science runs parallel to philosophical phenomenology in method and content. At first the psychological science was not yet separated from philosophical phenomenology.
5. The psychological science is an a priori and pure psychology; it can be called phenomenological psychology.
6. Phenomenological psychology is to provide the basic methodological foundation on which alone a scientifically rigorous, empirical psychology can be established.
7. Since phenomenological psychology is closer to our natural way of thinking than phenomenological philosophy, an outline of phenomenological psychology will be used in this article for the *Encyclopaedia* as an introduction to philosophical phenomenology.

In the "Amsterdam Lectures," which were written almost at the same time (1928) and constitute a further development and refinement of the *Encyclopaedia* article, Husserl provides us with some additional information that is of significance. By selecting the term "phenomenology" for the new method he had developed, one might have thought that Husserl might have been seeking affiliation with either Kant or Hegel. However, this appears not at all to be the case. In the "Amsterdam Lectures," Husserl points out first that his phenomenological method originated through a radicalization of the phenomenological method that already before his time had been demanded and practiced by some scientists. Scholars such as the physicist Ernst Mach and the psychologist Ewald Hering had already realized the meaning of this new method in their reactions against the threatening, groundless theorizing in the exact sciences of nature that makes use only of abstract conceptualization and mathematical speculation. This kind of conceptualization and speculation remains far from our immediate experience and thus is unable to bring clarity and genuine insight into the meaning of those theories and to secure their effectiveness. In addition, parallel to these developments in the exact sciences of nature, we also find psychologists and philosophers such as Franz Brentano engaged in an endeavor to systematically create a strictly scientific psychology on the basis of pure, internal experience and a rigorous description of its data.

Secondly, Husserl observes that it was the radicalization of these methodical tendencies, specifically in the psychological and the epistemological domains, which often were intertwined, that led to a new method for purely psychological research and, at the same time, to a new manner of dealing with philosophical questions of foundations. In these endeavors, which were called "phenomenological," a new form of scientificity also began to come to the fore.

Finally, Husserl states that in its further development, this radicalization gradually began to present itself in his own research in a remarkable way as having a dual meaning. On the one hand, this radicalization led to a new psychological phenomenology [*sic*] that is to serve as the radically foundational science for empirical psychology; and, on the other hand, it also led to transcendental phenomenology, which for its part in philosophy itself has the important function of being a first philosophy, that is, the science of all philosophical sources.

The clarification that Husserl provides in the "Amsterdam Lectures" is important. First of all, as was mentioned above, he makes it clear that the origin of his conception of phenomenology is not Hegel but rather ideas found in the works of thinkers such as Mach, Hering, and Brentano. Secondly, Husserl explicitly admits that at first he himself did not clearly realize the distinction to be made between the psychological and the philosophical sciences aimed at by the phenomenological method. Finally, Husserl introduces here the terminology that he will always use in all of his later works when he makes the distinction between phenomenological psychology and transcendental phenomenology.

In neither one of these two essays does Husserl mention the fact that he himself came to these ideas while he was engaged in research concerning the foundations of both mathematics and logic. It is thus of some importance in the commentary to follow to retrace Husserl's own development somewhat more closely. In my commentary, I shall focus on three basic themes: (1) the origin of Husserl's phenomenology, (2) phenomenology as a descriptive psychology, and (3) the origin of transcendental phenomenology. Some of the other issues mentioned above will be discussed in one of the chapters to follow.

Commentary

The Origin of Husserl's Phenomenology

Philosophy of Arithmetic — According to Walter Biemel, we must go back as far as 1887 if we want to understand Husserl's philosophical development and the genesis of his phenomenology.[1] At that time, Husserl was working on the first draft of his *Philosophie der Arithmetik,* in which he tried to provide a foundation for his investigations concerning the concept of number by using the logical and psychological ideas of his time. This attempt was in harmony with the special studies that he had made of mathematics, logic, and psychology in Leipzig, Berlin, and Vienna. As we have seen in the Introduction above, Husserl had received his doctoral degree in mathematics. His study under Weierstrass and others had given him a firm basis for his later work in logic, whereas Brentano had made him enthusiastic for the purely descriptive type of investigation used in empirical psychology. The fusion of these apparently diverse streams of scholarship in the realm of mathematics set the stage for his later career. As early as his *Philosophy of Arithmetic,* we find in Husserl's work several elements of his later phenomenology. For instance, he constantly speaks of achievement, reflection, and the method of disclosing the essences of things by going back to the origin of their meaning in consciousness and to the description of this origin. In these elements, we may also see the first indications of his later ideas about constitution, reduction, intentional analysis, and eidetic intuition. On the other hand, in *Philosophy of Arithmetic* Husserl remained within the horizon of psychologism, although he tried to find completely new ways by *starting from* the psychological investigations of Brentano and Stumpf.[2]

For this reason, a first point to be considered here is Husserl's initial training as a mathematician under Weierstrass, Kummer, and Kronecker. Husserl's mathematical studies at the universities of Leipzig, Berlin, and Vienna between 1876 and 1881 were concluded with a thesis on the calculus of variations. From 1884 till 1886, after returning to Vienna, he audited Brentano's lectures. This philosopher and psychologist lectured on philosophy, elementary logic and its necessary reforms, and also on selected psychological questions. At that time, Husserl himself was still in doubt whether he would devote himself to philosophy or remain in mathematics, but Brentano's lectures helped him decide the matter. His motivation for attending Brentano's lectures was partly curiosity—for Brentano was much discussed in Vienna—and partly the advice of his friend Tomas Masaryk, who became later president of Czechoslovakia.

Despite some initial prejudices, Husserl did not resist the power of Brentano's personality very long. Brentano soon aroused Husserl's interest in philosophy and in his new descriptive psychology, although Husserl's own questions were still restricted to the realm of mathematics, in particular the theory of numbers, which was of little interest to Brentano's own philosophy. These lectures, however, convinced Husserl that philosophy is a serious undertaking that can be pursued in the spirit of the most rigorous science. This conviction led him to dedicate his life to philosophy.[3]

Thus, when Husserl finally decided to accept a university position in philosophy at Halle under the direction of Brentano's former student Stumpf, he wrote his *Habilitationsschrift, On the Concept of Number: Psychological Analyses.* Subsequently his first book, volume 1 of his unfinished *Philosophy of Arithmetic* (1891), dedicated to Brentano, was described as "Psychological and Logical Studies."

In *Philosophy of Arithmetic,* it was not Husserl's intention to construct a system of arithmetic but merely to lay the scientific basis for a future system by means of a series of psychological and logical investigations in which both criticism and positive developments should be included. The objective of these studies in the philosophy of mathematics was to derive the fundamental concepts of arithmetic, and later also of Euclidean geometry, from certain psychological acts. For this purpose, these acts had to be traced in rigorous detail.

The tools for these attempts were taken from Brentano, Locke, Hume, and Berkeley. These thinkers had been Husserl's introductory readings in philosophy and remained of basic importance to him throughout his later development. For all practical purposes, however, Husserl borrowed most of his tools from Mill, whose *System of Logic* he had studied intensively.[4]

Philosophy as a Radical Study of the Essences of Beings —
In his *Philosophy of Arithmetic,* Husserl attempted to develop a philosophy of numbers. According to him, this philosophy is a study of the psychological sources from which our number concepts are derived. The first intention of this work, however, was

not to determine the nature of the psychological functions that are at the source of numeration but to understand number itself precisely as that which has been achieved by consciousness in its perception of numerable objects. It stands to reason that numbers as such cannot be perceived, but a certain mode of perceiving is connected with the operation of numbering the various numerable objects that results in numbers. It is also evident, according to Husserl, that a study of the numerable objects themselves does not enable us to determine what a number really is. To understand the essence of number, an accurate study must be made of the concepts that consciousness has constituted in itself; by numbering different numerable things, our consciousness imposes a determinate number upon them, and this number as such is constituted in consciousness by virtue of the data given in original perception.

Husserl was aware that many thinkers before him had considered numbers to be mental constructs. But for him this point was only the beginning. The problem that remained was to explain *how* exactly numbers are constituted by consciousness and what the fundamental meaning is of these constitutive activities of consciousness. Moreover, if it is possible to arrive at the essence of numbers by analyzing the concept of number itself, why is it not possible to attain the essence of anything else simply by examining the concept of the object known? The intelligibility of the things themselves must be limited, it seems, to that which can be conceptualized.

If this supposition is correct, our first task will be to determine exactly what is meant by "concepts" and especially what is meant by "consciousness," which is at the source of all our concepts. However, if consciousness is what psychology claims—namely, nothing but a describable function—then, Husserl says, consciousness itself simply belongs to the class of things or facts. But if consciousness is only a thing, then concepts and ideas, which are the results of the various activities of consciousness, can likewise only be things. Ideas, however, that are mere things are simply contingent facts; hence the possibility of knowledge, in any intelligible sense of the term, seems to be lost. In this supposition, therefore, skepticism will inevitably result, since to deny the necessary character of knowledge is to deny its very possibility. Skepticism, however, is completely inadmissible because it is self-contradictory. But if it is absolutely certain that there must be knowledge, then it is equally certain that knowledge is possible only on the condition that we are able to eliminate contingency in any form. Now, to eliminate the contingent is to eliminate the factual from our considerations. Thus, consciousness can be the seat of knowledge only if it belongs to a world completely separated from the world of facts. If it is possible to purify consciousness of everything factual, so that its content can truly be called knowledge in the proper sense of the term, then the objects of consciousness will be necessary objects and, therefore, *beings* in the full sense of the term. But to grasp beings in the full sense of the term is to grasp beings as absolutely necessary, and to grasp beings as absolutely necessary is to grasp the very essences of those beings. This, then, is for Husserl what philosophy must be: a radical and essential study of beings, that is to say, a radical study of the very essences of beings.[5]

These ideas, which were only latently present in Husserl's *Philosophy of Arithmetic,* implicitly contradicted the psychologism that his book explicitly tried to defend. Probably they were among the most important reasons why, in the following years, Husserl's ideas underwent a radical change with respect to the importance of psychology for mathematics and logic. Another factor in the reorientation of his thought was his exchange of ideas with Frege. Long before Husserl, Frege had contended that logic and psychology are fundamentally different studies. He had done so again with great clarity in his critique of Husserl's *Philosophy of Arithmetic.* Paul Natorp's critique of psychologism also influenced Husserl's development in this matter. Around 1894 Husserl began to develop a rigorous critique of psychologism in his lectures. Published in 1900 as *Prolegomena to Pure Logic* (the first volume of *Logical Investigations*), this critique immediately stirred up interest and even excitement among logicians and psychologists.[6]

Psychologism, Reactions — As Spiegelberg mentions, the term "psychologism" existed already before Husserl used it. Husserl himself credited it to Stumpf, who had used it as early as 1891 and who mentioned as its source the Hegelian historian Johann Eduard Erdmann. Compared with Stumpf's wider use, Husserl's was more specific, since at that time he was oriented to problems of mathematics and logic only. Husserl defined psychologism as the view that the theoretical foundation of mathematics and logic is supplied by psychology only, and especially by the psychology of knowledge. According to Husserl, therefore, psychologism is the view that psychology is both the necessary and sufficient foundation of mathematics and logic, a point of view that, for logic, was defended by Mill, Wundt, Christoph von Sigwart, and Theodor Lipps.[7]

One of the first reactions against psychologism was Stumpf's critique. He understood by psychologism the reduction of *all* philosophical problems, and especially of *all* epistemological issues, to psychological questions. We find an analogous critique of psychologism in Natorp's review of Lipps's *Basic Facts of Mental Life.*

Lipps, following Mill, regarded psychology as the basis of philosophy, whereas Natorp doubted the possibility of basing logic and epistemology upon psychology. According to Lipps, the genetic
derivation of the basic laws of knowledge from original facts of psychic life is identical with their epistemological foundation; the
theory of knowledge, therefore, is a branch of psychology.

Natorp pointed out that psychical facts are indeed represented
in the laws of knowledge and that these facts, as psychical, are also
objects investigated by psychology. But it is not correct, he argued,
to conclude from this that the axioms and statements of the different
sciences are merely psychological laws. On the contrary, our consciousness of truth is independent of any genetic explanation by
means of general psychological relations. If we want to explain scientific data as they manifest themselves to us, we must admit that
the principles of knowledge and truth have an independent objective
foundation. Hence it is not correct to reduce epistemology to psychology, for the critique of knowledge and the psychology of knowledge require and condition each other.

In another paper, Natorp argued that either logic is not founded
or it must be constructed entirely on its own ground and not borrow
its foundations from any other science. Those who make of logic a
branch of psychology assume that psychology is the basic science
and that logic is at best an application of psychology. Natorp as-
serted that not only the meaning of logic but the meaning of any objective science is denied and almost perverted into its very opposite
if we make the objective truth of knowledge dependent upon subjective experiences. To base logic upon subjective grounds would be to
abolish it as an independent theory regarding the objective validity
of knowledge.

According to Frege, Husserl also had become a victim of the
widespread philosophical disease known as "psychologism," for in
Philosophy of Arithmetic, Husserl had tried to explain the essence of
numbers by means of the psychological acts of consciousness. In
Frege's opinion, the mixture of psychology and logic is merely a
means of avoiding difficulties. Frege did not deny that it is possible
to study arithmetic from a psychological point of view, but, according to him, we must clearly distinguish a number as a representation from the objective meaning of that number. In the second part
of Husserl's book, however, Frege concedes, there are indications
that its author recognizes that our primary concern is with the
things themselves, of which we make representations, and not with
these representations themselves. The numbers in themselves are
objective in character and independent of our thinking. But, Frege
argues, if our representation of a number is not the number itself,

then the very foundation of the psychological viewpoint collapses insofar as the investigation of the essence of numbers is concerned.[8]

Husserl's Refutation of Psychologism — Husserl did not admit that all of these criticisms of psychologism were valid for his *Philosophy of Arithmetic*. On the other hand, he realized that he had made several mistakes. In an intensive study concerning the relation between psychology and logic, he came to the conclusion that psychologism really is untenable, and that he therefore should try to express what he really wanted to say in a more accurate way. In the decade following the year 1891, he came gradually to a strikingly new point of view, which was published for the first time in his *Logical Investigations* (1900–1901). The first volume, entitled *Prolegomena to Pure Logic,* contains, as is mentioned above, a detailed statement and critique of psychologism. It is characterized by thoroughness as well as by fairness to the authors examined. Husserl's critique was intended also as a correction of his earlier viewpoint, as is evidenced by his quotation of Goethe's saying that man is never more severe than with errors recently renounced.

In formulating his criticism of logical psychologism, Husserl extensively explained the absurdity of the consequences to which it leads and then assailed the underlying biases. One of the prime consequences with which Husserl was concerned here is psychologism's claim that the validity of logical axioms and principles depends ultimately on psychological laws. As one might expect, it was not too difficult a task for Husserl to show that it is impossible to interpret logical principles as psychological laws based only on our way of thinking.

A second conclusion to which Husserl turned his attention in this context was the fact that psychologism leads to skeptical relativism. If logical principles are made to depend upon the psychological characteristics of the logician, then they are concomitantly relativized in relation to this thinker; as a consequence, human beings in all their instability then become the standard against which everything else is to be measured. Relativism, however, Husserl held, is self-contradictory in that it negates the possibility of all knowledge and, at the same time, maintains that its own statements must be true.

Next, Husserl focused his attention on the biases of psychologism themselves. Among other matters, he pointed out, psychologism posits that the subject matter of logic consists only in psychological phenomena. In dealing with this prejudice, Husserl made a comparison between logic and mathematics. Mathematics is not concerned with our operations of counting but with numbers themselves. Similarly, the subject matter of logic is not constituted by the operations by which we form concepts, judgments, and inferences but with the products of these operations, namely, "ideal" concepts, propositions, and conclusions.

The criticism of psychologism's biases contained at the same time a first analysis and description of the logical realm as a domain of entities *sui generis*. Once he had dispensed with the idea that psychology can be of any help here, Husserl went on to develop his own view on "pure" logic free from every form of psychologism. But the details of this investigation need not engage our attention at this point.[9]

Husserl's "Conversion" — When the first volume of *Logical Investigations* appeared, most of Husserl's readers regarded him as a protagonist of realistic objectivism or perhaps even of Platonism, since his *Prolegomena to Pure Logic* clearly explains that mathematical and logical principles are true, regardless of whether or not they have ever been thought of by human beings. These truths must be independent of the human beings who think them, and therefore they must have a "being" that is independent of the factual functioning of consciousness. To be sure, there is no thought without a human being to think it, but it is only the *factual appearing* of this thought that depends on one's thinking; the *validity* of what is thought, however, is entirely independent of any psychic activity on the part of human beings. Moreover, if the concepts that are in our consciousness are independent of its psychic functions, then consciousness itself must transcend the sphere of these psychic functions, too.

Logical or mathematical propositions are true, but not because our thinking functions properly in formulating them; if they are true, it is because those propositions have validity in themselves. The laws of mathematics and logic are not concerned with our thinking as such but with our thoughts. They do not determine whether our mind is thinking properly but rather whether our thoughts are true. Thus we must conclude that mathematics and logic are "pure" if and only if they are independent of our factual thinking. That is why it is impossible to reduce them to a study of mental processes.

As Husserl sees it, the fundamental mistake of psychologism is that it has "naturalized" not only our ideas but also consciousness itself. In so doing, it did not see the necessity of making a clear distinction between the world of consciousness and the world of factual facts. What is true can possess validity, even though it is impossible for us to explain the correspondence between this truth and our thinking as a concrete event happening in a "real" world. Its "being" as an object of thought is somehow other than the being characteristic of our acts of thinking as concrete events. Its very transcendence as an object lies in that it transcends the thinking which, psychologically speaking, "produced" it. However, in Husserl's earlier works, it is not very clear what validity our thoughts precisely possess and what kind of being can be ascribed to truth.[10]

Phenomenology as Descriptive Psychology: Husserl's Original View

In *Philosophie der Arithmetik* and in *Logical Investigations,* Husserl looked for a universe of ideal objects—such as the world of numbers, geometrical entities, logical generalities—the validity of which is independent of the psychical activities by which the apprehension of these ideal objects is effected. But at the same time, he had to solve the problem of how exactly these ideal objects are given to consciousness, how they reach the state of being given.

In a manuscript of this period, Husserl argues as follows: We may manage to show in a fully evident way that ideal objects, although they take shape in consciousness, have a being of their own, a being in themselves. But even then, an important task is left, namely, to explain the typical correlation between these ideal objects belonging to the sphere of pure logic, and our subjective, psychical, lived experiences as the activities that constitute them. For we must keep in mind that the performance of certain psychical activities, which evidently are activities of a fully determined order, results in the successive formation and constitution of meanings and that the different ideal objects appear necessarily as products of these activities.[11] This text clearly indicates what already then was Husserl's concern and what was to constitute the characteristic theme of his later phenomenology.[12]

For anyone who on the basis of the first volume of the *Logical Investigations* had looked forward to a systematic development of the idea of a pure logic, it was a great surprise when the second volume appeared in 1901 under the title *Elements of a Phenomenological Elucidation of Knowledge.* This volume contained six essays: four shorter ones about matters of immediate interest to pure logic and two longer explanations bearing the strange titles "Intentional Experiences and Their Contents" and "Elements of a Phenomenological Elucidation of Knowledge." Especially the last two essays gave the impression of being relevant to psychology rather than to pure logic. Many readers thought therefore that Husserl had returned to the very psychologism that he had rejected in the first volume of *Logical Investigations.* However, to understand the reason of this seeming renewal of psychologism is to see the fundamental reasons that were to lead Husserl to his later phenomenology.[13]

The idea of a pure logic has sometimes been represented as an attempt to divorce logic completely from every kind of psychology. In the second volume of his *Logical Investigations,* however, Husserl's standpoint is precisely that such a separation is inadmissible and even impossible. In a manuscript written after 1920, he points out that the main problem discussed in *Logical Investigations* is the following: Hidden "lived experiences" are connected with every ideal entity. These experiences must be in harmony with corresponding fully determined achievements. How, then, must they manifest and present themselves in order that the subject will be able to be conscious of these ideal entities as objects in an at least ultimately evident act of knowledge?[14] For even ideal logical entities are given to us only in and through experience, even if this is an experience of a very special kind. No philosophical and critical logic, therefore, can ignore them.

But if this is true, then Husserl still seems to imply that a certain psychology of thinking must underlie a philosophical study concerning the foundations of logic. The psychology that prevailed in Husserl's days, however, was unequal to the demands of pure logic. All that Husserl wanted was a descriptive study of the processes by which the entities studied in pure logic are constituted.[15]

With respect to the meaning of the term "constitution" in this context, we must observe that the thinking subject is not able arbitrarily to constitute any meaning it wants, because the constitutive acts depend on the essences of the objects in question. In a letter to William Ernest Hocking dated 25 January 1903, Husserl explains that in *Logical Investigations* the expression "the objects constitute themselves in the different acts of consciousness" refers solely to that characteristic of an act by means of which it makes an object "presentable," and that there is no question here of constitution in the proper sense of the term.[16] In Chapter Six we shall deal with the problem concerning the meaning of the term "constitution" in Husserl's later publications (see also Chapter Ten).

In the introduction to the second volume of *Logical Investigations,* Husserl in passing refers to the new study, now called "phenomenology" taken as "descriptive psychology," using this latter term in the sense that was given to it by Brentano. He mentions here discussions of the most general kind that belong to the wider sphere of an "objective" theory of knowledge or to a "purely descriptive phenomenology" of experiences of thought and knowledge. This entire sphere must be investigated in an epistemological preparation and clarification of pure logic.[17]

In another passage, he specifies that it is not psychology as a complete science that is to be the foundation of pure logic. Certain types of description constitute a preliminary stage for the theoretical investigations of pure logic. These types describe empirical objects whose genetic connections psychology has to trace and which, at the same time, form the basis for those fundamental abstractions in which the logician grasps the essences of the ideal objects and their connections with evidence:

> Epistemologically it is of very great importance to separate the purely descriptive investigation of experiences of knowledge, which is not concerned with any question of interest to theoretical psychology, from the investigations which are really psychological and aim at empirical explanation and genesis. For this reason we shall do well to speak of phenomenology rather than of descriptive psychology.[18]

However, already in 1903 it was clear to Husserl that he had made several mistakes in his characterization of his new phenomenology. For, as with any other descriptive science, descriptive psychology as such is only interested in the experiences of human beings as they can be observed in concrete and individual cases. What Husserl wanted, however, was a description of the ideal types of logical experiences in their correspondence to ideal logical laws. He was especially interested in descriptive analyses of the various *kinds* of thinking, modes of intuitive consciousness, and forms of symbolic presentation, which seem to be paramount for a radical foundation of the laws of pure logic.

This study of the pure essences of these experiences must evidently divorce itself completely from that which happens in concrete and individual cases. The experiences as real events and everything that happens in them belong to the domain of empirical psychology. The new phenomenology, instead, is to study essential relationships, which as such are independent of concrete experiences. Only with such a study will philosophy be able to bring to light the ultimate foundations of our knowledge of logical entities and laws.[19]

For this reason, the second edition of Husserl's *Logical Investigations,* which appeared after the publication of *Ideas* in 1913, characterized "the purely descriptive phenomenology" in the following way: This new discipline, like the pure phenomenology of experience in general, described in *Ideas,* "is concerned with the experiences that can be grasped and analyzed intuitively in their essential generality but not with empirically apperceived experiences as real occurrences, as experiences of experiencing people or animals in the appearing world, posited as real facts of natural experience. The essences directly grasped in essential intuition and the connections based solely upon these essences are expressed *descriptively* in concepts of essences and logically correct statements about essences.

Every such statement is an a priori statement in the best sense of the term."[20]

What has just been said concerning the relationship between pure logic and phenomenology, understood here in a limited sense as a special study of the experiences that correspond to logical entities, contains an idea that in Husserl's later philosophy as a whole is of the greatest importance, namely, his view on "intentionality." According to this idea, the structures of the subjective act parallel those of its objective correlate. This parallelism constitutes the basis for investigations in which both these aspects of any phenomenon must be described in connection with each other. It leads to artificial abstractions if one tries to study one aspect without the other. Although there might be some value in such a separate study, it requires a reintegration of the aspects that in this way are brought to the fore, into the original phenomenon from which they have been drawn.[21]

Empirical and Phenomenological, or Descriptive, Psychology — In this historical sketch of the evolution of Husserl's thinking between 1887 and 1903, one point is of great importance for our understanding of his later phenomenological philosophy: the question of what exactly is to be understood by phenomenology as a descriptive psychology and what its relation is to empirical psychology.

As mentioned above, in the second volume of *Logical Investigations,* Husserl tried to present an epistemological preparation for, and clarification of, pure logic. In the first volume of this work, he had already explained that it is absolutely impossible to find this epistemological foundation in traditional empirical and experimental psychology. At first, Husserl thought that a descriptive psychology in Brentano's style could provide such an explanation. After the second volume of *Logical Investigations* was published, which explained this idea, Husserl realized its deficiency. It became evident to him that, although such a descriptive psychology is an important psychological discipline, it never will be able to provide a radical foundation for the epistemological aspects of our knowledge; for, to obtain such a foundation for the epistemological aspects of our knowledge, we must eliminate all transcendent interpretations of immanent data, including the psychological activities and conditions of real egos, physical things, and the experience of other persons.[22]

Moreover, it was never Husserl's intention to reject empirical psychology as such; he was simply opposed to those trends in psychology which he called "naturalistic" or "objectivistic." It had become evident to him that one has to make a sharp distinction between empirical psychology, descriptive or phenomenological psychology, and phenomenological philosophy, the latter understood as a *radical* study of consciousness. The role of phenomenological psychology is simply to fill the gap between the best possible type of empirical psychology and phenomenological philosophy. These insights are already implicitly present in Husserl's article "Philosophy as Rigorous Science" (1911) and more explicitly formulated in *Ideas* (1913).[23]

In 1903, however, Husserl did not yet have a clear idea about this phenomenological psychology as distinguished from phenomenological philosophy or about its concrete relations to empirical psychology. Later, he describes it, in line with his tentative views of 1903, as an a priori psychological discipline capable of providing the only secure basis for empirical psychology.[24] The task of phenomenological psychology lies in a systematic examination of the types and forms of intentional experience as such and in the reduction of their structures to "prime intentions" in order to discover the nature of the "psychical" as such and comprehend the very essence of the soul. A phenomenological psychologist will pay attention only to internal experiences, which are to be described as "phenomena," that is, exactly as they appear to consciousness. This reduction to the phenomena themselves, to the purely psychical, requires two steps: (1) the systematic and radical inhibition, or *epoche,* of every objectifying, positing act in every concrete experience; and (2) the recognition, comprehension, and description of the very essence of that which no longer appears as an object but only as a "unity of meaning." This phenomenological description itself comprises two phases: the description of the noetic aspect of the phenomena (the experiences) and the description of their noematic aspect (the experienced objects as such).

In this way, phenomenological psychology can be purified of every empirical and psychophysical element; but, purified in this way, it cannot deal with concrete matters of fact. However, Husserl claims, any closed field can be considered with respect to its essence, and we may disregard the factual side of the phenomena by using them as "examples" only. Thus we can ignore individual souls and societies to learn their a priori, essential structures.

Psychology in general, in both its empirical and its phenomenological branches, is a *positive* science, since it remains within the realm of our "natural attitude." Taking our starting point in phenomenological psychology, however, we need only use again the formal method of reduction in order to disclose the "transcendental" phenomena of transcendental-phenomenological philosophy.

In the preceding pages, I have anticipated part of Husserl's further development. This anticipation seemed to be desirable in order to bridge the gap between Husserl's original views and the final view he ultimately would come to. In the chapters to follow, I shall return to some of the issues involved. For the present, I wish to confine myself to the observation that the descriptive psychology of the second volume of *Logical Investigations* is identical with that discipline which Husserl later will call "phenomenological psychology."[25]

The Origin of Transcendental Phenomenology — A few years after the publication of the second volume of *Logical Investigations,* Husserl gradually began to realize that the position to which he had come in 1901 was really inconsistent. The descriptive psychology pursued in his work on the foundations of mathematics and logic appeared to be inadequate in regard to the most basic principles of philosophy. A rather thorough study of the first two of Descartes's *Meditations of First Philosophy* and of Kant's *Critique of Pure Reason* had made this evident to him. Yet it would still take several years before Husserl was able to unfold a philosophical position that in principle would be capable of dealing with the most pressing issues. Since the genesis of these new ideas is of importance for our understanding of Husserl's transcendental phenomenology,[26] it is necessary to dwell on them.

Five years after he had published the first volume of his *Logical Investigations,* Husserl's philosophical evolution had come to a crisis. He realized that in his philosophical investigations concerning the foundation of pure logic, he had discovered a new philosophical discipline that perhaps could lead to a completely new ideal of philosophy itself. But at the same time, he realized that he had not yet discovered the right way to explain his new ideas. In 1906 the Board of Education of the University of Göttingen had proposed him as a full professor, but the university itself had explicitly rejected this proposal. In the summer of 1906, Husserl began to seriously doubt himself and to wonder whether it would not be better to abandon his philosophical career. On 25 September 1906, he noted in his diary:

> In the first place there is the general problem which is to be solved if I wish to call myself a philosopher; I mean a critique of reason, a critique of logical, practical, and valuing reason. If, in general lines at least, I cannot clear up the important questions about meaning, essence, method, and other fundamental viewpoints of a *Critique of Pure Reason,* and if I should not be able to project, determine and provide a foundation for my ideas regarding these problems, it will be impossible for me to live truly as a philosopher.[27]

By the end of 1906, Husserl thought that he had already found the right approach to a transcendental philosophy under the influence of Kant's *Critique of Pure Reason*. It seemed possible to him to go beyond phenomenology as the descriptive psychology used in *Logical Investigations* and arrive at a transcendental phenomenology. This transcendental phenomenology would be able to give philosophy an absolute foundation by means of a wholly new process, which he called "phenomenological reduction." These main ideas were communicated for the first time in 1907 in the series of lectures entitled *The Idea of Phenomenology*.[28]

∎ N O T E S

1. Walter Biemel, "Les phases décisives dans le développement de la philosophie de Husserl," in *Husserl,* Cahiers de Royaumont: Philosophie, no. 3 (Paris: Minuit, 1959), 35.

2. Ibid., 39.

3. Farber, *The Foundation of Phenomenology*, 8–9; Spiegelberg, *The Phenomenological Movement*, 1:91–92.

4. Farber, *The Foundation of Phenomenology*, 25–26; Spiegelberg, *The Phenomenological Movement*, 92–93.

5. Quentin Lauer, *The Triumph of Subjectivity* (New York: Fordham University Press, 1958), 22–24.

6. Biemel, "Les phases décisives," 41–44; Farber, *The Foundation of Phenomenology*, 4–7, 37–38, 57–58; Spiegelberg, *The Phenomenological Movement*, 93.

7. Spiegelberg, *The Phenomenological Movement*, 94; Farber, *The Foundation of Phenomenology*, 4–5.

8. Gottlob Frege, "Dr. E. G. Husserl: *Philosophie der Arithmetik*," *Zeitschrift für Philosophie und philosophische Kritik* 103 (1894): 22–41; Spiegelberg, *The Phenomenological Movement*, 56–58; Farber, *The Foundation of Phenomenology*, 5–6, 57–58.

9. Spiegelberg, *The Phenomenological Movement*, 94–95.

10. Lauer, *The Triumph of Subjectivity*, 26–27; Louis Dupré, "The Concept of Truth in Husserl's 'Logical Investigations,'" *Philosophy and Phenomenological Research* 24 (1963–64): 345–54.

11. Husserl, MS. F I 36, 19, quoted by Biemel, "Les phases décisives," 45.

12. Biemel, "Les phases décisives," 44–45.

13. Spiegelberg, *The Phenomenological Movement*, 101.

14. Husserl, MS. F I 36, 19 b, quoted by Biemel, "Les phases décisives," 47.

15. Spiegelberg, *The Phenomenological Movement*, 102.

16. Biemel, "Les phases décisives," 45–46.

17. Husserl, *L.I.*, 1:194–95 (*L.U.* [1900–1901], 1:4).

18. English translation from Farber, *The Foundation of Phenomenology*, 198–99; Husserl, *L.I.*, 263 (*L.U.*, 1:81).

19. Spiegelberg, *The Phenomenological Movement*, 102–3. For Husserl's logical investigations, see also Suzanne Bachelard, *La logique de*

Husserl: Etude sur logique formelle et logique transcendentale (Paris: Presses Universitaires de France, 1957); Lothar Eley, "Logik und Sprache," *Kantstudien* 63 (1972): 247–60; Aron Gurwitsch, "Présuppositions philosophiques de la logique," *Revue de métaphysique et de morale* 56 (1951): 395–405; Robert Sokolowski, "The Logic of Parts and Wholes in Husserl's *Logical Investigations,*" *Philosophy and Phenomenological Research* 28 (1967–68): 537–53; Dallas Willard, *Logic and the Objectivity of Knowledge: A Study in Husserl's Early Philosophy* (Athens: Ohio University Press, 1984); J. N. Mohanty, *Readings on Edmund Husserl's "Logical Investigations"* (The Hague: Nijhoff, 1977).

20. Husserl, *L.I.,* 1:249 (*L.U.* [1921–22], 2:2; my translation).
21. Spiegelberg, *The Phenomenological Movement,* 103.
22. Farber, *The Foundation of Phenomenology,* 199.
23. Spiegelberg, *The Phenomenological Movement,* 149–50.
24. This is done in *Phenomenological Psychology* as well as in the *Encyclopaedia Britannica* article, as we shall see later.
25. Husserl, *L.I.,* 1:261–63 (*L.U.* [1921–22], 2:347–48).
26. Biemel, "Les phases décisives," 46–52.
27. Husserl, MS. X x 5, 17–18, quoted by Biemel, "Einleitung des Herausgebers," in *Die Idee der Phänomenologie,* vii–viii.
28. Ibid., vii–xi.

In this first division, Husserl explains why a pure or phenomenological psychology is possible and necessary in addition to empirical psychology. He describes its subject domain, its method, and its function. The subject matter of this new discipline consists in the experiences of the ego itself as well as in the experiences of communities of egos. The typical characteristic of these experiences is that they are all intentional experiences. Husserl also explains what is to be understood here by intentionality. In order to be able to demarcate the field of intentional experiences from everything else, a special phenomenological reduction appears to be necessary. In view of the fact that phenomenological psychology has to be a pure and eidetic science, a special eidetic reduction that leads us from concrete experiences to the essences of these experiences appears to be necessary in addition to the phenomenological reduction. Finally, Husserl explains here how in his view phenomenological psychology and empirical psychology are to be related to one another and what the precise function of phenomenological psychology is in regard to empirical psychology.

| **Pure Science of Nature and Pure Psychology**

Text

I. Die reine Psychologie, ihr Erfahrungsfeld, ihre Methode, ihre Funktion

1. Reine Naturwissenschaft und reine Psychologie

Die neuzeitliche Psychologie ist die Wissenschaft vom "Psychischen" im konkreten Zusammenhang der raumzeitlichen Realitäten, also von in der Natur sozusagen ichartig Vorkommendem mit all dem, was untrennbar dazugehört als psychisches Erleben (wie Erfahren, Denken, Fühlen, Wollen), als Vermögen und Habitus. Die Erfahrung bietet das Psychische als bloße Seinsschicht an Menschen und Tieren. Die Psychologie ist danach ein Zweig der konkreteren Anthropologie bzw. Zoologie. Animalische Realitäten sind zunächst einer Grundschichte nach physische Realitäten. Als das gehören sie in den geschlossenen Zusammenhang der physischen Natur, der Natur im ersten und prägnantesten Sinn, welche das universale Thema einer reinen Naturwissenschaft ist, d.i. einer in konsequenter Einseitigkeit von allen außerphysischen Bestimmungen der Realitäten absehenden objektiven Wissenschaft von der Natur. In diese ordnet sich die wissenschaftliche Erforschung der animalischen Körper ein. Soll nun demgegenüber die animalische Welt hinsichtlich ihres Psychischen zum Thema werden, so ist zunächst zu fragen, wiefern in Parallele mit der reinen Naturwissenschaft eine reine Psychologie möglich ist. In einem gewissen Ausmaß ist eine rein psychologische Forschung selbstverständlich zu betätigen. Ihr verdanken wir die Grundbegriffe vom Psychischen nach seinen eigenwesentlichen Bestimmungen, Begriffe, die in die übrigen, die psychophysischen Grundbegriffe der Psychologie [279] mit eingehen müssen. Keineswegs klar ist aber von vornherein, inwiefern die Idee einer reinen Psychologie als einer in sich scharf geschiedenen psychologischen Disziplin und als einer wirklichen Parallele zur rein physischen Naturwissenschaft einen rechtmäßigen und dann notwendig zu verwirklichenden Sinn hat.

I. Pure Psychology: Its Field of Experience, Its Method, and Its Function

1. Pure Natural Science and Pure Psychology

Modern psychology is the science dealing with the "psychical" in the concrete context of spatio-temporal realities, being in some way so to speak what occurs in nature as egoical, with all that inseparably belongs to it as psychic processes like experiencing, thinking, feeling, willing, as capacity, and as *habitus*. Experience presents the psychical as merely a stratum of human and animal being. Accordingly, psychology is seen as a branch of the more concrete science of anthropology, or rather zoology. Animal realities are first of all, at a basic level, physical realities. As such, they belong in the closed nexus of relationships in physical nature, in Nature meant in the primary and most pregnant sense as the universal theme of a pure natural science; that is to say, an objective science of nature which in deliberate one-sidedness excludes all extra-physical predications of reality. The scientific investigation of the bodies of animals fits within this area. By contrast, however, if the psychic aspect of the animal world is to become the topic of investigation, the first thing we have to ask is how far, in parallel with the pure science of nature, a pure psychology is possible. Obviously, purely psychological research can be done to a certain extent. To it we owe the basic concepts of the psychical according to the properties essential and specific to it. These concepts must be incorporated into the others, into the psychophysical foundational concepts of psychology.

It is by no means clear from the very outset, however, how far the idea of a pure psychology—as a psychological discipline sharply separate in itself and as a real parallel to the pure physical science of nature—has a meaning that is legitimate and necessary of realization.

| Synopsis

The next five sections of Husserl's article on phenomenology will be concerned with what he calls "pure psychology" but also "psychological phenomenology" or "phenomenological psychology." He is particularly interested in explaining its field of experience, its method, and its function.

The first section deals with the question of in what sense a pure psychology parallel to a pure science of natural entities is possible. Husserl begins by observing that there actually is an empirical science, called empirical psychology. Its subject matter is the "psychical" insofar as this is found in spatiotemporal real things of the objectively real world.

It is difficult to say what the psychical is; yet one could clarify the notion by saying that it consists in the living inner awarenesses of that which we designate as ego and everything that manifests itself as something that cannot be separated from an ego. In other words, the psychical is the domain of all ego-processes, the domain of all the immediate, lived experiences, such as seeing, thinking, feeling, willing, as well as the corresponding capacities, faculties, and habitual dispositions.

The problem is that experience gives us the psychical as a nonindependent ontological sphere in human beings and animals, which, according to a more fundamental sphere, are also physical realities. Psychology is therefore really a not-independent branch of zoology, and particularly of biological anthropology; these latter disciplines concern themselves with both the physical and the psychophysical. Real animal entities are first of all physical realities. As such they belong to the entities studied by the physical sciences of nature, such as mechanics, chemistry, biology, and zoology. All bodily entities taken as such can be studied by empirical sciences as well as by a pure natural science. The latter is an objective, eidetic science of nature that in deliberate one-sidedness excludes from consideration all extraphysical aspects of the bodily real things. The scientific investigation of the bodies of animals and human beings still fits within this large domain.

Although there is no doubt that an *empirical* psychology can be developed in detail, parallel to the empirical sciences of inanimate nature, the question must nevertheless be raised as to what degree a pure psychology can be developed that runs parallel to the pure science of nature. Husserl was convinced that pure psychological research can indeed be done to a certain extent. Pure psychology provides us with the basic concepts of the psychical that define the properties essential and specific to the psychical. Yet these concepts must later be related to, and incorporated into, the psychophysical concepts that also belong to the foundations of psychology.

Yet as mentioned above, it is by no means clear from the outset how far the idea of a pure psychology, sharply delineated in itself and running strictly parallel to the pure physical science of nature, has a meaning that is legitimate and, therefore, can also be materialized.

The view that Husserl describes here is one to which he ultimately had come in 1925 via a long process in which different phases can be distinguished. Furthermore, several issues touched on are by no means very clear. In the commentary to follow I thus shall deal with the following issues: (1) the genesis of the idea of phenomenological psychology; (2) Husserl's view on empirical psychology and eidetic psychology; (3) Husserl's view on empirical and eidetic, pure sciences; and (4) a more detailed account of the relationship between empirical psychology, pure psychology, and psychophysiology.

Commentary

The Genesis of the Idea of Phenomenological Psychology

From 1907 on, psychology is a constant pole of comparison in Husserl's explanations of the meaning of his phenomenological philosophy. Practically speaking, in every work dealing with the foundations of phenomenological philosophy, Husserl tries to explain his view on empirical psychology and to describe the difference and the relationship between these two sciences. Between 1911 and 1913, the problem concerning the relation between empirical psychology and phenomenological philosophy had Husserl's special attention again. Gradually it became clear to him that it is possible and even necessary to bridge the gap between empirical psychology and philosophical phenomenology with the help of a completely new science that at that time was called "rational psychology" or "eidetic psychology" and "phenomenological psychology" afterward. This view is explicitly expressed for the first time in *Ideas* (1913), although the first traces of these insights are already found in his *Logos* article.

Between 1913 and 1923, Husserl was especially concerned with the so-called constitutional problems. As a result of these investigations, it became apparent to him that his explication of the meaning of phenomenological psychology as presented in *Ideas* was not adequate, in that the distinction between phenomenological psychology and transcendental philosophy had not yet been founded in a radical way. It became apparent also that the new science, phenomenological psychology, was of such importance for the development of empirical psychology that a radical investigation of it seemed to be demanded. He thus dealt with the topic in different lecture courses between 1923 and 1927, and the results of these investigations were published posthumously in 1963 in *Phenomenological Psychology*. In this work, phenomenological psychology is described as an aprioric, eidetic, intuitive, purely descriptive, and intentional science of the psychical that remains entirely within the realm of the natural attitude (*Phen. Psych.*, 33–37 [46–51]). Husserl tried to found the necessity of such a new kind of psychology by pointing to the fact that traditional empirical psychology still lacks a systematic framework of basic concepts grounded in an intuitive clarification of the psychical essences. Whatever psychology has accumulated and is still accumulating by way of measuring and experimentation concerning objective correlations is wasted as long as there is no clear grasp of what it is that is being measured and correlated. According to Husserl, phenomenological psychology is destined to supply the essential insights needed to give meaning and direction to the research presented under the title "empirical psychology."

Exactly the same ideas are found in Husserl's *Encyclopaedia Britannica* article, his "Amsterdam Lectures," and *Cartesian Meditations.* In these publications Husserl mentions for the first time that a special reduction is essential and indispensable for a phenomenological psychology, too. In his last book, *Crisis,* Husserl returns to this point and in a detailed and minute inquiry tries to determine the very nature of this reduction and to found its necessity (*Crisis,* 235–65 [238–69]). In these investigations, he comes to strange conclusions regarding the relation between psychology and phenomenology, as we shall see in Chapter Nine.

Husserl's View on Empirical Psychology: "Eidetic Psychology"

Spiegelberg has rightly pointed out that Husserl never opposed empirical psychology as a whole, but only certain types of psychology, to which he referred with the epithets "naturalistic" and "objectivistic."[1] With these expressions, Husserl characterizes psychologies that, in mistaken imitation of the physical sciences, tried to get rid of the essential features of psychological phenomena.

To understand Husserl's point of view in regard to empirical psychology,[2] we must realize that the psychology of his day consisted of a combination of psychophysical and physiological investigations carried out to determine quantitatively and experimentally the relationships between objective stimuli and subjective responses.

Brentano and William James had evidently proposed several very important ideas to correct this fundamental misconception of psychology, but neither had materially altered the classical conception. The same holds true for Gestalt psychology, which was also still trapped in the prejudices of objectivism and scientism. According to Husserl, Dilthey was the first scientist who clearly saw the fundamental mistakes in the leading psychological schools, naturalism and objectivism. But even Dilthey was not able to indicate a new and correct way to psychology (*Phen. Psych.*, 4–13 [4–19]).

Husserl explained this view on empirical psychology for the first time in his *Logos* article, "Philosophy as Rigorous Science." Since it provided the basis for the first description of the new phenomenological psychology that Husserl introduced in his *Ideas,* a short summary of the most important insights proposed in the article is in order.

First Misconception of Traditional Psychology: No Pure Analysis — In the first part of the article, Husserl attempted to explain the necessity of a phenomenological philosophy. He described his phenomenology as a science of consciousness but distinguished it from psychology, a *natural* science about consciousness. Ultimately he concluded that there is a strong relationship between phenomenology and psychology, since both are concerned with consciousness, though in a different way and according to different orientations. Psychology is concerned with empirical consciousness, that is, with consciousness as an empirical being in the real world, whereas phenomenology is concerned with pure consciousness ("Phil. Rig. Sc.," 90–110 [299–315]).

From this it will be clear that, in principle, psychology is more closely related to philosophy than the other sciences, which do not deal with consciousness at all. However, what has been said here of a necessary relationship between psychology and philosophy does not apply to modern empirical psychology. For the fundamental conviction of this psychology is that pure analysis and description of the data that immediately manifest themselves in immanent intuition are to be put aside in favor of certain indirect, psychologically relevant facts brought to light by observation and experiment. Such a psychology does not see that without an analysis of the essence of conscious life, these facts are deprived of their real meaning. In other words, although it is true that empirical psychology is able to bring to light valuable psychophysical facts and laws, it nevertheless remains deprived of a deeper understanding and a definitive scientific evaluation of these facts as long as it is not founded in a systematic science of conscious life that investigates the psychical as such with the help of "immanent," intuitive reflection. By the very fact, therefore, that experimental psychology considers itself as already methodologically perfect, it is actually unscientific wherever it wishes to penetrate to a *real* psychological understanding. On the other hand, it is equally unscientific in all those cases where the lack of clarified concepts of the psychical as such leads to an obscure formulation of problems and consequently to merely apparent solutions. The experimental method is indispensable, particularly where there is a question of fixing intersubjective connections of facts. But this does not alter the fact that it presupposes what no experiment can accomplish, the analysis of conscious life itself ("Phil. Rig. Sc.," 92–94 [301–3]).

Some psychologists, such as Stumpf and Lipps, had recognized this defect of empirical psychology and, in the manner of Brentano, had tried to undertake thorough analytical-descriptive investigations of psychical experiences. The results of these investigations were denied recognition by most of the experimental psychologists, who disdainfully called them "Scholastic analyses." The only reason for this depreciation, however, was that Brentano, Stumpf, and Lipps took ordinary language as the starting point of their investigations. But if one reads these investigations, it becomes clear immediately that Brentano, Stumpf, and Lipps do not derive any judgment at all from word concepts but rather penetrate to the phenomena themselves, which immediately present themselves to one's intuitive reflection.

It is evident that the fixation of a scientific language presupposes a complete analysis of the original phenomena, and that as long as that has not been accomplished the progress of the investigations remains to a great extent in the realm of vagueness and ambiguity ("Phil. Rig. Sc.," 95–96 [303–5]).

Second Misconception of Traditional Psychology: Imitation of Physics — In the reactions against this so-called Scholasticism, it is very often brought out that "empty" word-analyses are meaningless and that one has to question the things themselves and to go back to experience, which alone can give sense and meaning to our words. The question is, however, what is to be understood here by "the things themselves," and what kind of experience it is to which we have to return in psychology. Are they perhaps the answers that the psychologist gets from his or her "patients" or subjects of experimentation? Or is the psychologist's interpretation of their answers the experience we must look for? Every experimental psychologist will say, evidently, that the primary experience lies in the subjects and that an interpretation of this experience presupposes certain self-perceptions of the psychologist that—whatever they may be—in any case are not "introspections" ("Phil. Rig. Sc.," 96–98 [305–9]).

Despite some exaggeration, there is something in this view that is unquestionably right. But there is also a fundamental error in this psychology, for it puts analyses realized in empathetic understanding of others' experiences and analyses based on one's own formerly unnoticed experiences on the same level with the analysis characteristic of natural science, in the belief that it is an experimental science of the psychical in fundamentally the same way as natural science is the experimental science of the physical. In so doing, however, it overlooks the specific character of consciousness and the psychical data.

Most psychologists believe they owe all their psychological knowledge to experience. Nevertheless, the description of the naive empirical data, along with an immanent analysis that goes hand in hand with this description, is effected with the help of psychological concepts whose scientific value will be decisive for all further methodological steps. These concepts, however, remain by the very nature of the experimental method constantly untouched but nevertheless enter into the final empirical judgments, which claim to be scientific. On the other hand, the value of these concepts was not present from the beginning, nor can it originate from the experience of the subjects or of the psychologists themselves. It cannot be logically obtained from any empirical determinations whatsoever. And here is the place for phenomenological, eidetic analyses ("Phil. Rig. Sc.," 98–102 [309–12]).

What has been constantly muddled in empirical psychology since its beginning in the eighteenth century is the deceptive idea of a scientific method modeled after that of the physiochemical sciences. The British associationists and the German experimentalists were implicitly convinced that the method of all empirical sciences, considered in its universal principles, had to be one and the same, and that it therefore ought to be the same in psychology as in the natural sciences. Just as metaphysics suffered for a long time from an imitation of the geometrical and physical methods (in the work of Descartes and many others), so psychology has suffered from an unacceptable simulation of the physical sciences. (It is not without significance that the fathers of experimental psychology [Gustav Theodor Fechner, Hermann von Helmholtz, and Wundt] were physiologists and physicists.) It is clear that in following these lines of thought, the typical characteristics of psychical phenomena must be denied. The true method has to follow the nature of the things to be investigated, not our prejudices and preconceptions ("Phil. Rig. Sc.," 102–3 [312–14]).

Since all psychological knowledge presupposes our knowledge of the essence of the psychical, and since such knowledge cannot be obtained by means of physical procedures, it is evident that only phenomenological analyses can give us a correct solution for the problems mentioned. It is the fundamental error of modern psychology that it has not recognized the necessity of a phenomenological method. For only a really radical and systematic phenomenology, carried out not incidentally and in isolated reflections but in exclusive dedication to the extremely complex and confused problems of consciousness and executed in an attitude free from all naturalistic prejudices, can give us a real understanding of the psychical. Only then will the plentitude of empirical facts and the interesting laws that have been gathered bear their real fruit as the result of a critical evaluation and psychological interpretation. Then, too, will it become clear in what sense psychology stands in close relationship to philosophy ("Phil. Rig. Sc.," 103–10 [314–22]).

Husserl's View on Empirical and Eidetic Sciences

When Husserl in the second volume of *Logical Investigations* for the first time introduced the term "phenomenology," he stressed the point that phenomenology, taken as descriptive psychology, is concerned primarily with the general essence of consciousness and with the essences of its various structures (*L.I.,* 2:2 [*L.U.,* 1:249].). Although after 1904 it became clear to him that this definition ambiguously and even incorrectly spoke of descriptive psychology, he never gave up the characterization of phenomenology as a science of the general essences of consciousness and its various structures. Although he also realized gradually that his study of the relation between facts and essences in *Logical Investigations* did not solve all the problems that can and must be asked in this context, he did not see in this limitation any reason to doubt the positive value of these inquiries or to minimize their fundamental importance for phenomenology. On the contrary, he repeatedly returned to the study of the relationship between facts and essences and, correlatively, between the sciences of facts and the sciences of essences. In these investigations, Husserl tried not only to solve the questions left open in his first examinations but also to give a more radical basis to the original insights that they had disclosed.

In the first part of the first volume of *Ideas* (*Ideas,* 1:5–48 [7–48]), which was added to the book after the other parts had already been completed, Husserl gave a systematic account of the "final" conception he had come to with respect to the distinction between facts and essences as well as the distinction between sciences of facts and sciences of essences, that is, between empirical and eidetic sciences. Since these ideas are of great importance to Husserl's phenomenology as a whole, in the pages to follow I shall present a brief overview of the most important ideas discussed in the first part of volume 1 of *Ideas*.

I Fact and Essence

Natural Knowledge and Experience: Fact and Essence — As Husserl sees it, all natural knowledge begins with experience and remains within experience. And since experience is experience of the world, the total field of possible research governed by our theoretical knowledge of the natural standpoint is the world. Accordingly, the sciences proper to this natural standpoint are sciences of the world. And, therefore, from this standpoint the meaning of the expressions "true being," "real being," and "being in the world" coincide.

Every science has its own domain of research. To all its correct assertions there correspond certain intuitions as the original sources of its scientific justification. In these intuitions, objects of the domain in question appear as self-given and, in part at least, as given in a primordial sense. The object-giving intuition of the first and natural sphere of knowledge and of all its sciences is "natural experience," and the primordial object-giving experience is "perception." In "external perception," we have primordial experiences of physical things, but memory and anticipating expectation cannot be called primordial experiences. We have a primordial experience of ourselves and of our own states of consciousness in "internal perception," but we do not have such an experience of others and their lived experiences, for those experiences occur in and through "empathy." We behold the lived experiences of others by perceiving their bodily behavior. Although this beholding in and through empathy is an intuitive object-giving act, it is no longer a primordial object-giving act. Human beings with their psychical lives are apprehended as "there in person" and as one with their own bodies, but, unlike the body, their psychical lives are not given to our consciousness in a primordial way.

The world is the totality of objects that can be known through experience and through theoretical knowledge based upon direct experiences. The sciences of the world—that is, the sciences of our natural standpoint—include not only the "natural sciences" but also sciences such as biology, physiology, and psychology, and the so-called *Geisteswissenschaften,* namely, history, the social sciences, and the different cultural sciences (*Ideas,* 1:5–6 [7–8]).

Sciences of experience are *sciences of fact.* Cognitive acts, which are ultimately based upon primordial experiences, posit reality in *individual* form; they posit it as having a spatiotemporal existence, as something existing here and at this point of time, as having this particular duration, and as having a real content whose essence could just as well be present in any other point of time. They posit it, moreover, as something that is present now at this place and in this particular physical shape, although the same real being, as far as its essence is concerned, could just as well be present in any other place and in any other form or shape. Every individual being as such is, generally speaking, accidental or contingent insofar as it is such and such but essentially could be other than it is.

Even if there are definite laws of nature according to which *these* particular consequences must in fact follow whenever *those* conditions exist, such laws express only an order that in fact does obtain but might be quite different. Presupposing that the objects thus ordered are, when considered in themselves, accidental and contingent, these laws refer already from the very beginning to the *essences* of the objects of possible experience. For when we state that every fact can be "essentially" other than it is, we express that it belongs to the meaning of every contingent thing and event to have an essential being and therefore an *eidos* that can be apprehended in all its purity. An individual object is not simply an individual, a "this-here," but being constituted thus, and so in itself it has its own mode of being, its own essential predicables that qualify it *qua* being as it is in itself. Whatever belongs to the essence of an individual can also belong to another individual (*Ideas,* 1:7–8 [8–9]).

Intuition of Essences and Intuition of Individual Things: Ideation — The term "essence" indicates that which is to be found in the very own being of an individual and tells us "what" it is. Every such "what" can be expressed in an idea. Empirical or individual intuition can be transformed into an intuition of the corresponding essence by *ideation.* The object of such an intuition is the corresponding *pure* essence, or *eidos,* regardless of whether this essence is the highest category, or a more specialized one, or even the fully "concrete."

The intuition that *gives* the essence and, in the last analysis, gives it in primordial form, can be *adequate,* but it can also be more or less imperfect or *inadequate.* In the case of an inadequate intuition, the inadequacy is not limited only to greater or lesser clearness and distinctness, for in certain categories of being essences can be given only one-sidedly, although evidently several, but never all, sides can be given successively. Hence, the concrete and individual particularities corresponding to these categories can be experienced and presented only in inadequate, one-sided, empirical intuitions. This assertion applies to every essence belonging to the realm of thinglike, physical, and material being.

No matter of what kind an individual intuition may be, whether adequate or inadequate, it can always change into essential intuition, and the latter, whether adequate or not, has the character of an object-giving act. This means that the essence (*eidos*) is a new type of object. Just as the datum of individual and empirical intuition is an individual and concrete object, so the datum of essential intuition is a pure essence.

It is very important to realize that there is no question here of a mere superficial analogy but rather of a radical correspondence in nature. Essential intuition is still intuition, and the eidetic object is still an object. The generalization of the correlative concepts "intuition" and "object" is therefore not accidental but is demanded by the very nature of things. Empirical intuition, and more specifically sense experience, is consciousness of an individual object and, as intuition, it brings this object to givenness; as perception, it brings the object to primordial givenness, to the consciousness of grasping the object in a primordial way in its authentic reality. In a similar way, essential intuition is the consciousness of something, of an object, a something toward which one's glance is directed, a something that is self-given within this glance.

Thus, every possible object—or, logically expressed, every subject of possibly true predication—has its own way of coming under a glance that presents, intuits, and meets it eventually in its authentic reality, its "bodily selfhood." Accordingly, essential intuition is intuition, and if there is a question of an intuition in the pregnant sense of the term, it is a primordial object-giving act that grasps the essence in its authentic reality. On the other hand, it is a fundamentally unique and novel kind of intuition.

It is undoubtedly intrinsically proper to the intuition of an essence that it should be based on a primary factor of individual intuition, namely, the striving for the "visible" presence of the individual fact. However, as is mentioned above, essential intuition does not presuppose any apprehension of the individual or any assumption as regards its reality. Consequently, no essential intuition is possible without the free possibility of performing an act of ideation and directing one's glance to the corresponding essence that exemplifies itself in every individual, visible thing. Nevertheless, the two kinds of intuition remain fundamentally different, although, as we have seen, they are essentially related, too. The essential relations between individual and concrete being and essence, between fact and *eidos,* thus correspond to the essential differences between the two kinds of intuitions (*Ideas,* 1:8–11 [10–12]).

The *eidos,* or pure essence, can be exemplified intuitively in the data of either experience or phantasy. Hence, if we want to grasp an essence itself in its primordial form, we can start either from the corresponding empirical intuitions or from intuitions of a purely imaginative order. If, in the play of phantasy, we create spatial forms of one kind or another or melodies, social events, fictitious events of everyday life, acts of satisfaction or dissatisfaction, or whatever we want to imagine, we can through ideation secure from this source a primordial and even, on occasion, an adequate insight into pure essences, for example, essences of spatial form as such, of melody as such, of social event as such, or essences of a relevant special type of them.

From all this it follows that the positing of the essence, with the intuitive apprehension that immediately accompanies it, does not at all imply the positing of any individual existence. Pure essential truths do not assert anything about facts. Consequently, from them alone we are not able to infer even the smallest truth about the real world (*Ideas,* 1:11–12 [12–13]).

Sciences of Facts and Sciences of Essences — We have seen above that each individual object has its own essence, just as to each essence there conversely corresponds a series of possible individuals as its factual individuations. This connection gives rise to a corresponding relationship between sciences of facts and sciences of essences.

There are pure sciences of essences, such as pure logic, pure mathematics, pure theory of time, pure theory of space, pure theory of movement. In all their considerations, these sciences are wholly free from positing any actual facts; in these sciences no experience *as* experience—that is, as consciousness which apprehends *reality*— can take over the function of offering a logical ground. If experience plays a role in these sciences, it is not *as* experience. For example, the geometrician who draws figures on the blackboard and experiences them provides as little ground for his seeing and thinking the geometric essences as does the "physical" act of producing those figures. Whether he draws his lines in an imaginary world or on the blackboard does not make any difference here. The physicist, however, acts quite differently. She observes and experiments, she determines what is concretely there just as she experiences it. For her, experience is an act that gives a foundation which mere imagining could never replace. It is for this reason that "science of facts" and "science of experience" are equivalent expressions.

Accordingly, the essential characteristic of pure eidetic science is that its procedure is exclusively eidetic. From start to finish, it discloses no factual meaning that is not eidetically valid, that is, a factual meaning which either is immediately open to primordial insight because it is directly based on essences in which we have a primordial insight or can be inferred through pure reasoning from axiomatic factual meanings of this type (*Ideas,* 1:15–17 [16–18]).

It is evident, then, that eidetic science is in principle unable to take over any of the theoretical results attained by empirical sciences, for the reference to reality that appears in the immediately valid premises of the empirical sciences reappears in all their derivative propositions. From facts nothing ever follows but facts.

Although eidetic science is intrinsically independent of any science of facts, the opposite holds for the sciences of facts themselves. No fully developed science of facts can exist without an admixture of eidetic knowledge; every science of facts depends on formal and material eidetic sciences. In the first place, it is obvious that an empirical science, no matter where it finds the ground on which it bases its judgments through mediate reasoning, must proceed according to the formal principles of logic. Generally speaking, since empirical science is directed toward objects, just as any other science, it is necessarily bound by the laws that pertain to the essence of the object in general. Hence it cannot be indifferent to the group of formal-ontological disciplines in which formal logic occupies the central place. Secondly, every fact includes an essential structure of a material order, and every eidetic truth, which pertains to the pure essence included therein, must lead to a law that governs the given concrete instance and, in general, every possible instance (*Ideas,* 1:17–18 [18]).

Regions and Regional Categories — Every concrete empirical object, together with its material essence, has its proper place in a highest material genus, a "region" of empirical objects. A "regional eidetic science," a "regional ontology," therefore corresponds to the pure regional essence. Accordingly, every empirical science that deals with the entities belonging to a given region will be essentially related to the regional and formal ontologies in question. In other words, every factual and empirical science has its essential theoretical basis in eidetic ontologies. For instance, an "eidetic science of physical nature in general" (the ontology of nature) corresponds to all the natural sciences insofar as an *eidos* that can be apprehended in its purity—namely, the essence "nature in general" with the limitless horizon of essential structures included in it—corresponds to actual nature. If we are to construct the idea of a completely rationalized empirical science of nature, obviously the realization of this idea will be essentially dependent on the cultivation of the corresponding eidetic sciences. It will depend not only on the cultivation of the formal *mathesis universalis,* which is related similarly to all

the sciences, but, in particular, on the constitution of material-onto-
logical disciplines that analyze in rational purity the essence of nature and all essential articulations of nature's objects as such. The
same holds good, of course, for all other regions.

To support this view, we may appeal again to the development
of the natural sciences. Their era of greatness in the modern age
arose precisely because geometry, which in the ancient world had
already been highly developed along pure, eidetic lines, was in one
sweep made fruitful for the physical method. It was clearly realized
that it is of the essence of a material thing to be a *res extensa* and
that consequently geometry is an ontological discipline concerning
an essential feature of such a thing, namely, its spatial form. But it
was also realized that the universal, regional essence of the things
goes much further. The evidence for this assertion is that, at the
very beginning of the modern era, a series of other sciences was created, and their purpose was to play a role analogous to the one
played by geometry in the rationalization of the empirical. A rich
variety of mathematical sciences originated from this impulse
(*Ideas,* 1:18–20 [19–20]).

▌Regional Ontologies and Phenomenology

The preceding pages briefly describe Husserl's view on the relation
between fact and essence and its logical consequences. For the
greater part, these considerations are found in the second and third
volumes of the second edition of *Logical Investigations* (1913). The
ideas mentioned contain many difficult problems that cannot be considered here in detail. There are, however, other problems with
which we must concern ourselves here because they appear to be
very important for the proper understanding of Husserl's phenomenology as a whole, and particularly of what he has to say about the
relationship between phenomenological psychology and empirical
psychology on the one hand, and about the relationship between
phenomenological psychology and transcendental phenomenology,
on the other. To these latter problems we shall turn next.[3]

Regional Ontologies and Empirical Sciences — There is no
doubt that in dealing with the so-called "regional ontologies,"
Husserl in 1913 took his starting point in the idea that in its many
directions the world of our immediate experience has already become the object of scientific determination in which everything that
our prescientific and daily experience finds merely in a vague and
naive way is grasped in exact concepts and explanatory theories.
Each science has its own domain of investigation, but it is not able to
furnish this domain for itself; this domain is pregiven inasfar as in

our prescientific experience, beings immediately manifest themselves as being comparable with, and distinguishable from, one another.

Our prescientific experience a priori precedes all sciences of experience and equally a priori delineates their different domains of investigation. We have just seen that Husserl calls the totality of objects that each science investigates, in its own and typical way, a "region." He thus speaks, for instance, of the "region of physical nature" and the "region of psychical beings." What all the objects of a certain region have in common, and what therefore characterizes them, is, according to Husserl, fixed in the categories germane to each region. Together they coconstitute the "regional categories," or the fundamental and basic concepts, of that region. In these basic concepts are all the a priori suppositions under which each multiplicity of the beings immediately given in our prescientific experience can be conceived and understood as belonging together in such a way that they can become the object and theme of one or the other science. Because these basic concepts constitute the typical mode of intelligibility and therefore also the object character of the objects of the sciences in question, the sciences in which the categories of a determinate region are discovered are called "regional ontologies." That is why every empirical science that is engaged in the scientific investigation of a determinate domain of beings is to be founded in a regional ontology in which the basic concepts of this science are to be explained in a radical way.[4]

According to Landgrebe, Husserl in 1913 considered these sciences to be philosophical sciences.[5] In my opinion, however, this cannot be so, for already in *The Idea of Phenomenology* (1907), Husserl characterized the difference between philosophical and nonphilosophical disciplines by pointing to the fundamental difference between the philosophical and the natural attitude, whereas in the same book the formal ontologies are explicitly classed under the sciences of the natural attitude (*The Idea,* 14–15 [17–19]). In a note of 1916 referring to the first lecture, Husserl adds the *material* ontologies and again makes the explicit remark that all these ontologies belong to the realm of the "natural" sciences, that is, to the sciences of the natural attitude. That Husserl in 1913 was of the same opinion is not only clear from the remark with which he concludes his "logical investigations" (*Ideas,* 1:39 [39]), but especially from the passage in which he explicitly says that the formal ontologies as well as the material ontologies must be "disconnected" through the transcendental reduction (*Ideas,* 1:135–141 [111–17]).[6] Here Husserl even claims "the absolute independence of phenomenology from all sciences, including the eidetic sciences," that is, from the formal and material ontologies; this claim is motivated by "the philosophical functions" that phenomenology has to perform (*Ideas,* 1:138 [114–15]). In the third volume of *Ideas,* which, according to Marly Biemel, was written in its first draft in 1912,[7] Husserl says that it is one of the most important tasks of phenomenological philosophy to give the eidetic, regional ontologies their ultimate foundation (*Ideas,* 3:76–92 [65–79]).

When Husserl claims that every empirical science is to be founded in a regional ontology, this evidently does not mean that the regional ontologies should have to precede the empirical sciences. On the contrary, it is Husserl's view that regional ontologies can be built up only by starting from a subsequent reflection on the conditions under which such a domain of beings could be delineated. Regional ontologies explicate what in unconditioned generality and necessity must belong to a certain object if it really is to be the object of investigation of the correlative empirical science; that is to say, regional ontologies must determine and describe the essential structures of every possible object of the different empirical sciences that deal with the entities belonging to the region in question. That is why Husserl also speaks of "eidetic sciences" in contradistinction to "sciences of facts." On the other hand, it also follows from the foregoing that, although the regional ontologies follow after the corresponding empirical sciences in the order of time, they nevertheless, as eidetic sciences, precede those sciences *de jure* (*Ideas,* 1:17–18 [18], 160–64 [132–36]).

Formal and Material Ontologies — In *Ideas* a formal ontology, which makes abstraction from all the regional distinctions of the different objects and deals with the formal idea of the object in general, is put ahead of the regional ontologies (*Ideas,* 1:17–18 [18]). Its subject matter consists in the conditions under which anything whatsoever can be a legitimate object of one's thought and science and thus can be described and explained by every science. Although, on the one hand, one could say that this formal ontology is a branch of logic as universal analytic, on the other hand, it is also true that it comprises the whole *mathesis universalis* (formal logic, arithmetic, pure analysis, set theory, etc.) (ibid., 20–21 [20–22]).

The regional or material ontologies try to investigate all the conditions that, from the point of view of their subject matters, are necessarily presupposed in the different empirical sciences. They have to focus attention on the *eidos,* that is, the universally operative and necessary essence of the objects of the empirical sciences. It is these essences that are investigated in formal ontology in the reduced form of "object-in-general." The subject matter of formal ontology, therefore, does not consist in the class of essences but in a mere essence-form, which is indeed an essence but a completely "empty" one (ibid.), that is to say, an essence that in the manner of an empty form fits all possible essences and in its formal universality has the highest material generalities subordinated to it (ibid.). However, the formal region is not on a par with the material regions; properly speaking, it is no region at all but the pure form of region in general only. Formal ontology, therefore, investigates a completely new dimension of being, namely, the necessary conditions of being-object (ibid.).

Let us try to explain this important distinction from a different point of view. It is Husserl's idea that the structure of being on which the material ontologies focus all their attention is not everywhere the same: different regions of being have a different constitution and therefore cannot be described with the help of the same categories (*Ideas,* 1:20–23 [20–23]). Certainly, one can universally apply the categories "object," "relation," etc., but the structure that is expressed in these concepts common to all regions of being is merely formal. Therefore, the concept "object-in-general" is *not* the supreme genus of which the basic concepts of the different material regions are to be the various species. The categories that express the material structure of being, which, for instance, defines nature as nature and consciousness as consciousness, are not mere specifications of formal categories; that is to say, they are not the results of the addition of a *differentia specifica* to a *genus proximum*. This is why Husserl stresses the difference between genus and form, between generalization and formalization, and between specialization and deformalization (ibid., 26–27 [26–27]).[8]

The General Ontology of the World of Immediate Experience — In 1913 Husserl had not yet mentioned the possibility or even the necessity of a "general material ontology of the world of immediate experience," which in the lecture series *Phenomenological Psychology* (1925) constitutes the core of his investigations. Once Husserl saw the necessity not only of a material ontology of nature as nature, consciousness as consciousness, society as society, etc., but, first and foremost, of a general material ontology of the world of immediate experience as such, it became clear to him that the subject matter of the different regional ontologies cannot be determined by taking one's starting point in the empirical sciences alone but must be drawn also from the general material ontology of the world of immediate experience. However, all that was said in 1913 about formal ontology as well as about the description of the meaning and function of the material ontologies is maintained in 1925. Husserl then only adds a new science, namely, the general ontology of the world of immediate experience as such, which has a foundational function in regard to the material ontologies. Evidently, the consequence of this is that the relation between regional ontologies and the corresponding empirical sciences is to be determined in a different way. But even then, Husserl explicitly maintains that every material ontology whatsoever must ultimately be founded in transcendental phenomenology (*Phen. Psych.,* 38–53 [52–72]).

We shall return to these questions in some of the chapters to follow because the development of Husserl's thought in this respect is closely connected with his view on phenomenological psychology.

Note on the Term "Ontology" — It appears that the term "ontology"[9] was used for the first time by Goclenius (1547–1628). In his *Lexicon Philosophicum,* he distinguishes three "contemplative sciences" and the degree to which they abstract from matter. If the science merely abstracts from the singular sensible matter, the subject matter of the science of "physics" will be the result. The mathematician abstracts from all sensible matter. The ontological abstraction that leads to ontology abstracts from all matter, sensible and intelligible, but only "secundum rationem," according to reason; ontology is the science of being as being as well as the science of the transcendental notions. Finally, there is a form of abstraction that abstracts from all matter both "secundum rationem et secundum rem," according to reason and according to the thing itself. This science of "transnatural" abstraction is the science of God and the "intelligences." It is clear that this distinction goes back to ideas first developed by Aristotle. While Aristotle does not explicitly speak of ontology and perhaps never explicitly made a distinction between the study of being qua being (ontology) and the study of the first being and the other "separate entities," in our tradition there have been a great number of commentators and scholars who have defended the view that such a distinction was indeed Aristotle's final view on what later would be called his metaphysics.

Several authors of the seventeenth and eighteenth centuries adopted the term "ontology," even though they did not always define it in the same manner with respect to other metaphysical disciplines. Yet, generally speaking, one can say that they used the term "ontology"—also called "ontosophia"—to refer to the systematic study of being as being. Leibniz, too, uses the term. In his *Introductio ad Encyclopaediam arcanam,* he gives a brief description of "general science" as the science of everything that is conceivable in the broadest possible sense, insofar as it is conceivable. This general science comprises a great number of sciences and "arts." At the end of the list, Leibniz, with some hesitation, adds ontology and defines it as the doctrine of something and nothing, being and nonbeing, thing and modality, substance and accident.

The clear and sharp distinction between ontology and natural theology is found for the first time in the works of Christian von Wolff and the entire Wolffian tradition. Ontology is the science of being in general, or of being insofar as it is being. This science is called first philosophy and also general metaphysics. It is followed by three types of special metaphysics: general cosmology, empirical psychology, and natural theology. Whereas in the entire Aristotelian tradition, ontology and natural theology had been taken to constitute a unity, in the Wolffian tradition ontology and natural theology become two different independent sciences, with the latter subordinated to the former. This separation had a deep influence on Kant. Once it was clear to him that a general ontology had been made impossible by the transcendental analytic, he saw himself forced to equally reject the three forms of *metaphysica specialis* in the transcendental dialectic. Says Kant:

> Accordingly, the transcendental analytic leads to this important conclusion, that the most understanding can achieve a priori is to anticipate the form of a possible experience in general. . . . [T]he understanding can never transcend those limits of sensibility within which alone objects can be given to us. Its principles are merely rules for the exposition of appearances; and the proud name of an ontology that presumptuously claims to supply, in systematic doctrinal form, synthetic a priori knowledge of things in general (for instance, the principle of causality) must, therefore, give place to the modest title of a mere analytic of pure understanding. (B 303–4)

Kant maintains the terms "metaphysics" and "ontology" but gives them a completely new meaning. "Metaphysics" in the narrow and proper sense of the term is either transcendental philosophy or physiology of pure reason: "The former treats only of the understanding and of reason, in a system of concepts and principles which relate to objects in general, but takes no account of objects *that may be given (Ontologia)*" (B 873).

In Husserl's philosophy, the term "ontology" receives a central place. Yet he uses the term in a completely new sense that may have been inspired by both the Aristotelian and the Wolffian conceptions of ontology. The distinction between formal and material ontologies and the distinction between a general material ontology and regional ontologies seem to be original with Husserl. The term "transcendental ontology," which he uses here in the *Encyclopaedia Britannica* article, may have been inspired by Kant's architectonic of pure reason.

As we shall see in Chapter Ten, in his later works Husserl also uses the term "ontology" to refer to his new, transcendental phenomenology insofar as it is the pure and transcendental science of *all* phenomena and of *all* synthetic activities in which these phenomena become constituted. Thus transcendental phenomenology presents us with the *logos* of all *onta;* it is *ontology* in the true and genuine sense of the term. Yet in his earlier works written before 1925, Husserl always reserves the term "ontology" for a "mundane," eidetic science, such as formal ontology or phenomenological psychology.

Empirical Psychology, Pure Psychology, and Psychophysiology

We must now finally try to apply the insights gained so far to the question of the relationship between pure, phenomenological psychology and empirical psychology.[10]

As Husserl sees it, contemporary empirical psychology, as the science of the psychical, taken insofar as this is concretely connected with spatiotemporal, real things, considers as its subject matter all that is present in the world as a living subject that perceives, strives, wills, thinks, etc. One could therefore call this concrete psychology a psychophysical psychology, since it seeks to study psychic life as it manifests itself in our immediate experiences and as it thus appears in the concrete connectedness with a living body. This psychophysical psychology often degenerated into naturalism when it tried to explain the psychical exclusively on the basis of material bodily happenings, as for instance in classical behaviorism. The unacceptability of this naturalism has already been the topic of a previous section, so we will not deal with it here again. The psychophysical psychology that we want to discuss now simply accepts the fact that the psychical never occurs in the world without a foundation in the physical. But at the same time, this psychology maintains that the psychical has its own typically essential characteristics and that it therefore commands its own realm of lawfulness.[11]

The first problem arising out of this consideration concerns the question of whether the *purely* psychical can be sufficiently separated from the physical to form the basis of a pure psychology that would operate in addition to psychophysical psychology. Before answering this question, we must first clarify the characteristics of psychical experience itself and of the psychical data that it brings to light. To that end, we must concentrate on our *immediate* experiences. These experiences allow us to discover the psychical only by means of reflection, by means of a change in our normal, natural attitude. In the natural attitude, we usually concentrate on objects, on their characteristics, their values, etc., but bypass the psychical acts of experience through which we get to know these objects. The act itself cannot be revealed except through reflection, and such a reflection can be applied to every experience. In this reflection, we turn away from things, from their values, purposes, or usefulness. Instead we try to contemplate the experiences in which things and their different aspects stand revealed. These appearances we call *phenomena*. The essential characteristic of a phenomenon is that it is a consciousness of its object. *Pure psychology* is concerned with these phenomena. Since these phenomena are essentially intentional, we can also speak of *intentional psychology*.

It is possible to assume two different theoretical positions in respect to these pure psychical phenomena: we can accept them as psychical facts and stop there, or we can shift our position and concentrate on the very essence that, at the same time, manifests itself in these facts. In the first instance, we achieve a *pure, factual scientific psychology*, or a psychology that investigates only psychical facts after removal of those components which in reality are always connected with the psychical. The object of such a psychology is the study of human experiences seen apart from all bodily and physical components. Actually this pure, factual scientific psychology is often closely related to psychophysical psychology. Together these sciences form what usually is called *empirical psychology*.[12]

The investigations of this pure, factual scientific psychology need to have as their foundation a pure eidetic psychology and an aprioric one. This latter psychology also restricts its activities to the realm of the purely psychical and concentrates on the very essence of the psychical phenomena rather than on their factual aspects. The best avenue of approach to this eidetic, or *phenomenological psychology*, is through a deeper understanding of intentionality.[13]

In the natural, nonreflective attitude, we direct our attention to objects that we know or toward which we strive. Reflection reveals to us that this intentionally being-directed-toward is an immanent process characteristic of all forms of experience. This process can assume any number of concrete forms or modalities. "To be conscious of something" does not mean simply to possess this something in consciousness. Each phenomenon has its own intentional structure, which in analysis can be shown to be an ever-expanding system of individual, intentional, and intentionally connected components. The perception of a house, for example, turns out to be a manifold synthesized intention, a continuous diversity of appearances of this house that answers the different points of view from which it is seen. This diversity of appearances also answers the different corresponding perspectives that are revealed when we observe the sides and the rear of the house after we have seen the front part. These latter perspectives originally remained hidden, were also relatively undetermined, and yet were always already presupposed. Seeing the front of the house already contains expectations concerning the sides and the back of the house. When we observe closely this stream of appearances and the manner in which they form a unity, we come to see that each phase of the total process is already by itself a consciousness of something, although these different acts of consciousness do not disrupt our distinct consciousness of dealing with one and the same thing. The intentional structure of a complete perceptual act must conform to a certain type if a certain physical object is to be perceived as an actually present, perceived thing. Something analogous to this must take place if we are to remember, to imagine, to judge, to value, or to strive for a particular object. We shall return to this in the next chapter.

The task of phenomenological psychology is to systematically investigate these types and forms of intentional experiences and to reduce their structures to a primary intention. The ultimate purpose is thus to explicate the very essence of the psychical and to come to an understanding of the being proper to, and characteristic of, the "soul" itself. The validity of this research reaches beyond the particular life of the investigating psychologist because psychic life is not only manifested in his own self-consciousness but also in his consciousness of other people. This last source of experience, that of other people, does not offer us a mere repetition of what we already found to be present in our own consciousness; on the contrary, it shows us the difference between what we experience as belonging to us and belonging to others and confronts us with the characteristics of social life. A further task of phenomenological psychology therefore directs itself to the intentionality operative in, and constitutive of, social life.

Phenomenological psychology therefore shares with pure, factual scientific psychology an interest in the conscious life of ourselves and in the experiences of others and of community that are derived from it. Its subject matter comes to light as soon as we remove all the nonpsychical aspects of a given reality by means of abstraction. It is not immediately clear how such an abstraction can be realized, how it can be consistently performed, and how it can be maintained without getting caught up time and again in physical and psychophysical considerations. It is this fundamental problem that, notwithstanding Brentano's discovery of intentionality as the fundamental characteristic of the psychical, has made psychologists

turn their backs to the many possibilities inherent in phenomenological psychology. The psychologist always finds his consciousness
of himself mixed with nonpsychical ingredients.

In the "Amsterdam Lectures," Husserl describes the main problems involved in a manner that indicates to what extent Husserl
thought there was an adequate answer to these problems.[14] Reflecting on the distinction between the empirical sciences of nature and
an aprioric, pure science of nature, one must ask to what extent, by
maintaining a one-sided orientation toward the psychical in animals and human beings—which manifestly is never found independently of their organisms—an experience and a kind of theoretical
research are possible that continually and consistently proceed from
one psychical phenomenon to another and thus never make the
physical the main point of concern. This leads immediately to the
question of whether a consistent and pure psychology is possible
that runs parallel to a consistently and purely developed science of
nature. Husserl is convinced that the last question cannot be answered in the affirmative. First of all, empirical psychology, as a science of empirical facts, can never consistently make abstraction of
the physical in the same manner in which the empirical science of
nature can make abstraction of everything psychical. Secondly, the
pure science of the psychical can be developed consistently up to a
point; yet beyond that point, it must take into consideration that
everything psychical is always found in animal and human bodies.

However far a consistently developed pure psychic experience
may reach and may be carried out by means of our theoretization, it
is and remains certain a priori that the pure psychical toward which
it tends in the real world always has its temporal and spatial determinations and that, as far as its real facticity is concerned, it can be
determined only through spatiotemporally local determinations,
just like everything real as such. Spatiotemporality, taken as a system of places, is the form of every mode of being that is factical, of
every mode of being in the world of facts. This implies that every
determination of real *facta* is founded upon spatiotemporal determinations. Spatiotemporality, however, belongs originally and also
immediately to nature, taken as physical nature. Spatiotemporal
situation and position belong to everything extraphysical, and to
everything psychical in particular, only through their foundation in
a physical corporeality. One can therefore easily understand why in
empirical psychology a purely psychological form of research can
never be clearly demarcated theoretically over against the psychophysical. Thus it is impossible that within psychology, taken as
an objective science of facts, an empirical science of the psychical can

ever be established as a self-contained discipline. It will never be possible to eliminate all thematic considerations of the physical and the psychophysical.

On the other hand, it is also clear that purely psychical research must be possible to some degree and must play an important part within every empirical psychology that strives for strict scientificity. For how else can one discover strictly scientific concepts of the psychical in its innermost essential structure and irrespective of its interwovenness with the physical? If we now realize that to these concepts must necessarily belong also such concepts that delineate the universal and essential form of the psychical in its innermost essential structure and without which the psychical as such cannot be thought, then we gain access to a possible, a priori science of essences that is concerned with the psychical purely as such. Thus the parallel referred to above is not one between physics as an empirical science of nature and empirical psychology but rather one between the science of the a priori constitutive of the essence of every conceivable nature as such and pure psychology as the science of the a priori constitutive of the essence of every conceivable psychic entity as such. While we usually do not speak of an a priori science of nature, one is nevertheless quite familiar with what is meant here insofar as we are all familiar with some of its basic subdisciplines, namely, the a priori doctrine of time, pure geometry, and pure mechanics.

▌NOTES

1. Spiegelberg, *The Phenomenological Movement,* 149–50.
2. For this section in general, see Joseph J. Kockelmans, *Edmund Husserl's Phenomenological Psychology* (Pittsburgh, Pa.: Duquesne University Press, 1967), 104–22.
3. For what follows, see Ludwig Landgrebe, "Seinsregionen und regionale Ontologien in Husserl's Phänomenologie," *Studium Generale* 9 (1956): 313–24; and idem, *Der Weg der Phänomenologie* (Gütersloh: Gerd Mohn, 1963), 143–62.
4. Landgrebe, "Seinsregionen und regionale Ontologien," 313–14.
5. Ibid., 314–15.
6. See Emmanuel Levinas, *Théorie de l'intuition dans la phénoménologie de Husserl* (Paris: Vrin, 1963), 21–22.
7. Marly Biemel, "Einleitung des Herausgebers," in Husserl, *Ideen,* 3:xvi.
8. Levinas, *Théorie de l'intuition,* 21.
9. See "Ontologie," in *Historisches Wörterbuch der Philosophie,* ed. Joachim Ritter and Karlfried Gründer (Stuttgart: Schwabe, 1971–), 6:1189–1200; *Opuscules et fragments inédits de Leibniz,* ed. Louis Couturat (Paris: Alcan, 1903); Heinz Heimsoeth, "Christian Wolffs Ontologie und die Prinzipienforschung Immanuel Kants," in *Studien zur Philosophie Immanuel Kants,* 2 vols. (Cologne: Kölner Universitäts Verlag, 1956–71), 1:1–92.

10. See Max Drüe, *Edmund Husserls System der phänomenologischen Psychologie* (Berlin: de Gruyter, 1963), 55–92.

11. Ibid., 56–57.

12. Ibid., 57. Husserl, *Phen. Psych.,* 166–70 [217–22]; *Crisis,* 211–15 [215–19], 224–26 [227–29].

13. Drüe, *Edmund Husserls System,* 58–61. Husserl, *Phen. Psych.,* 33–37 [46–51], 170–79 [222–34]; *Crisis,* 233–57 [235–60]; *Cart. Med.,* 33–37 [72–75], 72–131 [107–59], 141–48 [168–74].

14. Husserl, *Phän. Psych.,* 303–5.

The Purely Psychical as Given in Experience: Intentionality

Text

Das rein Psychische der Selbsterfahrung und Gemeinschaftserfahrung. Die universale Deskription intentionaler Erlebnisse

Für eine Begründung und Entfaltung dieser Leitidee bedarf es als ein Erstes der Klärung des Eigentümlichen der Erfahrung und insbesondere der reinen Erfahrung von Psychischem und dieses rein Psychischen selbst, das sie offenbart und das zum Thema der reinen Psychologie werden soll. Wir bevorzugen naturgemäß die unmittelbarste Erfahrung, die uns je unser eigenes Psychisches enthüllt.

Die Einstellung des erfahrenden Blickes auf unser Psychisches vollzieht sich notwendig als eine Reflexion, als Umwendung des vordem anders gerichteten Blickes. Jede Erfahrung läßt solche Reflexion zu, aber auch jede sonstige Weise, in der wir mit irgend welchen realen oder idealen Gegenständen beschäftigt sind, etwa denkend oder in der Weise des Gemüts und Willens wertend, strebend. So, geradehin uns bewußt betätigend, sind in unserem Blick ausschließlich die jeweiligen Sachen, Gedanken, Werte, Ziele, Hilfsmittel, nicht aber das psychische Erleben selbst, in dem sie als solche uns bewußt sind. Erst die Reflexion macht es offenbar. Durch sie erfassen wir statt der Sachen schlechthin, der Werte, Zwecke, Nützlichkeiten schlechthin die entsprechenden subjektiven Erlebnisse, in denen sie uns "bewußt" werden, uns in einem allerweitesten Sinne *"erscheinen"*. Sie alle heißen daher auch *"Phänomene"*, ihr allgemeinster Wesenscharakter ist es, zu sein als "Bewußtsein von", "Erscheinung-von—*von* den jeweiligen Dingen, Gedanken (Urteilsverhalten, Gründen, Folgen), von den Plänen, Entschlüssen, Hoffnungen usw. Daher liegt im Sinne aller Ausdrücke der Volkssprachen für psychische Erlebnisse diese Relativität beschlossen, wahrnehmen von etwas, sich erinnern oder denken an etwas, etwas hoffen, befürchten, erstreben, sich entscheiden für etwas usw. Erweist sich dieses Reich der "Phänomene"

The Purely Psychical in Self-experience and Community Experience. The Universal Description of Intentional Experiences

To establish and unfold this guiding idea, the first thing that is necessary is a clarification of what is peculiar to experience, and especially to the pure experience of the psychical—and specifically the purely psychical that experience reveals, which is to become the theme of a pure psychology. It is natural and appropriate that precedence will be accorded to the most immediate types of experience, which in each case reveal to us our own psychic being.

Focusing our experiencing gaze on our own psychic life necessarily takes place as reflection, as a turning about of a glance which had previously been directed elsewhere. Every experience can be subject to such reflection, as can indeed every manner in which we occupy ourselves with any real or ideal objects—for instance, thinking, or in the modes of feeling and will, valuing and striving. So when we are fully engaged in conscious activity, we focus exclusively on the specific thing, thoughts, values, goals, or means involved, but not on the psychical experience as such, in which these things are known *as* such. Only reflection reveals this to us. Through reflection, instead of grasping simply the matter straight-out—the values, goals, and instrumentalities—we grasp the corresponding subjective experiences in which we become "conscious" of them, in which (in the broadest sense) they "appear." For this reason, they are called "phenomena," and their most general essential character is to exist as the "consciousness-of" or "appearance-of" the specific things, thoughts (judged states of affairs, grounds, conclusions), plans, decisions, hopes, and so forth. This relatedness [of the appearing to the object of appearance] resides in the meaning of all expressions in the vernacular languages which relate to psychic experience—for instance, perception of something, recalling *of* something, thinking *of* something, hoping *for* something, fearing something, striving *for*

als mögliches Feld einer reinen, ausschließlich auf sie [280]
bezogenen psychologischen Disziplin, so versteht sich nun deren
Kennzeichnung als *phänomenologische Psychologie*. Der temino-
logisch aus der Scholastik herstammende Ausdruck für jenen
Grundcharakter des Seins als Bewußtsein, als Erscheinung von
etwas ist *Intentionalität*. In dem unreflektierten Bewußthaben
irgendwelcher Gegenstände sind wir auf diese "gerichtet", unsere
"intentio" geht auf sie hin. Die phänomenologische Blickwendung
zeigt, daß dieses Gerichtetsein ein den betreffenden Erlebnissen
immanenter Wesenszug ist, sie sind "intentionale" Erlebnisse.

Überaus mannigfaltige Artungen und Besonderungen fallen
unter die Allgemeinheit dieses Begriffs. Bewußtsein von etwas ist
nicht ein leeres Haben dieses Etwas, jedes Phänomen hat seine
eigene intentionale Gesamtform, zugleich aber einen Aufbau, der
in der intentionalen Analyse immer wieder auf Komponenten
führt, die selbst intentional sind. So führt z.B. die im Ausgang
von einer Wahrnehmung (etwa eines Würfels) geübte phänomenologische Reflexion auf eine vielfältige und doch synthetisch
vereinheitlichte Intentionalität. Es treten die kontinuierlich sich
abwandelnden Unterschiede in den Erscheinungsweisen wech-
selnder "Orientierung" hervor, des Rechts und Links, der Nähe
und Ferne mit den zugehörigen Unterschieden der "Perspektive".
Ferner Erscheinungsunterschiede zwischen der jeweils "eigentlich
gesehenen Vorderseite" und der "unanschaulichen" und relativ
"unbestimmten", jedoch "mitgemeinten" Rückseite. Im Achten auf
das Strömen der Erscheinungsweisen und die Art ihrer "Synthesis" zeigt sich, daß jede Phase und Strecke schon für sich
"Bewußtsein-von" ist, aber so, daß sich im stetigen Auftreten
neuer Phasen das synthetisch einheitliche Bewußtsein von dem
einen und selben Gegenstand herstellt. Der intentionale Aufbau
eines Wahrnehmungsverlaufes hat seine feste Wesenstypik, die in
ihrer außerordentlichen Komplikation notwendig verwirklicht
werden muß, wenn ein körperliches Ding schlicht wahrgenommen
sein soll. Ist das selbe Ding in anderen Weisen anschaulich, z.B. in
der Weise der Wiedererinnerung, der Phantasie, der abbildlichen
Darstellung, so kehren gewissermaßen alle intentionalen Gehalte
der Wahrnehmung wieder, aber alle in entsprechenden Weisen
eigentümlich abgewandelt. Auch für jede sonstige Gattung psy-
chischer Erlebnisse [281] gilt Ähnliches: das urteilende, das
wertende, das strebende Bewußtsein ist nicht ein leeres Bewußthaben der jeweiligen Urteile, Werte, Ziele, Mittel. Sie konsti-
tuieren sich vielmehr in einer strömenden Intentionalität mit
einer ihnen entsprechenden und festen Wesenstypik. —Für die
Psychologie eröffnet sich hier die universale Aufgabe: die

something, deciding *on* something, and so on. If this realm of what we call "phenomena" proves to be the possible field for a pure psychological discipline related exclusively to phenomena, we can understand the designation of it as *phenomenological psychology*. The terminological expression, deriving from Scholasticism, for designating the basic character of being as consciousness, as consciousness of something, is *intentionality*. In unreflective holding of some object or other in consciousness, we are turned or directed towards it: our *"intentio"* goes out towards it. The phenomenological reversal of our gaze shows that this "being directed" [*Gerichtetsein*] is really an immanent essential feature of the respective experiences involved; they are "intentional" experiences.

An extremely large and variegated number of kinds of special cases fall within the general scope of this concept. Consciousness of something is not an empty holding of something; every phenomenon has its own total form of intention [*intentionale Gesamtform*], but at the same time it has a structure, which in intentional analysis leads always again to components which are themselves also intentional. So for example in starting from a perception of something (for example, a die), phenomenological reflection leads to a multiple and yet synthetically unified intentionality. There are continually varying differences in the modes of appearing of objects, which are caused by the changing of "orientation"—of right and left, nearness and farness, with the consequent differences in perspective involved. There are further differences in appearance between the "actually seen front" and the "unseeable" [*"unanschaulichen"*] and relatively "undetermined" reverse side, which is nevertheless "meant along with it." Observing the flux of modes of appearing and the manner of their "synthesis," one finds that every phase and portion [of the flux] is already in itself "consciousness-of"—but in such a manner that there is formed within the constant emerging of new phases the synthetically unified awareness that this is one and the same object. The intentional structure of any process of perception has its fixed essential type [*seine feste Wesenstypik*], which must necessarily be realized in all its extraordinary complexity just in order for a physical body simply to be perceived as such. If this same thing is intuited in other modes—for example, in the modes of recollection, phantasy or pictorial representation—to some extent the whole intentional content of the perception comes back, but {with} all aspects peculiarly transformed to correspond to that mode. This applies similarly for every other category of psychic process: the judging, valuing, striving consciousness is not an empty having knowledge of the specific judgments, values, goals, and means. Rather, these constitute themselves, with fixed essential forms corresponding to each

typischen Gestalten der intentionalen Erlebnisse, ihrer möglichen Abwandlungen, ihrer Synthesen zu neuen Gestalten, ihres strukturellen Aufbaus aus elementaren Intentionalitäten systematisch zu durchforschen und von da aus zu einer deskriptiven Erkenntnis des Ganzen der Erlebnisse, des Gesamttypus eines Lebens der Seele fortzuschreiten. —Offenbar liefert die konsequente Verfolgung dieser Aufgabe Erkenntnisse, die nicht nur für das eigene seelische Sein des Psychologen Gültigkeit haben.

Seelenleben ist uns nicht nur zugänglich durch Selbsterfahrung sondern auch durch Fremderfahrung. Diese neuartige Erfahrungsquelle bietet nicht nur Gleichartiges mit der Selbsterfahrung sondern auch Neues, sofern sie die Unterschiede des "Eigenen" und "Fremden", sowie die Eigenheiten des Gemeinschaftslebens für uns alle bewußtseinsmäßig und zwar als Erfahrung begründet. Eben damit ergibt sich die Aufgabe, auch das Gemeinschaftsleben phänomenologisch nach all den zugehörigen Intentionalitäten verständlich zu machen.

process, in a flowing intentionality. For psychology, the universal task presents itself: to investigate systematically the elementary intentionalities, and from out of these [unfold] the typical forms of intentional processes, their possible variants, their syntheses to new forms, their structural composition, and from this advance towards a descriptive knowledge of the totality of mental process, towards a comprehensive type of a life of the psyche [*Gesamttypus eines Lebens der Seele*]. Clearly, the consistent carrying out of this task will produce knowledge which will have validity far beyond the psychologist's own particular psychic existence.

Psychic life is accessible to us not only through self-experience but also through experience of others. This novel source of experience offers us not only what matches our self-experience but also what is new, inasmuch as, in terms of consciousness and indeed as experience, it establishes the differences between own and other, as well as the properties peculiar to the life of a community. At just this point there arises the task of also making phenomenologically understandable the mental life of the community, with all the intentionalities that pertain to it.

I Synopsis

In this important section, Husserl states that in order to establish and unfold the idea of phenomenological psychology, which is to guide us in our subsequent reflections, we must first try to clarify what is peculiar to *experience* and especially to *psychical experience;* more specifically, we must attempt to clarify the purely psychical, which psychical experience reveals, for it is the *purely psychical* that is to become the subject matter of pure psychology. In so doing, it is appropriate that we focus primarily on the most immediate types of experiences, which in each case reveal to us our own psychic being.

One can focus on one's own psychic life in experience only by means of acts of reflection. *Reflection* is a turning about of the experiencing gaze, which had previously been directed elsewhere, in order to focus on our psychic life itself. Every experience and every act in which we occupy ourselves with real or ideal entities can be the subject of such reflection.

When we are fully engaged in a conscious activity, we focus exclusively on the specific entity with which we happen to be concerned, but not on the psychic experience in which this entity is given. In reflection we can grasp the corresponding subjective experience in which we become conscious of the relevant entity and in which this entity appears. If an entity is taken as appearing in a conscious act, we call it a *phenomenon;* its most general, essential characteristic is that it exists as the "consciousness of" or "appearance of" the specific thing. The relatedness of the appearing in an act of experience to the object of appearance is characteristic of all psychic experiences: perception *of* something, thinking *of* something, hoping *for* something, etc. To designate the basic characteristic of all conscious acts, which consists in this relatedness, this being-directed-at, Husserl uses the term *intentionality.* All experiences are intentional experiences.

In view of the fact that pure psychology has as its subject matter the domain of all phenomena (taken in the sense indicated), it is called also *phenomenological psychology.*

The term *intentional experience* refers to an extremely large and variegated number of kinds of special cases. Furthermore, even though every phenomenon has its own form of intention in which it is given as a whole, it nevertheless also has a structure, which in *intentional analysis* leads always to components that themselves are also intentional. One and the same thing can be given in modes of appearing that show continually varying differences. Observing the flux of the modes of appearing and the manner of their *"synthesis,"* one finds that every phase of the flux is already in itself "consciousness-of," but in such a manner that within the constant emerging of new phases, the synthetically unified awareness is formed that this is nonetheless one and the same object.

Also, the intentional structure of any act of perception has its fixed essential type, which must be realized in all concrete cases in order for a physical body simply to be perceived as such. If this same physical body is intuited in other modes of consciousness, such as recollection or phantasy, to some extent the whole intentional content of the perceptual act comes back, but all aspects are then peculiarly transformed to correspond to that new mode. This holds good for every other category of psychic processes.

The universal task of phenomenological psychology can now be defined: to investigate systematically the elementary intentionalities, and from these to unfold the typical forms of intentional processes, their possible variants, their syntheses to new forms, their structural composition, in order to advance toward a descriptive knowledge of the totality of all experiences and thus toward a comprehensive, descriptive knowledge of the life of the soul.

If this task is carried out systematically, it will lead to results that have validity far beyond the psychologist's own particular psychic being. For psychic life is accessible to us not only through self-experience but also through *experience of others*. This new source of experience offers us not only what matches our self-experience but also new phenomena insofar as, in terms of consciousness and as experience, it establishes the difference between what is our own and what is other. It also must establish the properties that are characteristic of the *life of a community*. At this point, there finally arises the task of making phenomenologically understandable the life of the community with all the intentionalities that pertain to it.

In the sections to follow, I shall present a brief commentary on the following topics: (1) experience, intuition, evidence; (2) experience of the purely psychical; and (3) intentionality. There are several other important issues that Husserl touches on in this rich section, but for practical reasons I have decided to raise them explicitly in some of the chapters to follow, where they seem to fit better because a thorough discussion of them would imply that the transcendental reduction would already have been performed. This is true particularly for what was said about synthesis and intersubjectivity (the life of the community).

Commentary

Experience, Intuition, Evidence

Experience — The concept of experience plays an essential role in Husserl's thought. The first volume of *Ideas* begins with a statement that manifestly was inspired by the first page of Kant's *Critique of Pure Reason:* "Natural cognition begins with experience and remains *within* experience." There are many forms and types of experience. What is given in these forms of experience can become the subject matter of a theoretical, scientific approach. Each science has its own realm of entities that constitutes the domain of its investigations. And to all its cognitions there corresponds, as primal sources of the grounding that guarantees their legitimacy, certain intuitions (*Anschauungen*) in which the entities belonging to the domain become *themselves given* as existing and, at least some of them, as *given originarily.* The giving intuition belonging to the natural sphere of cognition and to all the sciences of the natural attitude is natural experience (*natürliche Erfahrung*), and the natural experience that gives something of that realm *originarily* is perception. We have originary experience of concrete physical entities in *external perception;* we have originary experience of ourselves and of our states of consciousness in *internal perception* or self-perception.

In every primordial experience, we "see" a thing to be and to be thus. If we have such a seeing, we speak of *evidence,* which is, "in an extremely broad sense, an experiencing of something that is, and is thus; it is precisely a seeing of something itself" (*Cart. Med.,* 12 [52]). Evidence, which in fact includes all experiencing in the usual and narrower sense, can be more or less perfect.

Before going on to other issues, two observations are in order here. First of all, Husserl makes a distinction between *Erlebnis* and *Erfahrung.* The former is called a highest genus (*Ideas,* 1:25 [31]). It encompasses all awareness a subject can have. *Erfahrung* is a more limited category; it is an *Erlebnis* concerning things that belong to the *real* world; psychic phenomena can also belong to this world. We are concerned here with *Erfahrungen* in the strict sense of the term. Secondly, experience (*Erfahrung*) cannot ever be understood to mean "sense impression" in Hume's sense, even though a "sense impression" might have been called an *Erlebnis.* Instead, *Erfahrung* means the full-fledged experience or act of consciousness in which something real is given to consciousness as what it genuinely is. Obviously, a thing can be given in different ways and with different degrees of evidence.

Intuition and Evidence — Intuition (*Anschauung, Intuition, Sehen*) also plays an essential role in Husserl's phenomenology. The word "intuition" is mentioned at almost all levels of his philosophical reflections, and it is always referred to in the strongest language possible. Yet Husserl very seldom speaks *about* intuition and its implications. Like almost all other fundamental concepts of his phenomenology, intuition, too, remains for the most part an "operative concept," that is, a concept which Husserl uses to explain and justify his views, without ever explicitly thematizing it.[1]

In Husserl's view, intuition and self-evidence are essentially related concepts (*The Idea*, 28 [35]). Phenomenology attempts to answer the question concerning the meaning of being (*F. tr. L.*, 15 [19], 166 [174]; *Cart. Med.*, 56–57 [91–92]). In this attempt, the phenomenologist is guided by the principle of evidence, whereas self-evidence is rooted in each case in an act of intuition (*Ideas*, 1:44–45 [43–44]). These insights guided Husserl throughout his entire career. And although his conception of phenomenology may have changed somewhat over the years, his ideas concerning the relationship between self-evidence and intuition, and their fundamental significance within the phenomenological enterprise, always remained the same.[2]

When Husserl formulated his conception of phenomenology for the first time in 1907, he described phenomenology as a system of scientific disciplines to be developed with the help of a new method, the phenomenological method. Among these disciplines, a general phenomenology of knowledge and a universal science of being in the absolute sense must have a privileged position, in that they are to constitute the beginning and the end of the entire phenomenological enterprise (*The Idea*, 18–19 [23]). In both these disciplines, it is assumed that what is adequately self-given is beyond question. What is adequately self-given can and must be taken as an absolute beginning. It is assumed further that everything that is given in consciousness in an *immediate* act of seeing is adequately self-given (ibid., 4 [2], 24 [31]). Self-givenness in the absolute sense rules out any meaningful doubt; it consists of an *absolutely immediate seeing* and apprehending of the intended object itself *as it is;* it constitutes the precise concept of evidence understood as immediate evidence (ibid., 28 [35]). The seeing or grasping of what is given, insofar as it is actual seeing, and actual self-givenness in the strictest sense, not another sort of givenness that points to something which is not given: that is an ultimate. *That is absolute self-evidence* (ibid., 39–40 [50]).

The same insights are formulated on many occasions in *Ideas*. Suffice it to quote here two important passages only. "*Immediate seeing,* not merely the sensuous, experiential seeing, *but seeing in the universal sense as an originally presentative consciousness of any kind whatever* is the ultimate legitimizing source of all rational assertions" (*Ideas,* 1:36 [36]). Thus, Husserl argues, we may formulate the following as the basic principle of our entire phenomenological philosophy: No conceivable theory can mislead us in regard to the principle of all principles, namely, that every primordial intuition is a legitimate source of knowledge, and that whatever presents itself in intuition in primordial form, in its authentic reality and bodily selfhood, is to be accepted simply as that which it presents itself to be, but obviously only within the limits in which it thus presents itself (ibid., 44–45 [43–44]).

It is obvious to Husserl that although evidence denotes the quite eminent mode of consciousness that consists in the self-giving of any object that is in the final mode "it itself there," immediately intuited and given originally (*F. tr. L.,* 157–58 [166]), there is very little that is immediately philosophically relevant and yet given in immediate intuition. The entire history of philosophy shows abundantly how difficult it is to achieve apodictic evidence concerning basic philosophical issues. Although every experience implies a seeing of what is thus experienced, the seeing is nonetheless not always of the same degree of perfection, nor does it always have the same range. Thus one must make a distinction between different forms of intuition (seeing) and, correspondingly, between different forms of evidence. Firstly, most of our everyday experiences are inadequate evidences. Inadequacy as a rule signifies here an *incompleteness* and a *one-sidedness* that qualify the manner in which affairs themselves and affair complexes themselves are given. The meaning that is present to us in those experiences still contains *unfulfilled* components, that is, expectant and attendant meanings. Perfection of this experience takes place when, in the course of further harmonious experiences, these attendant meanings become fulfilled. We speak of *adequate* evidence when a state of affairs is present to us in such a manner that there are no longer any unfulfilled meaning components. Secondly, we must distinguish apodictic from assertoric evidences. Self-evidence is *apodictic* if our certainty concerning a state of affairs is such that the nonbeing of this state of affairs is absolutely unimaginable and inconceivable. However, if our certainty concerning a state of affairs is merely such that it excludes every reasonable doubt, our evidence is *assertoric.* A thing of the real world—for instance a three-dimensional object, such as a house—can appear only with imperfect and assertoric evidence because the perception in which it is given presents at each moment only one aspect of that object; in addition, the nonbeing of the state of affairs perceived is (at least in principle) always conceivable (*Cart. Med.,* 14–16 [55–57]). That is why Husserl can claim that the thing itself as given in external perception will always remain an "idea in the Kantian sense" (*Ideas,* 1:342–43 [297–98]).

Thus, on the one hand, Husserl defends the view that ultimately all philosophical knowledge must be founded upon apodictic evidence; on the other hand, he admits explicitly that we do not have an easy access to such evidence. That is why one must first ask precisely how apodictic evidence can be achieved in philosophy.

Husserl saw clearly that intuition implies that subject and object are immediately present to each other on the same level. Hence, if the "first origins and beginnings of philosophy" are to be intuited, one must try first to arrive at this "most basic field or world" ("Ph. Rig. Sc.," 146 [341]), in which these fundamental insights indeed can be intuited immediately. Husserl believed that his theory of reduction can lead us to this primordial field (*Ideas,* 1:112–14 [93–95], 131–41 [108–17]). As we shall see in the next chapter, by reduction Husserl means in general the methodic procedure by means of which one goes back from a given realm of not yet founded meaning to another realm of meaning where its foundation can perhaps be discovered (ibid., 322–25 [278–81]). He distinguishes different types of reductions. Here it is important to note that the basic function of all forms of reduction is to gradually disclose a field of *ultimate* experiences in which what is given there is given with apodictic evidence. This realm of ultimate experiences is called the *transcendental realm.* Once this realm has been opened up by the reductions, it must be possible, according to Husserl, to found every actual and possible knowledge on apodictic evidences by uncovering the entire field of transcendental experience in its universal structure (*The Idea,* 46–51 [58–63]).

One must realize here further that every conscious act necessarily implies its typical correlate. If, however, consciousness essentially is intentional, that is, consciousness of something, then not only is the conscious act itself present in evidence, but also what is given in it, provided one considers the latter solely insofar as it is immediately given in the conscious act (*Ideas,* 1:171–73 [141–44], 236–40 [201–5]). On closer investigation, it becomes quite clear that "pure and genuine Being" is not immediately found in the evidence of any conscious act. Thus it is not correct to think that after the reductions have been performed, all one has to do is simply intuit and grasp what is given there. Even in the transcendental sphere, the different "objects" are not found in our cogitations like matches in a box; they are constituted there in different types of syntheses. This is why analysis and description must bring to completion what was merely begun in the reduction (*The Idea*, 55–57 [70–72]).

Toward the Genuine Meaning of the Principle of All Principles — Husserl realized on many occasions that his conception of intuition and evidence was easily misunderstood. This misunderstanding had its origin in the fact that one simply identified evidence with absolute apodicticity only. Yet for Husserl, it was extremely difficult to see how absolute apodicticity could ever be ascribed to one single human activity torn from the essentially unitary context of a person's life. Evidence as such is thus not an absolute criterion of truth. If it were, then perceptual evidence would become impossible in principle.

Perception, indeed, gives something itself, but this giving-of-something-itself is not yet the giving of an object in the proper sense. Perception alone is never a full objectivating performance, the seizing of an object itself. One accepts *internal* perception as the seizing of an object itself only because one tacitly takes into account the possible recollections that are repeatable at will. When actualized, recollection gives us for the first time original certainty of the being of an object in the full sense, as something acquired originally and identifiable at will, something to which one can always return. Such a synthesis of recognition plays an analogous role in external perception, although in the latter case, the performance is still more complicated than in the case of internal perception, as we shall see.

Thus for Husserl, evidence refers to the *performance* on the part of intentional acts which consists in the giving of something *itself*. It is the universal and preeminent mode of intentionality, in which there is consciousness of the intended-to-objective affair in the mode: "it itself seized upon and seen." I am seizing upon it itself originally, as contrasted with seizing upon it in an image or some other sort of foremeaning. But I am not always seizing upon it in an absolute sense, for evidence obviously has different modes of originality.

Any time an experience is examined with respect to the mode of originality of its evidence, this is done by using evidences attained at a deeper level, by the phenomenological explication of that experience in the light of more primordial evidences. The deeper evidences themselves, in turn, can be understood in respect to their effect only by means of evidences belonging to a third level, and so on. Only in seeing, can I bring out what is truly present in an earlier seeing (*F. tr. L.*, 156–59 [165–68]).

The giving of something itself is thus, like every other intentional process, a function in the all-encompassing nexus of consciousness. The effect produced by a single intentional process, in particular its effect as evidence, is therefore not shut off in isolation. The single evidence, by its own intentionality, can implicitly require further acts that give the object itself; it can refer us to them for a supplementation of its objectifying effect. Generally speaking , one can say that the concept of intentionality and the concept of evidence (that is, the intentionality that gives something *itself*) are essentially correlates. From this it follows that any consciousness of anything whatsoever belongs a priori to an openly endless multiplicity of possible modes of consciousness that can always be connected synthetically to make one consciousness, as a consciousness *of the same*. In the final analysis, evidence is a universal mode of intentionality that is related to the whole life of consciousness.

In Husserl's view, it follows from these reflections that evidence is not the solution for all philosophical problems; rather, it is a theme for far-reaching and difficult investigations. One of these themes is that each category of objects has its own category of evidence. In other words, to every fundamental species of objects (taken as intentional unities that can be maintained throughout an intentional synthesis and, ultimately, as unities belonging to a possible "experience"), a fundamental species of "experience," that is, evidence, corresponds. Thus the task arises of exploring all these modes of the evidence in which the object intended shows *itself,* now less and now more perfectly, and thus of making understandable the extremely complicated performances, fitting together to make a synthetic harmony, and always pointing ahead to new ones. Yet, it is precisely because an imperfect experience is still an experience—that is, the consciousness of the having of something itself—that experience can adjust itself to experience and correct itself by experience (*F. tr. L.,* 159–65 [168–73]).

To all of this is still to be added the fact that in most cases when something presents itself to us in experience, it appears within a context of meaning or horizon. These horizons of meaning can be made explicit subsequently, but the intentionality that constitutes these horizons, without which the surrounding world would not be an *experienced* world, is always prior to its explication by someone who reflects. Thus here again it becomes clear that evidence is at first a "hidden" method that one must examine concerning its performance in order to know what one actually has as it itself, and in what horizons one has it, when one has something in evidence, that is, has something *itself* (*F. tr. L.,* 199–200 [206–8]).

I Experience of the Purely Psychical

Experience of the Psychical Comes About in Reflection — In phenomenological psychology, as in any other science, all claims must ultimately be founded upon basic truths that originate with some degree of evidence from the original sources of intuition; in the case of phenomenological psychology, the source is *inner perception.*[3] But such sources must still be disclosed in the proper manner. They become fruitful only if one lays hold of them systematically and unfolds their meaning from every possible point of view. Thus if we are to give a genuine foundation to phenomenological psychology, we must here, too, first turn to the experiencing intuition and then treat it methodically and unfold its meaning from every possible perspective. In this intuition the psychical as such is given in an original and concrete manner; it manifests itself there in the essential structure that is proper to it.

It is important to note here that every form in which we focus on something psychical, whether it be experiencing or some other act, is carried out by way of reflection. To live as an ego subject means to vividly experience various psychic phenomena. Yet this life, which we vividly experience, remains anonymous, as it were; it takes its course, but we do not focus on it. In our everyday life, we are always concerned with something; in most cases this is not something psychical. When we are perceiving, we are, for instance, concerned with a house; in memory, we are concerned with some important event that we remember; in thinking, we are concerned with certain thoughts; and in our feeling and valuing life, we may be concerned with something beautiful or something else that is valuable. When we concern ourselves with something in this straightforward way, we "know" nothing of the life that in so doing plays a vital part; we "know" nothing of the different peculiarities that essentially belong to it. It is in reflection, in which we turn our glance away from what straightforwardly was at first our theme of concern, that our psychic life comes into view. In a reflective experience, the psychical becomes grasped; thereby psychic life itself can become the theme of different forms of concern. Whatever becomes accessible to us through reflection has a remarkable general characteristic, that of being conscious of something, the character of intentionality. Intentionality is the essential characteristic of all psychic life taken in the strict and full sense of the term.

We must now return to the question of how a pure phenomenological experience and its disclosure can be brought about methodically. The term "phenomenological experience" is obviously nothing but that reflection in and through which we gain access to the psychical in its innermost essence.

The Meaning of the Concept of Purity in Phenomenology — The first question here is how this experience is methodically to be shown in practice, so that as *pure* experience it truly discloses what is to be intuited as far as the psychical's innermost essence is concerned.[4]

The purity at issue here manifestly means, first of all, independence of everything that is psychophysical. In the psychological-phenomenological attitude, psychic experiences are to be considered as real moments of animal and human realities; as such, they are always intertwined with something bodily. What is presented in the physical and psychophysical experiences must therefore remain unconsidered in phenomenological psychology; thus we must exclusively practice phenomenological experience and take into consideration only what becomes manifest in it. Considering the psychical as such, we must exclude from consideration whatever gives it position in, and ties it to, real nature. The same manifestly holds good for all considerations of conceivable psychological possibilities, that is, all data of possible psychic experience.

Here we encounter a first kind of difficulty: To what extent can one consistently practice purely phenomenological experience, that is, actual and, above all, possible experience? To what extent, if one begins with the self-given psychical and from there proceeds to something new, does one finally come to a uniform and purely psychical field of experiences that does not draw with it—even if extended ad infinitum—something that lies outside the innermost essence of the psychical into the unity of the purely intuitive context of meaning that is the "closed" domain of possible, pure, phenomenological intuitions? Secondly, pure experience obviously also signifies that one stays away from all prejudices, which, originating from other scientific spheres of experience, can actually blind one for what phenomenological reflection actually tries to exhibit.

Both these difficulties taken together have had a profound influence. One can only venture to say paradoxically that in the whole of psychology of the modern age, one has never come to a genuine performance of the intentional analysis. And this is the case even though modern psychology for centuries made an effort to be a psychology on the basis of inner experience, and at times even a descriptive psychology of the pure data of consciousness. As Husserl sees it, even Brentano and his school cannot be excepted here, although Brentano deserves the great merit of having introduced intentionality as the descriptive, basic characteristic of the psychical. Moreover, he advocated the development of an empirical psychology that was to be built on the foundation of a systematic and purely descriptive examination of consciousness. Yet the proper and characteristic meaning, as well as the method, of the pure analysis of consciousness remained hidden for him.

As far as the lingering prejudices are concerned that made many scholars unreceptive for what is to be accomplished in pure, descriptive psychology, they originated mainly from the fact that the natural sciences were taken to be the paradigm for psychology. These prejudices begin to manifest themselves already in the great originators of modern psychology—in Descartes and Hobbes, in Locke's *tabula-rasa* interpretation of the life of consciousness, and in the views of David Hume, who conceived of the life of consciousness as a bundle of psychic data. The universal blindness for the intentional was overcome by Brentano; yet he, too, did not overcome naturalism, so that his great discovery of intentionality remained fruitless. In the period that immediately followed the work of Brentano, the situation remained exactly the same. Combatting "psychic atomism" passionately, as many have done, is not yet tantamount to becoming really free from all naturalistic prejudices. Even the fashionable appeal to *Gestalt* qualities does not overcome naturalism. What is fundamental for naturalism in psychology could be brought to light for the first time only by phenomenology, in which a purely phenomenological experience was seriously enacted for the first time.

In Husserl's view, the ultimate source of all errors in the conception of the psychical is to be found in the identification of immanent temporality with objectively real time. Objective time is the extensional form of objectively real things and specifically and properly of physical nature. Yet the psychical, lived experiences do not have, in and for themselves, a real, unitary form of coexistence and succession of the kind found in the real, spatiotemporal world. The flowing that is characteristic for the unity of the stream of consciousness is not a genuine parallel form of natural spatiotemporality. The image of the stream is not without serious difficulties, and the intentional analysis of immanent temporality destroys this image while at the same time, it also clarifies its legitimate meaning.

This analysis also destroys the analogy between the analysis of consciousness and the analysis of natural things and events, just as it does that between the mode of being of consciousness and the mode of being of nature. The logical concepts used in the sciences of nature—such as thing and property, whole and part, connection and separation, cause and operation—are relevant only for natural things and therewith, in its basic determination, for the *res extensa*. In the transition to the domain of the psychical, these concepts lose their meaning; and what is left of them after the transition is nothing but the empty shell of the formal-logical concepts "object" and "disposition," just to mention a few.

The Purely Psychical as Found in the Experience of Self and the Experience of the Community — We must thus stay away from all prejudices of our tradition, even of the most universal and simple matters of traditional logic, because they all are closely connected with the meaning of the physical as such.[5] We must stick resolutely to what the phenomenological attitude offers us as consciousness and as what it is conscious of; we must thus strictly adhere to that which becomes truly and evidently self-given. In other words, we must examine the phenomenological experience with the exclusion of everything else by placing ourselves concretely into our reflective experiencing of consciousness without paying any attention to verification by factically occurring facts. This experience is first and foremost the experience of one's own self. In it alone are consciousness and the ego of consciousness given in completely original selfhood, as, when perceiving, I reflect on my perceiving. I, taken as a phenomenologist, disclose in this way my own life, my concrete life in its concretely actual and possible forms. The experience of someone else as well as the experience of the community is to be examined, also; yet one should notice that they are founded upon the immediacy of the experience of the self. We shall return to these issues in Chapter Ten.

▎ Intentionality

Although Husserl's doctrine of intentionality is already implicitly contained in his *Philosophy of Arithmetic,* he did not present a detailed and accurate description of it until he wrote the second volume of the *Logical Investigations.* The doctrine is presented there within the context of logical questions that are not essential to phenomenology as such. For this reason, Husserl reverted to the explanation of intentionality in *Ideas,* dealing there only with those elements and topics that are characteristic of phenomenology in the proper sense.

All of Husserl's later works presuppose the description of intentionality given in *Ideas,* and his conception of it never underwent any change, although the dynamic structure of intentionality was emphasized more in the later works. The same applies to the link between intentionality, on the one hand, and synthesis and constitution, on the other.[6] In this section, I shall limit myself to a brief paraphrase of Husserl's view on intentionality as the basic idea of phenomenology. Nevertheless, a few remarks on the ideas of intentionality found in Husserl's *Logical Investigations* seem to be indispensable. These remarks will be limited to points that seem necessary for an understanding of the evolution of Husserl's thought between 1901 and 1913.

I Intentionality in *Logical Investigations*

Between 1896 and 1900, Husserl developed the essential insights pertaining to his new philosophy of intentionality.[7] Our consciousness is intentional; it is "openness to," "relation to." This relation is, strictly speaking, identical with the fundamental and constitutive structure of consciousness; it is a relation between a "meaning" act and that which is "meant," its object, the latter being defined as meaning (*Sinn*).

It was during the preparation of *Logical Investigations* that Husserl discovered the concept of intentionality. At the time, he was seeking a radically philosophical explanation of mathematical and logical beings. In this process, and while also trying to arrive at their essential structures and indicate a foundation for their proper ontological status, Husserl formulated the thesis that the nature of these beings is exclusively as objects of consciousness. To say this is tantamount to saying that these logical and mathematical beings are, in the most fundamental sense, meanings-for-me. In this specific instance, he claims, intentional analysis demonstrates that consciousness is to be thought of as a relation *sui generis* to an apprehended object.

Husserl explicitly mentioned several times that he owed his conception of intentionality to Brentano. According to Brentano, every psychical phenomenon is characterized by what the medieval Scholastics called the intentional "inexistence" of an object. Brentano called this characteristic of every psychical phenomenon the "reference to a content" or "the directedness to an immanent object." This concept enabled Brentano to distinguish between psychical and physical phenomena. He held that everything psychical is characterized by such an intentional relation to an object. Any psychical phenomenon, he claimed, contains something as an object, but not always in the same way. Thus, in a presentation, something is presented; in a judgment, something is acknowledged or rejected; and in desire, something is desired. Brentano regarded this "intentional inexistence" as exclusively proper to psychic phenomena; for this reason, he defined them as phenomena that intentionally "contain" an object in themselves.[8]

There can be no doubt about Husserl's dependence on Brentano for the concept of intentionality and the field it opened to descriptive analysis. Nonetheless, Husserl thought that Brentano had failed to grasp what intentionality really is and make it philosophically useful. For Brentano, every intentional experience was a phenomenon, and the term "phenomenon" denoted an appearing object as such. In this sense, Brentano spoke of objects that "enter into consciousness," and he added that consciousness enters into relationship with objects in this or that particular way, or that intentional experiences contain something in themselves as an object. According to Husserl, such expressions are questionable, for they may lead to two misinterpretations: (1) that there should be a real relation between consciousness and the things known; (2) that there should be a relationship between two things found immanent in consciousness, namely, between act and intentional object; hence one psychical content is included in another.

Let us first consider the second misinterpretation. The expression "immanent objectivity" is used to denote the essential characteristic of intentional experiences. An object is "meant" in an intentional experience; it is "aimed at" in an experience of presentation, of judgment, or any other cognitive act. It is essential to such experiences that there be a reference to an object, that an object be "intentionally present." Such an intentional experience may occur even if the object does not exist. In that case, "meaning" the object is and remains an experience; but the object is merely "meant" and is really nothing. For example, if I present the god Jupiter, then this god is a presented object; it is "immanently present" in my act. Of course, the descriptive analysis of this intentional experience will not disclose the god Jupiter as being in it; hence, the "immanent" object does *not belong* to the descriptive immanent nature of the experience; therefore, it is not at all immanent. Neither is it "outside the mind"; that is, it really is not at all. That, however, does not prevent my presenting-the-god-Jupiter from being real. On the other hand, if the intended object does not exist, nothing needs to be changed phenomenologically. With respect to consciousness, the given is essentially the same, whether the presented object exists or is imaginary or even absurd. For this reason, it is better to avoid the term "immanent object" and to use the expression "intentional object," which is not open to similar objections.

As for the first-mentioned misinterpretation, there is no question of a real relation but only of an intentional relation between consciousness and the things known. Husserl therefore chose his own terminology in such a way that such disputable presuppositions and ambiguities were excluded as much as possible. He avoided the

expression "psychical phenomenon" and spoke instead of "experience" or, more exactly, of "intentional experience." The term "intentional" designates the characteristic of intention, the reference to
something objective. As a shorter expression, he also uses the term
"act." "Intention" is understood here in the sense of "aiming at" and
is applicable to acts of theoretical and practical aiming. "Aiming at,"
however, does not apply equally well to all acts; hence Husserl was
forced to distinguish a narrower and a wider concept of intention
(*L.I.*, 2:562–63 [2.1:377–80]).

Immediately after the publication of *Logical Investigations,*
Husserl realized the fragmentary nature of his first philosophical
investigation concerning intentionality. It became clear to him that
intentionality is not only a characteristic feature of the acts of consciousness, but that it is the very essence of consciousness itself. In
The Idea of Phenomenology (1907), in which he expressed this new
insight for the first time, Husserl's main interest was still mostly
epistemological. For this reason, he returned to the topic in *Ideas* in
order to explain the fundamental and full meaning of intentionality
as completely and clearly as possible (*Ideas*, 1:199–207 [167–77]).

The discussion of intentionality as we find it in the first volume
of *Ideas* constitutes a part of a series of analyses and reflections that
are transcendental in character and thus presuppose that the transcendental reduction already has been performed. In view of the fact
that this reduction will be introduced only in the second part of the
Encyclopaedia Britannica article, I have decided to describe in this
section only those ideas that directly pertain to Husserl's conception
of intentionality. The other issues discussed in the same part of
Ideas will be examined in some of the chapters to follow.

▌Intentionality in the Later Works

In section 84 of the first volume of *Ideas,* Husserl begins his reflections on intentionality by once more observing that intentionality is
a peculiarity distinctive of all experiences and mental processes.
Intentionality is the general theme of phenomenology taken in its
objective orientation. Later we shall see that there also is an orientation toward the ego in every intentional phenomenon. Yet for the
time being, Husserl prefers to limit himself to intentionality taken
in its orientation toward an object.

All experiences and all mental processes in some manner or
other share in intentionality. And yet we cannot say that *each* individual experience has intentionality in the same sense in which we
can say that each experience or mental process has a temporal
character. For it is really *consciousness* that is characterized by intentionality. This explains why intentionality justifies us in desig-

nating the whole stream of experiences as the stream of consciousness and as the unity of *one* consciousness.

Husserl understands by intentionality that the unique characteristic of every experience is consciousness *of* something. It is in the
explicit *cogito* that we first encountered this marvelous property, to
which all metaphysical enigmas of theoretical reason ultimately
lead us back: to perceive is to perceive something; to judge is to judge
something; to value is to value a certain value; to act concerns action; to do aims at a deed; to love, at the beloved; to rejoice, at the
object of joy. In every wakeful *cogito,* a regard of the pure ego is directed to the object of the correlate of consciousness then considered,
and the ego has consciousness of this object in one of its typical
variations.

However, as we have learned from phenomenological reflection,
this orientation of the ego in presenting, thinking, valuing, and so
on—this directedness toward the correlate object—cannot be found
in every experience, whereas intentionality may always be concealed in it. For instance, it is clear that the objective background,
from which the perceived object of cogitation emerges when it is
singled out by the glance of the ego, is an objective background in a
sense that can really be experienced. Even while we are turned toward the pure object in the mode of the *cogito,* various objects appear; we are intuitively aware of them; they blend into the unity of a
single intuition, the unity of a consciously grasped field of objects.
We face here a potential field of perception in the sense that a special
perception can be directed toward everything that appears in this
way.

But we cannot call it a *potential* field of perception in the sense
that the object in the field cannot be objectively grasped at all until
the ego's glance turns toward other objects in the field. The variations of the sensory perspective (for example, variations of the visual
perspective) are experienced as present in a single visual field as
soon as they first shape themselves into intuitive appearances of
objects.

Intentionality also includes experiences that proceed either
from the background of actual consciousness—such as the awakening of emotions, the first beginnings of judgments, and nascent
wishes—or from different depths of background; that is, they are
farther from or nearer to the pure ego, which, as it lives wakefully,
is the center of reference in the passing thoughts. A desire, a wish,
or a judgment can be fulfilled in a specific sense—namely, by the
ego, which plays an active role in this fulfillment. However, such
modes of consciousness may already be present and emerge in the
background without being "fulfilled" in this way. Yet in their own

essential nature, these emerging actualities are already a consciousness of something. Accordingly, we do not include in the essence of intentionality that which pertains specifically to the *cogito,* namely, the "glance-toward," the ego's "turning-to"; on the contrary, we take this cogitation to be a special modality of the general function called "intentionality" (*Ideas,* 1:199–201 [167–70]).

In the following pages, we must more accurately try to determine this original insight into the very essence of intentionality in both its static and dynamic aspects. As we shall see, the static consideration endeavors to determine everything that is concretely found in every lived experience; in other words, it is interested in its *real* components. The dynamic consideration, on the other hand, wants to describe the genesis and evolution of intentionality.[9]

▮ Static Description of Intentionality

Sensible *Hyle* and Intentional *Morphe* — Elaborating the first aspect of this subject, Husserl goes on to explain that in the static consideration of intentionality, we begin by making an essential distinction between experiences that we could call "primary contents" and experiences or phases of experiences that are bearers of the specific quality of intentionality.

To the primary contents belong unitary sense experiences, sense contents, such as the data of color, touch, and sound. They should not be confused with the appearing phases of things, such as their color qualities and their roughness, for these reveal themselves experientially only through the primary contents. The same applies to sense impressions, such as pleasure, pain, and tickling. Such concrete data of experience are found as components in concrete experiences of a more comprehensive type, which as a whole are intentional. With respect to these sensible phases, the latter are, as it were, an animating or meaning-giving layer that makes the concrete intentional experience take form and shape out of the sensible elements, which in themselves contain nothing intentional.

In the whole phenomenological domain, as Husserl explains it, this remarkable duality and unity of sensible *hyle* and intentional *morphe* play a dominant role. As a matter of fact, these "matter" and "form" concepts impose themselves when we consider clear intuitions or clearly formed valuations, volitions, and so on. Intentional experiences are there as unities that come about through the giving of meaning. Sense data offer themselves as material suitable for intentional "informing," or giving of meaning, at different levels.

The sensible *hyle* and the intentional *morphe* might also be called "formless materials" and "matterless forms." We may add in passing that the expression "primary content," which was used in

Logical Investigations, no longer covers the situation. The expression "sense experience" likewise should not be used any longer, since it indicates not only hyletic but also intentional experiences; even a sense experience consists of hyletic data and an intentional *morphe.* This is why we prefer to speak of "hyletic data," "material data," "materials," "sensible materials," or "sensory materials."

That which forms the materials into intentional experiences and thereby introduces the specific element of intentionality is identical with that which gives its specific meaning to our use of the term "consciousness." It is called "noesis" or "noetic phase."

To avoid every ambiguity, we will therefore say that the stream of phenomenological being has a double bed: one material and the other noetic. Phenomenological analyses that are specifically concerned with the material aspect may be called "hyletic-phenomenological analyses," and those that study the noetic phases may be referred to as "noetic-phenomenological analyses." Noetic analyses are the most important and fruitful analyses of phenomenology (*Ideas,* 1:203–7 [171–75]).

Noesis and Noema — It is easy to indicate the characteristic of intentional experience in its general form, for everyone understands the expression "consciousness is consciousness of something." It is more difficult, however, to obtain a pure and correct grasp of the phenomenological characteristics of the corresponding essence, since this "consciousness of something" (*Ideas,* 1:211–12 [179–80]) appears to be at the same time both very obvious and very obscure.

Concerning this aspect of intentionality, Husserl tells us that we must make a clear distinction between the real components of our intentional experiences and the intentional correlates or the components of these correlates. Thus, on the one hand, we have to distinguish the parts and phases disclosed by a real analysis of the experience that treats this experience as an object like any other. On the other hand, every intentional experience is the consciousness of something. Every intentional experience, by virtue of its noetic phase, is noetic; it is essential to it to contain in itself some kind of meaning or perhaps many meanings, and on the basis of, and in harmony with, this essential characteristic of giving meaning to develop further phases that, through it, become themselves "meaningful."

Examples of such noetic phases are: directing the pure ego's glance to the object intended by virtue of the regard's gift of meaning—that is, to that which the ego has in mind as something "meant"—apprehending this object, holding it in a steady grasp while the glance shifts to other objects that have come within its reach; likewise the effects of bringing out, relating, comprehending, and assuming such attitudes as belief, presumption, and valuation. All this may be discovered in the relevant experiences, no matter how different they may be in themselves. Just as this series of examples indicates that there are real components in the experiences, so also does it point, under the heading "meaning," to components that are not real. In this way, we come to the distinction, briefly indicated above, between noesis and noema. To the manifold data of the real noetic content there corresponds at all points a variety of data that can be displayed in truly pure intuition and in a correlative "noematic content," or "noema."

Perception, for instance, has its noema, and at the basis of this noema is its perceptual meaning, the "perceived as such." Likewise, recollection has as its own noema the "remembered as such." Everywhere we must take the noematic correlate, which, in a very broad sense, is here referred to as "meaning," precisely as it is immanent in experiences such as perception and judgment.

As phenomenologists, we now have to ask the essential question: What is the "perceived as such"? What are its essential phases as noema? We shall get the answer to these questions by yielding fully to what is essentially *given*. It will allow us faithfully to describe "that which appears as such" in the light of perfect self-evidence (*Ideas,* 1:213–16 [180–83]).

Continuing in this vein, Husserl claims that in phenomenologically pure experience we find indissolubly belonging to the essence of perception the "perceived as such," for instance under the headings "material thing," "plant," "tree." The quotation marks are important here, for they express the radical modification made in the sense of the words. The tree, for example, as it exists in nature, is quite different from this perceived tree as such. The former can be destroyed or burned, but the meaning of this perception is indestructible and cannot be separated from its essence.

It is to be noted that for the phenomenologist as well as for the psychologist, the perceived, as meaning, should not include anything that does not really appear in the perceptual manifestation of the appearing reality. Moreover, what appears must be included in the perceived precisely as it is presented to us in the actual perception. A special kind of reflection may lead to the discovery of this meaning, as it is immanent in perception. The phenomenological judgment has to adjust itself and give faithful expression only to that which is apprehended in this perception (*Ideas,* 1:216–17 [183–84]).

It is the fundamental characteristic of all intentionality that not only perception but every intentional experience has its intentional object, its objective meaning. To have a meaning is the cardinal characteristic of all consciousness; it is that on account of which consciousness is not only just experience but meaningful and noetic experience.

Husserl reminds us, however, that we must not forget that the meaning of an act does not exhaust the full noema. Likewise, the noetic side of an intentional experience does not consist exclusively in the strict meaning-giving phase, to which meaning specifically belongs as a correlate. As we shall show presently, the full noema consists in a chain of noematic phases, and the phase of specific meaning supplies only a kind of necessary nucleus. Further phases are essentially grounded in this nucleus, and for that reason they, too, should be called phases of meaning.

To state again the only clear conclusion we have reached, intentional experience is undoubtedly such that, from a suitable viewpoint, a meaning can be extracted from it. The situation that defines this meaning for us cannot remain concealed and is such that the nonexistence of the presented or ideally constructed object in its plain and simple sense cannot deprive the presented object, as such, from the relevant presentation. In other words, a distinction must be made between the presented object and its presentation. As a matter of fact, the Scholastic distinction between "mental," "intentional," or "immanent" object and "real" object points to the same correlation. However, from a first apprehension of a distinction affecting the nature of consciousness to its correct, phenomenologically pure determination and valuation is a giant step and one that Scholasticism failed to take.

Someone would perhaps suggest that the real object can be separated from the intentional object by saying that in experience the intention is given with its intentional object; however, this object, as such, belongs inseparably to it and therefore really lives in it. What the experience intends or presents is and remains with it, whether or not the corresponding "real object" exists in reality. However, when we try to separate the real object from the intentional object by making the latter a real factor immanent in experience, we face the difficulty that now two realities must confront each other, whereas only one of them is present and possible. For example, I perceive the tree in the garden; that tree and nothing else is the real object of the perceiving intention. Obviously, a second, immanent tree, or even an "inner image" of the real tree, is not *given,* and to assume that there is such a tree leads only to absurdity.

Husserl makes it clear that we must therefore restrict ourselves to what is given in pure experience. Through the phenomenological reduction, every "real" object is bracketed. Abiding by this suspension, we must therefore try to describe only that which is self-evidently contained in the "reduced" phenomenon. If we do this, it appears that every perception has its noematic meaning, its "perceived as such," which, as correlate, belongs to the phenomenologically reduced perception. In other words, any perception is a consciousness of a thing in the real world—the reality of which is placed between brackets—and this perceptually appearing thing can be described as such (*Ideas,* 1:217–21 [185–88]).

The Noema in Nonperceptual Experiences — According to Husserl, what has been said here concerning perception applies to all types of intentional experience. After reduction, memory yields the "remembered as such"; expectation, the "expected as such"; and phantasy, the "imagined as such." The object considered—for example, a tree in bloom—may appear in each of these experiences in such a way that the faithful description of what appears as such has to make use of the same expressions. Yet the noematic correlates are essentially different. In one case, the character of that which appears is described as bodily reality, in another as fiction, and in a third as recollection. The characters in question are not added to but rather found as inseparable features of the perceived, imagined, or remembered as such. They are features of the meaning of perception, that of imagination, and that of memory, and they are found to belong necessarily to those in correlation with the respective types of noetic experience. Within the complete noema, we must thus distinguish essentially different strata grouped around a *central nucleus.* This nucleus is the pure "objective meaning," that which in the above-mentioned examples could be described in identical objective terms regardless of the type of intentional experience (*Ideas,* 1:221–22 [188–89]).

We must now describe the meaning of noesis and noema in the case of a derivative act. Let us take as an example the predicative judgment. The noema of a judgment is the judged content of the judgment as such. But this content, at least insofar as its central nucleus is concerned, is nothing other than that which we ordinarily refer to as judgment. To grasp the full noema, we must grasp it as we find it in reality, in the full noematic concreteness in which we are conscious of it when we concretely judge. Note that the judged content of the judgment is not to be confused with the matter judged about. When the judging process takes place on the basis of a perceiving act that plainly posits something, the noema of this presenting act becomes part of the judging act taken in its full concreteness. The presenting noesis likewise becomes a constitutive part of the essence of the concrete noesis of the judgment. The "presented as such" receives the form of the apophantic subject or object. The object "concerning which," and in particular the object we use as subject of our judgment, is the matter judged about. The whole that is formed out of this matter, the content of the judgment as content, constitutes the full noematic correlate, the meaning of the judgment as experienced.

However, the phenomenological reduction must not be neglected here. If we wish to obtain the pure noema of our judgment as experienced, this reduction demands that we suspend the delivery of the judgment. If we do this, we find facing us in their phenomenological purity the full concrete essence of the judgment as experienced, that is, the noesis of the judgment, apprehended concretely as essence, and the noema of the judgment, which belongs to the noesis and is necessarily one with it, that is, the delivered judgment as *eidos* (*Ideas,* 1:226–31 [193–97]).

These remarks briefly indicate some very important features of the relationship between noesis and noema. We shall return to this fundamental phenomenological topic in the chapters to follow. The preceding descriptions suffice, we hope, as a preliminary idea of these two cardinal poles of the intentionality of consciousness.

I Dynamic Description of Intentionality

Functional Problems — Husserl leaves no room for doubt that as far as he is concerned, the greatest of all phenomenological issues are the "functional" problems, those involved in the constitution of the objective field of consciousness. They concern the way in which, for example, the noeses, which animate the hyletic material and merge into unitary manifolds and continuous syntheses, bring forth the consciousness of something in such a way that in and through it the objective unity of objects can be consistently and rationally determined.

The viewpoint of "function" is the central viewpoint of phenomenology. The inquiries to which it gives rise cover nearly the entire phenomenological sphere. All phenomenological analyses ultimately serve in one form or another as integral parts or lower grades of functions. Instead of analyzing, describing, and classifying single experiences, the study of details is governed by the teleological view of their function in making *synthetic unity* possible.

For instance, in the sphere of experience, the functional method concerns the many forms of conscious continua and of discontinua of conscious experiences that are internally united through a common bond of meaning, through the unifying consciousness of one and the same objective datum, which appears now in this perspective, and then in that, and presents itself either intuitively or as determined by thought. It seeks to discover how objective unities of every kind, immanent but not real, are "known" or "supposed"; how the identity of these suppositions is constituted by conscious formations of different types but essentially fixed structure; and how these formations should be described along strictly methodical lines. The functional method, moreover, investigates how the unity of the objective content of every objective region and category can and must, in accordance with conscious insight, be disclosed or exposed as corresponding to "reason" and "unreason," respectively.

We must therefore study in the most general and comprehensive fashion how objective unities of every region and category are consciously constituted. We must systematically show how all the connections of our real and possible consciousness of these unities as essential possibilities are fixed by the essential nature of the simple or secondary intuitions intentionally related to them: the thought formations of lower and higher levels, the confused and the clear, the expressed and the nonexpressed, the prescientific and the scientific, up to the highest formations of strictly theoretical science. All fundamental types of possible consciousness, and the modifications, fusions, and syntheses that essentially belong to them, must be made evident and systematically studied in their eidetic generality and phenomenological purity. We must also study how, through their own essence, they prefigure all possibilities of being; and how the existing objects, by virtue of absolutely fixed and essential laws, are the correlates of conscious connections having a definite essential content—just as, conversely, the being of systems thus articulated is equivalent to the existing objects. And in all these investigations, we have to keep in mind that they refer to all regions of being and all levels of generality (*Ideas,* 1:207–10 [176–79]).

Actuality and Potentiality of Intentional Life — As Husserl sees it, the most important problems of a genetic and dynamic study of intentionality are concerned with the different forms of synthesis: the synthesis uniting a multiplicity of aspects given in a multiplicity of acts into the experience of a single object, the synthesis uniting the different phases of a particular experience into the unity of a single total experience, and the synthesis uniting the whole of conscious life into an all-embracing *cogito* that synthetically comprises all particular conscious processes and intends the world as the horizon of every particular *cogitatum.* The fundamental form of this universal synthesis, which makes all other syntheses of consciousness possible, is the all-embracing consciousness of internal time. The correlate of this consciousness is immanent temporality itself as a constant infinite horizon (*Cart. Med.,* 77–81 [111–14]).

The multiplicity, however, of the intentionality that belongs to any *cogito* relating to the world is not exhausted by considering cogitations as *actual* lived experiences. On the contrary, every actuality implies potentialities that, rather than being empty possibilities, are intentionally prefigured with respect to content. In addition, they have the character of possibilities that can be actualized by the ego. This feature indicates another fundamental characteristic of intentionality. Every lived experience has a horizon that changes with the alteration of the links of consciousness to which the experience belongs and with the modification of the experience itself in the different phases of its flow. This horizon is an intentional horizon of references to potentialities of consciousness that belong to the experience itself. For example, to every external perception there belongs its reference from the genuinely perceived sides of the object of perception to the sides that are also "meant," though not yet explicitly perceived but only anticipated at first, with a nonintuitional emptiness as sides coming into view. There is a continuous "protention" that, in each phase of the perception, has a new sense. Moreover, the perception has inner horizons made up of other possibilities of perception that we could have if we actually took a different course of perception. Finally, every perception always has a horizon of the past as a possibility of recollections that can be awakened and that have their horizons of possible recollections.

All this was already mentioned in the foregoing. Here we want to focus attention on the fact that these horizons are *predelineated potentialities* in the sense that we can ask any horizon what lies in it; we can explicate, unfold, and uncover its potentialities. By doing this, we uncover the objective meaning that is implicitly meant in every actual *cogito,* though never with more than a certain degree of determination. This meaning, this *cogitatum* as *cogitatum,* is never present to our consciousness as a finished datum; it is clarified only through the explication of the given horizons.

The predelineation itself is always imperfect. But despite its indeterminateness, it has a determinate structure, that is, a determination and an openness that are both immediately given in any experience. This openness prior to further determinations is precisely what constitutes the horizon. As contrasted with the case of pure anticipating acts of imagining, there occurs here, by means of an actual continuation of perception, a "fulfilling" further determination, but it, too, always refers to new horizons.

Husserl explains thus that every consciousness is characterized essentially not only by being *somehow* able to change into continually new modes of consciousness of the same object but also by being able to do so according to these horizon intentionalities. The object is like an identity pole, always meant as having a meaning that is still to be actualized. In every moment of consciousness, it points to a noetic intentionality that pertains to it according to its meaning and that can and must be explained through intentional analyses.

Husserl tells us further that, as we have seen, every perceived object is perceived in an outer horizon. The horizon of all possible horizons is the world. This horizon, however, is a horizon *sui generis;* it is not the synthesis of all possible horizons, but this total horizon is pregiven to every concrete horizon. The world is indeed that to which every being refers but, at the same time, it is also that from which every being ultimately must be understood and has its sense and meaning. The same applies to every particular horizon. The world is the root and goal of the particular horizons; it is transcendent in the strict sense of this term.

This transcendent total horizon manifests itself in every being and shows how this being must be explicated. This world appears in a world experience in which everything is experienced but which itself is never experienced. Therefore, a very deep sense of transcendence manifests itself in every experience in which the ego experiences the world as a transcendent horizon from which and in which it understands every being and itself. The world is that to which the ego transcends itself in every concrete experience. The world as world experience and the ego as experience of the world are nothing but the final intentionality of consciousness. From the viewpoint of the ego, this intentionality is not a static consciousness of the world but a dynamic, continuous self-transcendence to the world; this intentionality *is* not, but it functions. That is why it is called "functioning intentionality" (*Cart. Med.,* 81–83 [114–16]).[10]

I Intentional Analysis

Function of Intentional Analysis within Phenomenology — In the foregoing, we have gained an understanding of the fundamental principle of phenomenology, according to which it wants to found all knowledge on an evidence that is immediately rooted in intuition. We have also seen that every *cogito* necessarily implies its *cogitatum.* If, however, consciousness essentially is consciousness of something, then not only the *cogito* itself but also its *cogitatum* has some degree of evidence, provided at least that we consider the *cogitatum* in question solely insofar as it is immediately given in this particular *cogito.* Thus the phenomenological reflection enables us to analyze and describe the *cogitata* exactly as they were "meant" (*noemata*) and to describe the noeses correlated to these *noemata* as they manifest themselves to be in reflection.

We must, however, Husserl warns us, be very careful here. At first sight, the "true and pure Being" of every phenomenon may seem to be already found in the actual evidence of every *cogito,* so that all we would have to do would be simply to intuit and grasp it. On closer investigation, however, it appears that in the domain of pure phenomena, the different objects are *not found* in the cogitations but are *constituted* in different types of syntheses, since what is meant (the object) is practically never identical with what immediately appears (noema) (*The Idea,* 55–57 [70–72]).

Every inquiry into consciousness implies two sides, a noematic and a noetic side, which, however, descriptively are inseparable. One of the most important points in our analysis and description will be to describe and explain the syntheses that occur in every act of consciousness and that have their noematic and noetic sides. A die, for instance, is given continuously in perception as an objective unity in a multiplicity of modes of appearing, and these modes are correlates of a multiplicity of individual noeses. How can we explain and describe that we experience a multiplicity of aspects, given in a multiplicity of individually different acts, as one and the same perception of one single object? Thus, once we have started the phenomenological task of describing consciousness concretely, an endless horizon of facts discloses itself, and all these facts can be characterized as facts of synthetic structures that give noetic-noematic unity to the individual cogitations and their *cogitata.* Only the elucidation of the peculiar operation called "synthesis" can make the disclosure of the *cogito* as "consciousness-of" fruitful for philosophy. This elucidation is the task of the *intentional analysis* (*The Idea,* 57–60 [72–76]).

The Proper Nature of Intentional Analysis — It should be evident that the intentional analysis of consciousness is wholly different from analyses in the usual, natural sense. Consciousness is not simply a whole made up of data of consciousness and therefore capable of being analyzed or divided into self-sufficient and non-self-sufficient elements or parts. Although, in certain themes, intentional analysis leads also to such distinctions and divisions, yet everywhere its peculiar attainment, as intentional, is to disclose the potentialities implicit in the actualities of consciousness. This disclosure results, on the noematic side, in an explication of what is consciously meant and, on the noetic side, in the explication of the possible intentional experiences themselves. Intentional analysis is guided by the fundamental principle that every consciousness is an intending of "what is meant," but that at any time, this something "meant" is more than what is given explicitly at that time. The intending beyond itself, which is implicit in any consciousness, must be considered an essential aspect of consciousness.

The phenomenologist's inquiry, however, does not arise from a naive devotedness to the intentional object purely as such. One wants also to describe the noetic manifolds of consciousness and their synthetic unity, through which alone we have one intentional object. When I as a phenomenologist explore everything objective with its content solely as a correlate of consciousness, I do not consider and describe it only as *somehow* referring back to the corresponding *cogito*. Rather, with my reflective glance, I penetrate an anonymous cogitative life and uncover there the definite synthetic courses taken by the manifold modes of consciousness. Beyond them, I uncover the mode of ego comportment, which leads to an understanding of how my consciousness makes it possible and necessary that this or that existing object with these determinations is intended in it, occurs in it as this or that meaning. It is to be noted here that the phenomenological explication of the perceived as such is not restricted to its perceptual explication. On the contrary, the phenomenological explication shows what is included and nonintuitively cointended in the very meaning of the *cogitatum* by making present in imagination the potential perceptions that will make the invisible visible.

By explicating their correlative horizons in this fashion, intentional analysis brings the highly diverse anonymous lived experiences to the fore, including those which have a constitutive function in relation to the objective meaning of the *cogitatum* in question. Only in this way can the phenomenologist explain how, within the immanence of conscious life and in the variously determined modes of consciousness, it is possible to intend anything like fixed and permanent objective unities, and how this marvelous operation of constituting identical objects is performed for each category of objects. The horizon structure that belongs to every intentionality makes phenomenological analysis and description follow a completely new kind of method (*Cart. Med.*, 46–49 [83–87]).

The most universal type, within which everything particular is included as special form, is indicated by our first universal scheme: *ego-cogito-cogitatum*. The most universal descriptions that we have attempted concerning intentionality refer to this type. In the particularizations of this type and their descriptions, the intentional object plays the role of "clue" to the typical infinite manifolds of possible cogitations.

The point of departure is the object given directly at this particular time. From it, reflection goes back to the mode of consciousness as it is at that moment and to the potential modes of consciousness included "horizonally" in that mode; next, it goes to those modes in which the object might be differently intended as the

107 I The Purely Psychical as Given in Experience

same, such as perception, retention, recollection, and expectation. And each of those types is further particularized in its whole noetic-noematic structure, as the intentional object is more particularized; for example, as *cogitatum* as such, as "anything whatsoever," as "a single object," a "concrete spatial thing," or "an animate being."

Each type disclosed by these clues is to be investigated in its noetic-noematic structure. It is to be systematically explicated with respect to the modes of the intentional flow pertaining to it and with respect to their horizons and the intentional processes implicit in them. No matter how fluid the modes of consciousness may be, they are always restricted to a set of structural types that remain invariably the same, as long as the object intended remains this one type of this determinate kind. To explicate systematically this set of structural types is precisely the task of phenomenology (*Cart. Med.*, 50–53 [87–89]).

Husserl concludes by making it clear that the peculiar attainment of intentional analysis is to disclose the potentialities implied in the actualities of consciousness. He sees intentional analysis as the general method of elucidation and explication of meanings and claims that as such it consists in disclosing and disengaging those constituents that are necessarily implied in a certain meaning experienced in a given situation.[11] Concerning the perceptual apprehension of a material thing, for instance, the method requires that the examination of a given perception be not confined to what presents itself in direct sense-experience. In fact, the meaning of a perception, the *cogitatum qua cogitatum,* the perceptual noema, the perceived thing as it presents itself before the experiencing subject's mind in and through the act under consideration, is only indicated implicitly by what is given in direct sense-experience. For a complete analysis and clarification of the perceptual meaning, a progressive explication of the inner horizon is required (*Cart. Med.*, 39–40 [77–78]). Thus, we resort to intentional analysis when, going beyond what is given in direct sense experience, we point out the inner horizon in its role as codeterminant of the perceptual meaning. From the noetic point of view, the explication of the inner horizon appears as a disclosure of anticipations with which the given perception is interwoven. These anticipations of potential perceptions, when actualized, will render visible what is unseen at the moment (ibid., 40–41 [78–79]). To subject a perception to intentional analysis amounts to considering it with regard to other perceptions, namely, the group of those related to the same thing. The material thing, as an objective unity, is constituted by perceptions concatenating themselves into one coherent, systematic group. The thing is that which it progressively reveals itself to be through those perceptions. Since the thing derives the sense of its existence from the systematic concatenation and intertexture of these perceptions, the investigation of a single act of perception by the method of intentional analysis is founded on the contribution of that perception toward the constitution of the appearing thing. Such an investigation is concerned with the role that the chosen single perception plays in the group to which it belongs and with which it is concatenated. In examining a single perception by the method of intentional analysis, we must concentrate upon the function that this single perception assumes in the synthesis of identification, which is the fundamental characteristic of the perceptual process (ibid., 41–43 [79–81]).

I NOTES

1. Eugen Fink, "Operative Begriffe in Husserls Phänomenologie," *Zeitschrift für philosophische Forschung* 11 (1957): 321–37.

2. Alwin Diemer, *Edmund Husserl: Versuch einer systematischen Darstellung seiner Phänomenologie* (Meisenheim am Glan: Hain, 1956), 150–59.

3. This section paraphrases "Amsterdamer Vorträge," in *Phän. Psych.*, 302–49, sect. 3, 306–8.

4. This section paraphrases ibid., sect. 4, 308–11.

5. This section paraphrases ibid., sect. 5, 311–12.

6. Diemer, *Edmund Husserl*, 45–72.

7. Cf. Husserl, *L. I.*, Investigation 5, 2:533–659. Spiegelberg, *The Phenomenological Movement,* 1:107–11 (see also 39–42); Ludwig Landgrebe, *Phänomenologie und Metaphysik* (Hamburg: Schröder, 1949), 59–69; Bernet et al., *Edmund Husserl,* 85–96; Quentin Lauer, *Phénoménologie de Husserl: Essai sur la genèse de l'intentionnalité* (Paris: Presses Universitaires de France, 1955), 56–59, 89–95; Diemer, *Edmund Husserl,* 45–56; Pierre Thévenaz, *What is Phenomenology?* trans. James M. Edie (Chicago: Quadrangle Books, 1962), 48–50.

8. Franz Brentano, *Psychologie vom empirischen Standpunkt,* ed. Oskar Kraus, 3 vols. (Leipzig: Felix Meiner, 1924), 1:125–26.

9. Diemer, *Edmund Husserl,* 77–79. Husserl, *Cart. Med.,* 10–11 [51–52], 77–81 [111–14].

10. See also Gerd Brand, *Welt, Ich und Zeit* (The Hague: Nijhoff, 1955), 13–25.

11. Gaston Bachelard, *Recherches sur les conditions de la connaissance* (Paris: Aubier, 1942), 101.

The Field of the Purely Psychical, the Phenomenological Reduction, and Genuine Inner Experience

Text

3. Das abgeschlossene Feld des rein Psychischen. — Phänomenologische Reduktion und echte innere Erfahrung

Die Idee einer phänomenologischen Psychologie ist durch die ganze Weite des aus der Selbsterfahrung und der in ihr fundierten Fremderfahrung entspringenden Aufgabenkreises umzeichnet. Aber es ist noch nicht klar, ob eine in Ausschließlichkeit und Konsequenz fortgeführte phänomenologische Erfahrung uns ein derart abgeschlossenes Seinsfeld verschafft, daß eine *ausschließlich* darauf bezogene, von allem Psychophysischen reinlich abgelöste Wissenschaft erwachsen kann. Hier bestehen in der Tat Schwierigkeiten, welche den Psychologen selbst nach *Brentanos* Entdeckung der Intentionalität die Möglichkeit einer solchen rein phänomenologischen Psychologie verdeckt haben. Sie betreffen schon die Herstellung einer wirklich reinen Selbsterfahrung und damit eines wirklich rein psychischen [282] Datums. Es bedarf einer besonderen Zugangsmethode zum rein phänomenologischen Feld. Diese *Methode der "phänomenologischen Reduktion"* ist also die Grundmethode der reinen Psychologie, die Voraussetzung aller ihrer spezifisch theoretischen Methoden. Letztlich beruht alle Schwierigkeit auf der Art, wie schon die Selbsterfahrung der Psychologen überall mit äußerer Erfahrung, der vom außerpsychischen Realen, verflochten ist. Das erfahrene "Äußere" gehört nicht zur intentionalen Innerlichkeit, obschon doch die Erfahrung selbst dazu gehört als Erfahrung *vom* Äußeren. Ebenso für jederlei sonstiges Bewußtsein, das auf ein Weltliches gerichtet ist. Es bedarf also einer konsequenten ἐποχή des Phänomenologen, wenn er sein Bewußtsein als reines Phänomen gewinnen will, einzelweise, aber auch als das Ganze seines reinen Lebens. D.h. er muß im Vollzug der phänomenologischen Reflexion jeden Mitvollzug der im unreflektierten Bewußtsein betätigten objektiven Setzungen inhibieren und damit jedes urteilsmäßige Hereinziehen

3. The Self-contained Field of the Purely Psychical.—Phenomenological Reduction and True Inner Experience

The idea of a phenomenological psychology encompasses the whole range of tasks arising out of the experience of self and the experience of the other founded on it. But it is not yet clear whether phenomenological experience, followed through in exclusiveness and consistency, really provides us with a kind of closed-off field of being, out of which a science can grow which is exclusively focused on it and completely free of everything psychophysical. Here [in fact] difficulties do exist, which have hidden from psychologists the possibility of such a purely phenomenological psychology even after Brentano's discovery of intentionality. They are relevant already to the construction of a really pure self-experience, and therewith of a really pure psychic datum. A particular method of access is required for the pure phenomenological field: the method of "phenomenological reduction." This *method of "phenomenological reduction"* is thus the foundational method of pure psychology and the presupposition of all its specifically theoretical methods. Ultimately the great difficulty rests on the way that already the self-experience of the psychologist is everywhere intertwined with external experience, with that of extra-psychical real things. The experienced "exterior" does not belong to one's intentional interiority, although certainly the experience itself belongs to it as experience—*of* the exterior. Exactly this same thing is true of every kind of awareness directed at something out there in the world. A consistent *epoche* of the phenomenologist is required, if he wishes to break through to his own consciousness as pure phenomenon or as the totality of his purely mental processes. That is to say, in the accomplishment of phenomenological reflection he must inhibit every co-accomplishment of objective positing produced in unreflective consciousness, and therewith [inhibit] every judgmental drawing-in of the world as it

der für ihn geradehin "daseienden" Welt. Die jeweilige Erfahrung
von diesem Haus, von diesem Leib, von einer Welt überhaupt ist
und bleibt aber ihrem eigenen Wesensgehalt nach, also unabtrennbar, Erfahrung "*von* diesem Haus", diesem Leib, dieser Welt,
und so für jederlei Bewußtseinsweise, die objektiv gerichtet ist. Es
ist ja unmöglich, ein intentionales Erlebnis zu beschreiben, auch
wenn es ein illusionäres ist, ein nichtiges Urteilen und dgl., ohne
das in ihm Bewußte *als* solches mit zu beschreiben. Die universale
Epoché hinsichtlich der bewußt werdenden Welt (ihre "*Einklammerung*") schaltet aus dem phänomenologischen Feld die für das
betreffende Subjekt schlechthin seiende Welt aus, aber an ihre
Stelle tritt die so und so *bewußte* (wahrgenommene, erinnerte,
beurteilte, gedachte, gewertete etc.) Welt "*als solche*", die "*Welt in
Klammern*" oder, was dasselbe, es tritt an die Stelle der Welt bzw.
des einzelnen Weltlichen schlechthin der jeweilige Bewußtseins-
sinn in seinen verschiedenen Modis (Wahrnehmungssinn, Erin-
nerungssinn usw.).

Damit klärt und ergänzt sich unsere erste Bestimmung der
phänomenologischen Erfahrung und ihrer Seinssphäre. Im
Rückgang von den in der natürlichen Einstellung gesetzten
Einheiten auf die mannigfaltigen Bewußtseinsweisen, in denen sie
erscheinen, [283] sind, als von diesen Mannigfaltigkeiten unabtrennbar, auch die Einheiten—aber als "eingeklammerte"—dem
rein Psychischen zuzurechnen und dann jeweils in den Erschei-
nungscharakteren, in denen sie sich darbieten. Die Methode der
phänomenologischen Reduktion (auf die reinen "Phänomene", das
rein Psychische) besteht danach 1) in der methodischen und streng
konsequenten ἐποχή bei jeder in der seelischen Sphäre auftre-
tenden objektiven Setzung, sowohl am einzelnen Phänomen als an
dem ganzen seelischen Bestand überhaupt; 2) in der methodisch
geübten Erfassung und Beschreibung der mannigfaltigen
"Erscheinungen" als Erscheinungen ihrer gegenständlichen
Einheiten und der Einheiten als Einheiten der ihnen jeweils in
den Erscheinungen zuwachsenden Sinnbestände. Es zeigt sich
damit eine doppelte "*noetische*" und "*noematische*" Richtung der
phänomenologischen Beschreibungen an. —Die phänomenologische Erfahrung in der methodischen Gestalt der phänomenologischen Reduktion ist die einzig *echte* "*innere Erfahrung*" im Sinne
jeder wohlbegründeten psychologischen Wissenschaft. In ihrem
eigenen Wesen liegt offenbar die Möglichkeit, kontinuierlich unter
methodischer Erhaltung der Reinheit fortgeführt zu werden *in
infinitum*. Die reduktive Methode überträgt sich von der Selbsterfahrung auf die Fremderfahrung, sofern im vergegenwärtigten
Leben des Anderen die entsprechende Einklammerung und

"exists" for him straightforwardly. The specific experience of this
house, this body, of a world as such, is and remains, however, according to its own essential content and thus inseparably, experience ["*of* this house"], this body, this world; this is so for every mode
of consciousness which is directed towards an object. It is, after all,
quite impossible to describe an intentional experience—even if illu-
sionary, an invalid judgment, or the like—without at the same time
describing the object of that consciousness *as* such. The universal
epoche of the world as it becomes known in consciousness (the "putting it in brackets") shuts out from the phenomenological field the
world as it exists for the subject in simple absoluteness; its place,
however, is taken by the world as given in *consciousness* (perceived,
remembered, judged, thought, valued, etc.)—the world *as such,* the
"world in brackets," or in other words, the world, or rather individual things in the world as absolute, are replaced by the respective
meaning of each in *consciousness* [*Bewusstseinssinn*] in its various
modes (perceptual meaning, recollected meaning, and so on).

With this, we have clarified and supplemented our initial determination of the phenomenological experience and its sphere of being. In going back from the unities posited in the natural attitude to
the manifold of modes of consciousness in which they appear, the
unities, as inseparable from these multiplicities—but as "bracketed"—are also to be reckoned among what is purely psychical, and
always specifically in the appearance-character in which they
present themselves. The method of phenomenological reduction (to
the pure "phenomenon," the purely psychical) accordingly consists
(1) in the methodical and rigorously consistent epoche of every objective positing in the psychic sphere, both of the individual phenomenon and of the whole psychic field in general; and (2) in the
methodically practiced seizing and describing of the multiple "appearances" as appearances of their objective units and these units as
units of component meanings accruing to them each time in their
appearances. With this is shown a twofold direction—the *noetic* and
noematic of phenomenological description. Phenomenological experience in the methodical form of the phenomenological reduction is
the only genuine "inner experience" in the sense meant by any well-
grounded science of psychology. In its own nature lies manifest the
possibility of being carried out continuously in infinitum with methodical preservation of purity. The reductive method is transferred
from self-experience to the experience of others insofar as there can
be applied to the envisaged [*vergegenwärtigten*] mental life of the
Other the corresponding bracketing and description according to
the subjective "How" of its appearance and what is appearing ("noesis"
and "noema"). As a further consequence, the community that is

Beschreibung nach Erscheinung und Erscheinendem im subjektiven Wie ("Noesis" und "Noema") vollzogen werden kann. In weiterer Folge reduziert sich die in der Gemeinschaftserfahrung erfahrene Gemeinschaft nicht nur auf die seelisch vereinzelten intentionalen Felder sondern auf die Einheit des intersubjektiven, sie alle verbindenden Gemeinschaftslebens in seiner phänomenologischen Reinheit (intersubjektive Reduktion). So ergibt sich die volle Erweiterung des echten psychologischen Begriffes von "innerer Erfahrung".

Zu jeder Seele gehört nicht nur die Einheit ihres mannigfaltigen *intentionalen Lebens* mit all den von ihm als einem "objektiv" gerichteten unabtrennbaren Sinneseinheiten. Unabtrennbar ist von diesem Leben das in ihm erlebende *Ichsubjekt* als der identische, alle Sonderintentionalitäten zentrierende *"Ichpol"* und als Träger der ihm aus diesem Leben zuwachsenden Habitualitäten. So ist dann auch die reduzierte [284] Intersubjektivität, in Reinheit und konkret gefaßt, eine im intersubjektiven reinen Bewußtseinsleben sich betätigende Gemeinschaft von reinen Personen.

experienced in community experience is reduced not only to the mentally particularized intentional fields but also to the unity of the community life that connects them all together, the community mental life in its phenomenological purity (intersubjective reduction). Thus results the perfect expansion of the genuine psychological concept of "inner experience."

To every mind there belongs not only the unity of its multiple *intentional life-process* [*intentionalen Lebens*] with all its inseparable unities of sense directed towards the "object." There is also, inseparable from this life-process, the experiencing *I-subject* as the identical *I-pole* giving a center for all specific intentionalities, and as the carrier of all habitualities growing out of this life-process. Likewise, then, the reduced intersubjectivity, in pure form and concretely grasped, is a community of pure "persons" acting in the intersubjective realm of the pure life of consciousness.

I Synopsis

In the preceding chapter, we have described the whole range of tasks that a phenomenological psychology encompasses; all of these tasks arise out of the experience of one's self and the experience of the other that is founded upon it. It is not yet clear, however, whether phenomenological experience can really provide us with a field of meaning that is properly closed off and self-contained so that phenomenological psychology can indeed focus on that field of meaning completely free of everything psychophysical. In Husserl's view, real difficulties exist here that have hidden from psychologists the possibility of a pure, phenomenological psychology, even after Brentano's discovery of intentionality. As Husserl sees it, a particular method of access is required that can demarcate the pure phenomenological field: the method of *phenomenological reduction.*

The method of "phenomenological reduction" is the foundational method of pure psychology and the presupposition of all its other theoretical methods. In the final analysis, the greatest difficulty rests in the manner in which the self-experience of the psychologist is everywhere intertwined with external experience and thus with that of extrapsychical real things. The experienced "exterior" things do not belong to one's intentional interiority, although certainly the experience itself and its intentional content belong to it as experience *of* what is exterior. In other words, a consistent *epoche* on the part of the phenomenologist is required, if he or she wishes to break through to his or her own consciousness. Even though it is quite impossible to describe an intentional experience without at the same time describing the object of experience as such, the phenomenologist must nevertheless replace all individual things in the world by the respective meaning of each of them in consciousness, and the latter is to be taken in its various modes as a perceptual meaning, a recollected meaning, a hoped-for meaning, and so on.

In going back from the unities posited in the natural attitude to the manifold modes of consciousness in which they appear, the unities, as inseparable from these multiplicities—but as bracketed and thus taken only as unities of meaning—are also to be reckoned among what is purely psychical; furthermore, they are always to be taken specifically with the appearance character in which they present themselves. Thus the method of phenomenological reduction to the pure phenomena, to the purely psychical, consists in two steps: (1) in the methodical and rigorously consistent *epoche* of every objective positing in the psychic sphere and (2) in the methodically practiced seizing and describing of the multiple phenomena as appearances of their objective unities; and these unities must be taken as unities of component meanings that accrue to them each time they appear. This explains why there is a twofold direction in the phenomenological analysis and description, one that focuses on the intentional acts and one that focuses on the intentional contents of these acts; thus the description is both noetic and noematic.

The phenomenological reduction can also be transferred from the experience of one's self to the experience of others. One can apply to the life of the other that which has been made present to the ego, the corresponding reduction; purified by the reduction, this life can then be analyzed and described with respect to its appearances (noeses) and in regard to what appears in them (noemata). In this case, both noesis and noema must be taken as they appear to the other subject.

As a further consequence, the community that is experienced in the ego's experience of community is reduced not only to the intentional fields of noeses and noemata that belong to each individual *psyche* but also, and even particularly, to the intersubjective life of the community that connects all of them, taken as a whole; the latter, too, is to be analyzed and described in its phenomenological purity (intersubjective reduction).

Finally, to every *psyche* there belongs not only the unity of its multiple intentional life with all the inseparable unities of meaning. There is also, inseparable from this life, the experiencing I-subject as the identical I-pole, which gives a center to all specific intentionalities and also functions as the carrier of all habitualities that develop out of this life. Likewise, then, the reduced intersubjectivity—provided it is concretely grasped in pure form—is also a community of pure persons who take an active part in the intersubjective, pure life of consciousness.

In this rich section, Husserl discusses a number of important issues. In order to avoid repetition, I have decided to limit myself in the commentary to what he has to say about the phenomenological reduction, the field of pure psychic phenomena that it brings to light, and what is characteristic of pure inner experience. The issues connected with the I-pole will be discussed in the commentary of Chapter Six, whereas the problems connected with intersubjectivity will be considered in the commentary of Chapter Ten, since it presupposes the transcendental reduction, which will be introduced in Chapter Eight.

Commentary

Phenomenological Reduction

Necessity of the Phenomenological Reduction

In the Introduction and preceding chapters of this book, we have already met the expressions "reduction"[1] and *"epoche"* several times. In Husserl's writings, these terms can have a variety of meanings. For this reason, Husserl usually added to the term "reduction" different qualifiers, such as "philosophical," "psychological," "eidetic," "phenomenological," or "transcendental." Although I shall limit myself in this section to the phenomenological reduction in the strict sense, I shall first briefly indicate the meaning of the other reductive processes. But to begin with, I should like to make a few terminological observations.

The terms "reduction" and *"epoche"* are both common logical expressions. *Epoche* means the suspension of judgment, either because one doubts that human beings are capable of knowing anything with certainty (radical skepticism), or because one wants to examine an issue before one feels confident to have a "definitive" opinion about it. The methodical doubt of Descartes and the reductions of Husserl are examples of the latter.

Epoche is a Greek word, derived from the verb *epechein;* the term means a (temporary) cessation, of a movement for instance. The term "reduction," on the other hand, is used for the process in which one replaces the not fully evident syllogistic forms of the second and third figures by the perfect and fully evident syllogistic forms of the first figure. In Husserl's case, the term "reduction" means the process in and through which one is led from something that is not yet evident to something that already has been made evident. On the other hand, the term *"epoche"* refers to the suspension of judgment in regard to everything that, in the transition from the not-yet-evident to what-is-evident, is to be left out of consideration because it cannot be accepted without further examination, or because no adequate evidence can be achieved in its regard.

In the Introduction, we have already seen that, speaking quite generally, reduction means the methodical procedure through which one returns to the origins of our knowledge, of which our everyday thinking has mostly lost sight (see 14–17). We have also seen that the reduction which Husserl calls the "philosophical *epoche*" has to lead us to a philosophical attitude that, in one way or another, is perhaps, at least implicitly, admitted by every philosopher. This *epoche* demands that the philosopher suspend judgment with respect to the solutions that in the course of history have been proposed for the different philosophical problems. Undoubtedly, in every philosophy, there is a historical element; nevertheless philosophy requires primarily one's personal insight. That is why I must at first adopt a neutral position with respect to the solutions of the problems in question. In developing my own philosophical insights, I cannot argue academically from a philosophical standpoint that was fixed in advance. I cannot base my personal insights on traditional or generally recognized philosophical theories; rather, I must try to base them on an immediate intuition. I must take the original phenomena exactly as they present themselves, without adding any hypotheses or interpretations, and without reading into them anything suggested by ancient or modern theories. Only positions taken up in such a way can be real principles and real "beginnings." When they are so general that they cover the all-embracing regions of being, they are certainly fundamental in a philosophical sense and belong themselves to philosophy. I must try not to presuppose anything, whether a science or a philosophy. The philosophical *epoche,* when explicitly formulated, should consist in this, that we abstain from making any judgment at all regarding the theoretical content of all previous philosophies, and that our whole discussion respect the limits imposed by this abstention up to the very end (*Ideas,* 33–34 [33–34]).

The eidetic reduction eliminates all references to the particular and individual in the immediately given phenomena. This reduction is needed in all ontologies as well as in philosophy because, unlike the natural sciences, all eidetic sciences are necessarily sciences of essences. In his earlier works, Husserl called this method "ideating abstraction"; in his later works, he often refers to it as "the method of free variation."

The term "psychological reduction" does not appear in Husserl's earlier works. As we have seen, about 1906 Husserl gradually came to the conclusion that there is an essential difference between phenomenological philosophy and descriptive psychology. At first, it was not easy for him to determine the function of descriptive psychology within the framework of his changing conception of transcendental phenomenology. Gradually, however, he realized that descriptive psychology is distinguished not only from empirical psychology but also from pure, transcendental phenomenology. It then became necessary to distinguish the psychological reduction of descriptive, or phenomenological, psychology from the transcendental reduction, which characterizes transcendental phenomenology.

Between 1906 and 1916, Husserl often used the expressions "phenomenological" and "transcendental" interchangeably. If used in connection with the term "reduction," both expressions *at that time* referred to a reductive process that had a dual function: to bring about the transition from what-is to the meaning of what-is, from "things" to phenomena, and the transition from what-is-given to the condition of its possibility, namely, the transcendental subject. After 1916 the term "phenomenological reduction" is always used for what I just called "the psychological reduction," which is characteristic of phenomenological psychology; the expression "transcendental reduction" is then always used for the reduction that is typical for transcendental phenomenology. In this section, I shall limit myself to the phenomenological reduction; the transcendental reduction will be discussed in Chapter Eight.

| Description of the
| Phenomenological Reduction

Phenomenological psychology is meant to make the life of the psyche, that is, of consciousness, taken in its pure, innermost essential structures, the universal and consistent theme of investigation. To this end, the phenomenological psychologist must turn to purely psychic experiences. The difficulty with the analyses of these experiences lies in the fact that we must leave out of consideration all that which relates to external experience, which necessarily refers to the physical. But how can this be done? We observed before, Husserl says, that all experiences are experiences of something, of the world, and that each reflection presupposes a direct experience of what is other.

In order to realize a pure phenomenological experience of my conscious life, in order to make this consciousness in its pure and unique being the universal theme of my research, I must put between brackets as nonpsychical the general thesis of our natural attitude, according to which the real world about me is at all times known as a fact-world that has its being out there. In doing so, the thesis of the natural attitude is still experienced as lived, but I make no use of it any more in order exclusively to focus attention on the psychical as such (*Phän. Psych.,* 312).

Yet I cannot deny that all consciousness is indeed consciousness of something. And in our direct experiences, that which we are conscious of is the natural world, the real, spatiotemporal world. It is thus impossible to describe the essential aspects of a perception or a memory without reference to *what* is perceived or remembered, without describing the concrete objects of these determinate activities. It follows that not just any reflection on consciousness suffices to reveal to us the psychical in its essential being and purity. First of all, we must suspend our natural belief in the reality of the world and place in brackets whatever it includes respecting its being-status. As phenomenologists, we should become disinterested bystanders watching our own conscious life. It is only in this manner that it can become a pure theme in our experience. Instead of living in the world, instead of investing it with our worldly interests, we must actually observe our life as somehow being conscious of this or that, as somehow being interested in itself. If we did not do this we again would be referring to the nonpsychical world. In this *epoche,* consciousness remains a consciousness, and this consciousness remains consciousness of something. The fact that every consciousness manifests itself as consciousness of something is precisely the essential aspect of consciousness as a psychic datum. That which we are conscious of, however, is not to be taken as such; that is to say, what we experience is not to be taken as a being in the real world but exclusively as that which is intended by consciousness. The object as being in the real world must be placed in brackets (*Phän. Psych.,* 312–13).

The phenomenological reduction is essentially determined by these considerations. It is of importance to note here that in this reduction, in addition to the noetic, the noematic is also maintained, even as an endlessly fruitful theme of phenomenological description. It is precisely through the phenomenological reduction that for the first time intentional objects are liberated as essential constituents of our intentional experiences (*Phän. Psych.,* 314).

The phenomenological reduction also has its consequences for our attitude toward the ego of our conscious experiences in that here, too, the human and the animal as real fall away. When real nature is reduced by the *epoche* to a noematic phenomenon, the real human ego of the natural attitude is reduced to a pure psychic life. That is to say, within the realm of the reduction, the ego no longer manifests itself as a real being in the real world but only as the center of the intentional activities that are correlative to the intentional objects mentioned (*Phän. Psych.,* 314–15).

The consequent uncovering of the noema, the object meant as such, can be turned into a consideration and analysis of the related noeses, of the different acts in and through which the ego is conscious of something. Besides these, the ego as center is something special; it is the *ego* in the *cogito,* the "I" that phenomenologically remains identical throughout the diverse acts. The ego is the center from which all the different acts flow and toward which all the different affects stream. In both these respects, this phenomenologically pure ego as center forms an important and comprehensive theme that is closely intertwined with all other phenomenological topics.

The faculties and habits of the ego as well belong to the specific egological topics that are phenomenologically relevant. The first and most important topic remains, however, the analysis of the pure life of the ego itself in its diverse modalities. And in this research concerning the life of the ego as well, it is essential to move in the direction of both the noema and the noesis (*Phän. Psych.*, 314–15).

The Dogmatic Natural Attitude: Possibility of the *Epoche* — According to Husserl, humans generally and ordinarily live in the natural attitude. Since we have already explained in detail what is meant by this attitude, we need only to summarize here its essential elements. With Husserl, in the natural attitude, I find continually present and "standing over against me" the one spatiotemporal factworld to which I myself belong, as well as all other people who are in this world and related to it in the same way as I. I find this factworld to be "out there," and I take it exactly as it gives itself to me as something existing out there. To doubt or to reject some data of the natural world does not destroy the general thesis of the natural standpoint itself. "The" world is a fact-world that is always there. At most, this world is here or there "other" than I supposed it to be; this or that particular point may be an illusion or a hallucination and therefore must be deleted from it. But the "it" itself always remains, in the sense of the general thesis, a world that has its being "out there." The goal pursued by the sciences of the natural standpoint is to know this world more comprehensively, more perfectly than is possible through naive explanations; they want to solve all the problems of scientific knowledge that offer themselves from the standpoint of the natural attitude (*Ideas*, 1:51–53 [48–50]).

Instead of persevering in this natural attitude, Husserl says, we want to alter it radically. First, however, we must convince ourselves that such an alteration is possible in principle. According to the general thesis of the natural standpoint, the real world around us is at all times known, not merely in general as something apprehended but as a fact-world that has its being "out there." This thesis, however, does not consist in an explicit existential judgment. It is and remains implicit during the entire time that this standpoint is adopted; that is to say, it perdures as long as our life runs its course of natural endeavor. What has been perceived at any time has in its totality and in all its distinct aspects the character of "being present out there." This character can function essentially as the basis of an explicit or predicative existential judgment that is in agreement with the character upon which it is founded. If we express the judgment in question, we know very well that we simply put into the form of a statement and express via a predication something that was already contained somehow in the original experience.

The unexpressed thesis can be treated in exactly the same way as the thesis of explicit judgment. A procedure of this kind that can be followed at any time is, for instance, Descartes's attempt to doubt everything. However, Husserl remarks, Descartes had an entirely different aim in mind, and the reduction is something completely different from the Cartesian doubt. Nevertheless, methodologically it has its advantages to compare the reduction with Descartes's doubt. The attempt to doubt everything is part of one's freedom at any moment. We can attempt to doubt everything, no matter how convinced we are of that which we doubt, even if the evidence that gives us certainty is wholly adequate.

Husserl invites us to consider the essential implications of such an act. One who attempts to doubt tries to doubt some form or other of being. This attempt does not affect the form of being itself. One who doubts whether an object, whose being one does not doubt, is constituted in this or that way, doubts only about the way it is constituted. It is clear, however, that we cannot both doubt the being of anything and, at the same time and in the same act of consciousness, bring what is contained in this being under the terms of the natural thesis, thereby conferring upon it the character of "being actually there." In other words, Husserl claims, we cannot at the same time both doubt and hold for certain one and the same quality of being.

It is likewise evident that the attempt to doubt any object of consciousness with respect to its actually being there necessarily implies a certain suspension of the natural thesis. This is precisely what interests us here. In phenomenology the suspension is not a transformation of the thesis into its antithesis, and neither is it a transformation of the thesis into a presumption, indecision, or doubt. Rather, it is something wholly unique, Husserl claims. For we do not relinquish the thesis we have adopted; we do not modify our conviction, but it remains unchanged in itself as long as we do not introduce new motives of judgment; and this is precisely what we abstain from doing here. Nevertheless, the thesis undergoes a modification; while remaining unchanged in itself, we put it out of action, we disconnect it, we bracket it. It still remains there "between brackets," as Husserl puts it. The thesis is a "lived" experience, but we make no use of it; and by that, of course, we do not mean that kind of nonuse resulting from ignorance of the thesis. As in all similar expressions, we are dealing here with signs pointing to a definite but unique form of consciousness that joins the original simple thesis—whether or not this thesis actually or even pre-dicatively posits existence—and changes its value in a very special way. This changing of value is an affair of our full freedom; it is the opposite of any cognitive attitude that would have a bearing on the thesis but would be incompatible with it.

If the attempt to *doubt* is applied to a thesis that, as we assume now, is certain and expressly adhered to, the "disconnection" takes place in and through a modification that leads to its antithesis; we suppose the nonbeing of the thesis so that this antithesis becomes the partial basis of the attempt to doubt. In Descartes's case, this is so predominant that his universal attempt to doubt is precisely an attempt at universal denial. However, Husserl points out, we may disregard this possibility here, for we are interested only in the phenomenon of bracketing or "disconnecting." Although this phe-nomenon can very easily be derived from the attempt to doubt, it obviously can appear in other contexts also, and even indepen-dently. This peculiar *epoche* can be used in relation to every thesis. As Husserl sees it, it is a certain refraining from judgment that is compatible with the *undoubted* and *indubitable* conviction based on self-evidence. The thesis is merely "put out of action," bracketed; it receives the modified status of being a "bracketed thesis," and the judgment in which it is founded simply becomes a "bracketed judgment."

Husserl adds in conclusion that nothing prevents us from speaking of bracketing with respect to an object that is posited, re-gardless of the region or category of being to which it belongs. Brack-eting, then, means that every thesis related to this object must be disconnected, changed into a bracketed thesis. Finally, the term "bracketing" is more suitable for the sphere of objects, and the ex-pression "to put out of action" better fits the sphere of acts of con-sciousness (*Ideas,* 1:57–60 [53–56]).

The Phenomenological *Epoche* — Husserl goes on to say now that the universal *epoche,* taken in the sharply defined new sense he has given to it, could replace the Cartesian attempt to doubt every-thing. However, there are good reasons for limiting the universality of the *epoche,* Husserl says, for if we leave it as inclusive as it is, there would be no room left for unmodified judgments. *Every* thesis and *every* judgment can be freely modified to any extent, and every object that we can judge can be placed between brackets. But our aim was precisely to discover a new scientific domain through the method of bracketing, and it is for this reason that its universality is to be limited.

Husserl is of the opinion that the following limitation is to be made. We put out of action the general thesis that is characteristic of the natural standpoint; we bracket whatever it contains concerning the nature of being. The entire natural world, therefore, which is continually "there for me" and will ever remain there, is a fact-world of which I remain conscious, even though I decide to put it between brackets. By doing so in absolute freedom, Husserl continues, I do *not deny* this world, as though I were a sophist; I do *not doubt* that it is there, as though I were a skeptic; but I use the "phenomenological *epoche,*" which completely bars me from making use of any judgment that concerns spatiotemporal factual being.

Accordingly, I disconnect all sciences concerning the natural world, even though they stand before me on as firm a foundation as ever; I even continue to greatly admire them. I merely make no use whatsoever of their principles and laws and do not make my own any of their propositions. None of their evident propositions serves me as a foundation—as long as any of them is understood as these sciences themselves understand it, as a truth concerning the real things of the world. I accept it only after I have bracketed it; I accept it only in the modified consciousness I have of the judgment as disconnected and not in the role it plays within the sciences in question, that is, as a proposition which claims to be valid and whose validity I recognize and utilize.

This *epoche* should not be confused with the one demanded by positivism but that positivism itself does not always respect. We are not concerned here with removing the prejudices that endanger the positive character of our research. Our aim is not to constitute a science free from theory and from metaphysics by reducing all its foundations to immediate data or to find the means to reach this aim. While we do not question the value of such undertakings, our demand goes in a different direction. The whole world as placed within the framework of nature and presented as real in experience, taken absolutely free from all theory, exactly as it is experienced in reality and as it is made manifest in and through our chains of experiences, is no longer valid for us; it must be bracketed as untested but also as uncontested. Likewise, all theories and sciences, positivistic or nonpositivistic, that are concerned with this world, no matter how good they may be, are subjected to the same reduction (*Ideas,* 1:60–62 [56–57]).

The Phenomenological Residuum — Although the preceding considerations show us the meaning of the phenomenological reduction, we still do not know how important this reduction may be. For what can possibly remain when the whole world is bracketed, including ourselves and our own thinking? Knowing that Husserl is interested in a new eidetic science, one would be inclined to reply that the world as fact is disconnected, but not the world as *eidos* or any other sphere of essential being. As a matter of fact, such a disconnection of the world does not mean that, for example, the number series and the arithmetic relative to it are disconnected.

Husserl, however, does not aim in this direction. His goal is to penetrate into a new region of being whose distinctive character has not yet been defined, a region of *individual* being, as is every genuine region. What exactly this region is will have to be determined more accurately at a later time. Now we want only to briefly indicate this region. We proceed, in the first instance, by disclosing simply and directly what we see. And because the being to be disclosed in this way is none other than that which we refer to on essential grounds as "pure experience," "pure consciousness" with its pure correlates of consciousness, on the one hand, and its pure ego on the other, it follows that we must start with the ego, consciousness, and experience as given to us from the natural standpoint. I, a real human being, am a real object like others in the natural world. I perform cogitations, acts of consciousness, and these acts, as belonging to this human subject, are events of the same natural world. The same holds true of the entire changing stream of my other experiences. The specific acts of the ego shine forth distinctively in this stream; they merge into one another, enter into combinations, and constantly undergo modifications.

Two points are to be noted here. First, in its widest sense, the term "consciousness" includes *all* experiences. Second, even in our scientific thinking, we are locked up in the natural attitude; we are grounded in habits that are firmly established, since they have never seemed to mislead us. For these reasons, we consider all these data of psychological reflection to be real world events, experiences of "animal" beings. It is so natural to see them only in this light that although we are familiar with the possibility of changing our standpoint and are in search of a new domain of objects, we failed to notice that the new domain emerges from those very centers of experience through the adoption of the new standpoint. Moreover, instead of keeping our eyes turned toward these centers of experience, we turned them away and sought the new objects in the ontological realms of arithmetic, geometry, and the like. But in these realms nothing truly new could be gained.

Thus, we must keep our eyes on the sphere of consciousness and study what we find immanent in it. At first, before we carry out the phenomenological reduction in the strict sense, we must subject the very essence of this sphere of consciousness to a systematic analysis, which, however, need not be exhaustive. What we lack most of all is a kind of general insight into the essence of consciousness in general, and more especially into the essence of consciousness insofar as in and through its essential being, the natural fact-world becomes known. In these studies, we must try to arrive at the full insight that we want to gain—namely, that consciousness in itself has a being of its own that is absolutely unique because it remains unaffected by the phenomenological reduction. Consciousness, therefore, remains as a "phenomenological residuum," as a region of being that is, in principle, unique and can become the domain of a new science: phenomenology.

Only through this insight will the phenomenological *epoche* deserve its name; it is the operation required to make accessible to us pure consciousness and subsequently the whole phenomenological region. In this way, we will be able to understand why this region and the corresponding new science were destined to remain unnoticed for such a long time. From the natural viewpoint, nothing can be seen save the natural world. As long as the possibility of the phenomenological attitude was not understood, and the method of referring the objects emerging in that sphere to a primordial form of apprehension had not been seen, the phenomenological world had to remain unknown.

Thus what is left over after the reduction has been performed is the entire domain of all phenomenologically purified phenomena as they are given in pure experiences. Whereas all other regional ontologies focus mainly on the noematic pole of the intentional phenomena, phenomenological psychology is interested mainly in the noetic side, in the various intentional activities of the ego. In addition, it is interested in a careful constitutive analysis of the ego itself.

▌ N O T E

1. For what follows here on reduction, see also Bernet et al., *Edmund Husserl,* 56–74; Eugen Fink, "Reflexionen zu Husserls phänomenologischer Reduktion," *Tijdschrift voor filosofie* 33 (1971): 540–58; Rudolf Boehm, *Vom Gesichtspunkt der Phänomenologie* (The Hague: Nijhoff, 1968), 119–40; Iso Kern, "The Three Ways to the Transcendental Phenomenological Reduction in the Philosophy of Edmund Husserl," in *Husserl: Expositions and Appraisals,* ed. F. Elliston and P. McCormick (Notre Dame, Ind.: University of Notre Dame Press, 1977), 126–49.

F I V E | The Eidetic Reduction: Phenomenological Psychology as an Eidetic Science

Text

Die eidetische Reduktion und die phänomenologische Psychologie als eidetische Wissenschaft

Inwiefern sichert die Einheit des phänomenologischen Erfahrungsfeldes die Möglichkeit einer darauf ausschließlich bezogenen, also rein phänomenologischen Psychologie? Nicht ohne weiteres einer empirisch reinen, einer von allem Psychophysischen abstrahierenden Tatsachenwissenschaft. Anders steht es mit einer apriorischen Wissenschaft. Jedes in sich abgeschlossene Feld möglicher Erfahrung gestattet *eo ipso* den universalen Übergang von der Faktizität zur Wesensform (*Eidos*). So auch hier. Wird die phänomenologische Faktizität irrelevant, dient sie *nur* exemplarisch und als Unterlage für eine freie aber anschauliche Variation der faktischen Einzelseelen und Seelengemeinschaften in a priori mögliche (erdenkliche) und richtet sich nun der theoretische Blick auf das sich in der Variation notwendig durchhaltende Invariante, so erwächst damit bei systematischem Vorgehen ein eigenes Reich des "Apriori". Es tritt damit der wesensnotwendige Formstil hervor (das *Eidos*), der durch alles mögliche seelische Sein in den Einzelheiten, den synthetischen Verbänden und abgeschlossenen Ganzheiten hindurchgehen muß, wenn es überhaupt "denkmöglich", das ist anschaulich vorstellbar soll sein können. Psychologische Phänomenologie ist in dieser Art zweifellos als *"eidetische Phänomenologie"* zu begründen, sie ist dann ausschließlich auf die invarianten Wesensformen gerichtet. Z.B. die Phänomenologie der Körperwahrnehmung ist nicht ein Bericht über die faktisch vorkommenden oder zu erwartenden Wahrnehmungen, sondern Herausstellung des invarianten Strukturensystems, ohne das Wahrnehmung eines Körpers und eine synthetisch zusammenstimmende Mannigfaltigkeit von Wahrnehmungen als solchen eines und desselben Körpers undenkbar wären. Schuf die

Eidetic Reduction and Phenomenological Psychology as an Eidetic Science

To what extent does the unity of the field of phenomenological experience assure the possibility of a psychology exclusively based on it, thus a pure phenomenological psychology? It does not automatically assure an empirically pure science of *facts* from which everything psychophysical is abstracted. But this situation is quite different with an a priori science. In it, every self-enclosed field of possible experience permits *eo ipso* the all-embracing transition from the factual to the essential form, the *eidos*. So here, too. If the phenomenological actual fact as such becomes irrelevant; if, rather, it serves only as an example and as the foundation for a free but intuitive variation of the factual mind and communities of minds *into* the a priori possible (thinkable) ones; and if now the theoretical eye directs itself to the necessarily enduring invariant in the variation; then there will arise with this systematic way of proceeding a realm of its own, of the "a priori." There emerges therewith the eidetically necessary typical form, the *eidos;* this *eidos* must manifest itself throughout all the potential forms of mental being in particular cases, must be present in all the synthetic combinations and self-enclosed wholes, if it is to be at all "thinkable," that is, intuitively conceivable. Phenomenological psychology in this manner undoubtedly must be established as an "eidetic phenomenology"; it is then exclusively directed toward the invariant essential forms. For instance, the phenomenology of perception of bodies will not be (simply) a report on the factually occurring perceptions or those to be expected; rather it will be the presentation of invariant structural systems without which perception of a body and a synthetically concordant multiplicity of perceptions of one and the same body as such would be unthinkable. If the phenomenological reduction contrived

phänomenologische Reduktion den Zugang zu den "Phänomenen" wirklicher und dann auch möglicher innerer Erfahrung, so verschafft die in ihr fundierte Methode der *"eidetischen* [285] *Reduktion"* den Zugang zu den invarianten Wesensgestalten der rein seelischen Gesamtsphäre.

a means of access to the phenomenon of real and also potential inner experience, the method founded in it of "eidetic reduction" provides the means of access to the invariant essential structures of the total sphere of pure mental process.

Synopsis

The question raised in this section is whether, and to what extent, the unity of the field of phenomenological experiences can guarantee the possibility of a pure phenomenological psychology. It is clear that this unity does not automatically assure an empirical pure science of facts from which everything psychophysical could be abstracted, for the facts studied by empirical psychology are all intimately intertwined with animal or human bodies. Yet the situation is quite different in the case of an a priori science. In an a priori science one can always go over from the factual to its essential form, or *eidos.* If one moves methodically from fact to *eidos,* the actual fact becomes as such irrelevant; it serves only as an example and as the foundation for a free but intuitive variation into the a priori possible and thinkable ones; this variation can be effected either by an individual soul (*Seele*), or by a community of souls.

If the theoretical eye focuses on the necessarily enduring invariant in the process of variation, then the realm of the a priori will arise, provided one proceeds systematically. In phenomenological psychology, it is thus possible to bring to light the eidetically necessary typical form, or *eidos,* of the psychic phenomena, such as perception, imagination, emotion, and so on. Phenomenological psychology in this manner can be established as an "eidetic phenomenology."

Just as the phenomenological reduction provided us with the means of access to the phenomena of the real, and also potential, inner experiences, so the method of "eidetic reduction," which is founded upon it, provides the means of access to the invariant, essential structures of the whole sphere of the soul.

The expression "eidetic reduction" refers to a process by means of which one can proceed methodically from concrete facts to the eidetic structures of these facts. Husserl sometimes refers to this methodical procedure with the expressions "eidetic intuition" or "the method of free variation."

Commentary

Eidetic Intuition

Every science essentially must make use of universal and necessary statements. This is true for the formal sciences, logic and mathematics; but it also holds good for the empirical and the eidetic sciences; finally, it is also true for philosophy.

The epistemological and ontological implications of universal and necessary statements, necessary for genuine science, have been the subject of philosophical reflections since the days of Plato. As is well known, different philosophers have suggested different solutions to the problems involved; and their attempts at justifying their claims have led to different assumptions. The following technical expressions may suffice to characterize briefly the most important conceptions suggested in the past in this connection: Plato's eternal Forms; Aristotle's *ousiai,* which at the same time are both substrata or subjects (*hupokeimena*) and essences (*eide*); the medieval nominalist, realist, and conceptualist theories concerning the problem of universals; Descartes's innate ideas; Leibniz's preestablished harmony; Kant's synthetic judgments a priori; and Mill's theory of induction. In Husserl's view, our universal statements and insights refer to *ideal* essences, and these essences themselves are the intentional correlates of our universal insights, which are given originally in *eidetic intuition.*

As we have seen, Husserl's view on essences, which was influenced by Bolzano's *Wissenschaftslehre,* has often been considered a new form of Platonic realism. Since the appearance of the second volume of *Logical Investigations* (1901), this remark has been made time and again in the literature.[1] Critics claimed that Husserl conceives of essences as entities to which one must ascribe "genuine reality," as to all other entities, and also the capacity of being intuited, as in the case of empirical realities. Husserl tried to refute this criticism by stating that (1) essences are not Platonic forms; (2) they are merely the *ideal* correlates of certain cognitive acts of consciousness; (3) they are intuited in an eidetic intuition that is totally different from perception; (4) "being" is most certainly not identical with empirical reality; and (5) the classical doctrine of abstraction is to be changed into a theory concerning ideation (*Ideas,* 1:39–44 [39–43]). We shall return to these theses shortly.

In developing his own ideas, Husserl tried first of all to avoid the pitfalls of all forms of empiricism and positivism. Anyone who denies the possibility of ideation is led into a skepticism that cancels itself through its own absurdity (*Ideas,* 1:37–39 [37–39]). It is in this context that Husserl wrote: "If by 'positivism' we are to mean the absolute unbiased grounding of all science on what is 'positive', i.e., on what can be primordially apprehended, then it is we who are the genuine positivists" (ibid., 39–40 [39–40]). Secondly, by developing his ideas on ideation, Husserl thought he could overcome what he considered one of the basic weaknesses of Kant's philosophy, namely, that Kant allows only for a purely formal a priori. For

Husserl, on the other hand, the expressions "a priori" and *"eidos"* mean the same (*F. tr. L.*, 248 [255] n; 255–66 [262–73]).

I *Eidos* and Ideation

I Introduction

In Chapter Two, we saw that according to Husserl every individual fact has its own essence (*Ideas*, 1:7–8 [8–9]), just as conversely to each essence there corresponds a series of possible individuals (ibid., 15–17 [16–18]). An individual object is not simply a mere "this-there" but, being constituted "in a specific way itself," it has its own proper mode of being, its own *eidos*, which can be apprehended in all its purity (ibid., 7–8 [9]). The term *"eidos,"* or "essence," is here taken to mean that which in the intimate self-being of an individual discloses to us "what it is" (ibid., [10]).[2]

Asking himself how we are able to know such an *eidos*, Husserl posits that every essence can be "set out as an Idea." Trying to explain this statement, Husserl continues that every empirical intuition can be transformed into an intuition of an essence by means of the process of *ideation*. Of whatever kind the empirical intuition may be, "it can always pass off into the intuition of an essence." Just as the datum of empirical intuition is an individual object, so the datum of "essential intuition" is a pure essence. And just as empirical intuition is consciousness of an individual object and intuitively brings it to givenness, so essential intuition is the consciousness of an "object" toward which consciousness directs its glance as toward something "self-given." And, finally, just as in perception, consciousness grasps the individual object in its "bodily" selfhood, so is genuine essential intuition a primordial, giving intuition grasping the essence in its "bodily" selfhood (*Ideas*, 1:8–11 [10–12]).

In developing this point of view, Husserl touches only in passing upon two problems that are very important for a proper understanding of his theory concerning the relation between fact and essence. These questions are: What mode of being is characteristic of essences *and* precisely how do we know essences? In formulating his own view on these questions, which are closely connected, Husserl first tries to define his position against empiricism and positivism, on the one hand, and classical idealism, on the other.

Empiricism and positivism deny that general essences can be considered to be given in the genuine sense of the term. Husserl tries to explain that in this matter the empiricist and the positivist suffer from a prejudice which prevents them from seeing that more is given than individual and singular data and more than singular facts. What phenomenology objects to, with respect to empiricism and positivism, is not their battle against unverified and unverifiable metaphysical "nonsense" but the fact that they dogmatically restrict givenness to particular experiences and thereby implicitly reject any intuition of general essences and general relations. Classical idealism, on the other hand, falls short inasfar as it never was able to develop a consistent theory of self-evidence, which is essential in every theory of intuition.

Against the background of this critical excursion, Husserl tries to define his own point of view concerning the questions mentioned. There it becomes clear that Husserl presupposes that self-evidence based upon intuition is the ultimate criterion of all truth and that the principle that intuition is the ultimate source which justifies all our knowledge is the leading idea of his phenomenology as a whole. That is why he finally explicitly formulates this basic principle and tries to elucidate its meaning and purpose. Let us try to explain this in more detail, taking up again the relationship between fact and essence discussed above.

▎ Naturalistic Misconceptions

Empiricism Identifies Experience with the Primordial Act —
We have seen that in his early years, Husserl grew up in a milieu in which empiricism was regarded highly. In his earlier publications, he defended some form of empiricism. Only gradually did he turn away from this position in the direction of his later transcendental phenomenology. Yet he always maintained a high regard for the positive contribution of empiricism to the philosophical debate in the modern era. What compelled him to oppose empiricism was the fact that "ideas," "essences," and "knowledge of essences" are denied by empiricism, whereas such a denial contradicts the immediately given phenomena (*Ideas,* 1:35–37 [34–37]). Husserl admits that empiricist naturalism has its origin in founded motives. Radically opposed to all "idols," it seeks to indicate and establish the right of autonomous reason to be the only authority in matters of truth. To pass rational judgment upon facts and things means to be guided by the things themselves, to get away from mere talk, to go back to the facts, to question them in their self-givenness, and to lay aside all prejudices foreign to their very nature. In the view of the empiricist, another way of expressing the same idea is to say that all science must arise from experience and that all mediated knowledge must be based upon immediate experience. Therefore, for empiricism genuine science means exactly the same as science of experience. Whatever does not belong to the world of facts is purely imaginary, and a science based on imagination is simply an imaginary science. Essences belong to the realm of speculative a priori constructions, by

means of which, in the first half of the nineteenth century, idealism in its ignorance of scientific knowledge of nature used to impede the progress of true science. Ideas and essences as opposed to facts are only Scholastic entities, metaphysical ghosts that are to be swept away by means of Ockham's razor. We must be grateful to modern natural science to have delivered us from these philosophical "spooks."

However, all those empiricist remarks are based on misunderstanding and prejudice, no matter how noble the motives may have been that originally inspired them. The basic mistake of empiricism is that it identifies the fundamental requirement of a return to the "things themselves" with the requirement that all knowledge must be founded upon experience. Accepting the naturalistic limitation of the realm of knowable "facts," it simply takes for granted that only experience can give facts themselves. But facts are not necessarily facts of nature. The fact-world in the ordinary sense of the term is not necessarily identical with reality as such, and it is only with the fact-world of nature that the primordial, giving act of "experience" is concerned. Immediate intuition—not only the sensory "seeing" of natural experience but "seeing" in general as primordial, giving consciousness of any kind whatsoever—is the ultimate source and justification of all rational statements. That is why for "experience" one must substitute the more general term "intuition." That is also why one must refuse to identify science in general with science of experience or empirical science (*Ideas,* 1:37–39 [37–39]).

Idealistic Obscurities — There are obscurities also on the opposite side: Idealism accepts only a pure thinking a priori and thus rejects the fundamental thesis of empiricism. However, Husserl says, it fails to explain in a convincing way what it genuinely means when it posits that there is such a thing as pure intuition in which essences are primordially given just as individual realities are given in empirical intuition. It also fails to realize that the concept of "giving intuition" encompasses every process of insight involving judgment, especially the insight into unconditionally universal truths. Idealism does not know that the concept of "giving intuition" can be differentiated in various ways and, in particular, that it has differentiations that are parallel to the logical categories. While there is a question of self-evidence in classical idealism, instead of considering it as a process of insight somehow connected with ordinary seeing, it speaks about a "feeling of self-evidence," which, like a mystical *index veri,* colors the judgment with a feeling. Such interpretations are possible only if one does not know how to analyze types of consciousness by viewing them purely in their essence, instead of making ethereal theories about them. These so-called feelings of self-evidence or of intellectual necessity are simply fictions (*Ideas,* 1:39–40 [39–40]).

∎ Existence and
∎ Our Knowledge of Essences

Husserl's Refutation of Platonic Idealism — It has often been said that Husserl's view on essences must be considered to be a new form of Platonic realism. As we have seen, the view developed in the second volume of *Logical Investigations* and his position developed in the article "Philosophy as Rigorous Science" were both said to go in the same direction. The criticism argues that Husserl conceives of essences as objects to which one has to ascribe "genuine Being"—as to all other objects—and the capacity to be intuited—as in the case of empirical entities.

Husserl refutes this criticism by positing that he never intended to defend the thesis that the term "object" is identical with "empirical object" and that "reality" and "empirical reality" are one and the same thing.[3] If "object" is to be defined as "anything whatsoever," then no one can deny that essences are objects, although they do not have the same status of being as this tree here before my window. Furthermore, all the critics who deny that essences are "genuine" objects seem to forget that they continually make use of essences in their thinking and speaking and that they explain them away only because of their epistemological a priori standpoints. These critics take their starting point in the epistemological presupposition that it is a priori impossible that there could be any such thing as essences and intuition of essences. When language suggests to us that there are such things, then they must be the consequences of certain "grammatical hypostatizations," which therefore do not give cause for abstruse "metaphysical" considerations. What we call essences, the critics say, are only the real mental products of our own "abstraction," which are somehow to be connected with our "real" experiences. Because of this abstraction, essences must be "concepts," and these concepts are "mental constructions" only. Therefore, the terms "essence," "*eidos,*" "Ideas," refer only to psychological facts.

In Husserl's view, essences are certainly concepts, but concepts are not mental products or psychological facts. Although it is true that my presentation of a number here and now is a psychological fact, this does not mean or imply that the number itself, which is presented here, *also* has to be a psychological fact. On the contrary, its nontemporal being is evident; to refer to it as a psychological fact or as a mental construct is therefore an absurdity. And if the term "concept" were to mean a "mental construct," then such things as pure numbers could not be concepts (*Ideas,* 1:40–42 [40–42]).

Essence and Fiction — However, one could say that no one can deny either that essences must have their origin in individual intuitions and that, therefore, a certain form of abstraction must play a role in the "construction" of essences. Furthermore, in many cases we just construct ideas at pleasure; especially in the latter cases it is clear that concepts must be psychological products.

In dealing with this objection, Husserl agrees with his opponents that those "conceptual constructions," just as in the case of free phantasy, certainly take place spontaneously, and that what is spontaneously produced must indeed be a product of the mind. However, Husserl says, one has to make a clear distinction here between the act of presentation and that which is presented in this very act, between the living experience of thinking or of imagining and the object qua thought or imagined. Whereas the thinking of a mathematical entity and the imagining of a centaur are spontaneous and therefore products of the mind, the objects meant in and by these acts are not mental products at all, but "ideal" entities. In other words, Husserl says, it is impossible to identify consciousness of essences with those essences themselves.

But are those essences not mere fictions, like the centaur mentioned above? And is speaking of the "existence" of essences, therefore, not very suspect? Husserl answers this objection by saying that here, too, there is an analogy between individual facts and essences. Things can be perceived and therewith recognized as "real," or as doubtful, or even as illusory. The same holds true of essences. Thus it follows that they, just like other objects, have meanings given to them that can be right and wrong. Husserl concludes that, notwithstanding all these objections, one must maintain the thesis that intuition of essences is a primordial, giving act that as such is analogous to perception and not to imagination (*Ideas,* 1:43–44 [42–43]).

Ideation — The preceding pages contain many difficult problems that cannot be considered here. There is, however, one point on which we must dwell here briefly because it appears to be very important for a proper understanding of Husserl's phenomenological methods, namely, the process of ideation.

As we have mentioned, Husserl uses the term "essence" to indicate what a thing is (*Ideas,* 1:8 [10]). Every essence can be expressed by an idea. Every empirical and individual intuition can be transformed into an essential insight by means of "ideation." The object of such an insight, called "pure essence" or *"eidos,"* is a new kind of object. Consequently, essential insight is a new kind of intuition (ibid., 8–9 [10–11]). However, Husserl claims, essential intuition, according to its very nature, is based on an individual intuition, although it does not presuppose any apprehension of an individual's reality. Hence it is certain that no essential intuition is possible when the ego cannot freely direct its regard to an individual counterpart. Conversely, no individual intuition is possible unless there is a free possibility of carrying out an act of ideation. All this, however, does not alter the fact that the two kinds of intuition are fundamentally different (ibid., 9–11 [10–12]).

Husserl does not go into detail here as far as the methodological aspects of this viewpoint are concerned. He focuses only on the following points: (1) phenomenology is either a science of essences or no science at all; (2) phenomenology is a science whose objects do not at all depend on mental constructs; (3) phenomenology is a science in which the essences known are in no way dependent on their concrete factual realizations; (4) nevertheless, it is true that our knowledge of essences must take its starting point in our knowledge of facts (*Ideas,* 1:8–11, 43–44 [42–45]). From this it necessarily follows that an essential insight into the very nature of things requires, among other things, that the essences of things, in one way or another, be disengaged from everything that is simply contingent and accidental to them. This is to be done by ideation.

I The Method of Free Variation

The first description of the process to which Husserl refers with the technical terms *"Wesensschau,"* "ideation," or "eidetic reduction" can be found in Husserl's *Logical Investigations* (*L.I.,* 2:786–88 [2.2:144–47]). This first tentative description of ideation, which originally occupied a central place in phenomenology, caused a great many misunderstandings. Husserl therefore tried to correct and clarify the method in his article "Philosophy as Rigorous Science" ("Phil. Rig. Sc.," 110–17 [315–19]). We find further elaboration and clarification of the method in the first volume of *Ideas* (*Ideas,* 1:7–12 [8–13], 156–60 [128–32]) and in *Phenomenological Psychology* (*Phen. Psych.,* 53–66 [72–87]). Later, Husserl continued this trend of thought in *Cartesian Meditations* (*Cart. Med.,* 69–72 [103–6]) and in *Formal and Transcendental Logic* (*F. tr. L.,* 208–12 [216–20]), where he tried to define the position and function of the eidetic reduction in its relationship to the other phenomenological reductions. The most exhaustive of Husserl's descriptions of the eidetic reduction appeared only much later, in his posthumously published book, *Expe-*

rience and Judgment (*Exp. J.,* 339–49 [410–21]). In the beginning,
Husserl seemed to imply that ideation takes place on the basis of the
particular experience of an individual member of a certain class.
Later we see an increasingly important role assigned to the imagination until ultimately Husserl saw the imagination as the essential
factor in the revealing of the essences of things. We will limit ourselves in this section to the explanation given in *Phenomenological
Psychology,* since we find there all that is needed for our present
purpose.

In order to explain and justify the method of ideation, or the
search for the essences of things, Husserl recommends that we start
with a concrete fact, which we then let freely vary in our imagination. We have to be careful to keep the free variations within the limits of possible individuals of the same type. The plurality of these
variations that now appear shows a certain unity, namely, the invariant essence of this type of thing. What is important here is that,
no matter how we imagine the different possible variants of a certain type to be, we nevertheless *necessarily* end up with an invariant
essence that can be grasped in immediate intuition once we are prepared in that way. All the imagined variations overlap in a certain
respect, and this is the essence, the *eidos,* the *Idea* in the Platonic
sense. Husserl makes use of the concept *"eidos,"* without, however,
attaching to it any metaphysical interpretation; he merely takes it to
refer to the essences as they appear to us immediately in intuition.

For example, if we take a sound as our point of departure,
whether we actually hear it or whether we have it present merely as
a sound in our imagination, then we obtain the *eidos* "sound" as that
which, in the course of arbitrary variations, is necessarily common
to all the variants in question. If we take as our point of departure
another phenomenon of sound in order to vary it arbitrarily, we do
not apprehend a different *eidos* "sound" in the new example. Comparing the first with the second, we see that the *eidos* is the same,
because the variants and the variations on both sides join together
in one single variation, and that different variants in both cases and
in like fashion are arbitrary particularizations of one and the same
eidos.

Furthermore, whether or not a particular variant actually exists is completely irrelevant as far as the *eidos* is concerned. The
variants that ultimately point the way to the *eidos* need only be
genuine possibilities of a particular species of things or entities. The
eidos is pure only to the extent that it remains independent of the
given world. In the natural attitude, the experienced world is always
presupposed as the universal and abiding basis for all our activities.
The attitude required for a completely free and pure search for es-

sences (*Wesensschau*) is therefore incompatible with the natural attitude (*Phen. Psych.*, 54–55 [72–74]).

When we compare the concept of variation with the concept of change, taken here in the sense of alteration, we find that despite their similarity they are essentially different concepts. We speak of change when we refer to a real thing that is affected by wear and tear and subject to duration and development. Change refers to the transition from one phase to the next and implies a unity because it is this particular identical, individual thing that is subjected to the change and survives all the manifold changes to which it is subjected. The unity, however, does not refer to the universal in the particular temporal phases; this unity is precisely the individual thing itself. While it is also possible from another perspective to approach the phases themselves as variants, we shall see that change is impossible when the phases of the changing process do not belong together. A color changes into a color; it does not change into a tone. Each change takes place within the limits of certain given conditions that cannot be superseded. However, the species comes to the fore as *eidos* only when we stand back from our involvement in that which actually exists. On the level of pure imagination, we can imagine possible variants of a concrete thing that takes part in the *eidos* and therefore possesses this *eidos* as "law of necessity." All that can be subjected to variation carries within itself a necessary structure, an *eidos,* and, therefore, a law of necessity (*Phen. Psych.,* 55–56 [75–76]).

The procedure is called intuition of ideas (*Ideenschau*) or ideation. Let us first summarize the most important steps of this procedure and then add some of the more important details. The fundamental step in this procedure is the formation of an open, endless multiplicity of variants of an experienced or imagined object. The open plurality does not, of course, command us to proceed indefinitely with the generation of variants of a particular thing. We do not need to project *all* possible variants. We need to form variants only to the point where we can truthfully say "and so on at will" (*Phen. Psych.,* 57–58 [76–78]). The intuition of the *eidos* takes place then on the basis of, and is founded in, the multiplicity of variants. The intuitive grasp of the *eidos* aims at the particular aspects that overlap each other in each of the variants. These overlapping aspects bring about the synthetic unity that only allows us truly to speak of variants of one and the same thing. We must then proceed to grasp this unity actively and immediately in our intuition, just as this unity shows itself in the series of variants as unchanging unity. It is important to note that the complete series of the variants should remain present in consciousness; the intuition of the essence

(*Wesensschau*) may never rest completely on the last of a chain of variants. Only if we hold onto the thing imagined earlier as a multiplicity in an open process, and only if we look toward the congruent and purely identical, do we gain access to an *eidos* (ibid., 58 [77–78]). One could object that Husserl's appeal to imagination seems unnecessary; why could we not rely on real individual cases to provide us with the needed variants? Husserl contends that an empirical generalization leads only to a generality, never to the *eidos*. This *eidos* can be reached only on the basis of an active, intuitive grasp, and this intuition needs to include all of that which only an unlimited, free play of our imagination can provide (ibid., 58–60 [78–81]).

We should realize that it is possible to proceed from one single example and nevertheless ultimately reach more than one *eidos;* a particular red can lead us to the *eidos* "red" and to the *eidos* "color." The intention of the variation determines which *eidos* we ultimately will find. Ideas can even be used themselves as variants; it is thus possible to intuit an idea out of many ideas. Thus, the *eidos* itself can likewise be subjected to variation. It is even possible to subject relationships, quantities, collections, or collections of relationships to ideation (*Phen. Psych.*, 60–63 [81–84]). In all these ways, we can come to an *eidos* that remains unaffected by any presuppositions of any real, factual occurrence whatsoever. Such an *eidos* is to be distinguished from an empirical generality. Furthermore, the intuition of essences is more than a mere vague speaking about, meaning, or intending. It refers to an active grasp in which I take a thing exactly in the way it is immediately present to me (ibid., 63–65 [84–87]).

It is essential in this method that we look upon the example from which we start as a pure possibility and not as a real thing: "[I]n a free doing a certain indifference comes here into play in regard to reality and in this way that which manifests itself as real becomes transposed into the domain of imagination." The *eidos* does not have an extension that is formed by facts but rather one formed by pure possibilities. These possibilities can include real facts, too, of course. However, the essential generality precedes all questioning concerning facts. Essential generalities constitute an a priori that precedes all facts and empirical truths (*Phen. Psych.*, 64 [86]).

In summary, we can say the following concerning the intuition of essences (*Wesensschau*). We start from a particular observation of a known individual specimen of a kind of thing, a meaning, act, etc. With the help of memory and through varying our position in regard to the object and, most importantly, by means of imagination, we detect how we could vary this object without violating its identity as this object, meaning, or act. The contribution of our imagination is of great importance because it is precisely our aim to produce random variations that do not remain bound up with experience and the experienceable world; the variants must remain free from positing the actuality of the object or act in question. This is evidently accomplished best in imagination. During the process of comparing the variants, the unchanging aspects come to light that form the necessary complex of characteristics without which we cannot think an example of this particular class of things. This invariant comes about in a seemingly passive manner when the objects of our many acts of imagination shift in front of each other and cover each other partially. This passively constituted and as yet imperfect content can then be grasped intuitively, through which we free the invariable, true, pure, universal, and always identical essence (*Phen. Psych.*, 64–65 [86–87]).

| N O T E S

1. Husserl, *Ideas*, 1:40–42 [40–42]. Husserl responds here to the charges and explains in what sense the claim is certainly not true.
2. For what follows, see Bernet et al., *Edmund Husserl*, 74–85; Levinas, *Théorie de l'intuition*, passim.
3. Husserl, *L. I.*, 2:337–432 [2.1:106–224]. See also Levinas, *Théorie de l'intuition*, 151–53.

The Function of Phenomenological Psychology for Empirical Psychology

Text

5. Die prinzipielle Funktion der rein phänomenologischen Psychologie für eine exakte empirische Psychologie

Die phänomenologisch reine Psychologie ist das unbedingt notwendige Fundament für den Aufbau einer "exakten" empirischen Psychologie, die nach dem Vorbild der exakten rein physischen Naturwissenschaft seit deren neuzeitlichen Anfängen gesucht worden ist. Der prinzipielle Sinn der Exaktheit dieser Naturwissenschaft liegt in ihrer Fundierung auf das apriorische, in eigenen Disziplinen (reine Geometrie, reine Zeitlehre, Bewegungslehre usw.) entfaltete Formensystem einer denkmöglichen Natur überhaupt. Durch die Verwertung dieses apriorischen Formensystems für die faktische Natur gewinnt die vage induktive Empirie Anteil an der Wesensnotwendigkeit und die empirische Naturwissenschaft selbst den neuen methodischen Sinn, für alle vagen Begriffe und Regeln die diesen notwendig zu unterlegenden rationalen Begriffe und Gesetze zu erarbeiten. So wesentlich naturwissenschaftliche und psychologische Methode auch unterschieden bleiben, darin besteht ihre notwendige Gemeinsamkeit, daß auch die Psychologie, wie jede Wissenschaft, ihre "Strenge" ("Exaktheit") nur schöpfen kann aus der Rationalität des "Wesensmäßigen". Die Enthüllung der apriorischen Typik, ohne die Ich, bzw. Wir, Bewußtsein, Bewußtseinsgegenständlichkeit und somit seelisches Sein überhaupt undenkbar wäre—mit all den wesensnotwendigen und wesensmöglichen Formen von Synthesen, die von der Idee einer einzelseelischen und gemeinschaftsseelischen Ganzheit unabtrennbar sind—schafft ein ungeheures Feld der Exaktheit, das sich, und hier sogar unmittelbar (ohne das Zwischenglied der Limes-Idealisierung), in die empirische Seelenforschung überträgt. Allerdings ist das phänomenologische Apriori nicht das vollständige der Psychologie, sofern der psychophysische

5. The Fundamental Function of Pure Phenomenological Psychology for an Exact Empirical Psychology

A phenomenological pure psychology is absolutely necessary as the foundation for the building up of an "exact" empirical psychology, which since its modern beginnings has been sought according to the model of the exact pure sciences of physical nature. The fundamental meaning of "exactness" in this natural science lies in its being founded on an a priori form-system—each part unfolded in a special theory (pure geometry, a theory of pure time, theory of motion, etc.)—for a Nature conceivable in these terms. It is through the utilization of this a priori form-system for factual nature that the vague, inductive empirical approach attains to a share of eidetic necessity [*Wesensnotwendigkeit*] and empirical natural science itself gains a new sense—that of working out for all vague concepts and rules their indispensable basis of rational concepts and laws. As essentially differentiated as the methods of natural science and psychology may remain, there does exist a necessary common ground: that psychology, like every science, can only draw its "rigor" ("exactness") from the rationality of the "essence." The uncovering of the a priori set of types without which "I," "we," "consciousness," "the objectivity of consciousness," and therewith mental being as such would be inconceivable—with all the essentially necessary and essentially possible forms of synthesis which are inseparable from the idea of a whole comprised of individual and communal mental life—produces a prodigious field of exactness that can immediately (without the intervening link of *Limes-Idealisierung**) be carried over into research on the psyche. Admittedly, the phenomenological a priori does not comprise the complete a priori of psychology, inasmuch as the psychophysical relationship as such has its own a priori. It

---

*By this expression (*Limes-Idealisierung*), Husserl would seem to mean idealisation to exact (mathematical) limits [tr.].

Zusammenhang als solcher sein eigenes Apriori hat. Es ist aber klar, daß dieses Apriori das der rein phänomenologischen Psychologie voraussetzt, wie nach der anderen Seite das reine Apriori einer physischen (und speziell organischen) Natur überhaupt.

[286] Der systematische Aufbau einer phänomenologisch reinen Psychologie erfordert:

1. die Deskription der zum Wesen eines intentionalen Erlebnisses überhaupt gehörigen Eigenheiten, wozu auch das allgemeinste Gesetz der Synthesis gehört: jede Verknüpfung von Bewußtsein mit Bewußtsein ergibt ein Bewußtsein.
2. die Erforschung der Einzelgestalten intentionaler Erlebnisse, die in einer Seele überhaupt in Wesensnotwendigkeit auftreten müssen oder auftreten können; in eins damit die Erforschung der Wesenstypik der zugehörigen Synthesen, der kontinuierlichen und diskreten, der endlich geschlossenen oder in offener Unendlichkeit fortzusetzenden.
3. die Aufweisung und Wesensdeskription der Gesamtgestalt eines Seelenlebens überhaupt, also die Wesensart eines universalen "Bewußtseinsstromes".
4. eine neue Untersuchungsrichtung bezeichnet der Titel "Ich" (noch unter Abstraktion von dem sozialen Sinn dieses Wortes) hinsichtlich der ihm zugehörigen Wesensformen der "Habitualität", also das Ich als Subjekt bleibender "Überzeugungen" (Seinsüberzeugungen, Wertüberzeugungen, Willensentscheidungen usw.), als personales Subjekt von Gewohnheiten, von wohlgebildetem Wissen, von Charaktereigenschaften.

Überall führt schließlich diese "statische" Wesensdeskription zu Problemen der Genesis und zu einer universalen nach eidetischen Gesetzen das ganze Leben und die Entwicklung des personalen Ich durchherrschenden Genesis. So baut sich auf die erste "statische Phänomenologie" in höherer Stufe die dynamische oder genetische Phänomenologie. Sie behandelt als erste fundierende Genesis die der Passivität, in der das Ich als aktives unbeteiligt ist. Hier liegt die neue Aufgabe einer universalen eidetischen Phänomenologie der Assoziation, eine späte Rehabilitation der großen Vorentdeckungen D. Humes, mit dem Nachweis der apriorischen Genesis, aus der für eine Seele eine reale Raumwelt in habitueller Geltung sich konstituiert. Es folgt die Wesenslehre der Entwicklung personaler Habitualität, in der das rein seelische Ich innerhalb invarianter Strukturformen als personales Ich ist und seiner in habitueller Fortgeltung bewußt ist als sich immerzu

is clear, however, that this a priori will presuppose that of a pure phenomenological psychology, just as on the other side it will presuppose the pure a priori of a physical (and specifically the organic) Nature as such.

The systematic construction of a phenomenological pure psychology demands:

1. The description of the peculiarities universally belonging to the essence of intentional mental process, which includes the most general law of synthesis: every connection of consciousness with consciousness gives rise to a consciousness.
2. The exploration of single forms of intentional mental processes which in essential necessity generally must or can present themselves in the mind; in unity with this, also the exploration of the syntheses they are members of for a typology of their essences: both those that are discrete and those continuous with others, both the finitely closed and those continuing into open infinity.
3. The showing and eidetic description [*Wesensdeskription*] of the total structure [*Gesamtgestalt*] of mental life as such; in other words, a description of the essential character [*Wesensart*] of a universal "stream of consciousness."
4. The term "I" designates a new direction for investigation (still in abstraction from the social sense of this word) in reference to the essence-forms of "habituality"; in other words, the "I" as subject of lasting beliefs or thought-tendencies—"persuasions"—(convictions about being, value-convictions, volitional decisions, and so on), as the personal subject of habits, of trained knowing, of certain character qualities.

Throughout all this, the "static" description of essences ultimately leads to problems of genesis, and to an all-pervasive genesis that governs the whole life and development of the personal "I" according to eidetic laws [*eidetischen Gesetzen*]. So on top of the first "static phenomenology" will be constructed in higher levels a dynamic or genetic phenomenology. As the first and founding genesis it will deal with that of passivity—genesis in which the "I" does not actively participate. Here lies the new task, an all-embracing eidetic phenomenology of association, a latter-day rehabilitation of David Hume's great discovery, involving an account of the a priori genesis out of which a real spatial world constitutes itself for the mind in habitual acceptance. There follows from this the eidetic theory dealing with the development of personal habituality, in which the purely mental "I" within the invariant structural forms of

fortbildendes. Eine besondere zusammenhängende Unter-
suchungsschicht höherer Stufe bildet die [287] statische und
dann die genetische Phänomenologie der Vernunft.

consciousness exists as personal "I" and is conscious of itself in habitual continuing being and as always being transformed. For further investigation, there offers itself an especially inter-connected
stratum at a higher level: the static and then the genetic phenomenology of reason.

I Synopsis

Let us suppose now that through the phenomenological reduction mentioned above we have put ourselves in the sphere of the purely psychological, and that with the help of intentional analyses and the method of free variation we have gained an insight into the essence of the psychical in its diverse modalities. The aprioric concepts that in this sphere are formed through eidetic reduction must then express an essentially necessary style to which every imaginable, factual, and real psychic life is tied. All empirical psychological concepts are governed by these aprioric concepts as well as by their logical "forms," just as analogically this is the case with physics and the general aprioric science of nature. It is self-evident, therefore, that the aprioric truths founded on these aprioric concepts possess an unconditional, normative validity in regard to the regions of being in question, and in this particular case, in regard to the empirical domain of the purely psychical (*Phän. Psych.,* 321–24).

In comparing phenomenology with the much more inclusive empirical psychology, phenomenological psychology is the absolutely necessary fundament for the development of an exact empirical psychology, a long-standing goal heretofore pursued in attempts to follow the example of the exact physical and natural sciences. It is necessary that empirical psychology somehow conform to the exactness required by modern natural science. Natural science, which was once also a vague, inductive, empirical science, owes its modern character to the a priori system of forms characteristic of nature as such; this system is constituted by pure geometry, pure mechanics, the pure science of time, etc. By theoretically referring the factual in experience to the a priori of these forms, the originally vague experience is able to participate in the essential necessity, which is the last root of the exactness of the physical sciences (*Phän. Psych.,* 324–25).

The methods of natural science and psychology are admittedly quite different, but the latter, like the former, can only reach exactness by means of a rationalization of what is essential. This means that in empirical psychology the exactness must be founded on the very essence of the psychical as such. As we have seen, the essence of the psychical as such must be brought to light through the investigations of phenomenological psychology, and phenomenological psychology thus has to provide us with the fundamental concepts that, describing the a priori structure of the psychical as such, must govern every possible psychological description (*Phän. Psych.,* 325).

Here, however, a typical problem arises, for the a priori of empirical psychology is more extensive than that which is explained by phenomenological psychology. Empirical psychology as a science of the psychical—which in the given world manifests itself as a real moment of, and thus belongs to, nature as psychophysical datum— is, therefore, also cofounded by the a priori of physical nature. The necessary consequence is that empirical psychology also is based on the empirical and apriorie sciences of nature. Ultimately it is even founded upon its own a priori, which belongs to the psychophysical as such. In other words, the a priori of empirical psychology is not exclusively phenomenological, for it depends not only on the essence of the psychical but also upon the essence of the physical, and more particularly upon the essence of the psychophysical of organic nature (*Phän. Psych.*, 326–28).

The systematic development of pure phenomenological psychology would have to include the following topics:

1. The description of the characteristics that belong to the essence of any intentional experience as such; this includes also the most universal law of synthesis.

2. The exploration of the various forms of intentional experiences that in essential necessity must present themselves in a soul or mind. Together with this, one must also explore the typology of the essences of the syntheses that belong to them; these syntheses may be continuous or discrete, finitely closed or to be pursued into an open infinity.

3. The unfolding and eidetic description of the essence of the total structure of the soul as such—in other words, a description of the essential mode of being of the universal "stream of consciousness."

4. The term "I" designates a new direction for investigation, still in abstraction from the social sense of this term. Here one must pay attention to the essential forms of habituality that belong to the ego as the subject of lasting beliefs, persuasions, convictions, decisions, and so on, as the personal subject of habits, of the kind of knowledge one attributes to a well-educated person, or of certain qualities of character.

Throughout all of this, the static description of essences ultimately leads to problems of genesis and to an all-encompassing genesis that governs the whole life and development of the personal "I" according to eidetic laws. In this way, we can build up a genetic phenomenology on the basis of our first static phenomenology. In genetic phenomenology, one must focus first on the passive genesis, in which the "I" as such does not actively participate in the genesis of meaning. In analyses concerning passive genesis, one must orient oneself toward the development of an all-encompassing eidetic phenomenology of association; here one can give an account of the

a priori genesis out of which the real spatial world becomes constituted before the mind in habitual validity. From this the eidetic
theory follows that deals with the development of all personal
habitualities, in which the purely psychic "I"—notwithstanding the
invariant, structural forms of consciousness—appears to exist as a
personal "I" that is conscious of itself as something that always remains what it is and yet also as always transforming itself. Finally,
there is the static and then the genetic phenomenology of reason.

In the commentary to follow I shall focus first on the basic issue
expressed in the title of this section, namely, the basic function of
phenomenological psychology for empirical psychology. Then I shall
turn to the topics that, in Husserl's view, phenomenological psychology is to address first and foremost. I have grouped these together under the heading "constitution."

Commentary

The Function of Phenomenological
Psychology for Empirical Psychology

The a priori concepts that can be brought to light through the eidetic
reduction express the essentially necessary form of style to which all
being and life of consciousness is tied.[1] All concepts of empirical phenomenology stand under them as under their logical forms, similar
to the manner in which all empirical concepts of the natural sciences
are rooted in the a priori concepts of nature. These a priori concepts
explain the self-evidence of the unconditioned normative validity of
the a priori truths that are grounded upon the a priori concepts for
everything empirical that belongs to a given region of beings. Phenomenological psychology, which brings the a priori concepts of the
psychical to light and then develops the relevant truths a priori, is
thus the unconditioned necessary foundation for the development of
a strictly scientific psychology that would be the genuine analogue of
the exact sciences of nature.

The exactness of the natural sciences ultimately rests upon its
own a priori, that is, upon the system of forms of any conceivable
nature as such described in specific regional ontologies, such as
pure geometry, theory of pure time, theory of pure space, and
theory of motion. By theoretically relating the facts of experience to
the a priori of the relevant forms, the vaguely given data of experience can participate in the essential necessity of the forms. By developing the relevant "exact" concepts and formulating basic principles,
the scientific statements of each science of nature can then be

brought to light methodically. The fact that in the natural sciences the a priori is something quantitative that can be expressed in magnitude and number is connected with the essence of nature as nature.

A similar exactness is required for every genuine science of facts, including empirical psychology. Empirical psychology, too, has its own basic, a priori concepts that govern all psychic facts. In other words, the domain of experience of psychology has its own a priori structural topology that defines the psychical as such; it is this a priori without which an ego, a consciousness, a community of egos, and so on, simply would be inconceivable. Phenomenological psychology is the eidetic science that is to reveal this a priori according to all the sides and dimensions that belong to noesis and noema. In so doing, it brings to light those rational, basic concepts that range over every conceivable psychology, insofar as it is concerned with the psychical, with the ego, with intentionality, etc.

Yet phenomenological psychology, as the a priori science of the psychical as such, does not exhaust the entire a priori of psychology insofar as empirical psychology is the science of the psychical that manifests itself in the real world as a real moment of a material thing, an organism that is alive. Thus the a priori of empirical psychology includes that of the natural sciences, in addition to that to be brought to light by phenomenological psychology. In the final analysis, empirical psychology rests on the a priori of the psychophysical as such; the latter constitutes a domain that until now has remained unexamined.

Thus far we have shown that a pure, phenomenological psychology is meaningful only as an *eidetic* science. Yet every genuine exact psychology, that is, every psychology that has the form of a rational science of *matters of fact* and is parallel to the rational sciences of nature, can also be called a phenomenological psychology. For it treats the real psychical, not on the basis of a vague empirical experience and of concepts that, because they are derived from vague experiences, are also vague themselves but rather on the basis of a universal phenomenological experience and of an eidetic, phenomenological doctrine of essences that is founded upon that experience.

From this presentation of empirical psychology, it could seem as if it would merely be an exact and positive science like all other such sciences and, correlatively, as if pure phenomenological psychology would just be an eidetic science like all others. Yet, even though the psychical at first appears as just another component of the real world, it nevertheless has the remarkable characteristic of relating intentionally to everything that is extrapsychical, to everything that is somehow conceivable. Human beings are in the world among other real things, but they have also conscious awareness of the world, including themselves. Because of these awarenesses, a world is constantly there for us, counts for us as being there. And the world is there for us because of the intentional achievements of our own consciousness.

In particular, the sciences that at each level can be developed, too, are intentional products that derive their sense of truth from the subjective or intersubjective, verifying achievements. A scientifically valid theory is a system of intersubjectively valid results that owe their objectivity to the intentional processes in and through which they became constituted and enriched in a subject. Yet the entire life of the subject that gives form to truth and science remains in the sciences outside of their theme of investigation. A complete and universal theory of science manifestly requires that the intentional achievements in which every science becomes constituted also be examined methodically and systematically. Such a kind of research would belong to a universal, pure phenomenology that would have to include every theory of knowledge, science, and reason.

Husserl observes here that the claims that have just been made seem to restore psychologism. In his view, this is most certainly not so. Thus far, it was merely argued that a universal phenomenology, insofar as it makes the theory of science understandable as the noema of the noeses that with essential necessity belong to it, at the same time includes a universal psychology of reason and of all its achievements. To such a psychology of reason obviously is to be added a phenomenology of unreason and a phenomenology of the entire passivity of consciousness, to which we usually refer with the term "association" (passive genesis of meaning).

It is important to note here that the phenomenological psychology of reason is and remains a science *of the natural attitude*. It is still a *positive* science, a not yet philosophical science. Phenomenological psychology becomes philosophical by the fact that it focuses on the a priori of the psychical just as little as geometry becomes philosophical by the fact that it aims at the spatial a priori by examining space. And yet, the psychological theory of knowledge and phenomenological psychology, taken as a whole, are very closely related to philosophy. Once phenomenological psychology is established and founded in full universality, one only needs the Copernican turn of the transcendental reduction to give a truly transcendental meaning to the entire phenomenology and doctrine of reason. The radical change of meaning comes about by eliminating through *epoche* the continuous assumption on which the positivity of all sciences, including empirical and phenomenological psychology, ultimately rest: the presupposition of the pregiven world that, according to universal conviction, needs no further justification because of its self-evidence. In the transcendental attitude, one no longer posits the world in advance but instead takes it as the noema of the ultimately constituting noesis of transcendental subjectivity. Only transcendental subjectivity is posited in an absolute way. The transcendental and absolute subjectivity in and through which the world becomes constituted cannot be identified with the animal subjects in the world. In other words, in the transcendental attitude the psychological, phenomenological reduction becomes changed into the transcendental, phenomenological reduction, and phenomenological psychology herewith changes into absolute and transcendental phenomenology (*Phän. Psych.*, 324–28). We shall return to this in the chapters to follow.

▌ Constitution

▌ Historical Introduction

Constitution: An "Operational" Concept in Husserl's Phenomenology — According to Fink, constitution is one of the concepts that Husserl never has explained accurately and completely. It is an "operational" concept with which he continually works, without thematizing it explicitly. Although for Husserl himself this concept must have had a precise meaning, for us it remains ambiguous, as are many other basic concepts of his phenomenology, such as "phenomenon," "production," "achievement," and "reduction." Despite the fact that Husserl sometimes—or in the case of "reduction," often—explicitly thematized them, in fact these concepts remained, to some degree, "operational."[2] Moreover, it is certain that Husserl's ideas underwent a long evolution with respect to this point. In his older phenomenological studies, he only spoke of the constitution of objects and objectivities in consciousness;[3] later, he mentioned the synthetical constitution of acts and of synthesis;[4] and finally he referred to the universal constitution of the whole of conscious life and even the transcendental constitution of the transcendental ego itself.[5]

Nevertheless, we should be prudent here. Without any doubt, Husserl's idea of constitution underwent a long and profound evolution with respect to the extent and the "how" of the constitution; on the other hand, it is also historically certain that he never changed his mind regarding the essence and meaning of constitution.[6] In his lecture series of 1907, *The Idea of Phenomenology,* Husserl presented the first outline of his transcendental phenomenology and tried to describe what constitution and constitutional problems really are and mean. When we compare this description with that offered in his *Cartesian Meditations,* which were written when Husserl was about seventy years old, we find that they are essentially the same. In 1906 Husserl describes the meaning of constitution in general as the "dissolution of Being in consciousness."[7] In other manuscripts of this period, he explicitly pointed out that his transcendental phenomenology is identical with a phenomenology of "constituting" consciousness.[8]

The Meaning of Constitution in *The Idea of Phenomenology* — It is very illustrative to see how this important concept for the first time is introduced in *The Idea* within the context of a theoretical treatise concerning the meaning of phenomenology as a whole. Since Husserl apparently was not completely satisfied with the first draft of the fifth lecture, in which this concept was explained in some detail, we shall follow here his summary written immediately after the last lecture, on 2 May 1907.[9]

In this summary, Husserl says that on the first and lowest level of the phenomenological considerations, it seems at first very easy to understand what is meant by evidence. Evidence seems to be only a question of seeing and intuiting: my intuiting grasp intuits the things that are simply there before me; they are there in consciousness in a really evident intuiting, and my intuiting glance simply looks at them, grasps them, and takes them just as they are in themselves. Any difference between the things and their givenness is founded, then, in the things themselves, which in themselves have all their distinctions.

On closer investigation and analysis, however, this intuiting glance appears to be completely different from such a simple "seeing." Although the indescribable and indistinct intuiting glance is to be maintained as "attention," it is meaningless to speak here of things that simply are there for me and only have to be intuited. This "simply being there" appears to imply a complex of different experiences possessing their own specific structures, such as perception, phantasy, memory, retention, and expectation. Things are not in consciousness as matches in a box; rather, in and through these experiences, things are *constituted* in such a way that they are in no way really contained in these experiences. For every thing "to be given" means in this or that way to come into being in and through our lived experiences and to be presented by them. Moreover, things are not there first and subsequently impress "pictures" of themselves on our consciousness. In our phenomenological reduction, the things are "in" the appearances, and only because they appear to us are they "given" in themselves. While they appear to be independent of this individual appearance, essentially they are inseparable from the appearing itself.

Everywhere we find the marvelous intentional relationship between the knowing act and the known object. The task of phenomenology is not only to intuit this relation and to describe it but also to explain how an object of knowledge is constituted in our knowing acts. Within the sphere of pure self-givenness and evidence, we must analyze and describe all the modes of presentation and the correlates that become manifest in them. Only in this way can we see how the transcendent real object is found and known in the acts of knowledge itself—namely, as that which at the outset was "meant" only—and how the sense of this meaning is continuously fulfilled in the progressing coherence of knowledge in an original act of synthesis. Then we will experience how the objects of knowledge are continuously constituted, and how this constitution is predetermined by the fact that these objects essentially require such a gradual constitution. Phenomenology studies in a scientific and radical way the constitution of objects of every kind of consciousness, the acts of consciousness and their correlates, phenomena in an active and a passive sense (*The Idea*, 8–12 [10–14]).

Constitution in Husserl's Later Works — In *Ideas* and especially in *Cartesian Meditations,* Husserl's description of the essence and meaning of constitution is much clearer and more radical. Also, the domain of constitution is considerably enlarged there. But with respect to the essence, these descriptions seem to be identical to those of *The Idea of Phenomenology.*

In these later works, Husserl clearly explains again that the main intention of his constitutional phenomenology is to identify being and intelligibility, to reduce being to reason (*Ideas*, 1:322–25 [278–81]; *Cart. Med.*, 56–57 [91–92]). According to this view, not only is knowledge constituted in consciousness, but the very being of that which is known is also so constituted. Only "absolute being" is being in the full sense, and only consciousness and being-in-consciousness are forms of "absolute being" and thus necessarily belong together. Since being is in consciousness only as constituted by consciousness, being is absolute only as constituted. Thus, intentional constitution becomes a universal explanation and clarification of being. Nothing is, except by a proper achievement of consciousness, whether actual or potential (*F. tr. L.*, 234 [241]). If, then, the task of philosophy is to understand being, it must penetrate the subjectivity wherein being has its source and clarify the original constitution of being in and by that transcendental subjectivity.[10]

Compared with the analyses given in Husserl's later works, those presented in *Ideas* appear relatively static. They give only the order in which the different constitutive layers rest upon one another and constitute themselves in consciousness. Husserl first tried to describe the constitution of the world of material things, then the constitution of our body, and, finally, that of the world of our personal life. A special feature of these constitutions is their final dependence on a pregiven *hyle,* the hyletic sense-data. The experience of such a *hyle* involves at first sight the dependence of the transcendental constitution on factors that are not dependent upon transcendental subjectivity. It is often said that this fact points to a "realistic" element in the very core of constitutive phenomenology. However, it is merely a sign that these analyses are not yet completely radical and that they have to be supplemented with more fundamental analyses. That is one of the reasons why Husserl's later works tried to trace the hyletic data back to a deeper kind of constitution.[11]

That there is no abrupt shift in Husserl's thinking but rather an evolution and a radicalization can readily be seen in his various constitutional analyses of time consciousness. This topic forms the major field in which Husserl tried to clarify the ultimate meaning of constitution and was originally inherited from Brentano. Studying the problems connected with our consciousness of internal time again and again, Husserl gradually came to the conclusion that it contained the clue to the universal phenomenological problem of constitution. In the investigations made between 1905 and 1910, he stressed the passive synthetic genesis of time, and these descriptions do not yet supply any evidence for an active constitution of time.[12] However, from these analyses it became gradually clear to Husserl that the constitution of internal time could throw more light on the constitution of the different types of objects.

His studies in this direction, performed between 1929 and 1938, are of great importance. But, as is clear from the investigations of Gerd Brand and Alwin Diemer, these studies do not offer more than the first indications of what Husserl hoped to demonstrate: the primal constitution of the stream of time by active hidden achievements of transcendental subjectivity, which is presupposed in all other constitutions, such as the constitution of the hyletic data themselves and the intentional objects based on those data. In this way, Husserl tried to establish a new form of transcendental idealism. The brief indications of the *Cartesian Meditations* and the analyses of the later manuscripts are suggestive, but they do not really show how all objects owe, together with their being known, their very being itself to active achievements of transcendental subjects.[13]

In *Cartesian Meditations,* Husserl introduces the constitutional problems in the following way. Every inquiry into consciousness implies two sides, a noematic and a noetic side, which, however, descriptively are inseparable. One of the most important tasks in our noetic-noematic analyses is to describe and explain the synthesis that takes place in every consciousness. For example, if I take the perceiving of a die as a theme of analysis and description, I see in pure reflection that this die is given continuously as an objective unity in a multiform and changeable multiplicity of manners of appearing. In their temporal flow, these acts of perception are not an incoherent sequence of lived experiences but rather merge in the unity of a synthesis in such a way that in them one and the same die is intended as appearing. The one identical die appears now in close appearances, now in distant appearances, in the changing modes of "here" and "there," over against an always cointended "absolute here." Moreover, each manner of appearance in such a mode shows itself to be the synthetic unity pertaining to a multiplicity of manners of appearance belonging to that mode. Thus, the die here nearby appears as the same, now from this side, now from that, and in every case shows me a determinate perspective. The same holds good for every aspect and property of the die: we always find the aspect in question as a unity belonging to a passing flow of multiplicities of acts. Thus, each passing *cogito* intends its *cogitatum* as a *cogito* possessing a describable structure of multiplicities that has a definite noetic-noematic composition that, by virtue of its essential nature, belongs only to this identical *cogitatum.* One must now ask: How can we explain and describe that we experience a multiplicity of appearances given in a multiplicity of *noeses* as the perception of one single thing? Only by clarifying the so-called synthesis can the discovery of the intentional character of the *cogito* become fruitful (*Cart. Med.,* 39–41 [77–79]).

The fundamental form of synthesis is identification. We first encounter it as an all-encompassing, passively flowing synthesis, in the form of a continuous consciousness of internal time. Every experience has its internal temporality. In the experience of a die, for instance, we can distinguish between the objective temporality of this die and the internal temporality of our die perceiving. The noetic appearing flows away with the temporal phases, which are the continually changing appearances of this identical die. The unity of these phases is a unity of synthesis. It does not consist in being stuck to one another externally but in a connectedness that makes possible the unity of a single consciousness in which the unity of one intentional object as the same object, belonging to multiple modes of appearance, becomes *constituted.* The one identical die taken as appearing is continuously immanent in the flowing stream of consciousness; it is descriptively *in* it, not as a real intrinsic component but as something intentional, as its immanent objective meaning. This object of consciousness, taken as identical with itself during the flowing experience, does not come into the experience from without but is an intentional effect produced by the synthesis of consciousness itself. Thus, also the immanent objective sense as a whole is constituted in and by consciousness.

One and the same die can also be intended in completely different types of acts, simultaneously or successively in separate perceptions, recollections, expectations, and so on. Here again, it is a synthesis that gives rise to consciousness of identity of one and the same immanent objective meaning.

Moreover, there is a synthesis in every consciousness of a plurality and of a relational complex. And finally, the whole of conscious life is unified synthetically: it is an all-embracing *cogito,* synthetically comprising all particular conscious experiences and intending the world as the horizon of every particular horizon (*Cart. Med.,* 41–43 [79–81]).

The fundamental form of this universal synthesis, the form that makes all other syntheses brought about by consciousness possible, is the all-encompassing consciousness of internal time, which has as its correlate immanent temporality. In conformity with immanent temporality, all the intentional processes that belong to the ego, and can ever be discovered reflectively, must present themselves as temporally ordered, as beginning and ending, as simultaneous or successive, or as ordered in another temporal way within the constant "infinite" horizon of immanent time. It is the task of the constitutional analyses of phenomenology to analyze and describe the constitution that takes place in all these syntheses (*F. tr. L.,* 270–71 [276–78]).

I Constitutional Problems

A More Accurate Description of Constitution — In the preceding sections, we spoke often of "synthesis," "constitution," and "genesis" without describing these terms accurately or precisely indicating their meaning in the whole of phenomenology. Because these expressions point at the very heart of phenomenology, we must try to explain them now by describing the problems to which they refer, the methods to be used in order to solve these problems, and the solutions themselves.[14]

Husserl claims that hitherto it was irrelevant to our intentional analyses whether their objects were being or not being. Now, however, we must try to deal with this distinction explicitly under the heading reason and unreason as a correlative expression for being and nonbeing.

By our *epoche* we have effected a reduction to our pure meaning act (*cogito*) and the object meant (its *cogitatum*) purely as meant. The predicates "being" and "nonbeing" now refer to the "meant," not as an object but as an objective sense; truth and falsity refer to the meaning act.

Husserl claims that, as is evident from the study of intentional analysis, these predicates are not ipso facto given as phenomenological themes when meaning act and objective sense are given and described. On the other hand, these predicates have their phenomenological origin in these correlative entities. As we have seen, the multiple modes of consciousness that belong together synthetically and pertain to every object meant appear to be founded on an initial intending act that has the typical nature of a verifying and, in particular, an evidently verifying synthesis. When such a synthesis occurs, the object meant has correlatively the characteristic of "being" or "existing"; or there are nullifying syntheses, and then the object meant has the characteristic of "nonbeing" or "nonexisting." These synthetic occurrences are intentionalities of a higher level that essentially and, in exclusive disjunction, pertain to every objective sense from the side of the acts and their correlates that in principle can be produced by the ego. Reason thus refers to the possibility of verification, which the subject in principle always has, and verification refers to making evident. We must thus return here to one of the preceding sections in which the concept of evidence was explained (*Cart. Med.,* 56–57 [91–92]). (See Chapter Three above.)

Being and Reality as the Correlates of Evident Verification
— Husserl points out that in the broadest sense evidence indicates a universal primal phenomenon of our intentional life, namely, the mode of consciousness that consists in the self-appearance, the self-giving, of a thing or state of affairs in the final mode of "it itself here," "immediately intuited" and "given originally." For the ego, this signifies not aiming confusedly at something with an empty expectant intention but being with it itself, seeing and intuiting it itself. Every experience in the ordinary sense of the term is evident in this broadest sense.

In the case of most objects, evidence is only an occasional occurrence in conscious life; nevertheless, it is also a possibility that could be the aim of an actualizing intention in any particular case. Thus, it is an essential, fundamental characteristic of all intentional life.

Any consciousness, without exception, either is itself already to be characterized as evidence, giving its intended object originally, or it essentially tends toward conversion into an original presentation of its object and therefore toward syntheses of verification that belong essentially to the domain of the "I can."

Within the realm of the phenomenological reduction, we can ask any vague consciousness whether and to what extent—as long as the identity of the object meant is preserved—the meant object in the mode of "it itself" corresponds to that consciousness. During the process of verification, however, verification can turn into its negative. Then it appears that nonbeing must be conceived of as a modality of being in the sense of certain being. Evidence thus appears to be correlated with being and with all the modal variants of being possible, being probable, being doubtful, and so on (*Cart. Med.,* 57–58 [92–93]).

All these differences, moreover, are split into two by a difference extending throughout the whole sphere of consciousness, namely, that between reality and the "as-if reality" of phantasy. Thus a new universal concept of possibility arises that repeats in modified form all the modes of being as modes belonging to purely imagined nonrealities, in contrast to the modes belonging to reality itself in all its modalities.

Correlatively, all modes of consciousness are divided into those of *positionality* and those of *quasi-positionality*. And to each of these modes there corresponds both a particular mode of evidence of its object meant and one of potentialities of making these objects evident. All this must be explained in phenomenology in an original process of *clarification* that ultimately is founded on a prefigurative intuition. This prefigurative intuition of a verifying fulfillment as such, however, furnishes a realizing evidence, not that the content in question is but only that it could be. Such an intuition only contains the meaning in an implicit way; if it were a direct, self-giving act, it would fulfill and verify its meaning with respect to its existential sense (*Cart. Med.,* 58–59 [94]).

These brief observations refer first of all to formally universal problems of intentional analysis and to investigations concerning the phenomenological origin of the principles and fundamental concepts of formal logic. At the same time, however, they also make it evident that these concepts in their formal-ontological universality point to a universal conformity of the structural laws of our conscious life, a harmony by virtue of which alone truth and reality are able to have meaning for us. True, the fact that objects in the broadest sense—such as real things, lived experiences, or numbers—exist for me says nothing immediately about evidence itself; it says only that objects are accepted by me, they are for me as *cogitata* intended in the positional mode of "certain believing." However, we know also that we should have to abandon that acceptance if a course of evident identifying syntheses were to lead to conflict with an evident datum, for we can be sure that something is real only as long as a synthesis of evident verification takes place. It is clear that truth and the true reality of objects are to be obtained only from evidence, and that it is through evidence alone that a really existing, true, and rightly accepted object has meaning for us. Every claim of being right comes from evidence and therefore from the subject itself (*Cart. Med.,* 59–60 [94–95]).

Constitution and World — Neither the identity of any object meant nor that of a truly existing object nor the identity constituted in the adequation of the object meant as such with the object that truly is, is really an intrinsic moment of the transient lived experience of evidence and verification. However, we have here an *ideal immanence* referring to further complexes of possible syntheses that play an essential role. Every evidence founds for me an abiding possession, and I can always return to this reality beheld in itself in a series of new evidences securing the first evidence. For instance, in the case of evidence of immanent data, I can return to them in a series of intuitive recollections that, as a potential horizon, creates the "I can always do so again." Without such possibilities, there would be for me no fixed and abiding being, no real or ideal world, for both of these exist for us only thanks to the evidence, or the presumption, that we will always be able to "make evident" in the future or to repeat acquired evidences of the past.

Thus, the particular evidence itself does not as yet produce for us any abiding being. We must distinguish here between everything that exists "in itself" and the accidental "being for me" of this particular act with its particular noema. On the other hand, the "in itself" refers us also to a certain evidence, not to a particular evidence as a factual experience and its correlate but to determinate potentialities that are grounded in the pure ego and its life, namely: (1) the infinity of intending acts that all relate to something as identical and (2) the potential evidences that, as particular and factual experiences, are repeatable ad infinitum (*Cart. Med.,* 60–61 [95–96]).

In another, even more complicated manner, evidences refer to infinities of evidences relating to the same object. They make their object itself given with an essential one-sidedness because of the perspectivism and the inner and outer horizons we have spoken of. This one-sidedness is found not only in the totality of evidences of the real and objective world but also in every particular object in it.

The evidence pertaining to particular objects in the real objective world is rooted in "external experience"; in this case, there is no other mode of self-presentation. This kind of evidence has an essential one-sidedness that entails a multiform horizon of unfulfilled anticipations that are in need of fulfillment. This imperfect evidence can be made more and more perfect by means of the actualizing synthetic transitions from evidence to evidence, but there is no imaginable synthesis here that is ever completed as an adequate evidence because any such synthesis must always involve unfulfilled meanings. At the same time, there always remains the open possibility that the belief in being will not be fulfilled and that what seemed to be does not exist. The external experience verifies objects of external experience only as long as the passively or actively continuing experiences together constitute a harmonious synthesis. That the being of the world is, and necessarily remains, transcendent to consciousness does not at all alter the fact that it is only by our conscious life that everything transcendent becomes constituted as something inseparable from consciousness; only conscious life, as world-consciousness, bears within itself inseparably the meaning "world," "this really existing world." Only an uncovering of the horizon of experience ultimately clarifies the reality and transcendency of the world and, at the same time, shows the world to be inseparable from the subjectivity that ultimately constitutes the reality of meaning and being. We must therefore conclude that "true being" and "truth" indicate, in the case of any object meant or even able to be meant by me as ego, a structural differentiation among the infinite multiplicities of actual and possible cogitations that relate to the object in question and thus can somehow together make up the unity of an identifying synthesis.

A really existing object indicates a particular synthesis within this multiplicity, namely, the system of evidences relating to this object and belonging together in such a way that they make up one, perhaps infinite total evidence. This would be an absolutely perfect evidence that would present the object itself just as it is. It is completely impossible to produce such an evidence: it is an idea in the Kantian sense only (*Ideas,* 1:340–43 [295–98]).

The task of the constitution of really existing objects is to clarify, with respect to all essential structures, the intrinsic structure of the dimensions of infinity that systematically make up the ideal infinite synthesis of this evidence. Besides those formally universal investigations that confine themselves to the formal-ontological concept of any object whatsoever as such, we have to explain the immense problems of that constitution which occur with respect to each region of objects, such as "physical nature," "living being," "human being," "human community," "culture." Yet in every case, we meet essentially the same problem and have to use the same method. Some of the things argued for here will have to be taken up in transcendental phenomenology, which shows that the ultimate source of all meaning and being is to be found in transcendental subjectivity.

▌ Constitutional Problems
▌ Pertaining to the Ego

On the Ego as Pole of Activities and Habitualities — In the preceding, we have seen that in an intentional analysis the observing phenomenologist can turn his or her attention to the object given in an intentional act, the noema; one can also turn to the corresponding noesis, the act of the subject in which a given object meant was intended as such. In addition, one can turn one's attention to the subject, the ego, because every intentional act is obviously the act of a given subject.[15]

The first issue that one encounters here is the realization that for a human being to perceive, for example, means to have appearances of what appears by them and what is perceptually meant. When we have appearances in perception, then the thing appears visually in seeing, tactually in touching, and so on. This realization leads us to our body as the unity of our perceptual organs. But this means that the study of the intentional acts in which things become perceptually constituted and brought to givenness cannot be carried out without a study of the corresponding intentionality of one's own body in its perceiving functions.

What is very peculiar in this case is that the body is at the same time both a thing and a function. In a completely developed phenomenological psychology, one would thus need a new type of intentional analysis in which the kinesthetic systems of hand movements, head movements, movements of the eyes, movements of walking, and so on are constituted intentionally and are joined together in the unity of one total functioning system. One should note here that the clarification of the peculiarity of kinesthetic processes has its proper place here also, as does the clarification of the two-sidedness of every bodily organ with regard to its movement as objective spatial movement and as kinesthetic movement. The same is true also for the intentional clarification of the uniqueness of the living body, which is simultaneously "a spatial externality and a subjective internality," a spatial, material thing and, at the same time, an organ, a habitual system of subjective functions that is always ready to pass over into actual subjective functioning (*Phen. Psych.*, 147–53 [192–99]). In *Phenomenological Psychology,* Husserl discusses the functioning of the body only in outline. More detailed analyses of the kind Husserl has in mind here can be found in

Merleau-Ponty's *Phenomenology of Perception.*[16] It is not possible to dwell on this important theme of phenomenology, and we must turn now to constitutional problems connected with the pure ego itself.

We have seen that many perceptual acts may all pertain to the same thing meant; they are all oriented toward one identical pole, the thing meant—for example, the house in several acts of perceiving it. Thus, from everything that is given directly as an object, reflection can lead us to the constituting lived experiences in which the object is constituted as a pole. A similar move is possible that is directed toward one and the same identical ego. This ego is the subject of all lived experiences and the subject for all its objects; it is a pole of unity of all its intentionalities. Yet the ego is itself not a lived experience. In a noematic analysis of the perception of a house, for example, one sees that the object as appearing in the multiplicity of lived experiences and meant as existing is nevertheless not a real moment of these experiences, for it is one and the same identical object given in a number of experiences all separated by internal time. Yet the object pole is obviously ideally contained in all of them, insofar as in each one of them the same thing is consciously given— one and the same house, for instance—in perception; this means that this same house, taken noematically, is the same meant house; at the same time, it inseparably belongs to each of the acts and is thus nothing less than a real moment of each of them. In other words, as meaning it is immanent, not transcendent. When we turn in reflection to the ego, we find something similar, for the ego, too, is not to be found in the real stream of experiences, neither as a lived experience nor as a part or a real moment of the lived experiences. It, too, is one and the same subject of all these experiences. I, who now perceive this house and actually perform this perception, am identically the same as the one who found himself at an earlier moment in recollection of the death of a friend. I recognize the identity immediately in reflection. It appears that all my lived experiences are related to me, as the one, identical, same "I." And, in and through my lived experiences, all objects that are constituted in them as object-poles are also related to me. Of course, it is nonetheless also true that every reflection in which I relate to myself and every synthesis of reflection in which I find myself as identical are themselves also lived experiences. They make me objective, objective for myself (Kant's transcendental ego) (*Phen. Psych.,* 157–59 [206–8]).

It is clear that an all-encompassing synthesis runs through the streaming of all lived experiences and all entities synthetically constituted in them. By means of this synthesis, even without me performing an act of reflection, I am constantly a pole of identity in relation to which everything else is "objective" (synthesis of transcendental apperception in Kant). But when I do perform an act of reflection and turn to myself, then I am, as the subject of the reflecting act, a functioning ego; on the other side, as object of the reflection, I am just an object, which I designate as *me*. Thus, standing above everything that can be an object is the functioning ego as an ideally identical pole for all objects.

Yet we must note here that this ego is not this human being in the world, even though in the natural attitude I say, "I, this human being." As we have seen, as is every spatial object, so too, the body that I claim to be mine is a unity of appearances. I am the pure ego of these lived experiences that are mine; I am also the pure ego for which the experiential unity of these experiences—namely, my body—is constituted. This pure ego, which Kant must have had in mind when he spoke of the ego of transcendental apperception, is not an empty or dead pole of identity. Rather, it is the ego of all affections and actions, and it lives in the stream of its lived experiences precisely because, on the one hand, it is the source of all intentional lived experiences with whose intentional objects it actively is concerned, and because, on the other hand, it is affected and stimulated by these objects; in feeling it is touched by them, it is attracted to them and is motivated by them to act in a certain way. All of this is true for the ego insofar as it actually is awake. But the ego can also be asleep, and then nothing stands out as far as either immanent or transcendent objects are concerned; everything has then just flowed together so that nothing can be distinguished from anything else. The ego is then no longer a prominent functioning subject pole. The peculiarities of the sleeping ego can, of course, be revealed only from the perspective of the waking ego. As a matter of fact, sleep has meaning only in relation to waking and implies a potentiality for awakening (*Phen. Psych.*, 159–60 [208]). A detailed analysis of falling asleep, which is just one aspect of the phenomenon that Husserl is referring to here, has been developed by Jan Linschoten.[17]

The waking ego is engaged in activities of various kinds. For example, I perceive attentively, I consider something carefully, I explain something, I relate a thing to other things. The ego is constantly present in such occurrences and can be exhibited as a center or pole that can be shown.

Every *actus* [sic] has the character of something that arises from the ego-pole; it does not passively flow forth from it but goes out from it in an active way. Yet every such *ego cogito* presupposes that the ego was previously affected; this means that a passive intentionality in which the ego did not yet hold sway had already constituted in itself an object by which the ego-pole had been affected and "determined" to perform the *actus*. On the other hand, every *actus*, taken just as it has been put into action by the ego, is itself a lived experience that belongs to the same stream of experiences to which the passive experience also belongs.

This leads to an enrichment of the world of objects, which, once they are constituted, can time and again affect and motivate new activities of the ego, whereby in each case even new objects produced by the ego are constituted and inserted into the world of the ego. Thus the ego does not simply turn toward what is already given passively. Rather, it is always active: by comparing, it constitutes likeness; by relating things to each other, it constitutes relations, states of affairs, complexes of relations, and so on. In addition to these formal relations, the ego also constitutes relations of value, practical relations, means for goals, etc. Even these objects have their original mode of givenness. Their originality, too, is the result of an activity of the ego on the basis of something given passively beforehand, and only as issuing forth from the activities of the ego are they there for it. Once they are there for the ego, they are henceforth its enduring acquisition, something to which the ego can return repeatedly in different activities (*Phen. Psych.*, 160–61 [209–10]).

Once we have gained insight in the notion of the ego as the point of origin of all producing activities and their intentional correlates, two domains of research immediately become of interest to us: the higher levels of the surrounding world of objects that have come into being by the activities of the ego, on the one hand, and the correlative change that thereby takes place in the ego itself, on the other. The pure ego-pole is numerically and identically the same; it is the center of the entire, pure subject with which we become progressively acquainted. Just as the object-pole, in the progress from appearance to ever new appearances that can be connected in a harmonious synthesis, is and remains the same in numerical identity and yet is ever new, determined by ever new objective components, so it is with the ego. Of course, the ego is not a mere object in the manner of a thing that is constituted as a unity of appearances; the ego performs activities. Yet it is not just an empty, ideal polar point, determined by the point of intersection of the activities that flow forth from it; rather, it is also a pole of corresponding habitualities. But these are not in it as material properties given in perception; rather, they are dispositions that accrue to it by the fact that the ego has performed the relevant acts. With the first decision, the ego becomes originally the one who has thus decided. In this way, the ego has its own history, and on the basis of that history it creates an ego that persists for itself habitually as one and the same ego (*Phen. Psych.*, 161 [210–11]).

On the Ego That Founds Meaning and the Ego That Follows Others — Next Husserl turns to a series of analyses in which he uses the German words *Stiftung* and *stiften*. The verb, *stiften,* has a number of meanings: to found (*gründen*), to endow or give (*schenken*), to cause, produce, bring about (*verursachen*), and establish or institute (*einrichten*). I shall translate the term with the verb that fits best in the context and thus may use any of the verbs mentioned. Sometimes I shall even use the verb "to constitute."

The ego has no properties in the common sense of the term; it has the determinate mode of being that it has exclusively because of the convictions that it itself has instituted. First of all, it brings about its own foundations of meaning, and by so doing it establishes itself in a correlative way as an ego of self-founded, original convictions. Yet living in a community, it also understands and follows other egos in their self-foundation and originally founding activities. It shares their beliefs and values and, in so doing in its foundational activities, follows by assent, by accommodating itself to the other's motivations and convictions. The convictions that are instituted in the ego in this way do not flow from the ego itself, nor are they originally established by it. Rather, the ego follows after another and is guided by his or her convictions and motivations.

In this case, both egos can have an opinion in two ways: (1) there can be an opinion, a decision, a conviction based on rational insight and rational motives; or (2) the opinion can be based on blind motives that perhaps can be explained and justified rationally but at the moment are accepted as being explicitly understood, so that its rationality still has to be determined. One can also make a distinction here between rational motivation and that which motivates me to adopt teachings of reason wherever I encounter them. In the latter case, I follow the other rationally and decide according to his or her reason but at the same time also according to my own. My decision is then a decision fashioned after that of another person, and yet I also have decided by free exercise of reason. Thus I can always justify it to myself. Yet it is and remains true that it does not stem purely from me. But we must first also distinguish between going along passively and deciding by free deliberation in favor of the other's decision on the basis of reason. Thus we can have the following possibilities: (1) convictions arrived at by mere suggestion, (2) freely following another person by means of convictions arrived at by assent, and (3) convictions of assent arising from one's own reason. On the one hand, I can originally establish my own convictions on my own; but I can also follow convictions established by someone else whose example I follow. In that case, I am freely motivated by others (*Phen. Psych.,* 162–63 [211–13]).

Every change of conviction is a change of the ego. I do not have convictions in the way in which I have fleeting lived experiences; rather, I have them as abiding properties that I have on the basis of my own activities, either by formulating my own convictions or by somehow following someone else's convictions. As long as I do not give up my convictions, I, as who and what I now am, am the one who is thus and thus convinced on the basis of a decision. But taken in and by itself, the ego has no properties at all. It receives its characteristics by the decisions it makes. The concept of personality, character, and individuality, taken insofar as they refer to the ego, also refer to the field of convictions that are to be established by the ego and then define it as the ego it is.

The ego also has its typical way of enduring through time; it is an enduring ego, notwithstanding the fluctuations in its activities and convictions. What we call an ego in the proper sense means an entity with personal individuality. Notwithstanding changes and fluctuations, the ego preserves an individual style that can be recognized by others.

In inductive experiences that make use of association, we can form expectations as to how a certain person will behave in accordance with his or her past behavior. The same is true of myself. It is important to note here that the ground of this expectation can be disclosed intelligibly, for the decisions of an ego themselves imply a predelineation of possible consequences for further decisions that can be made intelligible in principle (*Phen. Psych.*, 163–65 [213–15]).

The Static and Genetic Investigation of the Subject as Monad — When Husserl had come to this point in his lecture course, the semester was almost over. He thus limited himself to briefly indicating important topics for further analysis and description. Yet he felt that what he had said was adequate to give his students an idea of the constitution of pure subjectivity. If we take pure subjectivity in its concretely complete context, it comprises the concrete but pure subjectivity called the *monad*. Thus the term "monad" does not here refer to a concept introduced by some metaphysical system; it is merely the name for an important theme of phenomenological, constitutive analyses.

The monad can be examined in static phenomenology when one simply unfolds whatever relatively self-contained connections are to be made prominent at any particular time by pursuing everything that is immanently real and ideal in all essential correlations. Genetic investigation explores the passive and active geneses in which the monad develops and evolves and in which the monadic ego acquires its personal unity and becomes a subject of a surrounding world. At the highest level, the monadic ego becomes the subject of a history.

Finally, one more essential step would have to be added, namely, the transition from the concrete monadic ego to a community of egos. Until now, we have limited ourselves to an investigation of the pure subjectivity of a concrete monad taken as *solus ipse*. Thus a pure phenomenology of intersubjectivity would still have to be added (*Phen. Psych.*, 165–66 [216–17]). The issues mentioned by Husserl will be taken up from the perspective of transcendental phenomenology in Chapter Ten.

❚ NOTES

1. For what follows, see section 9 of the "Amsterdam Lectures," in *Phän. Psych.*, 324–28.
2. Fink, "Operative Begriffe in Husserls Phänomenologie," 321–22, 335–37.
3. Husserl, *The Idea*, 52–60. See also Biemel's introduction to the original German edition, viii–ix.
4. Husserl, *Ideas*, 1:207–10 [176–79], 283–85 [246–47], 331–33 [286–89].
5. *Cart. Med.*, meditations 3 and 4.
6. Biemel, "Les phases décisives," 32–34.
7. See Biemel's introduction to *Die Idee*, viii.
8. Ibid., ix.
9. See the report on the manner in which the text of the lectures was composed by the editor, ibid., 87–88. In what follows, I shall make use of the critical notes about the text, ibid., 89–93 and, above all, of the "Train of Thoughts in the Lectures" found in *The Idea*, 2–12 [4–16], particularly 8–12 [10–16].
10. Lauer, *The Triumph of Subjectivity*, 79–80.
11. Spiegelberg, *The Phenomenological Movement*, 1:147.
12. See, for instance, Husserl's *On the Phenomenology of the Consciousness of Internal Time* (1893–1917), 77–103 [73–98].
13. Brand, *Welt, Ich und Zeit*, 54–141 passim; Diemer, *Edmund Husserl*, 143–75. See also Spiegelberg, *The Phenomenological Movement*, 146–49.
14. For what follows, in addition to the literature quoted already, see Robert Sokolowski, *The Formation of Husserl's Concept of Constitution* (The Hague: Nijhoff, 1964); Ludwig Landgrebe, "Reflexionen zu Husserls Konstitutionslehre," *Tijdschrift voor filosofie* 36 (1974): 466–82; Roman Ingarden, "Le problème de la constitution et le sens de la réflexion constitutive chez Husserl," in *Husserl*, Cahiers de Royaumont: Philosophie, no. 3 (Paris: Minuit, 1959), 242–64; Bernet et al., *Edmund Husserl*, 181–89.
15. For what follows, see *Phen. Psych.*, 147–66 [192–217]; "Amsterdamer Vorträge," section 7, 315–21.
16. Maurice Merleau-Ponty, *Phenomenology of Perception*, trans. Colin Smith (London: Routledge & Kegan Paul, 1962), parts 1 and 2.

17. Jan Linschoten, "On Falling Asleep," in *Phenomenological Psychology: The Dutch School,* ed. Joseph J. Kockelmans (The Hague: Nijhoff, 1987), 79–117. In an appendix to this essay, Linschoten has included a brief essay by Husserl on "The Unconscious I—Sleep—Impotence" (ibid., 115–17).

From Phenomenological Psychology to Transcendental Phenomenology

In this part of his essay on phenomenology, Husserl explains why phenomenological psychology cannot be the basic philosophical discipline and thus why a more radical type of phenomenology, called *transcendental phenomenology,* is necessary. He begins his exposition with a brief note on the history of modern philosophy and describes how Descartes had seen the need for a completely new and radical type of "first philosophy." This idea was taken up by Locke, who misunderstood it and steered it in the wrong direction.

Next, Husserl explains what is understood by the *"transcendental problem"* and why psychology is unable to deal with it. Any effort to try to do this leads into a transcendental circle (psychologism). Finally, Husserl explains that a *transcendental reduction* is necessary to make a transcendental phenomenology possible. The nature of transcendental phenomenology will be explained in the third part of the article.

At the end of this section, Husserl points out that phenomenological psychology and transcendental phenomenology have practically the same subject matter, so that the one seems to be a duplication of the other. Husserl explains why these two sciences nonetheless are completely different, even though phenomenological psychology is an excellent propaedeutic to transcendental phenomenology.

I have grouped sections 6, 7, and 8 together in view of the fact that they constitute a unity. Sections 9 and 10 are considered separately because the one deals with the transcendental reduction and the other with the relationship between phenomenological psychology and transcendental phenomenology.

The Transcendental Problem: Its Origin and Its Quasi-Solution by Psychologism

Text

II. Phänomenologische Psychologie und transzendentale Phänomenologie

6. Descartes' transzendentale Wendung und Lockes Psychologismus

Die Idee einer rein phänomenologischen Psychologie hat nicht nur die soeben dargelegte reformatorische Funktion für die empirische Psychologie. Aus tiefliegenden Gründen kann sie als Vorstufe für die Freilegung des Wesens einer transzendentalen Phänomenologie dienen. Auch historisch ist diese Idee nicht aus den eigenen Bedürfnissen der Psychologie selbst erwachsen. Ihre Geschichte führt uns bis auf J. *Lockes* denkwürdiges Grundwerk zurück und auf die bedeutsame Auswirkung der von ihm ausgehenden Impulse durch J. *Berkeley* und D. *Hume.* Schon bei *Locke* war aber die Beschränkung auf das rein Subjektive von außerpsychologischen Interessen bestimmt. Die Psychologie stand im Dienste des durch *Descartes* erweckten Transzendentalproblems. In seinen *meditationes* war der Gedanke zu dem für die erste Philosophie leitenden geworden: daß alles Reale und schließlich diese ganze Welt *für uns* seiende und soseiende nur ist als Vorstellungsinhalt unserer eigenen Vorstellungen, als urteilsmäßig vermeinte und bestenfalls evident bewährte unseres eigenen Erkenntnislebens. Hier lag die Motivation zu allen, ob echten oder unechten Transzendentalproblemen. *Descartes'* Zweifelsmethode war die erste Methode der Herausstellung der "transzendentalen Subjektivität", sein *"ego cogito"* führte auf deren erste begriffliche Fassung. Bei *Locke* wandelt sich *Descartes'* transzendental reine *mens* in die reine Seele (*human mind*), deren systematische Erforschung durch innere Erfahrung *Locke* in transzendental-philosophischem Interesse in Angriff nimmt. Er ist so der Begründer des *Psychologismus* als einer Transzendentalphilosophie durch eine Psychologie aus innerer Erfahrung. Das Schicksal der wissenschaftlichen Philosophie hängt an einer radikalen Überwindung jedes Psychologismus, die nicht nur seinen prinzipiellen Widersinn bloßlegt,

II. Phenomenological Psychology and Transcendental Phenomenology

6. Descartes' Transcendental Turn and Locke's Psychologism

The idea of a purely phenomenological psychology does not have just the function described above, of reforming empirical psychology. For deeply rooted reasons, it can also serve as a preliminary step for laying open the essence of a transcendental phenomenology. Historically, this idea too did not grow out of the peculiar needs of psychology proper. Its history leads us back to John Locke's notable basic work, and the significant development in Berkeley and Hume of the impetus it contained. Already Locke's restriction to the purely subjective was determined by extra-psychological interests: psychology here stood in the service of the transcendental problem awakened through Descartes. In Descartes' *Meditations,* the thought that had become the guiding one for "first philosophy" was that all of "reality," and finally the whole world of what exists and is so *for us,* exists only as the presentational content of our presentations, as meant in the best case and as evidently reliable {as meant, and in the best case as evidently verified} in our own cognitive life. This is the motivation for all transcendental problems, genuine or false. Descartes' method of doubt was the first method of exhibiting "transcendental subjectivity," and his *ego cogito* led to its first conceptual formulation. In Locke, Descartes' transcendentally pure *mens* is changed into the "human mind," whose systematic exploration through inner experience Locke tackled out of a transcendental-philosophical interest. And so he is the founder of *psychologism*—as a transcendental philosophy founded through a psychology of inner experience. The fate of scientific philosophy hangs on the radical overcoming of every trace of psychologism, an overcoming which not only exposes the fundamental absurdity of psychologism but also does justice to its transcendentally significant kernel of truth. The sources of its continuous historical power are drawn from out of a

sondern auch seinem transzendental bedeutsamen Wahrheitskern genugtut. Die Quelle seiner beständigen historischen Kraft schöpft er aus einer [288] Doppeldeutigkeit aller Begriffe von Subjektivem, die alsbald mit der Aufrollung der transzendentalen Frage erwächst. Die Enthüllung dieser Zweideutigkeit bedeutet in eins mit der scharfen Trennung zugleich eine Parallelisierung der rein phänomenologischen Psychologie (als der wissenschaftlich strengen Gestalt der Psychologie rein aus innerer Erfahrung) und der transzendentalen Phänomenologie als der echten Transzendentalphilosophie. Zugleich rechtfertigt sich so die Vorausschickung der reinen Psychologie als Zugangsmittel zur echten Philosophie. Wir beginnen mit der Klärung des echten Transzendentalproblems, das in der zunächst unklaren Labilität seines Sinnes so sehr geneigt macht (und das trifft schon *Descartes*), es auf ein abwegiges Geleise zu verschieben.

| 7. Das transzendentale Problem

Zum wesentlichen Sinn des transzendentalen Problems gehört seine Universalität, in der es die Welt und alle sie erforschenden Wissenschaften in Frage stellt. Es erwächst in einer allgemeinen Umwendung jener *"natürlichen Einstellung"*, in der wie das gesamte alltägliche Leben so auch die positiven Wissenschaften verbleiben. In ihr ist uns die Welt das selbstverständlich seiende Universum der Realitäten, beständig vorgegeben in fragloser Vorhandenheit. So ist sie das allgemeine Feld unserer praktischen und theoretischen Betätigungen. Sowie das theoretische Interesse diese natürliche Einstellung aufgibt und in einer allgemeinen Blickwendung sich auf das Bewußtseinsleben richtet, *in dem* die Welt für uns eben "die" Welt, die für uns vorhandene ist, sind wir in einer neuen Erkenntnislage. Jeder Sinn, den sie für uns hat (dessen werden wir nun inne), ihr unbestimmt allgemeiner wie ihr nach realen Einzelheiten sich bestimmender Sinn, ist in der Innerlichkeit unseres eigenen wahrnehmenden, vorstellenden, denkenden, wertenden Lebens bewußter und sich in unserer subjektiven Genesis bildender Sinn; jede Seinsgeltung ist in uns selbst vollzogen, jede sie begründende Evidenz der Erfahrung und Theorie in uns selbst lebendig und habituell uns immerfort motivierend. Das betrifft die Welt in jeder Bestimmung, auch in der selbstverständlichen, daß, was ihr zugehört, *"an und für sich"* ist, wie es ist, ob ich oder wer immer seiner zufällig bewußt wird oder nicht. [289] Ist einmal die Welt in dieser vollen Universalität auf die Bewußtseinssubjektivität bezogen worden, in deren Bewußtseinsleben sie eben als "die" Welt des jeweiligen Sinnes auftritt, so

double sense [an ambiguity] of all the concepts of the subjective, which arises as soon as the transcendental question is broached. The uncovering of this ambiguity involves [us in the need for] at once the sharp separation, and at the time the parallel treatment, of pure phenomenological psychology (as the scientifically rigorous form of a psychology purely of inner experience) and transcendental phenomenology as true transcendental philosophy. At the same time this will justify our advance discussion of psychology as the means of access to true philosophy. We will begin with a clarification of the true transcendental problem, which in the initially obscure unsteadiness of its sense makes one so very prone (and this applies already to Descartes) to shunt it off to a side track.

| 7. The Transcendental Problem

To the essential sense of the transcendental problem belongs its all-inclusiveness, in which it places in question the world and all the sciences investigating it. It arises within a general reversal of that "natural attitude" in which everyday life as a whole as well as the positive sciences operate. In it [the natural attitude] the world is for us the self-evidently existing universe of realities which are continuously before us in unquestioned givenness. So this is the general field of our practical and theoretical activities. As soon as the theoretical interest abandons this natural attitude and in a general turning around of our regard directs itself to the life of consciousness—*in which* the "world" is for us precisely that, the world which is present *to us*—we find ourselves in a new cognitive attitude [or situation]. Every sense which the world has for us (this we now become aware of), both its general indeterminate sense and its sense determining itself according to the particular realities, is, within the internality of our own perceiving, imagining, thinking, valuing life-process, a conscious sense, and a sense which is formed in subjective genesis. Every acceptance of something as validly existing is effected within us ourselves; and every evidence in experience and theory that establishes it, is operative in us ourselves, habitually and continuously motivating us. This [principle] concerns the world in every determination, even those that are self-evident: that what belongs *in and for itself* to the world, is how it is, whether or not I, or whoever, become by chance aware of it. Once the world in this full universality has been related to the subjectivity of consciousness, in whose living consciousness it makes its appearance precisely as "the" world in its varying sense, then its whole mode of being acquires a dimension of unintelligibility, or rather of questionableness. This "making an appearance" [*Auftreten*], this being-for-us of

erhält ihre gesamte Seinsweise eine Dimension der Unverständlichkeit bzw. Fraglichkeit. Dieses "Auftreten", dieses Für-uns-sein der Welt als der nur subjektiv zur Geltung gekommenen und zur begründeten Evidenz gebrachten und zu bringenden, bedarf der Aufklärung. Das erste Innewerden der Bewußtseinsbezogenheit der Welt in seiner leeren Allgemeinheit gibt kein Verständnis dafür, *wie* das mannigfaltige, kaum erschaut ins Dunkel zurücksinkende Bewußtseinsleben es zu solchen Leistungen bringt, wie es das sozusagen macht, daß in seiner Immanenz irgend etwas *als* an sich seiend auftreten kann und nicht nur als Vermeintliches sondern als sich in einstimmiger Erfahrung Ausweisendes. Offenbar überträgt sich das Problem auf jederlei "ideale" Welten und ihr "An-sich-sein" (z.b. die der reinen Zahlen oder der "Wahrheiten an sich"). Die Unverständlichkeit greift in besonders empfindlicher Weise *unsere* Seinsart selbst an. Wir (Einzelne und in Gemeinschaft) sollen es sein, in deren Bewußtseinsleben die reale Welt, die für uns vorhanden ist, als solche Sinn und Geltung gewinnt. Wir als Menschen sollen aber selbst zur Welt gehören. Nach unserem weltlichen Sinn werden wir also wieder auf uns und unser Bewußtseinsleben verwiesen, als worin sich für uns dieser Sinn erst gestaltet. Ist hier und überall ein anderer Weg der Aufklärung denkbar als der, das Bewußtsein selbst und die in ihm bewußt werdende "Welt" als solche zu befragen, da sie eben als von uns je gemeinte nirgendwoher sonst als in uns Sinn und Geltung gewonnen haben und gewinnen kann?

Machen wir noch einen wichtigen Schritt, der das "transzendentale" (den bewußtseinsrelativen Seinsinn des "Transzendenten" betreffende) Problem auf die prinzipielle Stufe erhebt. Er liegt in der Erkenntnis, daß die aufgewiesene Bewußtseinsrelativität nicht nur das Faktum *unserer* Welt angeht, sondern in eidetischer Notwendigkeit jede erdenkliche Welt überhaupt. Denn variieren wir in freier Phantasie unsere faktische Welt, sie in beliebige erdenkliche Welten überführend, so variieren wir *uns* deren Umwelt sie ist, unweigerlich mit, wir wandeln uns je in eine mögliche Subjektivität, deren Umwelt je [290] die erdachte Welt wäre, als Welt ihrer möglichen Erfahrungen, möglichen theoretischen Evidenzen, ihres möglichen praktischen Lebens. Diese Variation läßt freilich die rein idealen Welten der Art, die ihr Sein in der eidetischen Allgemeinheit haben, zu deren Wesen ja die Invarianz gehört, unberührt; aber es zeigt sich doch in der möglichen Variierbarkeit des solche Identitäten erkennenden Subjekts, daß ihre Erkennbarkeit, also ihre intentionale Bezogenheit nicht nur unsere faktische Subjektivität angeht. Mit der eide-

the world as only subjectively having come to acceptance and only subjectively brought and to be brought to well-grounded evident presentation, requires clarification. Because of its empty generality, one's first awakening to the relatedness of the world to consciousness gives no understanding of *how* the varied life of consciousness, barely discerned and sinking back into obscurity, accomplishes such functions: how it, so to say, manages in its immanence that something which manifests itself can present itself *as* something existing in itself, and not only as something meant but as something authenticated in concordant experience. Obviously the problem extends to every kind of "ideal" world and its "being-in-itself" (for example, the world of pure numbers, or of "truths in themselves"). Unintelligibility is felt as a particularly telling affront to *our* very mode of being [as human beings]. For obviously we are the ones (individually and in community) in whose conscious life-process the real world which is present for us as such gains sense and acceptance. As human creatures, however, we ourselves are supposed to belong to the world. When we start with the sense of the world [*weltlichen Sinn*] given with our mundane existing, we are thus again referred back to ourselves and our conscious life-process as that wherein for us this sense is first formed. Is there conceivable here or anywhere another way of elucidating [it] than to interrogate consciousness itself and the "world" that becomes known in it? For it is precisely as meant by us, and from nowhere else than in us, that it has gained and can gain its sense and validity.

Next we take yet another important step, which will raise the "transcendental" problem (having to do with the being-sense of "transcendent" relative to consciousness) up to the final level. It consists in recognizing that the relativity of consciousness referred to just now applies not just to the brute fact of *our* world but in eidetic necessity to every conceivable world whatever. For if we vary our factual world in free fantasy, carrying it over into random conceivable worlds, we are implicitly varying *ourselves* whose environment the world is: we each change ourselves into a possible subjectivity, whose environment would always have to be the world that was thought of, as a world of its [the subjectivity's] possible experiences, possible theoretical evidences, possible practical life. But obviously this variation leaves untouched the pure ideal worlds of the kind which have their existence in eidetic universality, which are in their essence invariable; it becomes apparent, however, from the possible variability of the subject knowing such identical essences [*Identitäten*] that their cognizability, and thus their intentional relatedness does not simply have to do with our de facto subjectivity. With

tischen Fassung des Problems wandelt sich auch die erforderliche
Bewußtseinsforschung in eine eidetische.

8. Die psychologistische Lösung als transzendentaler Zirkel

Die Herausarbeitung der Idee einer phänomenologisch reinen
Psychologie hat die Möglichkeit erwiesen, in konsequenter phänomenologischer Reduktion das Eigenwesentliche der Bewußtseins-
subjekte in eidetischer Allgemeinheit zu enthüllen, nach allen
seinen möglichen Gestalten. Das befaßt auch diejenigen der Recht
begründenden und bewährenden Vernunft und damit alle Gestalten möglicherweise erscheinender und als an sich seiend durch
zusammenstimmende Erfahrung auszuweisender und in theore-
tischer Wahrheit zu bestimmender Welten. Danach scheint diese
phänomenologische Psychologie in ihrer systematischen Durchführung die gesamte Korrelationsforschung für Sein und Bewußtsein
und von vornherein in prinzipieller (eben eidetischer) Allgemeinheit in sich zu fassen, also die Stätte aller transzendentalen
Aufklärungen zu sein. Demgegenüber darf aber nicht übersehen
werden, daß die Psychologie in allen ihren empirischen und
eidetischen Disziplinen "positive Wissenschaft" ist, Wissenschaft
in der natürlichen Einstellung, in der die schlechthin vorhandene
Welt der thematische Boden ist. Was sie erforschen will, sind die
in der Welt vorkommende Seelen und Seelengemeinschaften. Die
phänomenologische Reduktion dient als psychologische nur dazu,
das Psychische der animalischen Realitäten in seiner reinen
Eigenwesentlichkeit und seinen rein eigenwesentlichen Zusam-
menhängen zu gewinnen. Es behält, auch in der eidetischen
Forschung, den Seinssinn von weltlich Vorhandenem, nur bezogen
auf mögliche reale Welten. Der Psychologe ist auch als eidetischer
Phänomenologe transzendental naiv, er nimmt die möglichen
"Seelen" (Ich-subjekte), [291] ganz dem relativen Wortsinn gemäss, als
solche schlechthin vorhanden gedachter Menschen und Tiere
einer möglichen Raumwelt. Lassen wir aber anstatt des natürlich-
weltlichen das transzendentale Interesse theoretisch maßgebend
werden, so erhält die gesamte Psychologie den Stempel des
transzendental Problematischen, sie kann also der Transzendentalphilosophie keinerlei Prämissen beistellen. Die Bewußtseinssubjektivität, die als seelische ihr Thema ist, kann nicht
diejenige sein, auf die transzendental zurückgefragt werden soll.

Um an diesem entscheidenden Punkte zu einsichtiger Klarheit zu kommen, ist der thematische Sinn der transzendentalen
Frage scharf im Auge zu behalten und zu erwägen, wie sich ihm

the eidetic formulation of the problem, the kind of research into consciousness that is demanded is the eidetic.

**| 8. The Solution by Psychologism as a
| Transcendental Circle**

Our distillation of the idea of a phenomenologically pure psychology
has demonstrated the possibility of uncovering by consistent phenomenological reduction what belongs to the conscious subject's own
essence in eidetic, universal terms, according to all its possible
forms. This includes those forms of reason [itself] which establish
and authenticate validity, and with this it includes all forms of potentially appearing worlds, both those validated in themselves
through concordant experiences and those determined by theoretical truth. Accordingly, the systematic carrying through of this phenomenological psychology seems to comprehend in itself from the
outset in foundational (precisely, eidetic) universality the whole of
correlation research on being and consciousness; thus it would seem
to be the [proper] locus for all transcendental elucidation. On the
other hand, we must not overlook the fact that psychology in all its
empirical and eidetic disciplines remains a "positive science," a science operating within the natural attitude, in which the simply
present world is the thematic ground. What it wishes to explore are
the psyches and communities of psyches that are [actually] to be
found in the world. Phenomenological reduction serves as psychological only to the end that it gets at the psychical aspect of animal
realities in its pure own essential specificity and its pure own specific essential interconnections. Even in eidetic research [then], the
psyche retains the sense of being which belongs in the realm of what
is present in the world; it is merely related to possible real worlds.
Even as eidetic phenomenologist, the psychologist is transcendentally naive: he takes the possible "minds" ("I"-subjects) completely
according to the relative sense of the word as those of men and animals considered purely and simply as present in a possible spatial
world. If, however, we allow the transcendental interest to be decisive, instead of the natural-worldly, then psychology as a whole receives the stamp of what is transcendentally problematic; and thus
it can by no means supply the premises for transcendental philosophy. The subjectivity of consciousness, which, as psychic being, is its
theme, cannot be that to which we go back in our questioning into
the transcendental.

In order to arrive at an evident clarity at this decisive point, the
thematic sense of the transcendental question is to be kept sharply
in view, and we must try to judge how, in keeping with it, the regions

gemäß die Regionen des Fraglichen und Unfraglichen scheiden.
Das transzendentalphilosophische Thema ist eine konkrete und
systematische Aufklärung jener mannigfaltigen intentionalen
Bezogenheiten, die einer möglichen Welt überhaupt als Umwelt
einer entsprechenden möglichen Subjektivität wesensmäßig
zugehören, für die sie die vorhandene, praktisch und theoretisch
zugängliche wäre. Diese Zugänglichkeit bedeutet für die Sub-
jektivitäten hinsichtlich aller Kategorien für sie vorhandener
Weltobjekte und Weltstrukturen Regelungen ihres möglichen
Bewußtseinslebens, die in ihrer Typik erst enthüllt werden
müssen. Solche Kategorien sind "leblose Dinge", aber auch Menschen und Tiere mit ihren seelischen Innerlichkeiten. Von hier aus
soll sich der volle und ganze Seinssinn einer möglichen vorhandenen Welt im Allgemeinen und hinsichtlich aller für sie konstitutiven Kategorien klären. Wie jede sinnvolle Frage setzt diese
transzendentale einen Boden unfraglichen Seins voraus, in dem
alle Mittel der Lösung beschlossen sein müssen. Dieser Boden ist
hier die Subjektivität desjenigen Bewußtseinslebens, in dem eine
mögliche Welt überhaupt als vorhandene sich konstituiert. Andererseits ist es eine selbstverständliche Grundforderung vernünf-
tiger Methode, daß dieser als unfraglich seiend vorausgesetzte
Boden nicht mit solchem vermengt wird, was die transzendentale
Frage in ihrer Universalität als in Frage stehend meint. Das Reich
dieser Fraglichkeit ist das gesamte der transzendentalen Naivität,
umfaßt also jede mögliche Welt als die in natürlicher Einstellung
schlechthin in Anspruch genommene. Danach sind alle positiven
Wissenschaften transzendental eine [292] Epoché zu unterwerfen
so wie alle ihre Gegenstandsgebiete, also auch die Psychologie und
das gesamte in ihrem Sinne Psychische. Es wäre also ein transzendentaler Zirkel, die Beantwortung der transzendentalen Frage
auf die Psychologie zu stützen, einerlei ob auf empirische oder
eidetisch-phänomenologische. Die Subjektivität und das Bewußtsein—hier stehen wir vor der paradoxen Zweideutigkeit—, auf das
die transzendentale Frage rekurriert, kann also wirklich nicht
diejenige Subjektivität und das Bewußtsein sein, von dem die
Psychologie handelt.

of the problematical and unproblematical are set apart. The theme of transcendental philosophy is a concrete and systematic elucidation of those multiple intentional relationships, which in conformity with their essences belong to any possible world whatever as the surrounding world of a corresponding possible subjectivity, for which it [the world] would be the one present as practically and theoretically accessible. In regard to all the objects and structures present in the world for these subjectivities, this accessibility involves the regulations of its possible conscious life, which in their typology will have to be uncovered. [Among] such categories are "lifeless things," as well as men and animals with the internalities of their psychic life. From this starting point the full and complete being-sense of a possible world, in general and in regard to all its constitutive categories, shall be elucidated. Like every meaningful question, this transcendental question presupposes a ground of unquestioned being, in which all means of solution must be contained. This ground is here the [anonymous] subjectivity of that kind of conscious life in which a possible world, of whatever kind, is constituted as present. However, a self-evident basic requirement of any rational method is that this ground presupposed as beyond question is not confused with what the transcendental question, in its universality, puts into question. Hence the realm of this questionability includes the whole realm of the transcendentally naive and therefore every possible world simply claimed in the natural attitude. Accordingly, all possible sciences, including all their various areas of objects, are transcendentally to be subjected to an epoche. So also psychology, and the entirety of what is considered the psychical in its sense. It would therefore be circular, a transcendental circle, to base the answer to the transcendental question on psychology, be it empirical or eidetic-phenomenological. We face at this point the paradoxical ambiguity: the subjectivity and consciousness to which the transcendental question recurs can thus really not be the subjectivity and consciousness with which psychology deals.

∎ Synopsis

In section 6, Husserl explains that the idea of a phenomenological psychology not only has the function of providing the foundation for empirical psychology; it can also serve as an introduction to transcendental phenomenology; and this is so for fundamental reasons. Furthermore, it can also be shown historically that this idea did not grow out of the peculiar needs of empirical psychology.

The history of this idea leads us back to Locke, whose insights were developed further by Berkeley and Hume. Locke's decision to restrict himself in his reflections to the purely subjective was determined by extrapsychological interests. His "psychological" investigations stood in the service of the transcendental problem, first formulated by Descartes in his *Meditations*. In Descartes's view, metaphysics can show that all of reality, and the entire world of what exists for us, exist only as the content of our cognitive acts, as meant in judgments and, in the best case, as verified with evidence. It is here that we find the motivation for all transcendental problems.

Descartes's method of doubt was the first method developed to exhibit the "transcendental subject," and his description of the *ego cogito* provided its first conceptual formulation. Locke replaced Descartes's transcendentally pure mind with a "human mind"; yet he continued to examine and explore this *human* mind through inner experience because of a transcendental-philosophical concern. In this manner, Locke became the father of psychologism, that is, of a "transcendental philosophy" that allegedly can be founded through a psychology of inner experience.

Husserl was convinced that the fate of philosophy depends on the radical overcoming of every form of psychologism. In the effort to do so, one must show not only the basic error of psychologism but also the kernel of truth that it contains. The basic error is that it confuses the transcendental subject with the mundane subject; the kernel of truth lies in the fact that one indeed must turn to the subject if one is to provide philosophy with a solid foundation.

The fact that empiricism and psychologism have been historically so powerful is to be explained by the fact that all the concepts of the subjective are ambiguous; they can all be taken in a transcendental and in a mundane sense. The uncovering and clarification of this ambiguity will help us to clearly distinguish phenomenological psychology from transcendental philosophy, while at the same time treating them in a parallel manner. In doing so, it will be possible also to justify the approach chosen here, namely, of using a critical discussion of phenomenological psychology as a means of access to true phenomenological philosophy.

In section 7, Husserl stresses first the all-encompassing scope of the transcendental problem; it includes everything; it places everything in question, the entire world and all the sciences examining it. This problem arises when we turn from the natural to the transcendental attitude. In the natural attitude, we take the world as the self-evidently existing universe of all real entities that are continuously before us in unquestioned givenness. In the transcendental attitude, we turn around, away from the field of all theoretical and practical activities in the world, and focus instead consistently on the life of consciousness, in which the "world" is precisely no more than the world that is present to us. After the change of our attitude in regard to the world, every meaning that the world has for us is now a conscious meaning, a meaning that is formed in subjective genesis and is found only within our own perceiving, imagining, thinking, valuing life.

Once the world in its entirety has been related to the subjectivity of consciousness, in whose life it makes its appearance precisely as "the" world, its whole mode of being becomes questionable. Its "making an appearance" in consciousness, its being-for-us as only having come to acceptance, as only subjectively brought, or to be brought, to evident presentation, requires clarification. When one becomes aware of the relatedness of the world to consciousness, one has at first absolutely no understanding of *how* the life of consciousness in its various modalities can accomplish such a function, how it manages that something which manifests itself in its immanence can also present itself as something existing "in itself," not only as something meant but as something authenticated in harmonious experience. What is claimed here for the real world manifestly also holds good for all ideal worlds, such as the world of numbers, and "truths in themselves." This unintelligibility affects our own mode of being in a particularly sensitive manner insofar as it is implied that it is we who are the ones, individually or in community, in whose conscious life the entire real world that is present to us as such receives both meaning and validity. But as human creatures we, too, precisely belong to this world. Thus it is according to our own mundane sense, that is, taken as beings in the real world, that we are referred back to ourselves and our conscious life as that wherein for us meaning is first formed. But how can that be? There does not seem to be another way to elucidate this enigma than to interrogate consciousness itself and the "world" that becomes known in it. For it is precisely as meant by us, and from nowhere else, that the world, and we ourselves as mundane entities, have gained meaning and validity.

We must now still take another important step. This will raise the "transcendental" problem, which has to do with the meaning of being of everything "transcendent" relative to consciousness, up to the final level. It consists in realizing that the relativity of everything in regard to consciousness applies not only to our own de facto world but in eidetic necessity also to every conceivable world whatever. But if we vary our factual world in various ways in our imagination and thus carry it over into merely conceivable worlds, we implicitly are also varying *ourselves,* whose environment our world is: we each change ourselves into a *possible subject,* a subject whose environment would always have to be the world that was perceived or thought, that is to say, a world of the subject's possible experiences, its possible theoretical experiences, and its possible practical life.

The variation mentioned leaves untouched the ideal worlds referred to earlier because these worlds are essentially invariable; however, it is apparent from the possible variability of the subject that knows the entities of these ideal worlds, such as the world of numbers, that their intentional relatedness does not simply have to do with our de facto subjectivity. The important point here is to realize that if the transcendental problem is taken in an eidetic manner, then the kind of research that is demanded in dealing with the problem must itself also be eidetic in nature.

In section 8, Husserl states that if anyone were to try to find a solution for the transcendental problem while remaining within the natural attitude, he or she would eventually run into a circle, a transcendental circle. But this is precisely what every form of psychologism has tried to do. Thus Husserl sets out to show that the solution which psychologism proposes for the transcendental problem did indeed end up in a transcendental circle.

The idea of phenomenological psychology that has been developed thus far has demonstrated that it is possible in consistent phenomenological reduction to uncover in eidetic universality whatever belongs to the very essence of the conscious subject with respect to all its possible forms. This includes also those forms of reason itself that provide foundation and validity, and with them all forms of potentially appearing worlds. Accordingly, the systematic development of phenomenological psychology seems to comprehend in itself in foundational, and even eidetic, universality the entire research that examines the correlation between being and consciousness; thus phenomenological psychology seems to be the proper place for all transcendental elucidations.

Yet one cannot forget that phenomenological psychology is and remains a "positive science," a science that operates within the natural attitude and in which the simply present world is the ground for all thematization. What phenomenological psychology in all its forms wants to examine are the souls and the community of souls that are actually to be found in the world. The phenomenological reduction is applied with the intention of separating the purely psychical as such from the psychophysical, with which it is essentially connected, so that the psychical as such can be examined in its own essential specificity and interconnections. Even in eidetic research, the psychical retains the ontological meaning of something that belongs to the realm of what is present in the world, although it is true that it is then related merely to possible worlds. Thus, even in eidetic research, the phenomenological psychologist is transcendentally a naive person; he or she takes the possible souls, the I-subjects, as those of people and animals considered merely as present in a possible world. If we now move from the natural to the transcendental attitude, phenomenological psychology as a whole becomes immediately transcendentally problematic. Thus phenomenological psychology can never provide the premises for transcendental philosophy. The conscious subjectivity, which as psychic is its subject matter, cannot be the subjectivity to which we go back in our questioning into the transcendental.

In order to avoid any possible confusion, one must keep the transcendental question sharply in view and attempt to judge how, in keeping with it, one can carefully separate what is problematic from what is unproblematic. The subject matter of transcendental philosophy is a concrete and systematic elucidation of the multiple intentional relationships that, in conformity with their essences, belong to any possible world whatever as the world of a corresponding possible subjectivity for which the world would be present as practically and theoretically accessible.

Like every meaningful question, this transcendental question presupposes a ground of unquestioned being in which all means for a solution must be contained. This ground is the subjectivity of that conscious life in which any possible world can be constituted as present. However, a self-evident requirement of any rational method is that this ground, presupposed here as beyond question, is not confused with what the transcendental question in its universality precisely puts into question. Hence the realm of what is questionable in this case includes the entire realm of what is transcendentally naive, and thus also every possible world simply claimed in the natural attitude. Consequently also all the sciences, including all their various domains of objects, are transcendentally to be subjected to an *epoche*. This is true also for phenomenological psychology and everything that it considers. It would therefore be circular to base the answer to the transcendental question on psychology, be it empirical or phenomenological. Thus it is clear that the subjectivity and consciousness to which the transcendental question must recur can really not be the subjectivity and consciousness with which phenomenological psychology is concerned.

In the commentary to follow, I shall focus on two topics: (1) the origin of psychologism and the need for a transcendental turn and (2) the precise meaning of the term "transcendental" in Kant and Husserl.

Commentary

On the Origin of Psychologism and the Need for a Transcendental Turn

From Descartes to Kant — On several occasions, Husserl focused on the historical origin and the true meaning of psychologism. We are already familiar with part of the story insofar as Husserl himself started in psychologism and from there moved in the direction of his later transcendental philosophy. In what follows I shall present a brief paraphrase of what Husserl says in his last major publication, *Crisis,* about the origin of psychologism and the need for a transcendental turn. There Husserl writes that in his view psychologism originated in the works of Locke under the influence of ideas that Locke had discovered in the philosophy of Descartes. When Husserl describes how psychologism in philosophy gradually came about, he is aware of the fact that he is not involved in historical investigations in the usual sense of the term. He is not interested in historical-critical analyses of texts and documents but rather in an effort to make understandable the teleology in the historical development of philosophy, and of modern philosophy in particular. There is also a second aim involved here: to achieve clarity about ourselves, who are the actual bearers of this teleology and who take part in carrying it out. In so doing, Husserl hopes to understand the unity that runs through all the philosophical projects of modern history.

If philosophers turn to the great ideas developed in our philosophical tradition, then this is done not with the hope of finding there a system that can passively be taken over but rather with the intention of carrying forward, through their own self-reflection, the self-reflection of their forebears. The latter necessarily implies a responsible form of criticism. If these philosophers decide to think for themselves and become autonomous philosophers with the will to liberate themselves from all ideas that are simply taken for granted without any critical examination, they must know that all the things one takes for granted are prejudices, and that all prejudices are obscurities arising out of a sedimentation of our tradition—not merely judgments whose truth is as yet undecided (pre-judgment, *Vor-Urteile*).

Husserl was convinced that the origin of psychologism was to be found in the philosophy of Descartes, who is the father of the modern idea of an objectivistic rationalism but also of the transcendental motif that eventually would explode it. After Galileo had provided the foundation of a new science of nature, Descartes set himself the task of systematically developing the new idea of a universal philosophy in the form of a mathematical rationalism, of a philosophy as universal mathematics. What Descartes intended to achieve has not yet fully materialized even today, even though since Leibniz many great thinkers have made important contributions to its final realization. Thus what Descartes actually developed was not a genuine mathematical but rather a physicalistic form of rationalism.

Yet it was not merely because of the inauguration of this idea that Descartes became the founder of modern philosophy. In his *Meditations,* in which he attempted to provide us with a radical foundation for this new type of rationalism, he also developed ideas that eventually would explode his form of rationalism by uncovering its hidden absurdity. The very ideas that were meant to give a foundation to his new rationalism as "eternal truth" bear within themselves a deeply hidden meaning that, once brought to light, would completely uproot it (*Crisis,* 70–74 [71–76]).

Descartes's Turn to the *Ego Cogito* and the Meaning of the Cartesian *Epoche* — In his first two meditations, Descartes describes how he came to realize the need to turn to the *cogito,* and particularly to the *ego* of the *cogitationes* that essentially relate to the various *cogitata*. In Husserl's view, in these first meditations there is a depth that is so difficult to bring to light that even Descartes was unable to do this; as a matter of fact, he did not fully understand the importance of his discovery and let slip away the great discovery he had just made. To see this, it is not enough just to repeat what Descartes says; one must try to bring to light what is really involved in his thinking by separating what he himself thought from what still remained concealed from him because of ideas he simply took for granted.

For Descartes, philosophical knowledge is absolutely grounded knowledge that rests on a foundation of immediate and apodictic insights whose self-evidence excludes all conceivable doubt. In an effort to discover that foundation, Descartes started with a radical, methodical, skeptical *epoche* that puts in question all his hitherto accepted convictions. This "Cartesian *epoche*" shows a form of radicalism never heard of before, for it encompasses not only the validity of all the existing sciences, including mathematics, but also the validity of all pre- and extra-scientific life, including the world of sense experience, which is constantly pregiven and is taken for granted unquestioningly, as well as everything that is developed on its basis.

Descartes performs this *epoche* with the intention of discovering an absolute foundation for all systematically developed knowledge. But how can his *epoche* accomplish this? If it excludes all knowledge of the entire world and thus loses its grasp on the being of the world, how is it then that through this *epoche* an absolute ground of immediate and apodictic self-evidences can be exhibited? Descartes's answer is that if one refrains from taking any position on the being or nonbeing of the world, not every acceptance of being (*Seinsgeltung*) is prohibited within this *epoche*. Descartes thought that he, the ego carrying out the *epoche,* was not included in its domain of entities, but rather, if he really actually carried out the *epoche* radically and universally, the ego would have to be excluded in principle. The ego is necessary as the one who carries out the *epoche;* it is precisely herein that Descartes found the apodictic ground he was seeking, the one that absolutely excludes every possible doubt. No matter how far the ego may push its doubt, it is still absolutely self-evident that the ego, after all, would still exist as the doubter. Thus, during the universal *epoche,* the absolutely apodictic self-evidence of the "I am" is still at the ego's disposal. And within this self-evidence much more is comprised, for "I am as thinking" includes "I am thinking such and such cogitations oriented at such and such thought objects." In the final analysis, this includes all cogitations in which the world and all that the ego has attributed to it in thought still have acceptance of being for the ego, except that now, *as* one who is philosophizing, the ego may no longer straightforwardly accept them as beings that actually exist in the real world. Thus the life of the ego goes on, and all its activities continue; yet what formerly stood before me as "the" world, having being and validity for me, has now become a mere "phenomenon." In the *epoche,* all determinations and "the" world itself have now been transformed into the ideas of the ego; they have become merely the inseparable components of the ego's cogitations, as their *cogitata* as such.

In addition to this, something else must be added that is of the greatest importance. Through the *epoche,* the ego has penetrated into the domain of being, which in principle is prior to everything that conceivably has meaning and being for it. For Descartes, the ego performing the *epoche* is the only entity that is absolutely indubitable (*Crisis,* 75–78 [76–80]).

Descartes's Misinterpretation of His Own Discovery — Husserl next draws attention to the fact that the ideas of Descartes presented thus far really have a double meaning; one can take these ideas in two different ways, depending on whether or not one includes the ego itself in the *epoche.* In view of the fact that Descartes did not subject all his prior opinions to the *epoche,* everything that he actually brought to light remained in a sense superficial, in spite of the originality of his ideas and the enormous influence they have had over the centuries. After he had introduced the turn to the subject, he wondered about the ego discovered in the *epoche;* he asked what kind of ego it is, whether the ego is the human being, the sensibly intuited human being of everyday life. Then he excluded the body, because it, too, is part of the sensible world, and determined the ego accordingly as *mens sive animus,* as mind or soul.

In Husserl's view, one must ask whether the *epoche* is not related to the totality of what is given to me, including myself as a human being in the real world. The ego that Descartes intended to bring to light is not a residuum of the world but is that which is absolutely apodictically posited; and this is made possible by subjecting the entire world-validity to the *epoche.* The soul about which Descartes speaks is not only a part of the world, in that it is the soul of a real body, but is itself also the residuum of an earlier abstraction of the physical body. But this abstraction is not an essential component of the *epoche,* nor does it occur *in* the *epoche* but merely in the scientist's way of looking at things, which occurs on the ground of the natural world as pregiven and taken for granted.

It is important to realize that when Descartes identifies the ego with the soul, he is inconsistent. The great discovery of the ego becomes meaningless through this absurd move: a pure soul has no meaning in the *epoche* unless it is taken as a mere phenomenon in the phenomenological sense of the term. The difficulty in maintaining the unheard-of change of attitude that is implied in the radical and universal *epoche* is demonstrated by the fact that Descartes basically misunderstood the meaning of his own discovery, that the entire tradition following Descartes did not realize this, and that even in the twentieth century people continue to confuse phenomenology with Cartesianism (*Crisis,* 78–81 [80–83]).

Descartes's Two Basic Mistakes — In his *Meditations,* Descartes thus substituted his own psychic ego for the absolute and transcendental ego, and consequently a psychological immanence for an egological immanence, and the evidence of a psychic inner self-perception for the evidence of the egological self-perception. This was his first basic mistake. On this basis, he thought that it would be possible to establish the dualism of finite substances by means of inferences leading to what transcends his own soul, made possible by the first inference that leads to the transcendence of God. On the same basis, he also believed that in principle he had solved the problem of how the rational structures of the mathematical sciences can claim to have an objectively true validity for things that transcend the life of the soul. This problem will return in a modified form in Kant's critical philosophy, so that we can say in truth that with Descartes a completely new kind of philosophizing begins that seeks its ultimate foundation in the subject.

Descartes was able to persist in pure objectivism in spite of his turn to the subject because the mind or the soul, which in his philosophy functions as the absolute ground of knowledge and thus can provide a radical foundation to the objective sciences and philosophy, appeared at the same time to be grounded along with everything else as a legitimate subject matter within the objective sciences, particularly psychology. His interest in objectivism is thus the root of his basic errors.

Descartes did not realize that the ego, which has been deprived of the world by the *epoche* and in whose functioning cogitations the world has the ontological meaning it has and ever can have, cannot itself possibly turn up as subject matter in the world; for everything that is of the world derives its meaning precisely from these functions. Furthermore, he did not realize that the ego that comes to light in the *epoche* is not just an ego that can have other fellow egos outside itself. Descartes did not see that such distinctions as "I" and "you" as well as "inside" and "outside" first become constituted in the absolute ego. It is thus understandable once more why Descartes, in his haste to give a foundation to objectivism, did not set himself the task of systematically investigating the pure ego itself.

While Descartes really developed some kind of psychology in his *Meditations,* he did not at all focus on the intentionality of all conscious acts. And this was his second basic mistake (*Crisis,* 81–82 [83–84]).

Descartes's Philosophy as the Starting Point of Rationalism and Empiricism — Descartes's ideas were developed further by a number of rationalist philosophers, such as Nicolas de Malebranche, Spinoza, Leibniz, Wolff, Alexander Gottlieb Baumgarten, and this development led to impressive rationalist systems. These systems were developed on the basis of the conviction that *more geometrico,* an absolutely grounded, universal knowledge of the world taken as a transcendent in-itself, can be realized. English empiricism strongly reacted against the conviction that a rational metaphysical system of something transcendent can be developed, even though it, too, was deeply influenced by Descartes's turn to the subject. One finds skeptical empiricism already in the works of Hobbes, although from our perspective the works of Locke, Berkeley, and Hume are of greater relevance and importance because of the immense influence they would have on psychology and the theory of knowledge in the nineteenth century. This line of development is particularly significant in that it is an essential step toward the realization that the position of the psychologically misinterpreted transcendentalism of Descartes is really untenable and is to be changed into some kind of strictly transcendental philosophy, which one will find in the works of Kant and German idealism.

In empiricism, the new psychology, which in Descartes's thought was required as the correlate of the pure natural sciences, was given its first concrete form. One concerned oneself with investigations of introspective psychology. This psychology was then also used for the development of an empiricist theory of knowledge. Locke was the first to materialize these ideas. Locke presented his empiricist philosophy as a new attempt to accomplish what Descartes had tried to do in his *Meditations:* the epistemological foundation of the objectivity of all objective sciences. The skepticism that is inherent in such an approach to the problems of knowledge is evident from the start in the answers that Locke tried to give to questions of the scope, extent, and degrees of certainty of human knowledge. Locke had no idea of the depth of the Cartesian *epoche* and of the reduction to the ego. He took the ego to be a human soul that, in the self-evidence of its own self-experience, gradually becomes acquainted with its activities, capacities, and inner states. In Locke's philosophy, only what is given in immediate self-experience is self-evidently given; everything else, our knowledge of the external world, is inferred from this. Locke developed in this way a set of internal-psychological analyses purely on the basis of inner experience in which Locke naively made use of the experiences of other human beings, as well as of the conceptions resulting from the self-experience of what belongs to me, this one human being among other human beings. In this manner, the genuine philosophical problems that motivated Descartes's efforts simply disappeared in Locke and turned into problems of the psychological genesis of the real experiences and the faculties that belong to them.

Locke never mentioned the intentionality of conscious activities; instead he introduced "atomic" elements out of which complex experiences are to be built up. The data sensationalism that Locke developed, together with the doctrine of outer and inner sense, dominated psychology and the theory of knowledge for centuries; and in spite of the well-known criticism of "psychic atomism," the basic meaning of Locke's doctrine has been defended up to the present day.

Berkeley later reduced the material things that appear in our natural experience to the complexes of the sense data through which they appear. In his view, no inference is thinkable by which one could draw conclusions from these sense data about anything but other such sense data. Material things outside these sense data and whatever can be derived from them by association are mere philosophical inventions. In this way, Berkeley was led to a paradoxical form of idealism.

It is Hume who developed Locke's insights to the end. All the categories of the objective sciences, as well as the categories of our prescientific life, are for Hume no more than fictions. Take first of all the mathematical concepts, such as number, magnitude, continuum, and geometrical figure. For a phenomenologist, these entities are idealizations that methodically and necessarily can be derived from what is intuitively given. For Hume, they are mere fictions, and the same is true for mathematics as a whole. The origin of these fictions can easily be explained psychologically through the lawfulness of the associations and the relations between ideas. The same is true for the categories of our prescientific life, including those of the material world, such as the identity of persisting bodies, as well as the supposedly experienced identity of the person; all of these are mere fictions. In our everyday life, we make a distinction between the tree over there and its continuously changing manners of appearing. But immanently there is nothing there but these manners of appearing. These are ever more complex data, ultimately bound together and regulated by association, that can explain the illusion of experiencing something identical. The same is true for a person: an identical ego is not a datum but rather a ceaselessly changing bundle of data; its identity is a psychological fiction. To the fictions of this sort also belongs the category of causality, which Hume conceived of in terms of necessary connection. Speaking in general terms, one can say that in Hume's *Treatise of Human Nature,* the world, nature, the universe of material things, the world of identical persons, and all objective sciences through which we know these things in their objective truth are all transformed into fictions (*Crisis,* 82–88 [84–91]).

The Refutation of Objectivism as the Real Motif Hidden in Hume's Skepticism — After having criticized Hume's position rather severely, calling it an absurd form of skepticism, Husserl feels that he has to do justice to Hume's genius. He begins this re-evaluation with a question: Why was Hume's *Treatise* such an important historical event? In Husserl's view, it was important because it was able to show, in contrast to the claims of the rationalists and the leading mathematicians and physicists, that all knowledge of the world, the prescientific as well as the scientific, is and remains an enormous enigma. Classical rationalism was convinced that in principle one had succeeded in providing an absolute foundation to all methodical human knowledge, and the success of the mathematical and physical sciences seemed to point in the same direction. Then Hume came along and explained that the turn to the subject, as it was understood by Descartes, really leads to skepticism.

However absurd Hume's position may be from one point of view, it nevertheless revealed a completely new way of assessing the objectivity of the world and its entire meaning and, correlatively, the meaning of the objective sciences insofar as it denied their metaphysical claim of absolute truth. Through Hume's work, it became possible to realize that the life of consciousness is a life of accomplishment, the accomplishment of all meaning, both prescientific and scientific. Although Descartes had never contemplated the possibility that the whole world is no more than a *cogitatum* arising out of the universal synthesis of the various flowing cogitations, Hume's work nevertheless suggested this possibility. And the same is true for the entire scientific world insofar as the rational accomplishments of the scientific cogitations, built upon the prescientific ones, are constitutive of the scientific world. Through the work of both Berkeley and Hume, who each in his own way radicalized the basic Cartesian problem, dogmatic objectivism was shaken to its foundation (*Crisis*, 88–90 [91–93]).

The "Transcendental Motif" in Rationalism: Kant's Transcendental Philosophy — According to Kant's own testimony, Hume's work roused him from his dogmatic slumber. This does not mean that Kant's work is the continuation of a form of thought that begins in Descartes and through Locke and Berkeley results in the philosophy of Hume. The revolution of the way of thinking motivated by Hume's ideas is not directed against empiricism but rather against the post-Cartesian rationalism that Kant knew through Leibniz and Wolff.

In Husserl's view, we must now ask first of all what the meaning is of the dogmatism that Kant tried to uproot. Speaking generally, one can say that this was the dogmatism of classical rationalist metaphysics. Although Descartes's *Meditations* continued to exert influence, the radicalism that is implicit in it was not passed on to Descartes's successors. They passively accepted what Descartes had wanted to establish, namely, the absolute metaphysical validity of all objective sciences, of philosophy as the universal objective science, and—what comes to the same thing—the right of the knowing subject to let its rational constructs count as nature with a meaning that transcends the ego because of the self-evidences that occur in the ego's mind. The new conception of the natural world and the natural sciences related to it, as well as the correlative conception of a self-enclosed soul, and the task of a new psychology with a rational method according to the mathematical model were already established. Rational philosophy was under construction in every direction. Everyone was sharply focused on new discoveries, new theories, the rigor of the inferences made, and correspondingly on the general problem of method and its perfection. Knowledge was very much discussed everywhere, and this was done from a scientific point of view. Yet this reflection on knowledge was not transcendental but rather a mere reflection on the praxis of knowledge. This was a matter of what one usually calls logic.

The thematic direction of this kind of investigation was twofold: on the one hand, one wished to develop a systematic universe of logical laws, the theoretical totality of all the truths destined to function as norms for all judgments capable of being objectively true. To this domain belongs classical formal logic as well as the disciplines that Leibniz grouped together under the label *"mathesis universalis."* On the other hand, one also focused on those who make judgments and in so doing strive for objective truth: How is one to make normative use of those laws so that the self-evidence through which a judgment is certified as objectively true can appear?

As Husserl sees it, in all these laws, which are in the broad sense "logical" laws, metaphysical truth was contained automatically in the eyes of the rationalists. Thus the systematic development of the theory of these laws had to have the meaning of a general ontology. One finds in this ontology the scientific work of pure reason operating exclusively with concepts innate in the human soul. It was assumed as obvious that these concepts, laws, and theories contain metaphysical, objective truth.

One was aware of the fact that over against the faculty of pure a priori thinking, of pure reason, there is that of sensibility, the faculty of inner and outer experience. The knowing subject is affected in outer experience from the "outside" and thereby becomes certain of the affecting objects; yet in order to know them in their truth, one needs pure reason, that is, the system of all the norms in which reason displays itself as the "logic" for all true knowledge of the objective world.

This was the kind of rationalism against which Kant protested when he spoke about dogmatism. Kant's knowledge of Hume's *Treatise* had made him aware of the fact that between the pure truths of reason and the metaphysical objects there is and remains a gulf of incomprehensibility, namely, the question as to how the truths of reason can really guarantee the knowledge of things. Even the rationality of the mathematical, natural sciences, which was a model for all other sciences, was transformed into an enigma. Yet the rationalists had maintained that the rationality of modern physics is quite indubitable, that it owes its rationality to the a priori of pure, logical-mathematical reason, and that the disciplines of mathematical reason exhibit an unassailable pure rationality. One was aware of the fact that natural science is not purely rational, insofar as it depends on outer experience and sensibility; yet whatever is rational in the science of nature it owes to pure reason, which sets the norms. As for sensibility, the attitude of the rationalists was not consistent. On the one hand, it had been generally assumed that sensibility gives rise to the merely sensible data as a result of affection from the outside. Yet one also acted as if the experiential world of our prescientific attitude were the world pregiven by mere sensibility.

Hume had also shown that the notions of causality and necessary connection are enigmatic, and the same holds good for the notion of identity if applied to things of the material world. Thus he had to declare everything that for its being and explanation presupposes these notions to be fictions.

Kant realized that Hume substitutes sense data for perceptions that bring us into contact with things. Thus Hume overlooked the fact that mere sensibility, related to mere data of sense, cannot account for objects of experience. He thus overlooked the fact that these objects of experience point to hidden accomplishments of the mind. In Husserl's view, Kant said to himself that things undoubtedly appear, but this is so because the sense data, which are already brought together in a certain way, in concealment, through a priori forms of space and time, are made logical in the course of their alteration without any appeal to reason as manifested in logic and mathematics. Kant thus undertook to show that if common experience is really to be the experience of objects of nature, objects that can be known with objective truth in respect to their being and nonbeing, their being-such and being-otherwise, then the intuitively appearing world must already be a construct of the faculties of pure intuition and pure reason. But these are the same faculties that express themselves in an explicit form in mathematics and logic.

Thus reason appears to have a twofold way of functioning. One way is its systematic self-exposition and self-revelation in free and pure mathematizing, in the practice of the mathematical sciences. The other way is of constantly functioning in concealment, ceaselessly rationalizing sense data. The objective result in the first case is pure mathematics as theory, whereas the objective result of the second is the sensibly intuited world of objects, which is the empirical presupposition of all scientific thinking in the sciences of nature. Like the intuited world of material things, the whole world of natural science is a subjective construct of our understanding; only the material of the sense data arises from a transcendent affection by the things in themselves, so that the latter in principle are inaccessible to human knowledge.

Descartes conceived of natural science as a branch of philosophy taken as the ultimate science of what is; it is capable through its rationality to know the material things in themselves beyond the subjectivity of one's knowledge. For Kant, on the other hand, objective science is an accomplishment of reason that remains within subjectivity; as such it must be separated from philosophy. Philosophy itself is a theory of the accomplishments that are necessarily carried out within subjectivity; as such it is a theory of the possibility and scope of objective knowledge; it is able to reveal the naivete of the alleged rational philosophy of nature in itself.

Speaking in formal generality, one could say, according to Husserl, that Kant, reacting against the data positivism of Hume, outlined a great, systematically constructed scientific philosophy in which the Cartesian turn to conscious subjectivity is worked out in the form of a transcendental subjectivism. It should be noted here that Kant did not fully understand Hume's basic problem. As Husserl sees it, Hume's problem is that of how the naive obviousness of the certainty of the world in which we live, as well as of the world of science, is to be made understandable. Hume shows the impossibility of the naivete of the scientist who concerns himself with nature but is blind to the fact that all the truths he attains as objective truths, and the objective world as the subject matter of his claims, are really his own life-constructs developed within himself. In Husserl's view, this insight must come to anyone who seriously immerses oneself in Hume's *Treatise* (*Crisis,* 91–97 [93–100]).

Husserl concludes his historical observations with a brief note on the meaning that phenomenology attributed to the term "transcendental." He indicates that the meaning of the term as he uses it was inspired by Kant's transcendental philosophy. Yet he also states explicitly that phenomenology has the right to define the meaning of this important term in its own manner. In so doing, he makes it clear that for him the term "transcendental" includes con-notations of the basic conceptions of philosophy of both Kant and Descartes. Since what he says about the meaning of the term re-mains ambiguous, I shall add a brief reflection on the meaning of the term in modern philosophy, particularly in Kant and Husserl (*Crisis*, 97–98 [100–101]).

On the Meaning of the Term "Transcendental" in Kant and Husserl

In our Western philosophical tradition, the term "transcendental" has been used in several senses. The best known of these are the ones propagated by medieval theology and philosophy, by Kant's critical philosophy, by Husserl's transcendental phenomenology, and by Heidegger's analytic of *Dasein*. We shall be concerned here mainly with the views of Kant and Husserl. Yet in view of the fact that in one instance Kant explicitly refers to the medieval use of the term, I shall add a few comments on the medieval conception of the so-called transcendentals as well.

The Medieval Doctrine of the Transcendentals — The medi-eval conception of the transcendental[1] has a rather strange history. The idea underlying the doctrine is Aristotelian, and Aristotle him-self explicitly expounded the transcendental character of the "one." Yet Aristotle never extended what he claims for the "one" to other similar concepts or notions.[2] To some degree, the doctrine of the transcendentals is a creation of Christian theology, where the three basic transcendental notions, namely, the one, the true, and the good, were used to explain an aspect of the doctrine of the Trinity. At a later time, the doctrine found its way into philosophy and was de-veloped there systematically.

In medieval philosophy, it was generally accepted that what one conceives first, is most evident, and to which one can reduce all other concepts is the concept of being. Thus all other concepts of our understanding can be described as additions to the concept of being. Obviously, nothing can be added to "being," as though it were some-thing not already included in being, in the way in which a specific difference is added to a genus or an accident to a substance. For ev-erything is essentially a being. Yet some predicates may be said to "add" something to the concept of being insofar as they *explicitly* ex-press a mode of being not so expressed by the term "being" itself.

Metaphysics also shows that predicates may add to the concept of being in more than one way. First, there is the case of the predica-ments. The concept of substance does not add a difference to the con-cept of being by signifying something that is to be added to being.

Rather, it simply expresses a special *manner* of being that is different from the manner of being of the accidents. Second, there is the case of those concepts that express a *mode of being* that is common to *all* beings without exception. These latter concepts are known in the tradition as the transcendental concepts, the *transcendentals*. The notions "one," "something," "what is true," and "what is good" are transcendental notions because they fulfill these conditions. By "one," we mean to express that a being is undivided; "something" expresses that it is distinct from all other beings; "what is true" signifies that the being is taken in relation to the intellect, whereas "what is good" expresses a relation to the appetitive power.[3]

These few remarks may suffice to understand Kant's reference to the transcendental notions that his categories were meant to replace.

On Kant's Conception of the Transcendental — It is well known that Kant defines the concept of transcendentality in more than one way, and these definitions are not easily combined with each other.[4] Each definition, taken separately, seems perfectly clear; yet if one compares the various definitions given, it becomes clear that Kant may not have been as certain as the isolated individual definitions seem to suggest.

Boehm has shown that if one compares the statements about the meaning of the term "transcendental" that Kant formulated between 1772 in a letter to Marcus Herz and the final definition of the term in the second edition of the *Critique of Pure Reason,* it is clear that not all of these claims can be brought into harmony with each other.[5] It is reasonable to assume that originally Kant was not totally clear about the precise nature of the transcendental kind of knowledge he had discovered. Let me give just a few examples to justify Boehm's claim. In his letter to Herz mentioned above, Kant wrote that he was searching for the sources of our intellectual knowledge because he was in the process of determining the nature as well as the limits of metaphysics. To succeed in this difficult task, he had to divide metaphysics into different sections and then to try "to bring transcendental philosophy, i.e., all the concepts of the pure understanding, into a limited number of categories."[6] Transcendental philosophy is here thus defined as the philosophical discipline that is concerned with all the *concepts of the pure understanding.* The sources of all our intellectual understanding must be found in these basic concepts.

In the first edition of the *Critique of Pure Reason* (1781), Kant wrote: "I entitle transcendental all knowledge which is occupied not so much with objects as with our a priori concepts of objects in general. A system of such concepts might be entitled transcendental philosophy" (A 12). Transcendental philosophy thus presents a system of concepts that here are called simply *"concepts a priori";* these concepts a priori are said to be concepts of *"objects in general."*

In the *Prolegomena* of 1783, Kant made the observation that "the word 'transcendental' . . . does not signify something passing beyond all experience, but something that indeed precedes it a priori, but that is intended simply *to make knowledge of experience possible.* If these conceptions overstep experience, their employment is termed transcendent . . ."[7]

In the second edition of the first *Critique,* Kant reformulated the definition of the transcendental given in the first edition (A 11–12) to read as follows: "I entitle transcendental all knowledge which is concerned not so much with objects as with *the mode of our knowledge of objects,* insofar as this mode of knowledge is to be possible a priori" (B 25). One should note here that in this definition, no explicit use is made of the term "concept," even though the next sentence defines transcendental philosophy as the system of such concepts. Furthermore, transcendental knowledge is defined here for the first time as *knowledge of knowledge,* not of every kind of knowledge but rather of the possible knowledge a priori of objects in general. Before 1787, Kant called *all* knowledge that is concerned with the possible knowledge a priori of objects transcendental knowledge; here, Kant claims that transcendental knowledge has to do with the possibility of a *particular type of knowledge.* Further, he opposes transcendental philosophy as ontology to the physiology of pure reason:

> The former treats only of the understanding and of reason, in a system of concepts and principles which relate to objects in general, but takes no account of objects that may be given (*ontologia*); the latter treats of nature, that is, of the sum total of given objects (whether given to the senses or to some other kind of intuition), and is therefore *physiologia,* although only *rationalis.* (B 873)

Transcendental philosophy is here thus called "ontology" if it is taken as a system *of all concepts and principles* that relate to all objects in general, irrespective of any transcendental philosophy as the system of these concepts.

In the second edition of the first *Critique,* Kant also adds an idea never explicitly mentioned before. He writes:

> In the transcendental philosophy of the ancients there is included yet another chapter containing pure concepts of the understanding which, though not enumerated among the categories, must, in their view, be ranked as a priori concepts of objects. This, however, would amount to an increase in the

> number of the categories, and is therefore not feasible. They
> are propounded in the proposition, so famous among School-
> men, *quodlibet ens est unum, verum, bonum.* (B 113)

Kant thus knew that there is a connection of analogous intentions
between his transcendental philosophy and the ancient doctrine
concerning the transcendentals, that is, classical ontology.

In his *Über die Fortschritte der Metaphysik* (1791), Kant explicitly wrote in this connection that *ontology* is that science, that part of
metaphysics, which develops a system of all concepts and principles
of the understanding, but only insofar as they pertain to the objects
that are given by the senses and thus can be verified by experience.
Ontology, as the entrance hall of metaphysics proper, is called *transcendental philosophy* because it contains the conditions and the
first elements of all our knowledge a priori.[8]

Even if we limit ourselves to Kant's final view on the meaning of
the term "transcendental," it is not easy to define its meaning unam-
biguously. When he introduces the term for the first time in the second edition of the first *Critique,* he writes: "I call transcendental all
knowledge which is occupied not so much with objects as with *the
mode of our knowledge of objects,* insofar as this mode of knowledge
is to be possible a priori" (B 25). Yet the term is not exclusively used
for a certain way of knowing objects. Kant also speaks of "transcendental deduction," "transcendental negation," "the transcendental
employment of faculties," and "transcendental hypotheses." Usually
he immediately explains what the term "transcendental" means in a
given expression.

When he introduces the term "transcendental logic," for example, he explains that this kind of logic is concerned with the origin, scope, and objective validity of that kind of knowledge in which
we think objects entirely a priori because—unlike general logic,
which has to deal with both empirical and pure knowledge of reason—it concerns itself with the laws of our understanding and of
reason solely insofar as they relate to a priori knowledge (B 81–82).
The term "a priori" is used to qualify knowledge that is independent
of experience and even "of all impressions of the senses" (B 2). A
priori modes of knowledge are entitled "pure" when there is no admixture of anything empirical (B 3). Thus in Kant's opinion, not every kind of knowledge that is a priori can be called transcendental,
but only that kind by which we know that, and also how, certain concepts or intuitions can be employed or are possible purely a priori.
Thus the term "transcendental" signifies such knowledge as concerns the a priori possibility of knowledge, or its a priori employment (B 80–81). Transcendental aesthetics is called transcendental
because it shows that our intuitions of space and time are pure. The

transcendental exposition of a concept is the explanation of a concept as a principle from which the possibility of other a priori synthetic knowledge can be understood. The transcendental deduction of the categories is the explanation of the manner in which they can relate a priori to objects.

It is not easy to bring the various ways in which Kant uses the expression "transcendental" together in one brief description or definition. Yet generally speaking, one could say that in expressions such as "transcendental affirmation," "transcendental negation," and "transcendental hypothesis," the term is always meant in a sense that would be relevant only in a transcendental conception of knowledge such that, in the latter case, the term is taken as Kant defined it in his *Critique,* B 25.

Husserl's Reformulation of the Meaning of the Transcendental — Husserl uses the terms "transcendental phenomenology" and "transcendental philosophy" quite regularly without, however, carefully defining their meaning. Only on a few occasions does he give us a hint as to how the term is to be understood. In *Ideas,* he writes: "In its purely eidetic attitude 'excluding' every sort of transcendence, on its own peculiar basis of pure consciousness, phenomenology necessarily arrives at this entire complex of *transcendental problems in the specific sense,* and *on that account* deserves the name *transcendental phenomenology*" (*Ideas,* 1:209). In the same work, Husserl spells out the meaning of the expression in greater detail,[9] yet this further explanation does not at all eliminate ambiguities or clarify legitimate questions one might have. One thing is clear, though: for Husserl, transcendental phenomenology concerns itself with transcendental problems insofar as, on its own peculiar basis of pure consciousness, phenomenology in its pure eidetic attitude excludes every sort of transcendence.

Although the term "transcendent" was used quite often in his earlier works, the term "transcendental" appears there only rarely and is never carefully defined. This changes after 1915, when Husserl began to occupy himself more and more with the philosophy of Kant and German idealism. In the works of the twenties, the term appears regularly; Husserl then speaks of such concepts as "transcendental reduction," "transcendental subjectivity," "transcendental ego," and "transcendental constitution." When he makes an effort to explain the meaning of "transcendental," he continues to refer to the meaning of the expression "transcendent." Yet he then immediately adds that these terms are to be understood exclusively from phenomenology's own situation. To clarify their meaning, Husserl merely mentions that, just as the reduced ego is not a piece of the world, so, conversely, neither the world nor any worldly object is a piece of my ego, to be found in my conscious life as a really inherent part of it. This "transcendence" is part of the intrinsic meaning of anything that belongs to the world, despite the fact that anything that belongs to the world necessarily acquires all the meaning determining it, along with its ontological status, exclusively from my experiencing, my objectivating, thinking, valuing, or doing; the status of an evidently valid being is one that it can acquire only from my own evidences, my grounding acts. If this "transcendence," which consists in being nonreally included in consciousness, is part of the intrinsic meaning of the world, then by way of contrast, the ego itself, which bears in itself the world as an accepted meaning and which thus is necessarily presupposed by this meaning, is legitimately called *transcendental* in the phenomenological sense of the term (*Cart. Med.,* 26 [65]).

Later, Husserl returns to the issue in *Crisis* and relates his use of the term to that of the tradition since Kant. He says there that the expression "transcendental philosophy" has been used often since Kant, particularly for types of philosophy deeply influenced by Kant.

> I myself use the term transcendental *in the broadest sense* for the original motif . . . which through Descartes confers meaning upon all modern philosophies, the motif which, in all of them, . . . seeks to attain the genuine and pure form of its task and its systematic development. It is the motif of inquiring back into the ultimate source of all formations of knowledge, the motif of the knower's reflecting upon himself and his knowing life in which all the scientific structures that are valid for him occur purposefully, are stored up as acquisitions and have become and continue to become freely available. Working itself out radically, it is the motif of a universal philosophy which is grounded purely in this source and thus ultimately grounded. This source bears the title *I-myself,* with all of my actual and possible knowing life and, ultimately, my concrete life in general. The whole transcendental set of problems circles around the relation of *this,* my "I"—the "ego"—to what it is at first taken for granted to be—my soul—and, again, around the relation of this ego and my conscious life to the *world* of which I am conscious and whose true being I know through my own cognitive structures. (*Crisis,* 97–98 [100–101])

Husserl is of the opinion that this notion cannot be justified by means of an appeal to historical texts. It is a notion that is at work in all modern philosophies and also guides his own way of thinking. The description given is obviously still provisional and to be made concrete in the rest of *Crisis* (*Crisis,* 98 [101]).

From this description, it is clear that Husserl understands the transcendental character of his philosophy mainly in terms of

Descartes's search for a *fundamentum inconcussum,* and not primarily in terms of Kant's concern with the nature and limits of finite knowledge. Furthermore, Husserl limits the meaning of the term to a theory of knowledge that is transcendentally motivated; yet what he actually claims about this theory is so general that his determination fits almost any theory of knowledge. Husserl also posits that any theory of knowledge that considers the *ego* itself to be the last and pure source of all knowledge and its contents is without further ado also a universal philosophy that has an ultimate foundation. Finally, Husserl suggests that he has presented us here with a delineation of the entire transcendental problematic.

I NOTES

1. See H.-D. Gardeil, *Initiation à la philosophie de S. Thomas d'Aquin,* vol. 4: *Métaphysique* (Paris: Éditions du Cerf, 1966), 71–89, 181–88; and James F. Anderson, *Introduction to the Metaphysics of St. Thomas Aquinas* (South Bend, Ind.: Regnery-Gateway, 1953), 44–98.

2. Aristotle, *Metaphysics,* 1.1052a15–1059a15.

3. Cf. St. Thomas Aquinas, *Quaestio disputata de veritate,* I, l, c.

4. For what follows, see Rudolf Boehm, "Omlijning van een nieuw begrip van transcendentaalfilosofie," *Tijdschrift voor filosofie* 34 (1972): 407–33; and O. J. Duintjer, *De vraag naar het transcendentale, vooral in verband met Heidegger en Kant* (Leyden: Universitaire Press, 1966). See also the review of this book by R. Bakker in *Tijdschrift voor filosofie* 30 (1968): 366–74.

5. Boehm, "Omlijning van een nieuw begrip van transcendentaalfilosofie," 409–10.

6. Kant, *Werke,* ed. Hartenstein, 8.690–91, quoted by Boehm, "Omlijning van een nieuw begrip van transcendentaalfilosofie," 410.

7. Kant, *Prolegomena to Any Future Metaphysics,* trans. Lewis White Beck (Indianapolis, Ind.: Bobbs-Merrill), 122–23n.

8. Kant, *Werke,* 3:520.

9. Husserl, *Ideen,* 3:138–62.

Text

9. Die transzendental-phänomenologische Reduktion und der transcendentale Schein der Verdoppelung

"Wir" sollten also doppelt sein, psychologisch als wir Menschen Vorhandenheiten in der Welt, Subjekte seelischen Lebens und zugleich transzendental als die Subjekte eines transzendentalen weltkonstituierenden Lebens? Diese Doppelheit klärt sich durch evidente Aufweisung. Die seelische Subjektivität, das konkret gefaßte "ich" und "wir" der alltäglichen Rede, wird in ihrer reinen psychischen Eigenheit erfahren durch die Methode phänomenologisch-psychologischer Reduktion. In eidetischer Abwandlung schafft sie den Boden für die rein phänomenologische Psychologie. Die transzendentale Subjektivität, auf die im transzendentalen Problem hingefragt und die in ihm als Seinsboden vorausgesetzt ist, ist keine andere als wiederum "ich selbst" und "wir selbst", aber nicht als die wir uns in der natürlichen Einstellung des Alltags und der positiven Wissenschaft vorfinden, apperzipiert als Bestandstücke der für uns vorhandenen objektiven Welt: vielmehr als Subjekte des Bewußtseinslebens, *in* dem sich diese und alle Vorhandenheit—für "uns"—durch gewisse Apperzeptionen "macht". Als Menschen, seelisch wie leiblich in der Welt vorhanden, sind wir für "uns"; wir sind Erscheinendes eines sehr mannigfaltigen intentionalen Lebens, "unseres" Lebens, *worin* sich also dieses Vorhandene apperzeptiv mit seinem ganzen Sinnesgehalt "für uns" macht. Das vorhandene (apperzipierte) Ich und Wir setzt ein (apperzipierendes) Ich und Wir voraus, *für* das es vorhanden ist, das aber nicht selbst wieder im selben Sinn vorhanden ist. Zu dieser transzendentalen Subjektivität haben wir direkten Zugang durch eine transzendentale Erfahrung. Wie schon die seelische [293] Erfahrung zur Reinheit einer reduktiven Methode bedarf, so auch die transzendentale.

9. The Transcendental-Phenomenological Reduction and the Semblance of Transcendental Duplication

Are we then supposed to be dual beings—psychological{ly}, as human objectivities {things present} in the world, the subjects of psychic life, and at the same time transcendental{ly}, as the subjects of a transcendental, world-constituting life-process? This duality can be clarified through being demonstrated with self-evidence. The psychic subjectivity, the concretely grasped "I" and "we" of ordinary conversation, is experienced in its pure psychic ownness through the method of phenomenological-psychological reduction. Modified into eidetic form it provides the ground for pure phenomenological psychology. Transcendental subjectivity, which is inquired into in the transcendental problem, and which subjectivity is presupposed in it as an existing basis, is none other than again "I myself" and "we ourselves"; not, however, as found in the natural attitude of everyday or of positive science; *i.e.*, apperceived as components of the objectively present world before us, but rather as subjects of conscious life, *in* which this world and all that is present—for "us"—"makes" itself through certain apperceptions. As men, mentally as well as bodily present in the world, we are for "ourselves"; we are appearances standing within an extremely variegated intentional life-process, "our" life, *in which* this being on hand constitutes itself "for us" apperceptively, with its entire sense-content. The (apperceived) I and we on hand presuppose an (apperceiving) I and we, *for* which they are on hand, which, however, is not itself present again in the same sense. To this transcendental subjectivity we have direct access through a transcendental experience; just as the psychic experience requires a reductive method for purity, so does the transcendental.

Wir wollen hier so vorgehen, daß wir die *"transzendentale Reduktion"* einführen als aufgestuft auf die psychologische Reduktion, als eine weitere an dieser jederzeit zu vollziehende Reinigung und abermals mittels einer gewissen Epoché. Diese ist eine bloße Konsequenz der universalen Epoché, welche zum Sinn der transzendentalen Frage gehört. Fordert die transzendentale Relativität jeder möglichen Welt deren universale "Einklammerung", so fordert sie auch die der reinen Seelen und der auf sie bezogenen rein phänomenologischen Psychologie. Dadurch verwandeln sich diese in transzendentale Phänomene. Während also der Psychologe innerhalb der für ihn natürlich geltenden Welt die vorkommende Subjektivität auf die rein seelische Subjektivität—in der Welt—reduziert, reduziert der transzendentale Phänomenologe durch seine absolut universale Epoché diese psychologisch reine auf die transzendental reine Subjektivität, auf diejenige, welche die Weltapperzeption und darin die objektivierende Apperzeption "Seele animalischer Realitäten" vollzieht und in sich in Geltung setzt. Z.B. meine jeweiligen reinen Wahrnehmungserlebnisse, Phantasieerlebnisse usw. sind psychologische Gegebenheiten der psychologischen inneren Erfahrung in der Einstellung der Positivität. Sie verwandeln sich in meine transzendentalen Erlebnisse, wenn ich die Welt, mein Menschsein inbegriffen, durch radikale Epoché als bloßes Phänomen setze und nun dem intentionalen Leben nachgehe, worin die gesamte Apperzeption "der" Welt, im besonderen die Apperzeption meiner Seele, meiner psychologisch realen Wahrnehmungserlebnisse usw. sich gestaltet. Der Gehalt dieser Erlebnisse, ihr Eigenwesentliches bleibt dabei voll erhalten, wenn schon er nun sichtlich ist als Kern einer vordem psychologisch immer wieder betätigten aber nicht in Rechnung gezogenen Apperzeption. Für den Transzendentalphilosophen, der durch einen vorausgehenden universalen Willensentschluß in sich die feste Habitualität der transzendentalen "Einklammerung" gestiftet hat, ist auch diese in der natürlichen Einstellung nie fehlende Verweltlichung des Bewußtseins ein für allemal unterbunden. Demgemäß ergibt für ihn die konsequente Bewußtseinsreflexion immer wieder transzendental Reines, und zwar anschaulich [294] in der Weise einer neuartigen, der *transzendentalen "inneren" Erfahrung.* Aus der methodischen transzendentalen Epoché entsprungen, eröffnet sie das endlose transzendentale Seinsfeld. Es ist die Parallele zum endlosen psychologischen Feld, sowie seine Zugangsmethode die Parallele ist zur rein psychologischen, derjenigen der psychologisch-phänomenologischen Reduktion. Und wieder ebenso ist das transzendentale Ich und die transzendentale Ichgemeinschaft, gefaßt in der vollen Konkretion des transzendentalen

We would like to proceed here by introducing the *transcendental reduction* as built on the psychological reduction—as an additional part of the purification which can be performed on it any time, a purification that is once more by means of a certain epoche. This is merely a consequence of the all-embracing epoche which belongs to the sense of the transcendental question. If the transcendental relativity of every possible world demands an all-embracing bracketing, it also postulates the bracketing of pure psyches and the pure phenomenological psychology related to them. Through this bracketing they are transformed into transcendental phenomena. Thus, while the psychologist, operating within what for him is the naturally accepted world, reduces to pure psychic subjectivity the subjectivity occurring there (but still within the world), the transcendental phenomenologist, through his absolutely all-embracing epoche, reduces this psychologically pure element to transcendental pure subjectivity, [*i.e.,*] to that which performs and posits within itself the apperception of the world and therein the objectivating apperception of a "psyche [belonging to] animal realities." For example, my actual current mental processes of pure perception, phantasy, and so forth, are, in the attitude of positivity, psychological givens [or data] of psychological inner experience. They are transmuted into my transcendental mental processes if through a radical epoche I posit as mere phenomena the world, including my own human existence, and now follow up the intentional life-process wherein the entire apperception "of" the world, and in particular the apperception of my mind, my psychologically real perception-processes, and so forth, are formed. The content of these processes, what is included in their own essences, remains in this fully preserved, although it is now visible as the core of an apperception practiced again and again psychologically but not previously considered. For the transcendental philosopher, who through a previous all-inclusive resolve of his will has instituted in himself the firm habituality of the transcendental "bracketing," even this "mundanization" [*Verweltlichung,* treating everything as part of the world] of consciousness which is omnipresent in the natural attitude is inhibited once and for all. Accordingly, the consistent reflection on consciousness yields him time after time transcendentally pure data, and more particularly it is intuitive in the mode of a new kind of experience, *transcendental "inner" experience*. Arisen out of the methodical transcendental epoche, this new kind of "inner" experience opens up the limitless transcendental field of being. This field of being is the parallel to the limitless psychological field, and the method of access [to its data] is the parallel to the purely psychological one, *i.e.*, to the psychological-phenomenological reduction. And again, the transcendental I [or

Lebens, die transzendentale Parallele zum Ich und Wir im ge-
wöhnlichen und psychologischen Sinn, wieder konkret gefaßt als
Seele und Seelengemeinschaft mit dem zugehörigen psychologischen Bewußtseinsleben. Mein transzendentales Ich ist also
evident "verschieden" vom natürlichen Ich, aber keineswegs als
ein zweites, als ein davon *getrenntes* im natürlichen Wortsinn, wie
umgekehrt auch keineswegs ein in natürlichem Sinne damit
verbundenes oder mit ihm verflochtenes. Es ist eben das (in voller
Konkretion gefaßte) Feld der transzendentalen Selbsterfahrung,
die jederzeit *durch bloße Änderung der Einstellung* in psychologische Selbsterfahrung zu wandeln ist. In diesem Übergang stellt
sich notwendig eine Identität des Ich her; in transzendentaler
Reflexion auf ihn wird die psychologische Objektivierung als
Selbstobjektivierung des transzendentalen Ich sichtlich, und so
findet es sich als wie es in jedem Moment natürlicher Einstellung
sich eine Apperzeption auferlegt hat. Ist der Parallelismus der
transzendentalen und psychologischen Erfahrungssphären als
eine Art Identität des Ineinander des Seinssinnes aus bloßer
Einstellungsänderung verständlich geworden, so auch die daraus
sich ergebende Folge des gleichen Parallelismus und des im
Ineinander *implicite* Beschlossenseins der transzendentalen und
der psychologischen Phänomenologie, deren volles Thema die
doppelsinnige reine Intersubjektivität ist. Es ist dabei nur in
Rechnung zu ziehen, daß die rein-seelische Intersubjektivität,
sowie sie der transzendentalen Epoché unterworfen wird, ebenfalls
zu ihrer Parallele, der transzendentalen Intersubjektivität führt.
Offenbar besagt der Parallelismus nichts weniger als theoretische
Gleichwertigkeit. Die transzendentale Intersubjektivität ist der
konkret eigenständige absolute Seinsboden, aus dem alles Tran-
szendente (darunter [295] alles real weltlich Seiende) seinen
Seinssinn schöpft als Sein eines in bloß relativem und damit
unvollständigem Sinne Seienden, als den einer intentionalen
Einheit, die in Wahrheit ist aus transzendentaler Sinngebung,
einstimmiger Bewährung und wesensmäßig zugehöriger Habitualität bleibender Überzeugung.

ego] and the transcendental community of egos, conceived in the full concretion of transcendental life are the transcendental parallel to the I and we in the customary and psychological sense, concretely conceived as mind and community of minds, with the psychological life of consciousness that pertains to them. My transcendental ego is thus evidently "different" from the natural ego, but by no means as a second, as one *separated* from it in the natural sense of the word, just as on the contrary it is by no means bound up with it or intertwined with it, in the usual sense of these words. It is just the field of transcendental self-experience (conceived in full concreteness) which in every case can, *through mere alteration of attitude,* be changed into psychological self-experience. In this transition, an identity of the I is necessarily brought about; in transcendental reflection on this transition the psychological objectivation becomes visible as self-objectivation of the transcendental I, and so it is as if in every moment of the natural attitude the I finds itself with an apperception imposed upon it. If the parallelism of the transcendental and psychological experience-spheres has become comprehensible out of a mere alteration of attitude, as a kind of identity of the complex interpenetration of senses of being, then there also becomes intelligible the consequence that results from it, namely the same parallelism and the interpenetration of transcendental and psychological phenomenology implied in that interpenetration, whose whole theme is pure intersubjectivity, in its dual sense. Only that in this case it has to be taken into account that the purely psychic intersubjectivity, as soon as it is subjected to the transcendental epoche, also leads to its parallel, that is, to transcendental intersubjectivity. Manifestly this parallelism spells nothing less than theoretical equivalence. Transcendental intersubjectivity is the concretely autonomous absolute existing basis [*Seinsboden*] out of which everything transcendent (and, with it, everything that belongs to the real world) obtains its existential sense as that of something which only in a relative and therewith incomplete sense is an existing thing, namely as being an intentional unity which in truth exists from out of transcendental bestowal of sense, of harmonious confirmation, and from an habituality of lasting conviction that belongs to it by essential necessity.

I Synopsis

Husserl begins this section with an important question: Are we then supposed to be twofold, (1) psychologically seen as human things present in the real world, the subjects of psychic life, and (2) transcendentally seen as the subjects of a transcendental, world-constituting life? This duality can, in his view, be clarified and shown with evidence.

The psychic subject, the concretely grasped "I" or "we" taken in the ordinary way of speaking, can be experienced in its own psychic ownness through the method of the phenomenological reduction. Eidetically modified through eidetic intuition, it provides the ground for *pure* phenomenological psychology. Transcendental subjectivity, on the other hand, on which the transcendental problem focuses and which, in the formulation of that problem, is presupposed as the foundation of its being, is again none other than "I myself" or "we ourselves"; not however, as found in the natural attitude of our everyday life or as found in the positive sciences—that is, apperceived as components of the world of objects that are present to us—but rather as subjects of conscious life in which this world and all that is present in it "constitutes" itself for us through certain apperceptions. As human beings, in body and soul present in the world, we are before "us"; we are appearing entities of a very variegated life, "our" life, in which this being present at hand constitutes itself "for us" apperceptively, with its entire meaning-content. The apperceived "I" or "we," which is present to us, presupposes an apperceiving "I" or "we," for which it is present at hand; yet it is not itself present to itself in the same sense. We have direct access to this transcendental subject through a transcendental experience. Just as the psychic experience requires a reduction in order to be pure, so does the transcendental.

Husserl says that he prefers in this section to introduce the transcendental reduction as built upon the psychological reduction, as an additional part of the purification process that can be performed on it. This second purification again requires a certain *epoche,* but this *epoche* is merely a consequence of the all-embracing *epoche* that belongs to the meaning of the transcendental question. In view of the fact that in the transcendental attitude the relativity of any possible world in regard to the transcendental subject requires that any possible world be put between brackets, this relativity requires also that the pure souls, and the phenomenological psychology that makes them its theme of investigation, be bracketed. The souls, as well as pure psychology, change in this manner into transcendental phenomena. Thus, whereas the psychologist, who works within the world of the natural attitude, reduces the subject occurring there to a pure psychic subject, but in so doing still remains within the world, the transcendental phenomenologist, through the all-embracing transcendental reduction, reduces this psychological subject to transcendental pure subjectivity. This is the subjectivity that performs and posits within itself the apperception of the world and therein also the objectifying apperception called "souls of animals, real things." For example, my pure experiences of perception, of phantasy, and so forth are, in the attitude of a positive science, such as phenomenological psychology, psychological data of psychological inner experience. They change into my transcendental experiences if, through a radical *epoche,* I posit as mere phenomenon the world, including me as a human being, and now examine that intentional life wherein the entire apperception of the world, and particularly the apperception of my psychologically real perceptual experiences, become formed.

The content of these experiences, what is included in their own essences as such, remains fully preserved herein, although it now manifests itself only as the core of an apperception that was practiced again and again psychologically, but previously never taken into consideration. In the natural attitude, the mundanization of consciousness is unavoidable. For the transcendental philosopher who has decided once and for all to maintain the transcendental reduction, such a mundanization is prohibited once and for all.

Accordingly, the consistent reflection on consciousness provides the transcendental philosopher time and again with data that are transcendentally pure and given intuitively in the form of a new kind of experience called transcendental experience. Arisen out of the transcendental reduction, this new kind of "inner" experience opens up for the philosopher the limitless transcendental field of being. This field of being is parallel to the limitless field of meaning of phenomenological psychology; and the transcendental reduction runs parallel to the phenomenological reduction of psychology. And finally the transcendental "I," or the transcendental community of egos, are parallel to the "I" and the "we" one encounters in phenomenological psychology.

My transcendental ego is thus evidently "different" from the natural and mundane ego, but it is by no means a second ego separated from the natural ego. The field of transcendental self-experience in every case can be changed into that of the psychological self-experience through a mere alteration of attitude. In the transition from the one attitude to the other, the identity of the "I" is necessarily brought about.

What has been said here about transcendental subjectivity and psychological subjectivity holds good also for the transcendental and psychological intersubjectivities. In other words, if we turn to pure intersubjectivity, taken in its dual sense, we shall find the same parallel. As soon as the purely psychological intersubjectivity of pure psychology is subjected to the transcendental reduction, it immediately leads to its parallel, transcendental intersubjectivity. The latter parallelism means nothing less than *theoretical equivalence.*

Transcendental intersubjectivity is the concretely autonomous, *absolute* basis of all meaning and being out of which *everything transcendent,* and thus everything that belongs to the real world, obtains the meaning of its being. Since the meaning of every transcendent being is constituted by transcendental intersubjectivity, each transcendent being appears to be a being that only is in a *merely relative* and incomplete sense; it is the meaning of an intentional unity that in truth only is through the transcendental bestowal of meaning and subsequently through a harmonious confirmation and lasting, habitual convictions that belong to it by essential necessity.

In this rich and complicated section, Husserl touches on a number of important issues. In the commentary, I shall focus on the following themes: (1) the meaning of "transcendental reduction," (2) absolute, pure consciousness as the theme of transcendental phenomenology, (3) the difference between natural and transcendental reflection, and (4) the doctrinal content of the transcendental reduction. What Husserl says about the relationship between the phenomenological and transcendental reductions will be discussed in Chapter Nine, and his conception of intersubjectivity will be dealt with in Chapter Ten.

Commentary

The Transcendental Reduction

We have already seen that at first Husserl did not make an explicit distinction between the phenomenological and the transcendental reduction.[1] Only when he began to concern himself with phenomenological psychology did it become clear to him that such a distinction would be necessary and that a transcendental reduction was thus to be added to the phenomenological reduction. The phenomenological reduction is essential for phenomenological psychology, whereas the transcendental reduction is constitutive for transcendental phenomenology.[2]

What is to be understood by the transcendental reduction can be explained in more than one way, and Husserl himself used several of them. Sometimes he employs the "Cartesian way" to explain what transcendental reduction is; sometimes he begins in phenome-

nological psychology and proceeds from there to transcendental phenomenology by means of a process of further radicalization; sometimes he explains the reduction from the perspective of the world in
which we live. The Cartesian way was used in the first volume of
Ideas as well as in *Cartesian Meditations*. The road from phenomenological psychology is described in the *Encyclopaedia* article, the
"Amsterdam Lectures," and *Crisis*. The road from the life-world was
used in *Crisis*. The merits and limits of these approaches have been
discussed at length in the second volume of *Erste Philosophie,* where
the editor in his introduction also discusses other approaches that
Husserl contemplated (*E. Phil.,* 2:xii–xlii, particularly xxx–xlii).

Generally speaking, Husserl understands by the transcendental reduction that methodical procedure by means of which we suspend judgment in regard to everything that is not apodictically
evident or that cannot be made apodictically evident with the help of
phenomenological methods. This procedure ultimately leaves nothing but the absolute, transcendental subjectivity that in and
through its transcendental experiences is the ultimate source of the
meaning and being of all that is.

In the Cartesian way, Husserl begins by explaining that transcendental phenomenology must be a genuine science. Genuine science in the most radical sense of the term must rest on basic insights
that are apodictically evident. An evidence is apodictic if it excludes
not only every doubt and every possible doubt but also the absolute
unimaginableness of the relevant situation's nonbeing. Where there
is apodictic evidence, there cannot be any doubt. Apodicticity can be
achieved by adequate and inadequate evidences. An evidence is inadequate if there are components of meaning in the experience that
are still expected and anticipated without having been explicitly fulfilled. If one wants to make such an evidence more perfect, one must
start a methodical process that can fulfill these anticipated meanings. The experience comes to perfection when adequate evidence
has been achieved. One could say that Husserl's demand for apodictic evidence in phenomenology corresponds to Descartes's principle of absolute indubitability in first philosophy. Yet it should
immediately be added that where Descartes demands a radical methodical doubt, Husserl asks for a transcendental reduction that
does not imply any doubt, whether methodical or otherwise (*Cart.
Med.,* 9–16 [50–57]).

We must now ask whether and how a demand for apodicticity
can help us find an acceptable starting point for transcendental phenomenology. We need (1) evidences that are *first* and thus precede
all other imaginable evidences, since otherwise they would not be
first principles, and (2) evidences that are *strictly apodictic,* since

otherwise they would not be providing us with the radical foundation we are seeking. If such evidences were still to be inadequate, they must at least possess a recognizable apodictic content and give us something that is firmly confirmed and secured once and for all, absolutely (*Cart. Med.,* 16 [56–57]).

One is inclined to believe that the question of evidences that are first in themselves and apodictically evident can be answered rather easily: Does not the existence of the world present itself immediately as such an evidence? For the existence of the world is presupposed in all of our prescientific and scientific actions. If we think about the issue carefully, however, we shall see that the evidence of the world's existence is not apodictic; furthermore, its evidence is not absolutely primary, either. That the evidence of the world's existence is not apodictic is clear from the fact that the nonbeing of the world is neither impossible nor inconceivable. The existence of the world may perhaps later become a primary evidence, but only after its evidence has been critically examined in regard to validity and range. As things stand now, the being of the world cannot simply be taken for granted. We can hold on to it only as a phenomenon that has validity, as *a phenomenon that claims to have actuality* (*Cart. Med.,* 17–18 [57–58]).

But, if we put the entire world between brackets and reduce it to a large set of phenomena, is there then anything left for us on which we can build transcendental phenomenology? Does philosophy as a whole not come to a halt if one tries to begin in this manner? But what if there were to be a being that is intrinsically prior to the world and functions as the basis for the existence of the world? Husserl suggests at this point that we follow Descartes in his turn to the ego. If we make the reversal in the proper manner, we shall be led to transcendental subjectivity. The proper turn to the *ego cogito* is the ultimate and apodictically certain basis for all our judgments; on this foundation, any radical philosophy can be grounded because the reduction leads to apodictic insights insofar as it shows apodictically that the being of the transcendental ego is antecedent to the being of the world (*Cart. Med.,* 18n.3).

After we perform the reduction and bracket the entire world, we, as radically reflecting philosophers, have neither a world nor a science left. Instead of being accepted naturally by us in its existence, the world is now for us only something that claims to be actual. With the world, all intramundane beings, including all human beings and animals, are affected, as is our social and cultural life and their respective correlates. The entire life-world is from now on for us only a *phenomenon of being,* a *Seinsphänomen.*

Regardless of its ontologic status after the reduction has been performed, the world as phenomenon is not nothing. Even if I do not accept the actual being of the experienced world, this abstaining from making a commitment is still what it is, and it exists, together with the entire stream of experiences that constitute my life. Moreover, this life is continually there for me. Taken as a field of the present, it is given to me continually in perception, with the most originary originality as it itself. In memory I can make present certain aspects of it that already have been present so that now these and now other parts of the world are given to consciousness.

In reflecting, I can at any time look at this original living and note certain particular things and grasp what is present as present and what is past as past. And I do this now as the ego who philosophizes while exercising the transcendental reduction. Meanwhile, the world that is experienced in my reflectively grasped life goes on being for me as a phenomenon, but experienced as before, and experienced with the same content. The only difference is that, as radically reflecting philosopher, I take the world merely as a phenomenon (*Cart. Med.,* 18–20 [58–60]).

The same is true for all the processes of meaning that belong to the stream of my entire life in addition to the processes in which I experience the world: the nonintuitive processes in which objects are meant, the processes of seeking ends, selecting means, and all other activities. But in all these cases, too, the reduction is to be applied; I cannot take any position in regard to the actual being of the objects meant. All of this, too, is to be taken only *as a mere phenomenon.*

Thus the putting out of action of all positions in regard to the existence of the world and of the human beings and the things found in it does not leave me empty-handed. Through this process, we also acquire access to our own pure living, with all the processes and activities that make up my pure living and with everything intended and meant in them; I am thus still left with the entire universe of all phenomena in the phenomenological sense of the term. Through the *epoche* and reduction, I apprehend myself purely, as ego, as having this conscious life, as having the entire objective world. All of this now exists for me as it is, precisely as it is for me. Anything belonging to the world exists for me in that I experience it. The entire world is for me nothing else but the world existing for me, accepted by me in and through my conscious acts. It received its entire meaning and its acceptance as existing exclusively from my cogitations.

In these cogitations, my entire "world-life" goes on, including my philosophical life. By my living and experiencing, I can enter no world other than the one that gets its meaning and acceptance in and from me. If I put myself above this entire life and refrain from all believing that takes the world as actually existing, if I thus direct my glance exclusively to this life itself, taken as consciousness of the world, I acquire at the same time myself as the pure ego with the pure stream of my cogitations.

Thus the being of the pure ego is antecedent to the natural being of the world; and the same is true for my pure cogitations. Natural being is a realm whose ontological status is secondary; it continually presupposes the realm of transcendental being. The subject that is brought to light by the transcendental reduction is rightly called transcendental subjectivity (*Cart. Med.*, 20–21 [60–61]).

Absolute Consciousness as the Theme of Transcendental Phenomenology

The Apodictic Evidence of the Transcendental Experiences of Transcendental Subjectivity — We have seen that for Husserl phenomenology cannot possibly be a genuinely radical philosophy if it cannot give a definitive foundation to its claims on the basis of primordial insights and principles that are apodictically evident. The investigation of the meaning and function of the transcendental reduction led to the insight that transcendental subjectivity is the ultimate source of all meaning and being of all that is. But this means that the transcendental experiences of transcendental subjectivity must be apodictically evident if they are to serve as the basis for apodictic judgments. It is therefore appropriate to ask: Does the transcendental reduction make possible apodictic evidence of the being of transcendental subjectivity? And what is the range covered by this apodictic evidence? As we have seen, undoubtedly there is apodicticity in the proposition "I am." However, the problem of the range covered by our apodictic evidence remains urgent, for undeniable self-experience offers only a nucleus that is *immediately* experienced with strict adequacy, namely, the ego's living present, while beyond this living present an indeterminately general presumptive horizon extends that comprises that which, strictly speaking, is not experienced but is necessarily "also-meant." The *implicit* presumption in the apodictic evidence of the *cogito* is subject, therefore, to critique with respect to the possibilities of its fulfillment and their range.

We have seen that adequacy and apodicticity of evidence do not have to go together. But even then, the following questions remain: To what extent can the transcendental ego be deceived about itself and its own life? And to what extent does it have components that are absolutely indubitable (*Cart. Med.*, 22–23 [61–63])?

In the wake of Descartes, it seems easy to grasp the pure ego and its cogitations. Nevertheless, his ideas contain several prejudices and much Scholasticism. Influenced by his admiration for the mathematical and natural sciences, he could easily fall for the prejudice that in the *"ego cogito"* one is dealing with an apodictic axiom which, together with other axioms, can serve as the basis for a deductively explanatory science patterned on geometry. Moreover, Descartes thought that in our apodictic pure ego we have saved a little remnant of the world, leaving us only with the problem of inferring and deducing the rest of the world from it through correctly conducted arguments based on our innate principles. In this way, the ego became a "thinking substance" and the starting point for inferences based on the principle of causality. In this manner, Descartes became the father of an absurd transcendental realism.

We can escape all these prejudices if we remain true to the principle of pure intuition and accept nothing but that which we find actually given in the field of pure consciousness (*Cart. Med.,* 23–25 [63–64]).

The Psychological and the Transcendental Egos — It is true, Husserl says, that the reduction leaves me and my life untouched in their existential status, regardless of whether or not the world exists. But we must emphasize here again that this ego with its life, which necessarily remains for me after the reduction, is *not itself a part of the world.* As apperceived in natural experience, I am a theme of positive and objective science—the psychic life, for instance, considered by psychology, is taken as psychical life in the world. However, for me, the meditating ego, who in the attitude of the transcendental reduction posits itself exclusively as the basis upon which all objective acceptances and their objective bases are accepted, there is no longer any psychological ego or any psychical phenomena.

Thus by the transcendental reduction I reduce my natural human ego and my psychic life to my transcendental-phenomenological ego, the realm of transcendental-phenomenological self-experience. The objective world, the only world that can ever exist for me, this world with all its objects, derives the entire meaning and existential status that it has for me from me as the transcendental ego. And this ego discloses itself only through the transcendental-phenomenological reduction.

The concepts "transcendental" and "transcendent," then, must be derived solely from our phenomenological attitude. Just as the transcendental ego is not a part of the world, so neither is the transcendent world a part of my ego. Its transcendence is essential to the intrinsic meaning of anything worldly, despite the fact that it is solely from my experiencing that anything worldly can acquire any meaning determining it. If this transcendence, which consists in being not really included in the ego, is essential to the intrinsic meaning of the world, then the ego itself, which contains within itself the world as an accepted meaning and which is necessarily presupposed by this meaning, is legitimately called transcendental, in the phenomenological sense of the term. Any philosophical problem arising from this correlation is said to be a transcendental-philosophical problem (*Cart. Med.*, 25–26 [64–65]).

A New Idea of Transcendental Grounding of Knowledge — In Husserl's view, we must still ask precisely what one can do with the transcendental ego. To answer this question, our meditating reflections require a development in a new direction.

We have seen that the transcendental ego is, in the order of knowing, prior to all objective being; in some sense, it is the basis and ground on which all objective knowledge ultimately rests. Thus the question here is not whether the ego is the ground, but rather in what sense it is the ground. What does grounding mean in this case?

Husserl states that he will not give up Descartes's basic idea and great discovery, even though he will try to avoid the fundamental mistakes that Descartes made in developing this idea in detail. He thus asks, Is it perhaps possible with the Cartesian discovery of the transcendental ego to disclose a new idea of the grounding of knowledge, namely, the idea of a transcendental grounding?

Thus, instead of following Descartes and attempting to use the *ego cogito* as an apodictically evident premise for arguments that allegedly imply some transcendent subject (namely, God), Husserl focuses on an infinite realm of being of a new kind that has been laid open by the transcendental reduction. This new realm of being is the sphere of a new kind of experience, transcendental experience, which demands a new type of science, transcendental phenomenology. What is left after the transcendental reduction is thus not a bare *ego cogito* but an *infinite realm of transcendental experiences* that constitute the life of transcendental subjectivity.

Furthermore, we still have to go from the concrete and actual to the universal and the possible with the help of the eidetic reduction or the method of free variation. On the basis of the two reductions mentioned, it will now be possible to construe an a priori science of the realm of the pure possibilities of the transcendental realm. Thus, instead of concerning ourselves methodically with actualities of the life of transcendental subjectivity, we must focus on its a priori possibilities, for these possibilities prescribe rules a priori for all actualities.

Yet there still remains a basic difficulty here: the apodictic evidence of the ego's existence is not necessarily also apodictic evidence for the existence of the manifold data of transcendental experience. Furthermore, the cogitations given to me as transcendental subject under the transcendental reduction cannot be claimed to be apodictic and absolutely indubitable with respect to their present and past existence. It is, however, possible to show that the absolute evidence of the *ego sum* necessarily extends into the manifold experiences of the self in which the ego's transcendental life and its habitual properties are given, even if in some cases there are limits that define the range of the relevant evidences; this is the case, for instance, with recollection and retention. Husserl formulates this as follows: "The bare identity of the 'I am' is not the only thing given as indubitable in transcendental experience of self. Rather there extends through all the particular data of actual and possible self-experience—even though they are not absolutely indubitable in every respect—a universal apodictically experienceable structure of the ego (for example, the immanent temporal form belonging to the stream of subjective processes)" (*Cart. Med.*, 28 [67]). Perhaps it can also be shown that the ego is apodictically predelineated for itself as a concrete ego that exists with a specific content made up of lived experiences, abilities, habitualities, and dispositions accessible to a possible self-experience that can be perfected and enriched without limit. All of this will have to be shown by detailed constitutional analyses. Phenomenology confronts us here with a quasi-infinite task (*Cart. Med.*, 27–29 [66–67]).

I Natural and Transcendental Reflection

Among the most general features pertaining to the essential structure of the pure sphere of experience, Husserl says, one has to consider reflection first of all. The reason is that reflection has a universal methodological function, since the phenomenological method proceeds entirely through acts of reflection. Let us begin by recapitulating what we already know and then seek to penetrate more profoundly into the matter by investigating that type of phenomenological study which is made both possible and necessary by reflection.

Every ego lives its own experiences, which include much that is real and intentional. The expression "it lives them" does not mean that it apprehends them explicitly after the manner of immanent experience. But it is ideally possible for every lived experience that is not explicitly included in the ego's glance to be apprehended by this glance. When this happens, a reflective act of the ego is directed toward this experience so that it becomes an object for the ego. Again, the reflections themselves are experiences and therefore can serve as the basis of new reflections, and so on to infinity.

The experience as really lived "now," as it first becomes the focal point of reflection, presents itself as really lived, as being "now." It presents itself also as "having just been" and, insofar as it was unnoticed, as "not reflected upon." In our natural attitude, we unthinkingly take it for granted that lived experiences do not exist only when we turn to grasp them in immanent experience and that, if in immanent reflection they are still objects of awareness as "having just been," then they were really existent and were really lived by us (*Ideas,* 1:174–75 [144–45]).

In continuing to clarify this idea, Husserl says, we are further convinced that that is also reflection which, in and on the basis of recollection, tells us about our former experiences that were "then" present, "then" immanently perceptible, although they were not immanently perceived. The same must be said, according to the naive natural view, for anticipation and foreseeing expectation. We have here first the immediate "protention," which is the exact counterpart of immediate retention. Next, we have the anticipation, which *re*produces in the more proper sense of the term and is the counterpart of recollection. In anticipation, what is intuitively expected—that to which one intends in foresight as "coming in the future"—has at the same time, due to possible reflection in anticipation, the meaning of something that will be perceived, just as the retrospectively remembered has the meaning of something that was perceived. Thus, in anticipation we can reflect also and become aware of our lived experiences as processes belonging to what was anticipated as such, even though in anticipation we are not focused on them—as we are whenever we say that we *shall see* what is coming when, on such occasions, our reflective seeing turns to the "coming" perceptive experience (*Ideas,* 1:175 [145–46]).

Let us now see what happens when we make use of the transcendental reduction. In the natural attitude we look upon the world as something that is already given as existing, even in our reflection, but in the transcendental reduction we give up this standpoint. The transcendental experience consists in this, that we look at and describe the particular "reduced" *cogito* but abstain from participating, as reflecting subjects, in the natural positing of existence by the original act of our natural ego. Moreover, we can transform every particular *cogito* into an example that illustrates an essential generality and make it our own within the framework of pure eidetic intuition.

In this way, Husserl emphasizes, we can examine all this from a phenomenological standpoint and even from an eidetic one, whether at a higher level of generality or at a level corresponding to the essential conditions proper to special types of experiences. The whole stream of experiences lived in the fashion of unreflecting consciousness, together with all its experiences as they occur in a reflectionally unmodified form, can thus be made the subject of a scientific study. This study and research should aim at systematic completeness and extend to all the possible intentional processes and aspects included in the experiences; and it should extend also to the experiences of modified consciousness that may be included in them and to their intentionalities.

The study of the stream of consciousness takes place through various acts of reflection. These acts themselves, in their turn, also belong to the stream of experiences, and in corresponding reflections on a higher level they can again become objects of phenomenological analysis and description. Analyses of this kind lay the foundation of a general phenomenology and of the methodological insights that are indispensable to its development.

The term "reflection," as the foregoing analysis shows, is an expression indicating the acts in which the stream of experiences, with its manifold events and intentionalities, can be grasped and analyzed in the light of its own evidence. Generally speaking, reflection modifies the previous experience in an essential fashion. The previous experience loses its original mode, and reflecting makes an object out of what previously was an experience, but does not make it objective. Thus, reflection does not repeat the original process but considers it and explains what can be found in it. Reflection is a new intentional experience that, with its characteristic of referring back to the earlier process, is awareness precisely of that earlier experience itself. It is an experiential knowing to which we owe all conceivable knowledge and cognition of our intentional life. This description holds also for our phenomenological reflection.

To put it differently, in phenomenological reflection there is a doubling of the ego: the transcendental ego establishes itself as a "disinterested onlooker" above the naively interested ego. This doubling itself can be experienced in a new reflection. As transcendental, this new reflection likewise demands the same attitude of looking on disinterestedly, for the ego's sole remaining interest is to see and describe adequately what it sees purely as it is seen, as that which is seen and seen in this or that fashion.

As Husserl sees it, it is in this way that all events of our life-turned-toward-the-world are made capable of description without any accompanying or expectant meanings and prejudices. Only in this purified condition can they become themes of a universal critique of consciousness, as is demanded by our aim to arrive at a radical grounding of philosophy. Evidently, however, everything depends here on keeping the description absolutely free of any prejudices so that we can satisfy the principle of pure evidence. This requirement means that we must restrict ourselves to the pure data of transcendental reflection; hence these data must be taken precisely as wholly free of any interpretation that reads into them more than is genuinely seen.

If we follow this methodological principle and remember that every *cogito* is a *cogito cogitatum,* it becomes evident that every description must have two sides: description of the intentional object as such (*noematic description*) and description of the modes of the *cogito* itself (*noetic description*). It should thus be clear that through the universal reduction the world is not simply lost for phenomenology. We retain it as *cogitatum,* not only with respect to particular realities but also with respect to the world itself as the necessary background of our whole natural life (*Ideas,* 1:177–81 [147–51]; *Cart. Med.,* 35–36 [73–75]).

The Doctrinal Content of the Transcendental Reduction

In the preceding pages, I have described Husserl's conception of the transcendental reduction as it appears in *Cartesian Meditations.* The view presented there, which I take to be Husserl's final view on the issue, is not found consistently in his earlier works, including *Ideas,* even though, as we have seen, in the 1950 edition several sections have been changed on the basis of indications made by Husserl himself. It thus seems desirable to conclude these reflections with a brief note on the genesis and development of the idea of the transcendental reduction and to focus for a moment on its doctrinal content.

Husserl first mentioned the transcendental reduction as a necessary condition for an absolutely radical and transcendental foundation of philosophy in the summer of 1906 in manuscripts written in Seefeld, later called the "Seefelder Blätter." However, in these notes he did not yet accurately describe his vaguely seen idea or determine the nature, function, and meaning of the phenomenological reduction. In *The Idea of Phenomenology,* the fundamental ideas concerning the phenomenological reduction were clearly expressed in their full meaning for the first time, and the essential relationship between reduction and constitution was likewise explicitly indi-

cated. In this same period, Husserl turned to Descartes as the model
of such a radical return to that which is given beyond every possible
doubt. However, he immediately emphasized that his reduction
should not be interpreted as a Cartesian doubt. Descartes denied, at
least temporarily, the existence of the things reduced, while Husserl
did not deny that existence but only placed it between brackets.

In this point also, Husserl's thinking underwent an evolution.
This becomes particularly clear when we study the manuscripts he
wrote between 1907 and 1913 and the innumerable writings of the
last fifteen years of his life that explicitly deal with this problem.
However, there is no doubt that this evolution reached, with respect
to the very essence of the phenomenological reduction as such, its
final stage before he published his *Ideas* in 1913, even though at that
time he did not yet make a clear distinction between the phenomenological and the transcendental reductions. In the 1950 edition of
Ideas, this distinction was made explicit on the basis of indications
by Husserl himself. After 1915 Husserl constantly restudied the
problems connected with the reduction without, however, changing
his mind about the cardinal aspects of this central idea of his phenomenological philosophy. In these new studies, he merely tried to
make the procedure more radical and to determine the positive
meaning and doctrinal content of the reduction more accurately
than he had done in his earlier writings.[3]

As Husserl proceeded in his phenomenological investigations, it
became increasingly clear to him that more was involved than a
mere suspension of existential belief. Yet it was not easy for him to
determine the additional aspects of the transcendental reduction.
Even in the last decade of his life, Husserl believed that no adequate
account of the transcendental reduction had appeared as yet; in fact,
his correspondence referred to it as the most difficult thing ever attempted in philosophy. The second part of Husserl's *First Philosophy* (1923–24), which was edited by Boehm and appeared under the
title *Theory of the Phenomenological Reduction,* provides us with
some information about the intermediate stages of the evolution. It
shows Husserl's struggle with the problems of the correct starting
point of the reduction, but it hardly clarifies the reduction itself and
certainly contains no significant change of its essence.[4]

The problems that drew Husserl's attention in the last fifteen
years of his life were the exact way in which the necessity of the reduction is to be justified; the relation between reduction and analysis, between reduction and constitution, and between the reduction
and the life-world; and the accurate description of the difference between the psychological and the transcendental reduction. Especially these issues explain why the transcendental reduction remains

one of the most enigmatic concepts of Husserl's philosophy, as is evident from the many different interpretations given to it by Husserl himself, his disciples, and his later interpreters.[5]

It is sometimes claimed that we must distinguish several different steps in Husserl's transcendental reduction. This claim is sometimes explained in the following way. First of all, the reduction has its positive and its negative aspects. In its negative aspect, the reduction guarantees that no foreign elements will be admitted into the later analyses. This negative aspect has its counterpart in the various levels of reduction. The constant application of the reduction therefore presents a gradual penetration into pure subjectivity as the sole ground and source of all objectivity. According to Quentin Lauer, Husserl nowhere explicitly describes the different stages of the process as a whole. However, Lauer claims, transcendental subjectivity can be understood only if we realize that there are at least six levels of reduction, each of which results in a subject of greater purity. Only when the subject is at its greatest purity do we have the strict science of phenomenology as Husserl understood it. Only when the subject has been purified to the extent of being absolutely pure subjectivity can it be the universal a priori source and ground of objectivity. And this constitutes the positive aspect of the reduction. According to Lauer, one has to wade through all of Husserl's works, published and unpublished, in order to discover just what the six levels of reduction are.[6]

Although there is some truth in this view, it seems to me that there is only one transcendental reduction that is to be clearly distinguished from the phenomenological reduction, the eidetic reduction, and the reduction of the world of culture to the original life-world. It is true that in the transcendental reduction we must make a distinction between a negative and a positive aspect. We may also admit several stages in the transcendental reduction, but these stages are so closely connected and interrelated that it seems to be more important to stress the unity of the procedure than its different phases.

We must now return to the important question raised above: What is the exact doctrinal meaning of the suspension of our existential belief in the world and the reduction of all meaning and being to transcendental subjectivity? In a remarkable study devoted to this issue, Van Breda has pointed out that one can perhaps summarize Husserl's final answer to this question in the following three theses: (1) The transcendental reduction is for Husserl that procedure which enables him to attain a genuinely philosophical level because it enables him to move from the naive, dogmatic, and mundane level of reflection to the transcendental level, which reveals the condition of its possibility. (2) This procedure prohibits Husserl from opting either for an objectivist or for a subjectivist attitude in philosophy; by radicalizing the subjectivist position as found in Descartes and Kant, Husserl was able to come to a position by which such oppositions can be definitively overcome; Husserl himself defines this position as "transcendental idealism of a new kind." (3) Finally, for Husserl the discovery of the true meaning of the transcendental reduction is solely the discovery of the ultimate foundation for any authentic metaphysics whatsoever.[7]

| N O T E S

1. For what follows here on the transcendental reduction, see Husserl, "Amsterdam Lectures," section 13, 336–42; and idem, *Erste Philosophie,* part 2, *Theorie der phänomenologischen Reduktion,* ed. Rudolf Boehm (The Hague: Nijhoff, 1959). See also Iso Kern, "The Three Ways to the Transcendental Phenomenological Reduction in the Philosophy of Edmund Husserl"; Rudolf Boehm, "Basic Reflections on Husserl's Phenomenological Reduction," *International Philosophical Quarterly* 5 (1965): 183–202; and Bernet et al., *Edmund Husserl,* 56–74.

It is important to compare what is said here about the transcendental reduction with what was said about the phenomenological reduction in Chapter Four above (118–27). See also Chapter Nine below.

2. See 14–17, 120–27 above.

3. See Biemel, "Les phases décisives," 55; and Spiegelberg, *The Phenomenological Movement,* 1:133–34.

4. See Boehm's introduction to Edmund Husserl, *Erste Philosophie,* 2:xii–xlii; and Spiegelberg, *The Phenomenological Movement,* 1:135–36.

5. Eugen Fink, "Operative Begriffe in Husserl's Phänomenologie," 321–22. See also Van Breda, "La réduction phénoménologique," in *Husserl,* 307–18, particularly 307.

6. Lauer, *Phénoménologie de Husserl,* 340n.4, 361n.1.

7. Van Breda, "La réduction phénoménologique," 307–8.

Pure Psychology as Propaedeutic to Transcendental Phenomenology

Text

10. Die reine Psychologie als Propädeutik zur transzendentalen Phänomenologie

Durch die Aufklärung der wesensmäßigen Doppeldeutigkeit der Bewußtseinssubjektivität und der auf diese zu beziehenden eidetischen Wissenschaft wird die historische Unüberwindlichkeit des Psychologismus aus tiefsten Gründen verständlich. Seine Kraft liegt in einem *wesensmäßigen transzendentalen Schein,* der unenthüllt fortwirken mußte. Verständlich wird auch durch die gewonnene Aufklärung auf der einen Seite die Unabhängigkeit der Idee einer transzendentalen Phänomenologie und ihrer systematischen Durchführung von derjenigen einer phänomenologisch reinen Psychologie, auf der anderen Seite doch die propädeutische Nützlichkeit eines vorausgeschickten Entwurfes reiner Psychologie für ein Aufsteigen zur transzendentalen Phänomenologie, eine Nützlichkeit, die die vorliegende Darstellung geleitet hat. Was das eine anlangt, ist es offensichtlich, daß sich an die Aufdeckung der transzendentalen Relativität *sogleich* die phänomenologische und eidetische Reduktion knüpfen läßt, und so erwächst die transzendentale Phänomenologie direkt aus der transzendentalen Anschauung. In der Tat war dieser direkte der historische Weg. Die reine phänomenologische Psychologie als eidetische Wissenschaft in der Positivität lag ja überhaupt nicht vor. Was fürs Zweite den propädeutischen Vorzug des indirekten Weges zur transzendentalen Phänomenologie über die reine Psychologie anlangt, so bedeutet die transzendentale Einstellung eine Art Änderung der ganzen Lebensform, die alle bisherige Lebenserfahrung völlig übersteigt, also vermöge ihrer absoluten Fremdartigkeit schwer verständlich sein muß. Ähnliches gilt für eine transzendentale Wissenschaft. Die phänomenologische Psychologie, obschon auch relativ neu und in der Methode intentionaler Analyse ganz neuartig, hat immerhin doch die Zugänglichkeit [296] aller positiven

10. Pure Psychology as Propaedeutic to Transcendental Phenomenology

Through the elucidation of the essentially dual meaning of the subjectivity of consciousness, and also a clarification of the eidetic science to be directed to it, we begin to understand on very deep grounds the historical insurmountability of psychologism. Its power lies in an *essential transcendental semblance* which [because] undisclosed had to remain effective. Also from the clarification we have gained we begin to understand on the one hand the independence of the idea of a transcendental phenomenology, and the systematic developing of it, from the idea of a phenomenological pure psychology; and yet on the other hand the propaedeutic usefulness of the preliminary project of a pure psychology for an ascent to transcendental phenomenology, a usefulness which has guided our present discussion here. As regards this point [*i.e.*, the independence of the idea of transcendental phenomenology from a phenomenological pure psychology], clearly the phenomenological and eidetic reduction allows of being *immediately* connected to the disclosing of transcendental relativity, and in this way transcendental phenomenology springs directly out of the transcendental intuition. In point of fact, this direct path was the historical path it took. Pure phenomenological psychology as eidetic science in positivity was simply not available. As regards the second point, *i.e.*, the propaedeutic preference of the indirect approach to transcendental phenomenology through pure psychology, [it must be remembered that] the transcendental attitude involves a change of focus from one's entire form of life-style, one which goes so completely beyond all previous experiencing of life, that it must, in virtue of its absolute strangeness, needs be difficult to understand. This is also true of a transcendental science. Phenomenological psychology, although also relatively new, and in its method of intentional analysis completely novel, still has the

Wissenschaften. Ist sie mindest der scharf präzisierten Idee nach einmal klar geworden, so bedarf es nur der Klärung des echten Sinnes transzendentalphilosophischer Problematik und der transzendentalen Reduktion, um sich der transzendentalen Phänomenologie als einer bloßen Wendung ihres Lehrgehaltes ins Transzendentale zu bemächtigen. In diese zwei Stufen verteilen sich die zwei Grundschwierigkeiten des Eindringens in die neue Phänomenologie, nämlich die des Verständnisses der echten Methode "innerer Erfahrung", die schon zur Ermöglichung einer "exakten" Psychologie als rationaler Tatsachenwissenschaft gehört, und die des Verständnisses der Eigentümlichkeit transzendentaler Fragestellung und Methode. An sich betrachtet ist allerdings das transzendentale Interesse das höchste und letzte wissenschaftliche Interesse, und so ist es das Richtige, wie historisch so weiterhin, die transzendentalen Theorien im eigenständigen absoluten System der Transzendentalphilosophie auszubilden und in ihr selbst mit der Aufweisung der Wesensart natürlicher gegenüber transzendentaler Einstellung die Möglichkeit der Umdeutung aller transzendentalen phänomenologischen Lehren in solche der natürlichen Positivität herauszustellen.

accessibility which is possessed by all positive science. Once this psychology has become clear, at least according to its sharply defined idea, then only the clarification of the true sense of the transcendental-philosophical field of problems and of the transcendental reduction is required in order for it to come into possession of transcendental phenomenology as a mere reversal of its doctrinal content into transcendental terms. The basic difficulties for penetrating into the terrain of the new phenomenology fall into these two stages, namely that of understanding the true method of "inner experience," which already belongs to making possible an "exact" psychology as rational science of facts, and that of understanding the distinctive character of the transcendental methods and questioning. True, simply regarded in itself, an interest in the transcendental is the highest and ultimate scientific interest, and so it is entirely the right thing (it has been so historically and should continue) for transcendental theories to be cultivated in the autonomous, absolute system of transcendental philosophy; and to place before us, through showing the characteristic features of the natural in contrast to the transcendental attitude, the possibility within transcendental philosophy itself of reinterpreting all transcendental phenomenological doctrine [or theory] into doctrine [or theory] in the realm of natural positivity.

I Synopsis

From our reflections on the dual meaning of subjectivity, it has become clear why it was historically so difficult to overcome psychologism. Its power and force lie in an essential, transcendental semblance that remained effective because it was never seen and disclosed.

We have also seen that transcendental phenomenology is independent of phenomenological psychology and can be developed independently of it. On the other hand, we have also learned that phenomenological psychology can be taken as a propaedeutic to transcendental phenomenology.

As for the independence of transcendental phenomenology from pure, phenomenological psychology, it is clear that the phenomenological and eidetic reductions taken together immediately lead to the transcendental relativity of the world and the mundane ego in regard to transcendental subjectivity; in this way, transcendental phenomenology springs directly out of transcendental intuition. In point of fact, this direct path was the historical path phenomenology took between 1903 and 1913. Pure psychology was at that time not yet developed. As for the propaedeutic preference of the indirect approach to transcendental phenomenology through pure psychology, one must realize that the transcendental attitude implies a change of focus in one's entire form of life; this form of life goes beyond all previous forms of experience; thus, because of its absolute strangeness, it is very difficult to understand. The same is true for the corresponding transcendental science. Phenomenological psychology is also a new science; yet, because it is a science of the natural attitude and thus a positive science, it is not so difficult to understand as is a transcendental science. Once the idea of phenomenological psychology has been explained in outline, only the clarification of the true sense of the transcendental-philosophical reduction and the field of experience that it opens up are needed in order for us to come into possession of transcendental phenomenology by means of a mere reversal of its doctrinal content into transcendental terms.

As for phenomenology as a whole, the basic difficulty consists in understanding both the phenomenological and the transcendental reductions.

One final observation is in order here. Simply considered in itself, the interest in the transcendental is the highest and scientifically the most important interest. Thus it is right to cultivate transcendental ideas and theories in the autonomous, absolute system of transcendental philosophy, and only later to bring to light, by showing the characteristic features of the natural and the transcendental attitudes, the possibility within transcendental philosophy itself of reinterpreting all transcendental phenomenological doctrines into doctrines in the realm of the positive science, phenomenological psychology. This has been so historically and should continue to be so.

In my commentary, I shall focus on the relationship between the phenomenological and transcendental reductions in Husserl's later life (1928–36), since, according to some scholars, there are reasons to believe that Husserl finally gave up his position on the relationship between phenomenological psychology and transcendental philosophy, which is defended here in the *Encyclopaedia* article.

Commentary

On the Phenomenological-Psychological and Transcendental Reductions in Husserl's *Crisis*

In section 10 of the *Encyclopaedia* article, Husserl suggests that it is easy to move from the domain of phenomenological psychology to that of transcendental philosophy; what is needed is only the transcendental reduction. One can equally easily move from transcendental phenomenological philosophy to phenomenological psychology; what is needed in this case is that one gives up the transcendental reduction. Finally, Husserl states that in his view the latter move is in some sense preferable over the first.

It is a well-known fact that the distinction between the two reductions, as well as the distinction between phenomenological psychology and transcendental phenomenology, gradually developed in Husserl's thought as a further specification of the two different types of phenomenology that he successively developed between 1901 and 1907, that is to say, in the second volume of *Logical Investigations* and in *The Idea of Phenomenology.*[1] Yet it is also the case that an *explicit* distinction between the phenomenological-psychological and transcendental reductions appears rather late in Husserl's work. To the best of my knowledge, this distinction is found explicitly for the first time in *Phenomenological Psychology,* the *Encyclopaedia Britannica* article, the "Amsterdam Lectures," *Cartesian Meditations,* and in various manuscripts written between 1925 and 1931.

There are reasons to believe that toward the end of his life Husserl may have changed his view on these issues. Husserl himself seems to suggest such a change of opinion in the concluding sections of *Crisis*[2] as well as in manuscripts of the same period. In addition, this idea is further corroborated by Fink in his outline for the continuation of *Crisis*.[3] Finally, in his book on Husserl's conception of psychology, Max Drüe has explicitly tried to defend and justify this view.[4]

I myself am not convinced that in his later life Husserl gave up the distinction between phenomenological psychology and transcendental phenomenological philosophy and the two relevant reductions. I shall thus focus on the following question: Is it indeed true that toward the end of his life Husserl abolished the radical distinction between phenomenological psychology and transcendental phenomenological philosophy and, therefore, also the distinction between the phenomenological-psychological and transcendental reductions?

I propose that in trying to answer these questions we turn first to two other important questions: (1) In the years between 1925 and 1931, how did Husserl specifically conceive of the relationship between phenomenological psychology and transcendental phenomenology, on the one hand, and the two corresponding reductions, on the other? (2) What does Husserl claim precisely in this regard in the final sections of *Crisis?* Once we have established Husserl's view in these two different phases of his development, we must then turn to the conceptions of Fink and Drüe in an attempt to reach our final conclusion.

The Reductions in the Period between 1925 and 1931

The question concerning the precise relationship between phenomenological psychology and transcendental phenomenology constitutes one of the central themes occupying Husserl's reflections between 1925 and 1931. In order to briefly characterize Husserl's view during this period of his life, I should like to take my point of departure in the "Amsterdamer Vorträge" (1928).[5]

Referring to phenomenological psychology, Husserl says here that the first problem is to clearly delineate the subject matter of such a pure psychology and to explain how one can gain access to this subject matter. As Husserl sees it, the subject matter of phenomenological psychology is the pure psychical, which is taken in this science as completely isolated from, and independent of, the physical, with which it is nonetheless essentially interwoven. One gains access to this domain not by a process of negative abstraction but by a special intuition that can occur only in the realm of reflection. What is now called phenomenological experience, Husserl says, is a very peculiar type of reflection, the nature of which is to be determined more accurately (*Phän. Psych.,* 303–8).

In order to materialize a pure, phenomenological experience, Husserl maintains, and to then be able to make consciousness in its pure and unique being the universal theme of my research, I must put between brackets as being not psychical all that is covered by the general thesis of our natural attitude, according to which the real world about me is at all times known as a fact-world that has its being out there. In so doing, the thesis of the natural attitude is still experienced as lived, but I make no use of it anymore in order to focus my attention exclusively on the psychical as such (*Phän. Psych.,* 312). In performing this reduction, I obviously cannot deny that consciousness is and remains intentional—consciousness of something—but as long as I decide to remain within the realm opened up by the reduction, I take that which I experience not as things in a real world but exclusively as that which is intended by consciousness, thus as unities of meaning, as phenomena (ibid., 312–13).

Phenomenological psychology is thus impossible without a reduction. At first sight, this conception seems to mean that pure— that is, phenomenological—psychology, in the final analysis, will be able to unravel all transcendental problems and will thus become identical with transcendental phenomenology. We must remember here, however, Husserl says, that phenomenological psychology is exclusively interested in the psychical as such, that is to say, in "souls" and "communities of souls," which as such are encountered in the natural world, which psychology therefore must still somehow presuppose. In other words, as a method of phenomenological psychology, the reduction serves *exclusively* to isolate and determine the purely psychical. Although it is reduced to phenomena in the phenomenological sense of the term, the psychical itself, which constitutes the immediate subject matter of psychology, is and remains the psychic life of concrete human beings within the real, spatiotemporal world—or, insofar as this psychology is eidetic, within a *possibly* real world. It is exclusively in this sense that in phenomenological psychology "the" world is always presupposed as a constant world at hand and that this psychology is still a "positing" science that therefore basically *remains within the realm of the natural attitude* (*Phän. Psych.,* 335–36).

Comparing phenomenological psychology with empirical psychology, on the one hand, and transcendental phenomenology, on the other, Husserl says that empirical psychology as a positive science studies the psychical as belonging to the always pregiven, spatiotemporal real world, which for this psychology remains the only valid one. As an eidetic science, phenomenological psychology seeks the *logos* of the psychical. Its thematic basis is not the real world as such but merely a possible real world, a world that is thought to be pregiven as real. The phenomenological-psychological reduction forms a necessary method through which it becomes possible to delimit and determine the psychical (especially in its character of being intentional) by means of an inactivation of all the transcendental positings that are found in this intentional life. Eidetic psychology, however, remains a *positive* science in that it retains the validity of the natural apperception of the world, at least insofar as the psychical itself is concerned. As soon as this latter aspect is inactivated, we enter the realm of transcendental phenomenology (*Phän. Psych.*, 338–341, 343–46).

In *Cartesian Meditations*, Husserl presents a similar view. In the fourth meditation, in speaking about the transcendental ego from an eidetic point of view, he says that what has been said about the transcendental ego can to a great extent be maintained in phenomenological psychology.

> To the transcendental *ego* there corresponds then the human *ego*, concretely as the *psyche* taken purely in itself and as it is for itself, with its psychic polarization: I as the pole of my habitualities, the properties comprised in my character. Instead of eidetic transcendental phenomenology we then have an eidetic pure psychology, relating to the *eidos* "psyche", whose eidetic horizon, however, remains unexamined. (*Cart. Med.*, 72–73 [107])

The Reductions in the Last Sections of *Crisis*

In *Crisis* Husserl's explanation of the difference and the relationship between empirical and phenomenological psychology does not contain essentially new insights, but his attempt to combine his conception of the life-world with his view on the meaning and function of the phenomenological-psychological reduction seems to entail that this reduction becomes identical to the transcendental reduction.[6] If this is indeed true, then there can no longer be an essential difference between phenomenological psychology and transcendental phenomenology. Therefore let us consider this idea more carefully.

Psychology, Husserl says, deals with the psychical, and phenomenological psychology is concerned with the *eidos* of the psychical. Since all psychic phenomena are intentional phenomena, the specific theme of eidetic psychology concerns the essence of the human soul seen exclusively as the subject of intentional life. Eidetic psychology studies the individual soul from the perspective of its intentional life. Every soul is intentionally connected with other souls in a community of souls; that is why phenomenological psychology in the final analysis is concerned with a community of pure subjects. In order to be able to bring to light the *eidos* of the pure ego and the community of the pure subjects, the psychologist has to perform the phenomenological-psychological reduction. This reduction places between brackets all the psychologist's existential convictions and judgments concerning the subject matter of his study. He is required to assume the position of a disinterested observer and witness to the intentional life of the pure subjects. This reduction includes all souls, all subjects, and the research psychologist is here no exception. Thus he must become a disinterested observer of himself as well as of other subjects. Unless he performs this reduction consistently, the phenomenological psychologist will never reach the essentially uniform and in itself absolutely closed "inner world" of the pure egos and the universal unity of intentional life, which is precisely the subject matter of his science (*Crisis,* 235–41 [238–44]).

Husserl states again that the universal reduction is merely the necessary and sufficient condition that must be fulfilled if one is to achieve access to the essentially intentional, psychic entities. Only by means of this reduction does it become possible to see the genuine meaning of the life of the pure egos as an *independent* theme of investigation. Only within the sphere of the reduction can this life be seen as intentional life, in which these subjects in various forms and modalities are directed toward, and concerned with, purely intentional objects. The task of psychology consists precisely in descriptively and adequately uncovering these manifold intentional relationships in all their immediate and mediate implications, at least insofar as all of this belongs essentially to the immanence of the pure egos. Husserl finally specifies again that all persons, including the observing phenomenologist, are in this way transformed into phenomena; this transformation reveals these egos as pure subjects of pure, intentional, conscious life (*Crisis,* 244–55 [247–58]).

After all of this, which is still in complete harmony with what is found in the earlier publications mentioned, Husserl quite unexpectedly continues by saying that it should be clear from what we already know on the subject that a full treatment of these ideas necessarily leads phenomenological psychology toward transcendental phenomenology because the phenomenological-psychological reduction necessarily turns into the transcendental reduction (*Crisis,* 255–56 [258–59]). The reason for this is that the descriptive psychology of intentionality must deal with the problem of the lifeworld as the intersubjective "product" of a quasi-infinite community of pure subjects whose lives are mutually interconnected, and that a logical development of this problem requires that we take the last step and perform the transcendental reduction. We want to solve the problem arising from those acts and systems of acts by means of which the absolutely isolated and pure ego is able to experience other egos and to enter into contact with them so that in their intersubjective cooperation an intersubjective world can emerge; but this can obviously be done only after the phenomenologist has made it possible for himself to experience himself as *absolute* ego.

In all sciences, psychology included, we search for objective knowledge. That is why, in dealing with human subjects scientifically, we try to achieve objectivity by excluding what is merely subjective. But this means that in order to achieve objective knowledge, we must eliminate ourselves, even as that functioning subjectivity in whose functioning the ontological meaning "world" precisely originates. As a scientist who searches for intersubjectively valid truth, I thus have to admit that (even in my investigations that aim at the intentional constitution of the world) there are other subjects with me whose being real as subjects I must admit on the basis of empathy and with whom I know myself to be communalized. But when I perform the reduction and apply it to myself and to the world, this reduction affects all other people, just as it affects the world in general, so that these people and the world in general become mere intentional phenomena for me. A radical and consistent reduction thus necessarily leads to an absolute and unique ego, the ego of the absolutely growing-lonely psychologist, who now no longer is a real human being in the world but the pure subject of his universal and pure intentionality. But this ego is an apodictic, transcendental ego (*Crisis,* 256–57 [259–60]).

In Husserl's view, the surprising result of these reflections can be summarized briefly as follows. A pure psychology within the realm of the natural attitude seems to be impossible; there is only a *transcendental* psychology or phenomenology. Husserl adds, however, that upon closer consideration one will see that this conclusion, although indeed containing a good deal of truth, cannot be entirely correct (*Crisis,* 257–58 [261–62]).

Further explanation of this remark does not help Husserl to transcend his ambiguous conclusion. On the one hand, he defends the thesis that phenomenological psychology and transcendental phenomenology cannot be completely identical (*Crisis,* 257 [261]), whereas on the other, he argues that the difference between the reductions cannot be maintained (ibid., 258–59 [261–63]). Drüe has collected a whole series of texts that seem to aggravate the difficulties.[7] I shall limit myself here to a brief indication of his most important considerations in this regard.

First of all, Drüe says, after performing the phenomenological-psychological reduction, the psychologist gradually becomes aware of the fact that his empirical ego is merely a mundane fixation of the transcendental ego, which precedes him in the realm of the transcendental, and furthermore that each transcendental ego is an individualized materialization of the transcendental subjectivity. But this latter insight leads the psychological reduction into the transcendental reduction, and phenomenological psychology thus changes into transcendental phenomenology.[8]

In a similar sense, Husserl writes that the separation between the pure, phenomenological-psychological and the transcendental attitudes—which is necessary at first—is later transcended and overcome by the phenomenologist, who tries to come to a higher level of self-understanding. Understood in the proper manner, phenomenological-psychological reduction is nothing other than the transcendental reduction that has not yet arrived at a complete self-understanding.[9]

Another argument can be developed along the following lines. From 1925 on, Husserl always maintained that we must make a clear distinction between the empirical-psychological ego and the pure ego of phenomenology (*Cart. Med.*, 25–26 [64–65]). We must furthermore make a clear distinction between the pure ego of phenomenological psychology and the transcendental ego dealt with in transcendental phenomenology (ibid., 72–73 [107]). Husserl described the empirical-psychological ego as "I, this man in the world" (ibid., 25 [64]). The phenomenological-psychological ego is determined as "the human ego, concretely as the psyche taken purely in itself and as it is for itself, with the psychic polarization: I as pole of my habitualities, that is the properties comprised in my character" (ibid., 72–73 [107]) and as "pure psychic subject with a pure psychic life" (*Phän. Psych.*, 342). In comparison with the transcendental ego, this phenomenological-psychological ego is still a mundane ego (ibid., 343–44). Husserl goes on to explain that phenomenological psychology studies the fundamental types of psychic phenomena. It deals only with psychic entities and events as "unities of meaning" as they appear to me in my intentional acts. Psychology is interested only in the essences of the psychic entities and events and describes them in intentional analyses. The necessary presuppositions of such a study are first, the eidetic reduction from facts to essences and then, a reduction from "objective and mundane things" to "unities of meaning" that are given to me (who is and remains here a real psychological entity in the world); this last reduction is what is called the phenomenological-psychological reduction (ibid., 335–44 passim). If one reflects upon this more carefully, it soon becomes quite clear that there is an inconsistency in the attitude of the psychologist. On the one hand, he performs the phenomenological reduction, and on the other, he refuses to perform the reduction consistently so as to include his own ego. It is this inconsistency that leads him to transcendental phenomenology by reducing his mundane ego to the transcendental ego, and then, in the final analysis, this transcendental ego is reduced in turn into transcendental subjectivity, which (as Husserl explicitly says) can no longer be understood as "personal."[10] In other words, a clear distinction between phenomenological psychology and transcendental phenomenology cannot be consistently maintained.

In another section of his book,[11] Drüe turns to certain reflections made by Fink in a first draft that he prepared for Husserl in 1936, suggesting some ideas for the remainder of *Crisis,* which at that time was still incomplete.[12] In this outline, Fink maintains that phenomenological psychology necessarily debouches into transcendental phenomenology. Nonetheless, Fink claims, there is and remains a difference between the two, even where the psychologist indeed passes completely from psychology to transcendental phenomenology. In other words, phenomenological psychology is not only different from transcendental phenomenology insofar as, and as long as, it is conceived of as a "preparatory phase" of transcendental phenomenology; but even when psychology has passed completely into transcendental phenomenology, there is still a difference between the two. Fink conceives of this difference in terms of the extension of interest spheres: phenomenological psychology is interested only in a limited realm of problems; within the domain of transcendental phenomenology, phenomenological psychology has a rather limited task and scope. Drüe agrees with these considerations and conceives of them as the final words one can say on the issue.

∎ Critical Reflections

I feel that these reflections do not give an adequate idea of Husserl's final view on the topic. I am convinced that there is a way of bringing together all the relevant texts (Husserl's manuscripts as well as Fink's project for the continuation of *Crisis*) into a harmonious synthesis, but this requires that we interpret all of these statements in a different way. In order to make my position as clear as possible, I should like first to make some introductory remarks and then to formulate my view in a few concise statements.

As I see it, Husserl never defended the view that phenomenological psychology and transcendental phenomenology are to be *identified.* First of all, we have a very impressive list of texts, written between 1913 and 1936, in which he explicitly claims that both disciplines are *essentially* different, in that psychology is a mundane science to be developed in the *natural* attitude, whereas transcendental phenomenology moves in the *philosophical* attitude. Furthermore, the meaning and scope of the second part of *Crisis,* taken as a whole, is certainly in conflict with the thesis that completely identifies psychology and transcendental phenomenology, since psychology (that is, empirical as well as phenomenological psychology) is described there as a road leading toward transcendental phenomenology. Third, if Husserl had been of the opinion in 1936 that the views he was developing at that time were in conflict with the ideas he had developed earlier in *Phenomenological Psychology* and *Cartesian Meditations,* he most certainly would have indicated this somehow. And finally, Husserl always maintained that regional ontologies are not to be identified with transcendental phenomenology, whereas phenomenological psychology is consistently referred to as the regional ontology of the psychical.[13]

On the other hand, I do subscribe to the view that a consistent development of phenomenological psychology will ultimately and of necessity lead to transcendental phenomenology. Husserl introduced phenomenological psychology as the eidetic science that must lay the foundations of empirical psychology. But obviously, phenomenological psychology is not the ultimate founding science; it itself is to be founded ultimately in transcendental phenomenology, just like every other regional ontology. The relationship between this particular regional ontology and transcendental phenomenology, however, is of a very peculiar type, not only because of the close relationship between the subject matters of phenomenological psychology and transcendental phenomenology but also, and even particularly, because of the fact that in phenomenological psychology a phenomenological reduction is necessary in addition to the eidetic reduction. This must be specified in greater detail.

Phenomenological psychology is a regional ontology. As such it remains in the natural attitude and thus outside the realm of the transcendental reduction. It is interested in bringing to light the *eidos* of the psychical, and in so doing it uses the eidetic reduction in order to make the transition from fact to *eidos* possible. Further, it employs the phenomenological-psychological reduction in order to separate the psychical from the physical, with which it is essentially connected. However, once this subject matter has been clearly demarcated, in phenomenological psychology as such there is no longer any need to maintain this reduction. Then the psychologist may return to the natural attitude and attempt to describe the intentional activities of the lives of the pure egos. Husserl follows this procedure exactly in *Ideas,* where, after introducing the phenomenological reduction and explaining its goal and scope, he continues: "We start now with a series of reflections within which we are not troubled with any phenomenological *epoche.* Directed to the 'outer world' and without forsaking the natural standpoint we reflect psychologically on our ego and its lived experiences . . . *on the essential nature of the consciousness of something . . .*"[14] In other words, phenomenological psychology as a science of the natural attitude remains oriented toward the real world and, as eidetic, toward a possibly real world; and its goal is to clarify the eidetic structures of real and possibly real egos and their conscious or psychic lives. Looking upon phenomenological psychology from this point of view, there are no serious problems.

However, if we turn to the question of how this particular science is precisely related to transcendental phenomenology, then it becomes evident that the position of the phenomenological psychologist is ambiguous. This ambiguity can be approached from different perspectives. One could say, for instance, that insofar as the psychologist himself is a human soul, a human subject, he belongs in principle to the subject matter of phenomenological psychology, and as such he is obviously objectified. As investigator, however, he is not an objectified ego but precisely the objectifying subjectivity. By returning now to the natural attitude, the psychologist is not able to justify his objectifying function. Such a function of the ego necessarily presupposes the transcendental reduction. One could also say that the moment the psychologist takes into consideration that a subject is not merely in his own world but also in an intersubjective life-world and tries systematically to account for the intersubjective validity of the world for everyone, he must realize that he can do so only if he occupies a privileged position in regard to all other egos as well as in regard to the world. But such a privileged position can be obtained only by means of the transcendental reduction.

The question that remains is whether these and similar considerations necessarily entail that phenomenological psychology debouches into transcendental phenomenology in such a way that phenomenological psychology cannot be maintained as an independent discipline essentially distinguished from transcendental phenomenology. The answer, in my view, is obviously in the negative. Such a consequence follows only if one is able to show that phenomenological psychology's task consists precisely in giving the *ultimate* explanation of the meaning and being of beings.[15] There is no doubt that, in Husserl's view, the goal of phenomenological psychology consists in laying bare the *eidos* of the psychical; the ultimate explanation of the meaning and being of all beings remains the task of transcendental phenomenology. When the phenomenological psychologist first performs the phenomenological reduction and then returns to the natural attitude, he is completely justified in doing so in view of the goal he wishes to achieve. But from the viewpoint of someone who desires to give an *ultimate* explanation, justification, and foundation, the psychologist's behavior is inconsistent. However, even though the transcendental phenomenologist sees this inconsistency, he cannot blame the psychologist for one important reason: the psychologist never pretended that his particular methodical procedure was ever meant to solve the problems of transcendental phenomenology. His sole legitimate claim is that his procedure enables him to attain the specific goal he originally set for himself.

▎NOTES

1. Husserl, *Phen. Psych.*, 14–33 [20–46]. See also Joseph J. Kockelmans, *Edmund Husserl's Phenomenological Psychology* (Pittsburgh, Pa.: Duquesne University Press, 1967), 87–137.

2. Husserl, *Crisis,* 235–65 [238–76].

3. Ibid., 397–400 [514–16].

4. Drüe, *Edmund Husserls System,* 227–45.

5. For what follows, see *Phän. Psych.,* 303–8, 312–15, 321–24, 331–47.

6. For what follows, see *Crisis,* 235–65 [238–76].

7. Drüe, *Edmund Husserls System,* 240–42.

8. Ibid., 241.

9. Husserl, MS. K III 1, 134, quoted by Drüe, *Edmund Husserls System,* 241.

10. Husserl, *Crisis,* 256–57 [259–60]; MS. B I 13, IV, 26, quoted by Drüe, *Edmund Husserls System,* 242.

11. Drüe, *Edmund Husserls System,* 243–45.

12. Husserl, *Crisis,* 397–400 [514–16]; *Krisis,* 557.

13. Husserl, *The Idea,* 11–12 [13–14]; *Die Idee,* 79; *Ideas,* 1:32 [32], 135–39 [111–15]; *Phen. Psych.,* 33–37 [46–51].

14. *Ideas,* 1:67 [60].

15. *F. tr. L.,* 14–15 [18–19], 165–66 [174–75].

In the last division of his article, Husserl gives a brief description of transcendental phenomenology and then tries to show that transcendental phenomenology in principle realizes the idea of philosophy as a universal science with absolute foundations. First he shows that transcendental phenomenology is able to actualize Leibniz's idea of a universal ontology, to be understood as the systematic unity of all conceivable a priori sciences. Next Husserl explains that transcendental phenomenology is able to overcome the crisis in the foundations of the exact sciences and provide a solid foundation to all empirical sciences. Phenomenology is even an all-embracing philosophy in the sense that it encompasses all knowledge. Finally Husserl shows that the problems that were described in the tradition as the ultimate and highest problems are in fact phenomenological problems, problems to which phenomenology is capable of providing the answer. Husserl ends his article by showing how phenomenology is able to overcome all philosophical antitheses, such as those between rationalism and empiricism, relativism and absolutism, subjectivism and objectivism, and ontologism and transcendentalism.

The reader will see that these last sections sometimes contain enigmatic statements, the precise meaning of which cannot be easily determined. Other sections are straightforward and do not require much commentary. I have grouped sections 11, 12, and 13 together, since they deal with issues that are intimately related, namely, the relationship between transcendental phenomenology and all other forms of knowledge. I have done the same for sections 14 and 15 because both are concerned with the nature of Husserl's philosophy as seen from the perspective of our tradition.

analytic or continental

Transcendental Phenomenology as Ontology: Its Function for the Eidetic and the Empirical Sciences

Text

III. Transzendentale Phänomenologie und Philosophie als universale Wissenschaft in absoluter Begründung

11. Die transzendentale Phänomenologie als Ontologie

In Erwägung der Tragweite der transzendentalen Phänomenologie ergeben sich merkwürdige Konsequenzen. In ihrer systematischen Durchführung verwirklicht sie die *Leibniz*sche Idee einer *universalen Ontologie* als systematischer Einheit aller erdenklichen apriorischen Wissenschaften, aber in einer neuen, den "Dogmatismus" durch die transzendental phänomenologische Methode überwindenden Begründung. Die Phänomenologie als Wissenschaft von allen erdenklichen transzendentalen Phänomenen und zwar je in den synthetischen Gesamtgestalten, in denen sie allein konkret möglich sind—denen von transzendentalen Einzelsubjekten, verbunden zu [297] Subjektgemeinschaften—ist *eo ipso* apriorische Wissenschaft von allem erdenklichen Seienden; aber dann nicht bloß von dem All des objektiv Seienden und nun gar in einer Einstellung natürlicher Positivität, sondern in voller Konkretion von dem Seienden überhaupt, als wie es seinen Seinssinn und seine Geltung aus der korrelativen intentionalen Konstitution schöpft. Das befaßt auch das Sein der transzendentalen Subjektivität selbst, deren erweisbares Wesen es ist, transzendental in sich und für sich konstituierte zu sein. Demnach ist eine durchgeführte Phänomenologie gegenüber der nur scheinbar universalen Ontologie in der Positivität die wahrhaft universale—eben dadurch die dogmatische Einseitigkeit und damit Unverständlichkeit der ersteren überwindend, während sie doch deren rechtmäßige Gehalte in sich befassen muß als in der intentionalen Konstitution ursprünglich begründet.

III. Transcendental Phenomenology and Philosophy as Universal Science with Absolute Foundations

11. Transcendental Phenomenology as Ontology

Remarkable consequences arise when one weighs the significance of transcendental phenomenology. In its systematic development, it brings to realization the Leibnizian idea of a universal ontology as the systematic unity of all conceivable a priori sciences, but on a new foundation which overcomes "dogmatism" through the use of the transcendental phenomenological method. Phenomenology as the science of all conceivable transcendental phenomena and especially the synthetic total structures in which alone they are concretely possible—those of the transcendental single subjects bound to communities of subjects—is *eo ipso* the a priori science of all conceivable beings. But [it is the science] then not merely of the Totality of objectively existing beings, and certainly not in an attitude of natural positivity; rather, in the full concretion of being in general which derives its sense of being and its validity from the correlative intentional constitution. This also comprises the being of transcendental subjectivity itself, whose nature it is demonstrably to be constituted transcendentally in and for itself. Accordingly, a phenomenology properly carried through is the truly universal ontology, as over against the only illusory all-embracing ontology in positivity—and precisely for this reason it overcomes the dogmatic one-sidedness and hence unintelligibility of the latter, while at the same time it comprises within itself the truly legitimate content [of an ontology in positivity] as grounded originally in intentional constitution.

12. Die Phänomenologie und die Grundlagenkrisis der exakten Wissenschaften

Überlegen wir das Wie dieses Enthaltens, so ist damit gemeint, daß jedes Apriori in seiner Seinsgültigkeit festgelegt ist *als* transzendentale Leistung, also in eins mit den Wesensgestalten ihrer Konstitution, der Arten und Stufen ihrer Selbstgebung und Bewährung und der zugehörigen Habitualitäten. Darin liegt, daß in und mit der *Feststellung* des Apriori die subjektive *Methode* dieser Feststellung durchsichtig gemacht ist, daß es also für die apriorischen Disziplinen, die innerhalb der Phänomenologie zur Begründung kommen (z.b. als mathematische Wissenschaften) keine "Paradoxien", keine "Grundlagenkrisen" geben kann. Hinsichtlich der historisch gewordenen apriorischen Wissenschaften, geworden in transzendentaler Naivität, ergibt sich als Konsequenz, daß nur eine radikale phänomenologische Begründung sie in echte, methodisch sich völlig rechtfertigende Wissenschaften verwandeln kann. Eben damit aber hören sie auf, positive (dogmatische) Wissenschaften zu sein und werden zu unselbständigen Zweigen der einen Phänomenologie als universaler eidetischer Ontologie. [298]

13. Die phänomenologische Begründung der Tatsachenwissenschaften und die empirische Phänomenologie

Diese unendliche Aufgabe, das vollständige Universum des Apriori in seiner transzendentalen Rückbezogenheit auf sich selbst und damit in seiner Eigenständigkeit und vollendeten methodischen Klarheit darzustellen, ist ihrerseits eine Funktion der Methode für die Erzielung einer universalen und dabei voll begründeten Wissenschaft von der empirischen Faktizität. Innerhalb der Positivität fordert echte (relativ echte) empirische Wissenschaft die methodische Fundamentierung durch eine entsprechende apriorische Wissenschaft. Nehmen wir das Universum aller möglichen empirischen Wissenschaften überhaupt und fordern eine *radikale,* von allen Grundlagenkrisen befreite Begründung, so führt das auf das universale Apriori in der radikalen, das ist phänomenologischen Begründung. Die echte Gestalt einer universalen Wissenschaft der Faktizität ist also die phänomenologische, als das ist sie universale Wissenschaft von der faktischen transzendentalen Intersubjektivität auf dem methodischen Fundament der eidetischen Phänomenologie als Wissenschaft von einer möglichen transzendentalen Subjektivität überhaupt. Danach versteht und rechtfertigt sich die

12. Phenomenology and the Crisis in the Foundations of the Exact Sciences

If we consider the how of this inclusion, we find that what is meant is that every a priori is ultimately prescribed in its validity of being precisely *as a transcendental achievement; i.e.,* it is together with the essential structures of its constitution, with the kinds and levels of its givenness and confirmation of itself, and with the appertaining habitualities. This implies that in and through the establishment of the a priori the subjective *method* of this establishing is itself made transparent, and that for the a priori disciplines which are founded within phenomenology (for example, as mathematical sciences) there can be no "paradoxes" and no "crises of the foundations." The consequence that arises [from all this] with reference to the a priori sciences that have come into being historically and in transcendental naiveté is that only a radical, phenomenological grounding can transform them into true, methodical, fully self-justifying sciences. But precisely by this they will cease to be positive (dogmatic) sciences and become dependent branches of the one phenomenology as all-encompassing eidetic ontology.

13. The Phenomenological Grounding of the Factual Sciences in Relation to {and} Empirical Phenomenology

The unending task of presenting the complete universe of the a priori in its transcendental relatedness-back-to-itself [or self-reference], and thus in its self-sufficiency and perfect methodological clarity, is itself a function of the method for realization of an all-embracing and hence fully grounded science of empirical fact. Within [the realm of] positive reality [*Positivität*], genuine (relatively genuine) empirical science demands the methodical establishing of a foundation [*Fundamentierung*] through a corresponding a priori science. If we take the universe of all possible empirical sciences whatever and demand a *radical* grounding that will be free from all "foundation crises," then we are led to the all-embracing a priori of the radical and that is [and must be] *phenomenological* grounding. The genuine form of an all-embracing science of fact is thus the phenomenological [form], and as this it is the universal science of the factual transcendental intersubjectivity, [resting] on the methodical foundation of eidetic phenomenology as knowledge applying to any possible transcendental subjectivity whatever. Hence *the idea of an empirical phenomenology* which follows after the eidetic is understood and justified. It is identical with the complete systematic universe of the

Idee einer empirischen, der eidetischen nachkommenden *Phänomenologie.* Sie ist identisch mit dem vollständigen systematischen Universum der positiven Wissenschaften, wofern wir sie nur von vornherein methodisch absolut begründet denken durch die eidetische Phänomenologie.

positive sciences, provided that we think of them from the beginning as absolutely grounded methodologically through eidetic phenomenology.

| Synopsis

In section 11, Husserl states that the importance of transcendental phenomenology becomes immediately clear when one focuses on its implications for philosophy and for the foundations of the formal, eidetic, and empirical sciences. He mentions first that the systematic development of transcendental phenomenology made it possible to realize Leibniz's idea of a universal ontology taken as the systematic unity of all conceivable sciences a priori. Through the use of the transcendental phenomenological method, phenomenology also made it possible to provide this ontology with a foundation that overcomes dogmatism.

To explain what is meant here, Husserl points out once more that transcendental phenomenology is the science of all conceivable transcendental phenomena and of all the synthetic activities and structures in which such phenomena alone can become constituted. These activities and structures are those of individual transcendental subjects, but also those of all subjects bound together to communities of subjects. Taken as such, transcendental phenomenology is at once the a priori science of all conceivable beings. One should note here that this science is not only the science of the totality of all objective entities, and most certainly not just the science of the objects of the positive sciences of the natural attitude; rather, in full concretion, it is the science of all beings as such. It explains how each being derives the meaning and validity of its being from the constituting activities of transcendental subjectivity. But this also encompasses the being of the transcendental ego itself, whose demonstrable essence is to be transcendentally constituted in and for itself.

Accordingly, if phenomenology is developed properly, it is the truly universal ontology that can overcome the dogmatism of the illusory ontology envisioned by Leibniz, which was conceived as a positive science of the natural attitude. And yet transcendental ontology comprises within itself the truly legitimate content of dogmatic ontology, but now to be taken as fully grounded originally in intentional constitution.

In section 12, Husserl explains that if one considers how the contents of the dogmatic ontology of the tradition are included in transcendental phenomenological ontology, it appears that also every conceivable a priori is ultimately determined in the validity of its being as the achievement of transcendental subjectivity. But this implies that the pure and a priori concepts of the entities that constitute the subject matters of the various *ontologies* are ultimately also determined in their being by the constituting activities of transcendental subjectivity. If these pure sciences are developed methodically, then there will no longer be "paradoxes" or "crises of foundations" in these sciences.

In Husserl's view, only a radical grounding by phenomenology can transform the pure, a priori sciences, which have come into being historically through transcendental naivete, into genuine, methodically fully self-justifying sciences. When this happens, these sciences will cease to be dogmatic, positive sciences and instead become dependent branches of phenomenology as the all-encompassing eidetic ontology.

Finally, in section 13, Husserl explains that phenomenology has a task not only in regard to the foundation of the pure, a priori sciences, the "exact sciences," but also in regard to the foundation of all *empirical* sciences. For if it is the case that transcendental phenomenology provides the foundation for the regional ontologies, and if it is the case, as we have seen before, that every genuine empirical science demands that its foundations be provided by a corresponding a priori, regional ontology, then it follows that transcendental phenomenology, in the final analysis, provides the foundations for the empirical sciences as well.

If we now take the universe of all possible empirical sciences and demand for them a radical grounding that will be free from all foundational crises, then we are gradually led to an all-embracing a priori that makes a radical, phenomenological grounding of these sciences possible. We can then speak of an all-embracing science of facts that derives its meaning and foundation from the factual, transcendental intersubjectivity, which itself in turn receives its foundation from transcendental subjectivity.

In this way, we can understand how Husserl legitimately could speak of an *empirical phenomenology* that follows after the eidetic phenomenology, which itself consists of several ontologies ultimately rooted in transcendental phenomenology. Empirical phenomenology is the complete, systematic universe of all positive sciences, provided we take them from the outset as absolutely grounded methodically through eidetic phenomenology.

In the commentary to follow, I shall focus on four important issues: (1) transcendental phenomenology and other forms of knowledge, (2) the transcendental self-constitution of the transcendental ego, (3) time and consciousness of time, and (4) intersubjectivity. Only the first, second, and fourth of these topics directly refer to sections 11, 12, and 13 of Husserl's text. The third topic has been placed here, even though in Husserl's text it was alluded to earlier, because an adequate treatment of the issue presupposes that the transcendental reduction already has been performed.

Commentary

Transcendental Phenomenology and Other Forms of Knowledge

▌ Phenomenology and Ontology

What Husserl claims in section 11 is in complete harmony with his conception of transcendental phenomenology as developed in his major works, beginning with the first volume of *Ideas*. Transcendental phenomenology is the pure and transcendental science of all conceivable transcendental phenomena, including the all-encompassing synthetic activities and structures by which such phenomena alone are concretely possible. Taken as such, transcendental phenomenology is the science of all conceivable beings; thus it provides the *logos* to all *onta*, it is *ontology* in the genuine sense of the term. It explains how each being derives its meaning and the validity of its being from the corresponding intentional acts of constitution.

It is peculiar here that Husserl refers to the fundamental science with the term "ontology." In all other works, he always uses the term "ontology" to refer to certain sciences of the natural attitude that are all pure and eidetic sciences. Specifically, Husserl uses the term "ontology" for formal ontology, the material ontology of the life-world, the general ontology of the world of immediate experience, and the various regional ontologies.[1] Since all these sciences are "positive" sciences developed on the basis of the natural attitude, they are always set apart from phenomenology as a transcendental science, even though it is true that the eidetic sciences, in some sense at least, are "included" in transcendental phenomenology. In Chapter Two, we saw that the reference to Leibniz makes matters even more complicated, since it is not clear from the text whether Husserl refers to Leibniz's *mathesis universalis,* his *scientia generalis,* his metaphysics, or to what Leibniz himself took ontology to be. The terminology is also puzzling because it does not seem to be completely in harmony with the terminology used in *Cartesian Meditations,* where Husserl deals with similar issues. Yet these *Meditations* were written only a few years later than the *Encyclopaedia* article.

In section 59 of *Cartesian Meditations,* almost at the end of the book, Husserl explains his view on the place of ontological explications within transcendental phenomenology. To clarify the issue, he first briefly summarizes the route he had just taken in his own meditations. Starting from the experiential world given beforehand as existent and—by subsequently employing the eidetic reduction—

starting from any experiential world whatever, he exercised the transcendental reduction. He then turned to the transcendental ego insofar as it constitutes in itself "givenness-beforehand and all subsequent modes of givenness"; performing again the eidetic reduction, he went back to any transcendental ego whatever (*Meditations,* I). The transcendental ego was then described as an ego that experiences in itself a world. Tracing the essence of its constitution and its various egological levels, he made visible an a priori of a completely new kind, namely, the a priori of constitution (*Meditations,* II–IV). Finally, he made a distinction between the self-constitution of the ego itself, taken in its own primordial essentialness, and, on the other hand, the constitution of everything that is other and may pertain to various levels. The result is the all-embracing unity of the essential form belonging to the total constitution accomplished in my own ego, as whose correlate the objectively existing world, for me and for every ego whatever, is continually given beforehand.

With those most radical and consistent explanations of what is intentionally included and what becomes intentionally motivated in "my" ego and its essential variants, it becomes apparent that the universal de facto structure of the given objective world is to a very high degree an essential necessity, so that eidetic sciences of the objective world are genuine possibilities. The passage that then follows is immediately pertinent to the issue concerning ontology at hand. Husserl states there that a necessary consequence of this is that the task of an a priori ontology of the real world is inevitable. Yet in the final analysis, this is not a philosophical science. Such an a priori ontology, such as the ontology of nature, for instance, does indeed give a relative intelligibility to the world of facts, but it does not confer philosophical intelligibility (*Cart. Med.,* 137 [164]). From this it is thus clear that in *Cartesian Meditations,* the term "ontology" is not used for transcendental phenomenology or an essential part of it but rather for the various eidetic sciences of the natural attitude. The same terminology is also maintained in *Crisis.*

And yet this is not yet all there is to it. For even though Husserl in *Cartesian Meditations* and *Crisis* uses the term "ontology" usually in the sense indicated, there is nonetheless in *Cartesian Meditations* one place where he uses the term in quite a different sense, and in complete harmony with the one given to the term in the *Encyclopaedia* article. In so doing, he maintains an idea that seems to have occurred to him for the first time shortly after he presented his lectures on first philosophy (*E. Phil.,* 1:187–88n.3).

In the concluding section of *Cartesian Meditations,* Husserl explicitly uses the term "universal concrete ontology" to refer to transcendental phenomenology if the latter is understood to form a *unity* with all the ontologies mentioned above. He states that he has been able to show the concrete possibility of the Cartesian idea of philosophy as an all-embracing science grounded on an absolute foundation. In Descartes's view, metaphysics, which for him was the radically founding science, constitutes the roots of a tree of which physics is the trunk, and all other sciences are the branches. Husserl feels that he still has to indicate how he sees the unity of the sciences as rooted not in classical metaphysics but rather in transcendental phenomenology.

He then goes on to say that our everyday life and all the sciences move in the natural attitude, which from a critical point of view is naive; at that level, one is completely unaware of the constituting activities that go on in the presentation of any form of meaning. The sciences are critical in regard to the assumptions made in our everyday life, but they themselves never engage in a *transcendental* critique of knowledge as such. This explains why one encounters at that level all kinds of difficulties, paradoxes, and anomalies. In each discipline, there are undetermined intentional horizons that are all products of unknown and only crudely and naively understood intentional functions and activities. This is true for all the traditional sciences that developed since Galileo but also for mathematics and formal logic. While some scientists have tried to develop a better grounding and understanding of the meaning of their scientific efforts, they always remained within the confinement of their own disciplines. They did not realize that there is only one radical self-investigation, and that is the kind that phenomenology makes possible. Radical and universal self-investigation is inseparable from the genuine phenomenological method of intentional self-explication of the transcendental ego carried out by constitutive analyses and made possible by the transcendental reduction as well as by a systematic description in the logical form of an eidetics that rests on intuition. Such universal eidetic self-explication implies that it must be able to encompass all conceivable constitutive possibilities harbored in the ego and in transcendental intersubjectivity.

A consistently developing phenomenology therefore constructs a priori, with a strictly intuited essential necessity and universality, the *forms* of all conceivable worlds as well as these worlds themselves. Moreover, it constructs them "originally" in correlation with the constitutional a priori of the intentional performances that constitute them. The basic concepts that transcendental phenomenology is capable of unfolding in this way appear to include the basic concepts to be used in the various sciences. This is clear from the fact that the investigations concerning the transcendental constitution of a given world with necessity lead to a radical clarification of the meaning and origin of the concepts that pertain to it, such as world, nature, space, time, psychophysical being, animate organism, human being, psyche, community, and culture. Once these concepts are brought to light *originarily* in the manner articulated by phenomenology, there can no longer be paradoxes and anomalies. This is true particularly of all the fundamental concepts that concern the concrete structure and the encompassing structural form of the sciences that relate to the various regions of beings. If one were to carry out the investigations mentioned, one would be led to all the concepts that function as the fundamental concepts of all the positing sciences. In this context, Husserl uses the expression "genuine universal ontology" to refer to transcendental phenomenology if the latter is taken in such a manner that it now includes all a priori sciences, that is, the formal, the material, and the regional ontologies (*Cart. Med.*, 155 [180]).

Now that we have clarified Husserl's use of the term "ontology," we must turn to his reference to Leibniz in this context. When Husserl introduces the term "the truly universal ontology" in the *Encyclopaedia Britannica* article to refer to phenomenology in its fully developed form, he does so by mentioning the idea that transcendental phenomenology in principle is able to fully realize Leibniz's idea of a universal ontology "as the systematic unity of all conceivable a priori sciences." Yet, as we have seen already in Chapter Two, it is not immediately clear precisely to what discipline projected by Leibniz Husserl here refers.

It appears that the term "ontology" is used by Leibniz only once, namely, in his description of the various disciplines that are included in the "general science" that Leibniz hoped to develop. In the *Introductio ad Encyclopaediam Arcanam,* Leibniz defines the general science as being "nothing other than the science of whatever can be thought taken generally and as such" ("Scientia generalis nihil aliud est quam Scientia de Cogitabili in universum quatenus tale est"). The general science encompasses a number of other disciplines, such as classical logic, the art of discovering new truths, the method to order things properly, synthesis, analysis, pedagogy, "gnostology," mnemonics, the *ars characteristica* and the *ars combinatoria* (the science of signs and the science of combinations), the art of sophistry, philosophical grammar, the art developed by Lullus, the cabbala, and natural magic. At the end of the list, Leibniz then adds: "and perhaps also ontology, i.e., the science of something and nothing, of being and nonbeing, of the thing and its modalities, of substance and accident."[2]

If one compares this description of ontology with those of metaphysics used in Leibniz's own time, it is clear that what is called here "ontology" is really identical with what the tradition of the time called general metaphysics. If this is correct, then Husserl seems to be referring to Leibniz's general science rather than to his ontology. Obviously, the eidetic sciences to be included in transcendental phenomenology are quite different from the subdisciplines mentioned by Leibniz. Yet the general perspective from which Husserl looks at our entire "intellectual globe" is certainly of Leibnizean inspiration. For Leibniz, philosophy in the true sense is the totality of all universal doctrines; as such it is opposed to the science of "history," which is concerned with singular things.[3]

Husserl often refers to another idea mentioned by Descartes and concretely developed by Leibniz, namely, the idea of a *mathesis universalis.* By *mathesis universalis,* Husserl understands a fully developed formal logic together with abstract mathematics. The "ontology" or "general science" to which Husserl refers in the eleventh section of the *Encyclopaedia* article, however, is not the *mathesis universalis* because the latter is a purely *formal* ontology (*F. tr. L.,* 72–85 [76–89]).

I Phenomenology and the Sciences

Another puzzling statement is the claim about phenomenology's task in regard to the foundational crises in the exact sciences. If one disregards the title of section 12 for a moment and simply reads the subsequent text, it is clear that Husserl speaks about all eidetic disciplines and all regional ontologies as well as formal ontology. While Husserl speaks of mathematical disciplines in the text, they are merely mentioned *as examples,* since paradoxes and foundational crises are there well-known events. Furthermore, it is not at all common to count the mathematical sciences among the exact sciences. The term "exakte Wissenschaften" is commonly used for those sciences that rest on measuring procedures that make it possible *to make use of* mathematical disciplines. Examples of exact sciences are physics, astronomy, and chemistry. Another somewhat puzzling point is the fact that in section 13 Husserl puts the sciences of fact opposite to the exact sciences; yet Husserl commonly uses the term "ontology" or "eidetic science" to refer to the "opposite" of the sciences of fact.

In the third version of the *Encyclopaedia Britannica* article, Husserl's treatment of these issues was much more detailed. Because what he claims there will help us solve some of these puzzling issues, I shall present here a brief paraphrase of the basic ideas contained in that passage (cf. *Phän. Psych.,* 519–21).

We have seen that transcendental phenomenology is the science of all conceivable transcendental phenomena as they appear in the all-encompassing synthetic formations in which alone they are concretely possible, namely, in the formations of transcendental subjects, who are connected with each other in communities of subjects. It is because of this that phenomenology is the absolute universal science of all being (*Seiendem*) insofar as each being receives its meaning as a being from intentional constitution. This is true also for the subjects themselves because their being is essentially being-for-themselves. Accordingly, transcendental phenomenology is not a special science among others but—assuming we take it in the form in which it would be if it already were systematically fully developed—is the realization of the idea of an absolutely universal science, specifically to be taken as an eidetic science. As such it must encompass all possible aprioric sciences in a systematic unity, and this by virtue of the fact that it takes into consideration all aprioric interconnections in an absolute grounding from every possible point of view.

By employing an expression that comes from our tradition and giving it a somewhat broader meaning, we can also say that transcendental phenomenology is the truly universal ontology that philosophers tried to develop already in the eighteenth century, without, however, being able to realize the idea. It is an ontology that does not get stuck in the naive one-sidedness of the natural, positive attitude, and, on the other hand, does not get stuck in formal generalities or even in esoteric, analytic explanations of concepts of the kind one finds in the ontology of Wolff and Baumgarten. It derives its insights from the original sources of a universal intuition that traces and investigates all essential connections, and so reveals the entire system of forms that belongs to every compossible universe of all possible being; and contained therein are also the forms of every possible world of things present at hand.

Leibniz already had the basic idea that for a genuine theoretical knowledge and science, the knowledge of possibilities must precede the knowledge of real things. Accordingly, he required for every real and ideal sphere of being corresponding aprioric sciences of pure possibilities (for example, also a pure grammar). In this way, he fully understood the true meaning of the typical achievements of the exact sciences of nature and of their exemplary character with respect to the formation of the method of all sciences of real things. Since the time of Francis Bacon, the modern world has searched for a universal knowledge of the world that would be a complete system of all sciences of the real world.

Later it appeared that if this knowledge indeed were to be a truly scientific one that could be developed with a rationally comprehensible method, this effort would be successful only if the a priori that belongs to the concreteness of the whole world were systematically discovered and unfolded in the systematic context of all a priori

sciences of the real world. It was mainly through Kant's critique of
the ontology that was developed in the school of Leibniz and Wolff
that Leibniz's idea lost its power, so that even the a priori of nature
was never developed completely in a systematic fashion. Whatever
was available in this regard was brought to light by the structure of
the exact method of the physical disciplines. Yet the preference for
this method does not at all mean that this method realizes the fundamentally perfect methodical form for these sciences.

Connected with all of this is the fact that the fundamental part
of the mathematical method to an increased degree proved to be inadequate; it has been shown also that the much-admired mathematical evidence is in need of critique and methodical reform. The
foundational crises in which today all positive sciences have ended
up pertain also, and even in the most sensitive manner, to the pure
mathematical sciences, which constitute the foundation for the exact sciences of nature. The battles about the "paradoxes," about the
legitimate or apparent evidence, of the fundamental concepts of set-
theory, arithmetic, geometry, the pure doctrine of time, just to mention a few, even the battle about the right on the part of the
empirical sciences of nature to change these disciplines according to
their needs instead of just taking their results over, have made it
clear that all these sciences cannot yet be considered to be sciences
in the full and genuine sense, that is, sciences which are methodically transparent.

Thus the realization of Leibniz's idea of a rational grounding of
all positive sciences through the development of all corresponding
aprioric sciences does not yet mean the realization of sciences of
facts of an adequate rationality, as long as the aprioric sciences
themselves have been developed merely on the evidence of a naive
positive attitude, for instance, of the kind we find in geometry. The
genuine basic concepts of all positive sciences, that is to say, of those
from which all scientific concepts of the real world are to be derived,
are necessarily also the fundamental concepts of the corresponding
aprioric sciences. If there is something lacking in the fully intuitive
method of their legitimate formation in which the knowledge of their
genuine meaning is to be grounded, then the lack of clarity will affect the entire a priori and thus also the entire theoretical composition of the empirical sciences.

Finally, it is important to mention once more that in the expression "the exact sciences" Husserl often uses the term "exact" in a
special sense. Even though he mentions the mathematical sciences
here explicitly when he speaks about the exact sciences, it nonetheless is clear that the term "exact" here is to be taken in the sense that
is characteristic for the "exactness" of the various ontologies that

owe their "exactness" to the basic a priori concepts that they unfold systematically.

▌ Constitutional Problems Pertaining to the Transcendental Ego Itself

▌ The Problem of the Self-constitution of the Transcendental Ego

We have seen that for Husserl objects exist for the transcendental ego, and that they are for the ego what they are only as objects of actual and possible consciousness. If this claim is to have any meaning, Husserl states, we must be able to explain what is concretely involved in this "existence as being-for-the-ego," to what kind of consciousness the claim refers, what the structure of consciousness precisely is, what exactly is meant here by "possibility," and other similar questions. As Husserl sees it, these questions can be answered only through constitutional analyses (*Cart. Med.*, 65 [99–100]).[4]

Moreover, only one method is possible here, the one required by the essence of intentionality and of its horizons, for the transcendental ego is what it is solely in relation to its intentional objects. Among these there are not only objects within its adequately verifiable sphere of immanent time but also world objects that are shown to be existent only in its inadequate and merely presumptive external experience. It is thus an essential property of the ego constantly to have systems of intentionality as actualities or potentialities. Each object that this ego ever "means," thinks of, or values indicates this object's correlative system and exists only as the correlate of that system. An important element, however, is still missing in our explanations. The ego itself is existent for itself by continuously constituting itself as existing: it transcendentally constitutes itself. The ego grasps itself not only as a flow of life but also as an "I" who lives through the cogitations of this flow as the same "I myself."

Hitherto, we have paid attention only to the intentional relation between the *cogito* and its *cogitatum* and to that synthesis which polarizes the manifolds of actual and possible consciousness toward identical objects as synthetic unities. Here, however, we meet a second polarization, a second type of synthesis, which encompasses all the particular manifolds of cogitations as belonging to the identical ego, which, as the active subject of consciousness, lives in all experiences as related through them to all object-poles (*Cart. Med.*, 66 [100]).

Note, however, that this "centering" ego is not an empty pole of identity. Rather, according to a law of transcendental genesis, it acquires a new abiding property every time an act emanates from it

262 I CHAPTER TEN

and has a new objective meaning. When, in an act of judgment, I decide for the first time that something exists or is this or that, the flowing act passes, but from now on, I am abidingly the ego who is thus decided: I am of this or that conviction. This does not mean merely that I remember that act now or can remember it later; rather, as long as the act and its correlate are accepted by me, I can return to them again and again, find them as mine, and correlatively find myself as the ego who is convinced in this or that way.

The temporal ordering of such determining properties of the ego is manifestly not a continuous filling of immanent time with lived experiences—just as the abiding ego itself, as the pole of the abiding ego properties, is not an experience or a continuity of lived experiences, even though the ego is so related to the stream of its lived experiences. Since, by its own active genesis, the ego constitutes itself as an identical substratum of ego properties, it constitutes itself also as a fixed and abiding personal ego (*Cart. Med.*, 66–67 [100–101]).

We must now distinguish the ego in full concreteness, which will be called the concrete monad, from the ego as the identical pole and substratum of habitual properties. The ego can be concrete only in the flowing manifold of its intentional life, along with the objects meant in its concrete acts. This is to be understood in the following way. As ego, I have a surrounding world that is continually existing for me and in which objects exist for me as already distinguished into objects with which I am acquainted and those which I only anticipate as objects with which I may become acquainted. The former, which are in the first sense existing for me, are such by an original acquisition of what I had never beheld previously and by my explication of it through particular intuitions of its features. In my synthetic activity, the object thereby becomes constituted originally, perceptively, in the explicit form of something identical having its manifold properties. My activity of positing and explicating being thus sets up a habituality of my ego by virtue of which the object, as having its manifold determinations, is mine abidingly. Such abiding acquisitions constitute my surrounding world, insofar as I am acquainted with it at this time, including its horizons of objects yet to be acquired but already anticipated with this formal object structure.

I exist for myself and am continuously given to myself in experiential evidence as "I myself." This is true of the transcendental ego and, correspondingly, of the psychologically pure ego; it is true, moreover, with respect to any sense of the word "ego." Since the monadic concrete ego includes the whole of actual and potential conscious life, it is clear that the problem of explaining this monadic ego phenomenologically must include all constitutional problems without any exception. Consequently, the phenomenology of self-constitution coincides with phenomenology as a whole (*Cart. Med.,* 67–68 [102–3]).

Only through a reform brought about by phenomenology can one liberate the modern sciences from their untenable position. Leibniz's basic quest for the development of all aprioric sciences must obviously be maintained. But the discovery of the idea of a new universal ontology that is contained therein must in an essential manner be perfected through the recognition of the essential dependence and methodical incompleteness of an ontology developed from the natural, positive attitude, and through the recognition of its belonging within the context of phenomenology, which alone is absolutely independent and absolutely universal. Once the ontological disciplines are reformed and developed as concretely full, constitutive ontologies, the radical method that was lacking in the positive attitude will be created intuitively.

Transcendental phenomenology includes thematically all conceivable achievements that come about in transcendental subjectivity; it also includes the natural attitude, together with the purely and simply existing world, just as it includes all habitual attitudes and the unitary structures that are constituted in them. Together with the world, phenomenology also includes all the positive sciences, which are related to this world, that is, all empirical and aprioric sciences. Transcendental phenomenology includes and treats these sciences and all their unitary structures together with the multiple acts in which they become constituted. In its systematic theories, in its universal apriori of all possible contents of transcendental subjectivity, the entire apriori that belongs to the natural attitude must also be included, not ready-made and in isolation but rather together with the apriori of the transcendental constitution that belongs to them. But this also means that, together with this a priori, the method through which it can be brought about must also be included, and this method is either imperfect or rationally intuitive once it has been developed completely.

Transcendental Analysis as Eidetic — With the doctrine of the ego as pole of its acts and as substratum of its habitual properties, we have reached the level of genetic phenomenology, which deals with the problems of phenomenological genesis. However, before we can clarify more precisely what genetic phenomenology is, we must once more reflect upon the phenomenological method. We must try to apply the eidetic reduction. In order to facilitate the approach to the constitutional problems, we have, in our considerations concerning analysis and constitution, made use of a merely empirical description, although this description remained in the sphere of transcendental experience. The method of eidetic description transfers all empirical descriptions into a new and fundamental dimension that is relatively easy to grasp now that we have given a number of empirical descriptions.

The method of transcendental reduction, Husserl continues, reduces each of us, as a Cartesian meditator, to his or her transcendental ego, with its concrete monadic contents, as this de facto and exclusively absolute ego. When I continue meditating, I find types that can be described and intentionally explicated and I am thus able to progress step by step in the intentional uncovering of my monad along the fundamental lines that offer themselves to me. In the course of our descriptions, such expressions as "essential necessity" and "essentially determined" forced themselves upon us. These phrases express a definite concept of the a priori that was first clarified and founded by phenomenology.

To clarify the matter, let us look at some particular examples. Any type of intentional, lived experience will do; therefore, take the perception of a particular table. Let us think of it as explicated and described by intentional analysis with respect to noesis and noema. This can signify—and so we have understood it up to now—that only a type of the de facto occurrence in the de facto transcendental ego is in question and that these descriptions have an empirical significance. But involuntarily our description was of such a universality that its results remain unaffected by the empirical facticity of the transcendental ego.

Starting from this particular perception, we are able to practice the eidetic reduction. Our analyses of perception are then essential or eidetic analyses. All that we have said concerning syntheses that belong to the type "perception," concerning horizons of potentiality, and so on, holds good essentially for everything that can be formed by this free variation and accordingly for every perception whatsoever. In other words, with absolute essential universality and with essential necessity this holds for every particular case and therefore for every de facto perception, since every fact can be thought of merely as an example of a pure possibility.

Though each single chosen type is thus raised from its environment within the empirically factual transcendental ego into the pure, eidetic sphere, the intentional outer horizons pointing to its uncoverable nexus within the ego do not vanish but rather become eidetic themselves. With each eidetically pure type, we find ourselves not inside the de facto ego, but inside the *eidos* "ego"; and constitution of one actually pure possibility among others implies, as its horizon, a purely possible ego, a purely possible variant of my de facto ego. Therefore, if we think of a phenomenology developed as an intuitively a priori science purely according to the eidetic method, all its eidetic researches are nothing other than uncoverings of the all-encompassing *eidos* "transcendental ego as such," which comprises all pure possible variants of my de facto ego and this ego itself as possibility. Eidetic phenomenology, accordingly, explores the universal a priori, without which neither I nor any transcendental ego whatsoever is imaginable. And since every eidetic universality has the value of an unbreakable law, eidetic phenomenology explores the all-embracing laws that prescribe for every factual statement about something transcendental the possible meaning of that statement. Thus, to me as the meditating ego, guided by the idea of philosophy as the all-embracing science, grounded with absolute strictness, it becomes evident now that, first of all, I must develop a pure eidetic phenomenology, and that in the latter alone the first actualization of a philosophical science as a first philosophy can take place.

After the transcendental reduction, my interest is directed to my pure ego. But its uncovering becomes genuinely scientific only if I go back to the apodictic principles that pertain to this ego as exemplifying the *eidos* "ego," that is, if I go back to the essential universalities and necessities by means of which the fact is to be related to its original fundaments. In this way, we arrive at the methodological insight that, along with the phenomenological reduction, eidetic intuition is the fundamental form of all particular transcendental methods. Both of them together determine the legitimate meaning of transcendental phenomenology (*Cart. Med.,* 69–72 [103–6]).

Genetic Phenomenology — After this digression dealing with the meaning of the eidetic reduction within the realm of the constitutional problems of transcendental phenomenology, Husserl continues, we must return now to our original task of discovering the most important constitutional problems of phenomenology. In the following, we shall confine ourselves to problems arising within the limits of a purely eidetic phenomenology, so that the de facto transcendental ego and the particular data given in transcendental experience serve henceforth merely as examples of pure possibilities.

A brief description of a systematic sequence of problems and investigations concerning the transcendental ego as such, Husserl goes on to say, involves extraordinarily difficult problems, all the more difficult, since we must try to find new approaches to the specific universal problems of the constitution characteristic of the transcendental ego itself. The universal a priori belonging to a transcendental ego as such is a definite *eidos* that contains an infinity of a priori types of life's actualities and potentialities, along with the objects that can be constituted in this life as really existing objects. But in a unitarily possible ego, not all possible single types that I find in my concrete ego are compossible, and not all compossible ones are compossible in just any order. For example, being scientific is only possible in a human being; and even then, it is not really possible in a child. Restrictions of this type have their origin in an a priori universal structure and in a conformity to universal eidetic laws of coexistence and succession in an egological time. Whatever occurs in my ego, and eidetically in any ego as such, has its temporality and so participates in the system of forms that belong to the all-encompassing temporality with which every ego constitutes itself for itself (*Cart. Med.,* 73–75 [107–8]). The eidetic laws of compossibility govern both actual and possible existence occurring simultaneously or in succession. They are laws of "causality" in a very broad sense. However, to avoid an expression that easily evokes the prejudices of naturalism, we prefer to speak of "laws of motivation."

The universe of lived experiences that are the ontological content of the transcendental ego is a compossible totality only in the universal and unitary form of a flux in which all particular experiences are concatenated as processes that flow within the flux. Accordingly, the most universal form, which belongs to all particular types of concrete lived experiences, together with the products that are flowingly constituted in its flux, is a form of motivation, connecting all, and governing within each single experience in particular. We may call it a formal regularity characteristic of a universal genesis, according to which past, present, and future become unitarily constituted time and again in a certain noetic-noematic form-structure of flowing modes of givenness. But within this form, life goes on as a motivated course of particular constitutive achievements with manifold particular motivations and motivational systems that, according to universal regularities governing the genesis, make the universal genesis of the ego into a unity. The ego constitutes itself for itself in the unity of a history. And if it is true that the constitution of the ego contains all the constitutions of all its objects, then we must add here that the constitutive systems by virtue of which such and such objects exist for it are themselves also possible only within the domain of a genesis that remains in conformity with certain laws. At the same time, however, they are governed by the universal genetic form that makes the concrete monadic ego possible as a unity. That nature, a cultural world, a society, and so on, exist for me as concrete monadic ego signifies: that possibilities of corresponding experiences exist for me, and that other modes of consciousness corresponding to them exist as possibilities for me that can be fulfilled or not fulfilled by certain experiences.

As Husserl claims, problems concerning the psychological origin of the "idea of space," the "idea of time," the "idea of physical thing," and so on present themselves in phenomenology as transcendental problems of intentionality, which have their particular places among the problems of a universal genesis.

Husserl holds that a systematic approach to the ultimate universalities pertaining to the problems characteristic of eidetic phenomenology is very difficult. The beginning phenomenologist has to take himself as his initial example. After the transcendental reduction has been performed, he finds himself as *the* ego, then generally as *an* ego who already has a world, a world with nature, sciences, culture, and so forth and also with personalities of a higher order, such as state and church. Although phenomenology developed at first on the static level, both the static and the genetic levels are essential, and the latter is the most fundamental (*Cart. Med.,* 75–77 [109–11]).

Active and Passive Genesis — If we consider first the principles of constitutive genesis, which have universal significance for us as possible subjects related to a world, we find that there are principles of two fundamentally different types: principles of *active* and of *passive* genesis.

In *active genesis,* the ego functions as productively constitutive by means of lived experiences, which are ego acts of a special sort—for instance, the achievements of practical reason. The characteristic feature of these ego acts is that they—through socialization concatenated in a certain community and combined in a manifold, specifically active synthesis—originally constitute new objects on the basis of objects already given in modes of consciousness. In this way, for instance, in collecting the collection is constituted; in counting, the number; and in dividing, the part. All these objects present themselves to consciousness as products. Original consciousness of universality is also an activity in which the universal becomes constituted objectively. Many other examples could have been given here, such as the transcendental constitution of all cultural objects. Most of these objects presuppose the antecedent constitution of a transcendental intersubjectivity, as we shall see later on.

But although the higher forms of activities and products of reason, all of which have the character of ideal objects, cannot be regarded as belonging to every concrete ego as such, it will be clear that, in regard to the lowest levels, such as experiential grasping, the situation will be different. But in *any* case, anything built up by active genesis necessarily presupposes, as the lowest level, a passivity that gives something beforehand; and by analyzing this passivity, we necessarily come upon the constitution by *passive genesis.* The ready-made objects that we meet in life as existent mere physical things, such as a star or a mountain, are given with the originality of the "it itself" in the synthesis of a passive experience. As such it is given before every mental activity that begins with the active grasping that is characteristic of active genesis.

We must, furthermore, remark here that while the mental activities are forming their synthetic products, the passive synthesis that supplies them their material still goes on. The physical thing given beforehand in passive intentions continues to appear in unitary intuitions. And no matter how much the thing may be modified therein by our active explanation, it continues to be given beforehand, the manifold modes of appearance continuously flow, and in their manifold passive synthesis, the one physical thing, with its typical shape and other characteristic features, appears. But even a synthesis of this form has its history, which becomes manifest in the synthesis itself. It is owing to an essentially necessary genesis that I, the meditating ego, can experience a physical thing and can do so even at first sight. That is why we had to learn to see physical things in infancy, and that such modes of consciousness had to precede all others genetically. In early childhood, the pregiven field of perception does not as yet contain anything that, at first sight, might be made explicit as a physical thing. But the meditating ego can pene-trate into the intentional content of the experiential phenomena themselves and thus find intentional references leading back to a history, accordingly bringing these phenomena to light as formations that presuppose other, essentially antecedent formations.

Husserl tells us that here, however, we soon come upon eidetic laws governing the passive forming of ever new syntheses. We encounter a *passive genesis* of the manifold apperceptions as formations that persist in a typical habituality that is characteristic of them. These appear as data formed beforehand; as soon as they become actual, they affect the ego that is their center and motivate its activities. Thanks to this passive synthesis, into which achievements of active synthesis also enter, the ego always has an environment of objects (*Cart. Med.,* 77–80 [111–13]).

Association — According to Husserl, the universal principle of passive genesis governing the constitution of all objects that are given completely prior to every constitution of active genesis, is to be indicated by the term "association." Association, however, is a matter of intentionality, and as such it can be brought to the fore descriptively in its primal constituting activity, which then manifests itself as being governed by eidetic laws. Owing to the principle of association, each passive constitution of lived experiences, of objects in immanent time, of all real natural objects belonging to the objective spatiotemporal world, can be made understandable. Taken in this way, association is a fundamental concept of transcendental phenomenology.

The traditional conception of association and of the laws of association, which were, for instance, proposed by Hume and other thinkers, is only a naturalistic misinterpretation of the corresponding genuine intentional concept. In phenomenology this concept receives an essentially new definition. Association is not defined here in terms of a conformity to empirical laws governing complexes of data comprised in a human soul but in terms of a conformity to eidetic laws that in a most comprehensive way rule the constitution of the pure ego. Association, therefore, refers here to a realm of the innate a priori without which an ego as such is inconceivable.

Only in the phenomenology of genesis does the ego come to light as an endless connection of synthetically concatenated achievements joined together in the unity of an all-encompassing genesis, at various levels, all of which conform to the universal abiding form, temporality. This form itself is built up in a continuous, passive, and completely universal genesis that, as a matter of essential necessity, embraces everything new. In the mature ego, this many-leveled structure persists as an abiding system of forms characteristic of apperception and, consequently, of the constituted objects; among these objects we also find those which belong to the objective universe with its fixed ontological structure. And this persisting itself, too, is merely a form of synthesis (*Cart. Med.,* 80–81 [113–14]).

▌ Transcendental Idealism

From the foregoing, it is clear that phenomenology can be rightly characterized as a transcendental theory of knowledge. Such an "epistemology," however, is to be clearly distinguished from the traditional theories of knowledge, Husserl claims.

The main problem of traditional epistemology is the problem of transcendence. This problem can be formulated in the following way: How can my knowledge, abiding wholly within the immanence of my own conscious life, acquire objective significance for a world out there? According to traditional epistemology, this problem is to be solved within the realm of the natural attitude. According to phenomenology, however, the whole problem becomes inconsistent in this way: How can I, as a natural human being in the world, ask seriously and transcendentally how I get outside of my island of consciousness, and how what presents itself in my consciousness can acquire objective significance for the world out there? It will be clear that, in formulating the question in this way, I apperceive myself as a natural human being in the world and, in so doing, I have already presupposed the world outside of me, which precisely is in question.

In Husserl's opinion, the execution of the phenomenological reduction is only one way to avoid this inconsistency. Only then, says Husserl, does that conscious life come to light by which transcendental questions about the possibility of transcendental knowledge can be asked. But as soon as one tries to perform such a reduction, it becomes clear that all that exists for the pure ego is constituted in and by consciousness itself and that transcendency is nothing but an immanent existential characteristic that is constituted within the ego itself. Every conceivable thing, whether immanent or transcendent, falls within the realm of transcendental subjectivity, taken as the subjectivity that constitutes all meaning and being. The world and consciousness belong together essentially, and as belonging together they are concretely one in the absolute concretion of transcendental subjectivity.

It will be clear, Husserl claims, that phenomenology is *eo ipso* transcendental idealism, though in a fundamentally new sense. It is neither a psychological idealism that tries to derive a meaningful world from senseless sensuous data, nor is it a Kantian idealism that believes in the possibility of a world of things in themselves; rather, it is a transcendental idealism as a consistently executed self-explication in the form of a systematic egological science (*Cart. Med.*, 81–88 [114–21]).

I Time and Consciousness of Time

I Some Historical Observations

In Husserl's treatises and lecture courses devoted to an exposition of transcendental phenomenology as a whole, temporality, time, and consciousness of time are discussed first in connection with the concept of intentionality and later in reflections on constitution.[5] I discuss some of the pertinent issues in this section rather than in preceding chapters because our discussion will have to turn to a level of analysis that presupposes that the transcendental reduction has already been performed.

In the preceding pages, we have already touched on issues directly pertaining to analyses of time and time consciousness. We had to limit ourselves in these cases to some observations that were pertinent to the main issues at hand. We must now turn to a more systematic treatment of this important subject.

Reflections on time and consciousness of time always had an important place in Husserl's philosophy from the very beginning. Investigations concerning consciousness of time occupied him al-

271 I Transcendental Phenomenology as Ontology

ready in 1893 in connection with analyses that focused on perception, recollection, and expectation. Consciousness of time would remain a very important focal point of his phenomenological analyses between 1904 and 1917, particularly during the years 1900–1901 and 1904 through 1911. The result of these investigations was made ready for publication in 1928 by Heidegger,[6] who was able to make use of Stein's earlier editorial work. A better and more definitive text of Husserl's phenomenology of the consciousness of internal time appeared in 1966 and was prepared by Boehm. Finally, in 1985 Bernet has proposed several important changes in Boehm's dating of several manuscripts.[7]

Since 1928 scholars who occupied themselves with Husserl's phenomenology of the consciousness of internal time have always assumed that the text prepared by Heidegger was a definitive, critically edited text. Careful and painstaking research by Boehm and Bernet has shown that this is not so; Stein and Heidegger did not carefully distinguish between texts written in the prephenomenological phase of Husserl's thought, texts written before the phenomenological reduction was introduced, and texts that presuppose that the transcendental reduction has already been performed. It would be improper to blame either Stein or Heidegger for the poor quality of the text that they have produced from a historical point of view. One should realize that both worked directly under Husserl's supervision, and Husserl studied the final version that the editors had prepared for publication. Husserl himself was manifestly more concerned about the issues than about historical scholarship. The new editions of the text of the lectures and the pertinent manuscripts make it possible to trace Husserl's development in his thinking about time and consciousness of time between 1893 and 1917 back to their starting point.

For a proper understanding of the development of Husserl's thought in regard to this issue, particularly in the period between 1904 and 1917, one must keep in mind the following factors. In 1904 Husserl had not yet discovered the phenomenological reduction; between 1906 and 1911, he already had access to the phenomenological reduction, but the latter was not yet clearly distinguished from the transcendental reduction. Consequently, the early analyses were written from the perspective of the natural attitude, whereas the latest reflections on the subject were written from a transcendental point of view. Moreover, Husserl's own ideas were at first deeply influenced by Brentano, Alexis Meinong, and Stumpf; he was only gradually able to bring to light basic errors and flaws in the investigations of the three authors mentioned. Finally, originally Husserl had given a *"schematic"* interpretation of the constitution of time consciousness in which he made use of the insights introduced in *Logical Investigations*. This kind of interpretation was abandoned in the latest investigations concerning time consciousness.[8]

For Husserl, reflections on time and consciousness of time are very important in phenomenology because consciousness of time is the most fundamental form of consciousness and is presupposed in all other structures and forms of consciousness. Time consciousness is an essential dimension of every conscious, intentional experience, so that the analysis of time consciousness in some sense must precede the analyses of all other forms of consciousness. Yet at first, Husserl found the analyses of time consciousness extremely difficult, so that in the first volume of *Ideas,* he decided to remain silent about time and consciousness of time, even though he had already dealt with the subject in several lecture courses and had dedicated numerous detailed analyses to the subject. In a lecture course given in Göttingen in 1906–7, Husserl once stated: "I do not at all intend to offer this analysis as a final one; it cannot be our task here to solve the most difficult of all phenomenological problems, the problem of the analysis of time. What matters to me here is only to lift the veil a little from this world of time-consciousness, so rich in mystery, that up until now has been hidden from me."[9]

Analysis of Our Consciousness of Inherently Temporal Objects

The analyses of time consciousness are really a very complex example of intentional and constitutional analysis. Consciousness of time exemplifies, and in some sense also makes possible, intentionality, the basic and universal structure of all conscious life. The phenomenologist must try to analyze and describe the essence of intentionality in its manifold forms and dimensions. Consciousness of time is one of these intentional experiences, but it occupies the central position insofar as it is an essential dimension of every other conscious experience. Neither time nor consciousness of time can ever be found independently from other experiences, yet, on the other hand, consciousness of time has a founding role in regard to all other experiences.

The phenomenon of time consciousness is so complex that Husserl was convinced that it should be dealt with at different levels. Thus he first focused on analyses concerned with conscious awarenesses of the time of external, or transcendent, inherently temporal objects, such as a tone, a melody, or a symphony. He then focused on analyses concerned with immanent, or internal, time, which is characteristic of the intending acts and the contents of consciousness through which transcendent temporal objects appear. Finally, at the deepest level, Husserl turned to the "absolute time-constituting flow of consciousness." The absolute flow constitutes the internal time of all intending acts and, through them, the transcendent time of all external objects. In addition, it also constitutes itself.[10]

In his analyses of our consciousness of inherently temporal objects, say a melody, Husserl took his point of departure from the theory developed earlier by Brentano and others. In Husserl's view, these authors approached the issue in the right way but tried to explain the relevant phenomena by an unfounded appeal to laws of association that would guide our imagination. For Brentano, time and temporal succession are not really perceived but rather are grasped by the reproductive and productive imagination. In his effort to show that time and temporal succession indeed are truly perceived, Husserl made a distinction in the perception of a melody between the original impression (*Urimpression*) of each individual tone or tone element, a continuity of ever new primary recollections (*primäre Erinnerungen*)—later called retentions—and finally the expectation, or protention, of what is still to come. Thus we in each case perceive a *now* surrounded by a temporal court or halo, a horizon of what is no longer and not yet. In this way, one can describe the first phase of the perception of a temporal object. One can then show how each phase goes over into every new phase, thus forming a continuous stream. As long as the melody lasts, there always is an ever new original impression, an ever new *now* that functions as the moving force of the constitution of time. This original impression changes over into the retention of the impression, and the latter again changes over into a retention of the retention of the impression, and so on. One can thus show that the original temporal field in its continuous change is indeed given in its primordial self-givenness. It is perceived and not reproduced or produced by the imagination.[11]

We have seen that for Husserl both time and the consciousness of time cannot exist and cannot be considered adequately by themselves, independently of objects and our experiences of these objects. Time is for him a form, but a form of individual objects. Objects obviously have many characteristics and properties beyond the form of time, so that time does not at all exhaust the objects that fall within time. Temporal objects are thus quite different from one another in respects other than time. Analyses of the temporal aspect of temporal objects are concerned only with the temporal features that the objects have in common, not with any other feature or characteristic that distinguishes them.

274 I CHAPTER TEN

Husserl distinguishes between transcendent and immanent temporal objects; an actually sounding melody is an example of the former, whereas the act of listening to the melody is an example of the latter. In both cases, time is the irreducible form of individual realities in their described modes.

All temporal objects have several features in common. The most important of them is their *duration*. Every experienced temporal object presents itself as enduring. The duration of the object is the time of that object. Duration is therefore called the form of an individual object. For a temporal object to endure is to possess the form of time, and for an object to possess the form of time is to become concrete. Each temporal object has a specific duration in which it either changes or remains constant; in addition, it presents itself as something that may come to an end. Furthermore, every temporal object is given as an individual by virtue of the fact that it possesses a particular temporal location.

The Exstases of Time as Modes of the Appearance of Temporal Objects — In the preceding we have seen that temporal objects present themselves in temporal modes of appearance: as *now, past,* and *future.* I am conscious of an object as enduring, concrete, and individual only to the extent that it appears to me in these three modes. The *now* occupies a privileged position among these modes because it functions as a point of orientation and because temporal objects appear as past or future in relation to it.

The *now* is not a part of the temporal object in the sense in which a given tone is part of a melody. When I say that the tone is now, I do not identify the tone with the *now;* I merely mean to say that the tone appears now. Thus the *now* is a mode of appearance for an object, not the object itself. It is precisely because object and mode are not identical that we can speak of the same object presenting itself in different modes. "One can intend the same tone successively as future, as now, and as past, which would be impossible if the tone were simply identified with the now."[12]

The *now* is not a thing capable of independent existence. Even as a mode of appearance, the *now* does not exist by itself but is always accompanied by the modes of past and future with which it forms the temporal horizon in which every temporal object is given. Yet even though past, now, and future form the temporal horizon in which temporal objects are given, they do not merge because they exclude each other. To the extent that now, past, and future are modes of appearance distinct from the temporal objects that appear in them, and thanks to the fact that as modes of appearance they are both distinct and inseparable from one another, an identical object can appear. Husserl also stresses the point that the immediately experienced present is an extended *now;* an indivisible *now* is something ideal created by abstraction.[13]

Immanent Time — On the next level of reflection, Husserl focuses on what he calls immanent time. In these analyses, he conceives of time as the condition of the possibility of the universal synthesis in which the whole of consciousness, consisting of numerous activities and processes of synthesis, is unified synthetically. In his view, the fundamental form of this universal synthesis—the form that makes all other syntheses of consciousness possible—is the all-embracing consciousness of internal time. The intentional correlate of this consciousness is immanent, or internal, temporality, in conformity with which all the ego's life processes that can ever be found reflectively must present themselves as temporally ordered, as beginning and ending, simultaneous or successive, within the constant infinite horizon of immanent time (*Cart. Med.,* 41–43 [79–81]).

Is Consciousness, Which Constitutes Time, Also in Time? — In his reflections on the temporalization of consciousness, Husserl first focuses on the question of whether consciousness that constitutes time is also in time. In his earlier manuscripts (1904–5), Husserl thought that each individual act is given as a *now.* Thus, in addition to the realization that I now perceive a tone, there is also the awareness that I now grasp my own awareness of the *now* belonging to the perception of the tone. This appears, indeed, to be correct as long as one remains in the natural attitude. Yet after one performs the transcendental reduction, it is not correct to say that the time of the perceiving act and the time of the perceived temporal object are not the same; nor can one say that they are simultaneous. After the reduction has been performed, and after one has moved from the mundane to the transcendental subject, one will see that the immanently enduring tone is indeed in each case given as *now,* but the constituting acts of perception, retention, and protention themselves are atemporal; they are not given in inner time. In other words, in view of the fact that all that is given as temporal (i.e., the perceived)—including the acts of consciousness insofar as they themselves are given as temporal—is constituted by consciousness, we must assume that the ultimate, everything-constituting consciousness itself cannot be temporal. In a sketch of 1908–9, Husserl writes:

> Is it inherently absurd to regard the flow of time as an objective movement? Certainly! On the other hand, memory is surely something that itself has its *now,* and the same *now* as a tone

for example. No. There lurks the fundamental mistake. The flow of the modes of consciousness is not a process; the consciousness of the *now* is not itself a *now*. The retention that exists "together" with the consciousness of the *now* is not "now," is not simultaneous with the *now,* and it would make no sense to say that it is.[14]

Different Kinds of Time: The Absolute Flow — Particularly in his later investigations concerning time and time consciousness, Husserl made a distinction between three basic kinds of time: (1) the perceived primordial time-field mentioned above; (2) "objective" time, which is constituted in reproduction and can in turn be distinguished in *objective time, transcendent time* (or the time of natural entities), and *objectively immanent time,* alluded to above; and (3) a prephenomenal and preempirical time that manifests itself in the stream of consciousness insofar as this is present to itself. These three kinds of time are constituted by absolute consciousness whose presence (*Urgegenwart*) is itself not a modality of time.

In reflections of this kind, Husserl often speaks of absolute consciousness as if it were a flow. Husserl is fully aware of the fact that in this case he is using a metaphor. Yet he feels that the metaphor is useful because it conveys the fact that absolute consciousness has phases, only one of which will be actual, whereas some of the others have passed and still others will come. Husserl is convinced that we are aware of the absolute flow and that it has a double intentionality, one by which it constitutes its own unity and appearance, and the other in which it constitutes the unity and appearance of the immanent object.

The flow has phases, and each of these phases possesses the three intentional moments of primal impression, retention, and protention; in this case, by primal intention one must understand the immediate consciousness of the now-phase of the immanent object. The retentional moment, however, is not immediately aware of the phases of the object that have just passed. Rather, it is immediately conscious only of the elapsed phase of the absolute flow. Thus retention refers to the intentional relation of a phase of consciousness to another phase of consciousness, and these phases themselves are not temporal objects.

On the other hand, since the elapsed phase of the flow originally did intend a phase of an object as being now, through its moment of primal impression and in retaining the just-elapsed phase of the flow, retention also retains the just-elapsed phase of the object in question. And since the retained phase of the flow itself possesses a retentional consciousness, that consciousness is obviously also retained. Thus we can always describe retention as retention of retention.

Husserl calls the retentional consciousness that intends the elapsed phase of absolute consciousness the horizontal intentionality (*Längstintentionalität*) of the flow, whereas the consciousness of the elapsed phase of the immanent object that the horizontal intentionality makes possible is called the transverse intentionality (*Querintentionalität*). The first constitutes the self-appearance of the flow, whereas the second constitutes the appearance of the immanent temporal object, that is, the act of perception, of memory, of imagination, and the like. If the constituted act is the consciousness of a transcendent temporal object, then the consciousness of the transcendent object in its temporal modes is also constituted.[15]

What has been said here is only a glimpse of the wealth of ideas that Husserl displays in his reflections on the consciousness of internal time. What has been said may have given the reader an idea of this most fundamental, but most difficult issue of transcendental phenomenology.

▎ Intersubjectivity

▎ The Problem of Intersubjectivity: Attempts at a Solution

Introduction — In the article for the *Encyclopaedia Britannica,* Husserl mentions on several occasions "the community of subjects."[16] This expression refers to an important issue that occupied Husserl ever since he began to take Descartes's *Meditations* and Kant's *Critique of Pure Reason* seriously. If, following Descartes and Kant, one begins the philosophical reflection with an individual meditating subject, one soon discovers that there are large realms of meaning for whose constitution an entire community of egos is necessary. As long as one does not make a transcendental turn, the problems created by this realization can all be solved in principle through careful intentional and constitutive analyses. A serious problem arises, however, with the transcendental reduction, for when this reduction brackets the entire world as transcending the consciousness of the meditating subject and as owing its entire meaning and being to its constitutive activities, the belief in the existence of other subjects is also suspended. The subsequent discovery that the entire world is ultimately the result of the achievements of transcendental subjectivity and is constituted by its intentional acts seems to make the conclusion inevitable that other egos are only projections of this solitary subject. If this conclusion were correct, the world constituted by transcendental subjectivity could not possibly have an objective meaning; it could not be a world for everybody. The issue is intimately related to phenomenology's claim to be a genuine transcendental philosophy and to the claim that, in the form of a constitutional theory remaining within the limits of the transcendentally reduced ego, it can solve all transcendental problems that pertain to the "objective" world.

In his efforts to deal with this basic problem, Husserl explicitly rejected solipsism as self-contradictory. On the other hand, he maintained that there can be no explanation of meaning and being in any form outside the intentional constitution, for meaning and being must be explained in terms of reason. In the preceding sections, we have seen how Husserl gives an account of the constitution of different types of objects as well as of the correlative constitution of one's own ego; yet the presence of other subjects as sources of meaning was never mentioned in that context. And yet only by means of the achievements of other subjects can a solipsistic phenomenology be transcended, but if other subjects are to be meaningful, they, too, must be constituted by the transcendental ego (*Cart. Med.*, 89–90 [121–22]).

Such a constitution, however, seems to be without any reason and even completely impossible. In the first place, it is difficult to understand how *constituted* other egos could help us to solve the transcendental problems pertaining to the *objective* world *for everybody.* Second, we face here a dilemma: the constitution cannot be objective in itself, since the term of the constitution is precisely a subject; nor can it be subjective, since subjective constitution necessarily means a self-constitution. Is there, then, perhaps a third kind of constitution that is neither subjective nor objective, or is there a kind of synthesis of objective and subjective constitution in which an object is constituted that is, at the same time, a subject?

Husserl's battle with this difficult problem began as early as 1905. Only in the last of the *Cartesian Meditations,* however, did he present a complete discussion of the matter. He tried to show there how the transcendental ego constitutes other egos as equal partners in an intersubjective community, which in turn forms the foundation for the objective, that is, the intersubjective world. The intersubjective community of egos, or transcendental intersubjectivity, is thus introduced here as the very presupposition of the objective world for everybody.[17] Whether his later theory, as explained in *Cartesian Meditations,* offers an adequate solution of the problem of solipsism is a point about which Husserl himself appears to have remained in doubt.[18]

According to Lauer, the problems concerning intersubjectivity arise as soon as, in the perspective of a phenomenological theory of constitution, we try to explain the universally valid objectivity of the world. We then need a universal subject; but, according to the requirements of transcendental phenomenology, this "universal" subject must also be a concrete subject. A concrete universal subject, however, can refer only to a concrete multiplicity of subjects. Since until now we have only met our own transcendental subjectivity as an example of the *eidos* "ego," we must now try to show by means of constitutional analyses that: (1) each subject must be self-constituted, for otherwise it can have no significance in a phenomenological context; (2) each subject must be constituted as such in each other subject, for otherwise a completely monadological universe will be the necessary result; (3) the constitution of the other must correspond to the other's self-constitution, for otherwise it will be invalid; (4) each subject must constitute a world of objects that is in some way identical with the world constituted by other subjects; (5) the world that each subject constitutes must be a world comprising oneself and others, for otherwise the unity of the world will be destroyed.[19] Finally, all these statements will be without any real foundation if they cannot be proved from the viewpoint of my transcendental ego. It is precisely this point that creates the greatest difficulties, as we shall see.

Empathy as the Way to a Solution — From the very beginning, it was evident to Husserl that we know the other as a subject. Although the supposition that every other consciousness that I posit in empathic experience does not really exist is not nonsensical, nevertheless *my* empathy itself is given in a primordial and absolute sense, not only with respect to its essence but also with respect to its existence (*Ideas,* 1:100–101 [85–86]). Thus, we must recognize in our field of objects some objects that are like none of the others. They present themselves not only as known by the knower but also as knowing the knower, and this also is an immediate phenomenon. To be a subject means to have experiences; to be experienced as a subject means to be experienced as having experiences. Somehow, therefore, the experiences of others must form part of my intentional life, without at the same time being my experiences. Hence we are obliged to find an intentional category comprising a kind of experience of the other's experience. Like Lipps, Husserl referred to this kind of experience as empathy, although he did not follow Lipps in his explanation of the phenomenon.

From the very beginning, Husserl maintained that he had found in empathy the key to a constituted world that would be objectively valid for everybody. In *Ideas,* he describes this thought clearly for both the natural and the phenomenological attitude. Describing our natural attitude, he says that whatever holds good for me personally also holds good for every other human being whom I find

present in my surrounding world. Experiencing them as human beings, I understand and accept them by means of empathy as ego subjects, units like myself and related to their natural surrounding
world (*Ideas,* 1:102–4 [86–87]). I do this in such a way that I apprehend the world about them and the world about me *objectively* as
one and the same world, which differs in each case only through affecting each consciousness differently. Despite these differences, we
come to an understanding with our neighbors and establish in common an *objective,* spatiotemporal fact-world as the world about us
that is there for all of us and to which we ourselves nevertheless belong (ibid., 55–56 [52]).

Speaking about constitutional problems, Husserl points out
that within the sphere of the transcendental reduction, the formation of the intersubjectively identical thing is a constitutive process
of a higher order than, for instance, the constitution of my own objects given in my lived experiences. Its constitution is related to an
indefinite plurality of subjects who stand in a relation of mutual
understanding. The intersubjective world is the correlate of the
intersubjective experience, which is mediated through empathy.
Here we are therefore referred to the various wholes of sensory
things already constituted individually by the many subjects and,
further, to the corresponding perceptual manifolds belonging to the
different personal subjects and streams of consciousness. The question of how this new factor of empathy plays a constitutive part in
objective experience and gives unity to those separate manifolds
must be explained in more detail (*Ideas,* 1:363–64 [316–18]).

Finally, it was evident to Husserl from the beginning that all
our knowledge of other subjects is to some extent indirect. We have
primordial experience of ourselves and our states of consciousness
in so-called inner or self-perception, but we do not have direct experience of others and their vital experiences in and through empathy.
We somehow see the living experiences of others through our perception of their bodily behavior. Although this seeing in the case of
empathy is an intuiting, giving act, it is no longer a primordial, giving act (*Ideas,* 1:6 [8]). The other is given to us not in a direct presentation but only by way of appresentation. Appresentation is a
process that acquaints us with aspects of an object that are not directly presented in themselves; we are familiar with such a process,
for example, in our acquaintance with the rear of a building when
we approach it from the front. In the latter case, direct presentations
may follow later on, but in the case of our knowledge of the other,
this is impossible. Rather, when we perceive a body other than our
own as "there" rather than as "here," we apperceive it at once as the

body of another ego by way of an assimilative analogy, a process that is not without problems.

On the basis of these principles, Husserl tried to develop a theory of intersubjectivity in the second volume of *Ideas.* In his third volume, however, he explained that the description of the problem of transcendental solipsism—that is more precisely, the relation between transcendental intersubjectivity and the objective world valid for me and for everybody as indicated in the first volume and explained in the second—is incomplete. This is because the central thesis of transcendental idealism posits that only the transcendental subjectivity originally has meaning with respect to its being and thus is an absolute being, whereas the "real" world is essentially relative to this absolute being; this central thesis is apodictically justified only if and when phenomenological explication of the transcendental ego succeeds in manifesting the other subjects that appear to me as *transcendental* in my transcendental life, within a *transcendental* we-community. Only in such a transcendental intersubjectivity is a real and objective world constituted as a world for everybody.[20]

It was for this reason that Husserl studied the problem again in *Formal and Transcendental Logic* and *Cartesian Meditations.* Since the ideas presented in *Cartesian Meditations* essentially agree with those given in *Formal and Transcendental Logic* and are more detailed and accurate, we will confine ourselves here to a brief description of the main ideas found in *Cartesian Meditations.*

| The Sphere of Transcendental Being as
| Monadological Intersubjectivity

The Problem of Experiencing Someone Else — In the foregoing, we have seen that the doctrine concerning the constitution of the transcendental ego seems to lead to transcendental solipsism. With respect to such a conclusion, one could say that the world constituted in the ego is indeed only a world for me and, therefore, only my idea; behind this idea there is somehow the world that exists in itself, and the problem is only to find a way from the first to the second world. One could also claim that those questions about an eventual transcendency of the world, and therefore the transcendency of the other egos, cannot be asked by phenomenology.

According to Husserl, it is much more fruitful to devote oneself to the task of a phenomenological explication of the explicit and implicit intentionalities in which other egos are verified in the realm of our own transcendental ego, instead of trying to follow up those suggestions and to present dialectical arguments and metaphysical

considerations in their favor. Only by means of such a phenomenological explication can the transcendental problem of the objective
world valid for everybody be solved (*Cart. Med.,* 89–90 [121–22]).

First of all, Husserl claims, in my intentional analyses concerning the other egos, my transcendental guide must be the experienced others themselves, precisely as they are given to me in
immediate and direct consciousness and manifest themselves there
with the noematic content belonging to them, and are taken now
purely as correlates of my own *cogito.* In other words, in many-sided
analyses I must try to describe the others just as I experience them,
namely, as beings, as world objects, as physical things, as governing
psychically their natural organisms, as psychophysical objects in
the world, as subjects for this world, as experiencing the world, and
as experiencing me myself.

Then, within the limits of my transcendentally reduced pure
conscious life, I experience the world, including the other subjects,
not as a formation of my own private synthesis but as an intersubjective world that is actually there for everyone. Yet everyone has
his or her own experiences, his or her own world phenomenon, while
the experienced world exists in itself, over against all experiencing
subjects and their phenomena of the world.

Then I have to ask myself: What is the explanation for this? I
hold fast, as I must do, to the insight that every meaning that any
being whatever can have for me with respect to its "what it is" and
its "that it is" is a meaning in, and arising from, my intentional life
and my constitutive syntheses. Therefore, I must begin with a systematic explication of the intentionality in which the being of the
others for me becomes established.

According to Husserl, the first problem is that of the "thereness
for me" of others. And this asks for a transcendental theory of experiencing someone else, a transcendental theory of empathy. Such a
theory contributes to laying the foundation for a transcendental
theory of the objective world valid for everybody (*Cart. Med.,* 90–92
[123–24]).

The Reduction to the Sphere of My Ownness — Husserl claims
that we must first perform, within the universal transcendental
sphere, *a new kind of reduction.* We must exclude from our thematic
field everything that is here in question, namely, all constitutional
achievements of intentionality relating to other subjectivities. This
reduction to the transcendental sphere of my ownness (*Eigenheits-
sphäre*)—that is, to the actual and potential intentionalities in
which the ego constitutes itself in its ownness—and thus to my transcendental concrete I myself, has an unusual sense, as we shall see.

In the natural attitude, I find myself distinguished from, and contrasted with, others. If I abstract from others, I alone remain. But such an abstraction is not yet radical, for such an aloneness does not modify the natural meaning of the world: to be experienceable by everyone. What we need here is a reduction by means of which I myself and all that refers solely and exclusively to me myself as this transcendental ego come to the fore. What is specifically proper to me as ego, my concrete being as a monad, purely in myself and for myself with an exclusive ownness, includes every intentionality and therefore the intentionalities directed to the other; but also these intentionalities and their correlates will at first remain excluded from our theme. If the ego in its ownness has been delimited, I can ask: How can my ego, within its ownness, constitute, under the heading "experience of something other," precisely something *other,* that is to say, the other as other? This question concerns, first, every possible other ego and, second, everything that acquires meaning from other egos—in short, an objective world in the proper and full sense of the term.

Let us try to characterize the ego's sphere of ownness and thus to perform explicitly the abstractive *epoche* yielding this new sphere. One remark, however, must be made in advance. The thematic exclusion of the constitutional achievements produced by the experience of something other—that is to say, the achievements referring to the other as other and all that presupposes the other as other—does not mean that we merely make a phenomenological *epoche* with respect to the naive acceptance of the other's being. The transcendental attitude is and remains presupposed here; everything that was previously for us in immediate consciousness is also here taken exclusively as a phenomenon, as a sense "meant." The above-mentioned abstractive *epoche,* then, is completely new but presupposes the transcendental reduction.

As ego in the *transcendental* attitude, I attempt first of all to delimit, within my horizon of transcendental experience, that which is particularly my own. I begin by freeing that horizon abstractively from everything that is alien (*Fremdes*). We thus abstract from what gives people and animals their specific meaning as egolike living beings and consequently also from all determinations of the phenomenal world whose meaning necessarily refers to and presupposes others as ego subjects. In this way, we retain a unitary coherent stratum of the phenomenon "world" that is the correlate of my continuously and harmoniously proceeding world experience. Despite our abstraction, we can continuously carry on our experiencing intuition while remaining exclusively in the retained stratum. This unitary stratum is distinguished by being essentially the *founding* stratum: I obviously cannot have the other as an experiential meaning without having this stratum in actual experience; the reverse is evidently *not* the case.

In this way, from the phenomenon "world," appearing with an *objective* sense, a substratum becomes separated as "nature" that is included in my ownness, a nature that must always be carefully distinguished from nature as the theme of the natural sciences. While nature as theme of the natural sciences is also the result of an abstraction—for it abstracts from everything psychical and from those predicates of the objective world that arise from persons—what is acquired by this scientific abstraction is still a stratum that belongs to the objective world itself and is therefore itself objective. But in the case of our abstraction, what is meant by "objective"—that is to say, the meaning of being constituted intersubjectively, of being experienceable by everyone and being valid for everybody—disappears completely. Thus a sense, "mere nature," that has lost precisely that "validity for everybody" is included in my ownness, as purified from every sense pertaining to other subjectivities.

Accordingly, this peculiar abstractive exclusion of the meaning of what is other leaves us still a kind of "world," a "nature" reduced to what is included in my ownness. As having its place in this nature because of my bodily organism, the psychological ego also remains, with body, soul, and personal ego; and finally, there are those predicates that get significance only and exclusively from this ego.

A paradox manifests itself in this case. The psychical life of my psychophysical ego, including my whole world-experiencing life and therefore my actual and possible experiences of what is other, is wholly unaffected by this reduction. Consequently, there belongs within my psychical being the whole constitution of the world existing for me and, by the same token, the differentiation of that constitution into the systems that constitute what is included in my ownness, and the systems that constitute what is other. I, the reduced human ego, am accordingly constituted as a member of the world with a multiplicity of objects outside me. But I myself constitute all this in my consciousness and bear it intentionally in me. The seeming paradox is thus that as constituting ego I must have the world-as-meaning within me as the correlate of my intentional activities (immanent); yet as concrete mundane ego I experience the world as external to me (transcendent) (*Cart. Med.,* 92–99 [124–30]).

Results of This New Reduction within the Sphere of the Transcendental Reduction — The preceding meditation has been carried out from the perspective opened up by the transcendental reduction. We must now ask how we can relate to one another the human ego reduced to what is purely its own and taken as being in the world that is equally reduced to a phenomenon, on the one hand, and the "I" as the transcendental ego, on the other. By means of the transcendental reduction, I have become aware of myself as the transcendental ego that constitutes in its constitutive life everything that is ever objective for me. I am aware of myself as the ego of all constitutions that exists in its own actual and potential lived experiences and constitutes in them not only everything objective but also itself as identical ego. If we now on this basis perform the second reduction, we can say that while I, as this transcendental ego, have constituted, and am continually further constituting as a correlate of my constituting activities, the world that exists for me, I can perform a mundanizing self-apperception in corresponding constitutive synthesis, an apperception in which my ego becomes constituted as a mundane ego, under the heading "ego in the usual sense."

By virtue of this mundanization, everything included in my ownness and belonging to my transcendental and ultimate ego enters as something psychical into my psyche. In so doing, I come upon the mundanizing apperception. And now, from the psyche as phenomenon and part of the phenomenon "human being," I can go back to the all-inclusive absolute or transcendental ego. In this ultimate transcendental ego and the universe of what is constituted in it, a division of this ego's whole transcendental field of experience takes place into the sphere of its ownness and the coherent stratum consisting in its experience of a world reduced to what is included in its ownness, and the sphere of what is other. Yet every consciousness *of* what is other belongs in the *former* sphere. Whatever the transcendental ego constitutes in that first stratum, whatever it constitutes as nonother, as its own, indeed belongs to this ego as a component of its own concrete essence. Within and by means of this ownness, the transcendental ego constitutes, however, the objective world as a universe of being that is other than itself, and constitutes, at the *first* level, the other in the mode "other ego" (*Cart. Med.,* 99–100 [130–31]).

Positive Characteristics of the Sphere of My Ownness — Husserl remarks that up to now we have only indirectly characterized the fundamental concept of that which is "my own" as nonalien (*Nichtfremdes*), a characterization that presupposes the concept of the other (*des Anderen*). We must try now to characterize it positively as the ego in its ownness.

When, in transcendental reduction, I reflect on myself as transcendental ego, I am given to myself perceptually as this ego in this perception that grasps it. I become aware that before this perception, I was already given, already there for myself as a possible object of original intuition, although I was not explicitly grasped as such. I am given with an open infinite horizon of still-undiscovered internal features of my own. As in a normal perception of a concrete material thing, my own being, too, is discovered by explication and gets its original sense by virtue of it. It becomes uncovered originally when my experiencing and explicating glance is directed to myself, to my perceptually and even apodictically given "I am," and to its abiding identity with itself in the continuously unitary synthesis of original self-experience. Whatever is included in this identical being's own essence is characterized as its actual or possible *explicatum,* that is, as that in which I merely unfold my own identical being as what it, as identical, is in particular, namely, "it in itself."

According to Husserl, there is, however, a difference between this self-perception and the explication of a perceptually given visual thing. Self-explication does not always go on in particular new perceptions in the proper sense. When explicating the horizon of being that is included in my own essence, one of the first things I run into is my immanent temporality: my existence has the form of a stream of lived experiences. Since this self-explication goes on in the living present, it can find, in a strictly perceptive way, only what is given in the living present. In the most original manner conceivable, it must uncover my own past by means of recollections. Therefore, although I am continually given to myself originally and can explicate progressively what is included in my own essence, this explication is carried out largely in acts of consciousness that are not perceptions of aspects of my ownness with all its actualities and potentialities.

This transcendental self-experience possesses an apodictic evidence, but only in a restricted sense. In unqualifiedly apodictic evidence, this self-explication brings to the fore only the all-encompassing structural forms in which I exist as ego. The explication of the single egological data, however, participates in this apodicticity only in an imperfect way; for example, as an evidence contained in my recollection of the past. Yet even here, perfect apodicticity is given at least as an idea (*Cart. Med.,* 100–103 [131–33]).

The ownness belonging to me as ego obviously extends not only to the actualities and potentialities of the stream of lived experiences. Just as it comprises the constitutive systems, so it comprises the constituted objects insofar as these are inseparable from the original constitution. This is true not only for hyletic data, which become constituted as my own as immanent temporalities within the limits of my ego, but also for all my habitualities, transcendent objects, and finally the entire reduced world. However, as soon as we exclude from our consideration the intentional achievements produced by empathy, we have a nature that is constituted as a unity of spatial objects transcending the stream of lived experiences, yet constituted merely as a multiplicity of objects of possible experience. This experience is purely my own life; and what is experienced in this experience is nothing more than a synthetic unity inseparable from this life and its potentialities.

In this way, it becomes clear that the concrete ego has a universe of what is peculiarly its own, which can be uncovered by an original explication of its apodictic self-consciousness. This explication is itself, at least in principle, also apodictic. Within this original sphere of original self-explication, we furthermore find a transcendent world that by reduction accrues to the ego's peculiar ownness on the basis of the intentional phenomenon "objective world" (*Cart. Med.*, 103–5 [134–35]).

Immanent and Objective Transcendency — The undeniable fact that my own essence can be contrasted with something else, and that I can become aware of something other than I, presupposes that not all my own modes of consciousness are modes of my self-consciousness. Since actual being is constituted originally by the fact that my experiences harmoniously grow together, my own self must contain, in contrast to my self-experience, yet other experiences united in harmonious systems. The problem is *how* it is to be understood that the ego can always have in itself intentionalities in and through which it wholly transcends its own being.

My experience of something that is not I manifests itself as experience of an *objective* world and of other egos therein. An important result of our new reduction was that it brought to light an intentional substratum in which a reduced *world* shows itself as an *immanent* transcendency. In the order characteristic of the constitution of a world alien to my ego, this reduced world is the primordial transcendency, the primordial world, and, notwithstanding its ideality, it is still a determining part of my own concrete being.

We must now try to explain *how,* at the higher and founded level, the sense bestowal of the constitutionally secondary objective transcendency, namely, the "objective world," takes place precisely as experience. And because the objective world is constantly there for me as already finished, this will entail a static analysis of this experience itself in which we must try to uncover the manner in which it precisely gives meaning (*Cart. Med.*, 105–6 [135–36]).

Constitution of the meaning of the objective world involves a number of levels. The first is the constitutional level of the other egos. Once the constitution of the other egos is explained, we must focus on the universal superaddition of meaning to my primordial world whereby the latter can manifest itself as an objective world, as the identical world for everyone, myself included. It is thus the other ego that makes it constitutionally possible for a new infinite domain of what is "other" to appear as an objective world to which all the other egos and I myself belong. But in this constitution of the objective world, the others do not remain isolated; on the contrary, an ego community as a community of monads becomes constituted in the sphere of my ownness, which in its communalized intentionality constitutes the one identical world. In this world all egos manifest themselves in an objectifying apperception as having the meaning "human being," as having the meaning "psycho-physical human beings as worldly objects."

As Husserl explains it, by means of the aforementioned communalization of intentionality, the transcendental intersubjectivity has an intersubjective sphere of its peculiar ownness in which it constitutes the objective world. This objective world, however, does not transcend the intersubjective sphere but inheres in it as an immanent transcendency. The objective world as the ideal correlate of an intersubjective experience is essentially related to intersubjectivity. Consequently, the constitution of the objective world necessarily implies a harmony of the monads mentioned (*Cart. Med.,* 106–8 [137–38]).

Appresentation — Husserl holds that after the definition and the articulation of the primordial sphere, it is especially the first of the above-indicated steps toward the constitution of an objective world that presents the greatest difficulties. These difficulties consist in the transcendental explication of experiencing someone else, taken in the sense in which the other did not yet attain the sense "human being."

In the case of experiencing other human beings, we generally say that the others themselves are there before us in person. Properly speaking, however, neither the other ego itself nor its lived experiences or its appearances themselves nor anything else belonging to its own essence is given in my experience *originally.* If that which belongs to the others' own essences were directly accessible, it would be merely a moment of my own essence, and therefore they themselves and I myself would be *the same.* And the same holds true for their bodies, if the latter were nothing but the bodies themselves, which are merely unities constituted in my actual and possible experiences. A certain mediating intentionality manifests itself here that, originating from the primordial world, makes present to consciousness a "there-with-me" (*Mit-da*) that nevertheless is not itself there and never can become an "itself-there." We thus have here a kind of *appresentation,* a making present with something else.

An appresentation occurs in external experience when, for example, the front of a house, which is actually seen, necessarily appresents its back. However, experiencing someone else cannot be a matter of just this kind of appresentation, since in external experience the verification by a corresponding fulfilling presentation is always possible, while such a possibility in the experience of someone else is excluded in principle. The question, therefore, is how the appresentation of another original sphere in my original sphere can be *motivated* as experience. It will be clear that a nonoriginal presentation can do so only in combination with an original one; and only as demanded by the original presentation can a nonoriginal presentation have the character of appresentation.

The perception that can function as the foundation here is our perception of the primordially reduced world. The problems, however, are: What in particular must be taken into account in the perception of the reduced world? How is the motivation to be built up? And how can the very complicated intentional achievement of the appresentation in question become uncovered?

The term "the other" means "alter ego," and the "ego" referred to in this expression is I myself, constituted within the sphere of my primordial ownness as the psychophysical unity, as primordial human being, as personal ego, governing immediately in my body and immediately producing effects in the primordial surrounding world. It is, moreover, the subject of a concrete intentional life and of a psychic sphere relating to itself and the world. All of that is already at our disposal; but as far as the intentionality by which it has become constituted is concerned, we have not yet investigated it here; that belongs to a different level and is the theme of investigations into which we have not yet entered.

Now, says Husserl, let us suppose that another human being enters my primordial sphere. Within the realm of the primordial reduction, this entrance must be described by saying that in the perceptual sphere belonging to my primordial world, a body is presented that, as primordial, is of course only an *immanent* transcendency. Since in *this* world my body is the only one that can be constituted originally as an animate organism, the body over there, which is nonetheless apprehended as an animate organism, must have derived its meaning from an apperceptive transfer of my animate organism. It will be clear then, that only a certain *similarity* within my primordial sphere connecting that body over there with my body can serve as the motivation for the analogizing apprehension of that body as another animate organism. There is thus a certain assimilative apperception, but by no means an inference from analogy, for apperception is not an act of thinking and therefore not an act of inference. Every apperception in which we apprehend at a glance objects given beforehand and in which we understand their meaning and its horizons immediately points back to a "primal instituting act" in which an object with a similar meaning became constituted for the first time. Even the physical things of the world that we have never seen are to some degree already known in regard to the type to which they belong. Thus each everyday experience involves an analogizing transfer of an originally instituted objective meaning to a new case, with its anticipating apprehension of the object as having a similar meaning. The manner in which apperceptions arise can vary greatly. There are different levels of apperception, corresponding to different layers of objective meaning. In the final analysis, we always return to the radical differentiation of apperceptions into those which, according to their genesis, belong purely to the primordial sphere, and those which present themselves with the sense "other ego" (*Cart. Med.*, 108–11 [138–41]).

The Concept of Pairing — If we attempt to describe the peculiar nature of that analogizing apprehension whereby a body similar to my own animate body within my primordial sphere becomes apprehended also as an animate body, we find that the primordially instituting original is always livingly present and therefore that the primal institution itself is always going on in a living manner; that what is appresented by virtue of the analogizing act can never attain actual presence and can never become an object of proper perception; and finally, that ego and alter ego are always and necessarily given in an original "pairing."

Pairing—that is, the configured occurrence as a pair and eventually also as a group—is a universal phenomenon of the transcendental sphere. It is a primal form of the passive synthesis that we call association, in contrast to passive synthesis of identification. The characteristic trait of a pairing association is that, in its most primitive form, two data are given intuitively in the unity of one conscious act, which, on this basis and essentially already in pure passivity, as data appearing with mutual distinctness, phenomenologically found a unity of similarity and thus are always constituted precisely as a pair—or in case there are more than two data involved, a group. We find here an intentional overlapping that comes about necessarily as soon as the data that undergo pairing become simultaneously intended; we find, more particularly, a mutual awakening and an overlapping of each other in regard to their objective meaning. This overlapping has its degrees, the limiting case being that of complete identity. The important point here is that, as the result of this overlapping, a mutual transfer of meaning takes place in the paired data.

In the apperception of the alter ego by the ego, pairing first occurs when the other enters my field of perception. I, as the primordial psychophysical ego, always occupy the central place in my primordial field of perception; my living body is always there and with primordial originality is equipped with the specific sense of an animate organism. In case there presents itself in my primordial sphere a body similar to mine and having determinations such that it must enter into a phenomenal pairing with mine, this body must appropriate its meaning "animate organism" from my body.

Husserl next asks whether or not this apperception is actually so transparent. What makes this organism another's rather than a second organism of myself? Obviously, the *second* fundamental characteristic of the apperception in question plays an important part here, namely, the fact that nothing of the appropriated meaning that is characteristic of bodily-hood as such can become actualized originally in my primordial sphere (*Cart. Med.,* 112–13 [141–43]).

But now, as Husserl explains, the problem of making such an apperception understandable in its possibility arises for us. How is it possible that the transferred meaning, as far as its ontological status is concerned, is appropriated as a set of psychic determinations existing in combination with that body over there, even though those determinations can never show themselves *as* themselves in the original domain belonging to the primordial sphere, which alone is accessible to me (*Cart. Med.,* 113–14 [143–44])?

My Experience of Somebody Else — As Husserl views it, the appresentation that gives the others' "psychic" determinations that are not accessible originally is combined with an original *presentation* of "their" bodies as parts of nature given in the sphere of my ownness. In this combination, the others' bodies and their egos are given in the manner characteristic of every transcending experience. Every experience points to further experiences that will probably fulfill and verify the appresented horizons. It will be clear then, that, in the case of an experience of someone else, the process of fulfillment can be effected only by *new appresentations* that proceed in a synthetical and harmonious way and themselves owe their existential status to their motivational connection with the changing presentations within the sphere of my peculiar ownness that necessarily belong to them. That is to say, the other organism that I experience continues to manifest itself as an actually animate body solely in its changing but incessantly harmonious behavior. This behavior has a physical side that appresentatively indicates something psychical that must present itself in original experience by means of a process of fulfillment. In this process, this organism may speak, like to eat good food, make gestures, or play the violin.

It is this kind of verifiable accessibility of what is not originally accessible that is characteristic of the existing other being. Whatever can be presented and evidently verified in the process of fulfillment originally is *something I am,* or else it belongs to the sphere of my peculiar ownness. Whatever is experienced in a different way is *other.* The other is therefore conceivable only as an *analogue* of something that is included in the sphere of my peculiar ownness. Because of the way its sense is constituted, it manifests itself necessarily as an intentional modification of that ego of mine, which is first to be objectified, or as an intentional modification of my primordial world: the other is phenomenologically a modification of myself. It will be clear that, together with the other ego, all that necessarily belongs to its primordial world and its fully concrete ego is appresented in the analogizing modification (*Cart. Med.,* 114–16 [143–45]).

However, what has been said does not suffice to give a really adequate explanation of the noematic complexes involved in the experience of what is other. We must now try to reach the point where the possibility of a transcendental constitution of the objective world can become manifest, and the real meaning of transcendental-phenomenological idealism can be explained.

It will be evident that in my primordial sphere my animate body is reflexively related to itself; it originally manifests itself as occupying the central *here.* Every other body appears in the mode *there.* This orientation to the *there* can be freely changed by means of my kinesthesias. I can always change my position in such a way that I convert any *there* into a *here.* This implies that not only the systems of appearances that belong to my current perceiving from *here* but also other systems of appearances that correspond to the possible change of position that would put me *there* belong constitutively to each physical thing.

Applying this to the experience of other subjects, we see that I do not apperceive the others simply as duplicates of myself. I do not apperceive them as having the spatial and other modes of appearance that are characteristic of me as being here; I apperceive them as having the spatial modes of appearance like those I would have if I should go over there and be where they are. Furthermore, the others are appresentatively apperceived as egos of a primordial world in which their animate organisms are originally constituted and experienced in the mode of the absolute *here.* In this appresentation, therefore, the bodies that present themselves in my monadic sphere in the mode *there* concretely indicate the same bodies that the other egos in their monadic sphere are supposed to experience in the mode *here* (*Cart. Med.,* 116–17 [145–46]).

What is *appresented* by the body over there in my primordial surrounding world is not my psychic life, for I am bodily here as the center of a primordial world oriented around me. Consequently, the entire sphere of my peculiar ownness as primordially given has the content of the *here*. On the other hand, the other ego must be appresented as an ego coexisting in the mode *there,* as I should be if I were there, because his body there enters into a pairing association with my body here and, being given perceptually, becomes the core of my appresenting experience of a coexisting ego. What is appresented by the body there is therefore appresented as an ego other than mine.

Equally easy to understand is the manner in which, as the effective association goes on continuously, such an appresentation of someone else continuously furnishes new appresentational contents by virtue of which a constant confirmation becomes possible. The first content obviously must be formed by the understanding of the others' bodies and their behavior, for instance, their hands functioning in pushing, or their eyes functioning in seeing. Through this, the ego at first is determined only as governing somatically in this particular form of behavior.

It is also quite understandable how certain contents belonging to the higher psychic sphere arise. These contents, too, are indicated bodily, namely, in the behavior of the body in regard to the world out there, for example, as the behavior of someone who is angry or cheerful, which I easily understand from my own behavior under like circumstances (*Cart. Med.,* 117–20 [147–49]).

Constitution of the Community of Monads — According to Husserl, however, it is more important to explain the community that develops at various levels between me and the appresentatively experienced other. The first thing that is constituted as a community and forms the foundation for all other intersubjectively common things is the fact that we have the same nature in common along with the pairing of the others' bodies and their psychophysical egos with my own body and my psychophysical ego.

Since the other's subjectivity, by appresentation within the sphere of my peculiar ownness, which exclusively and even essentially is mine, arises with the sense of a subjectivity that is essentially someone else's, it might at first seem to be a problem how even the first communalization in regard to a common world becomes established. The other body that appears in my primordial sphere is, first of all, a body within the realm of my primordial nature; and this is a synthetic unity belonging to me and therefore included in my own essence. If that body functions appresentatively, then in union with it,

the other ego becomes an object of my consciousness that shows itself as being *there;* primarily, however, the other ego with his own
body is given to himself as necessarily belonging to his absolute
here. How can one speak here at all of the *same* body? There seems
to be an unbridgeable cleft between the two primordial spheres in
question—namely, mine, which is for me as ego the original
sphere; and his, which is for me an appresented one. And if I
would be able somehow to cross the cleft, this would mean, after all,
that I should acquire an original, and not an appresenting, experience of someone else. How can the identification come about between the body belonging to my original sphere and the body
constituted quite separately in the other ego? This problem, however, appears only if the two original spheres have already been distinguished. And this does not seem to be necessary because a precise
explication of the intentionality that is actually observable in our
experience of someone else, and the discovery of the motivations
that are essentially implied in that intentionality, can help us to
solve the problem.

If one would follow this guide and discover the intentionality
mentioned, together with its motivations, it would become clear how
I can constitute in my monad another monad in such a way that I
can experience what is constituted in me as nonetheless other than
me, and how I can identify a nature constituted in me with a nature
constituted by someone else, or how I can identify a nature constituted in me with one constituted in me as a nature constituted by
someone else. This identification appears then to be no greater problem than any other synthesis of identification (*Cart. Med.,* 120–28
[149–56]).

Higher Levels of Intramonadic Community — It is in these
considerations, Husserl informs us, that we may find a brief indication of the first and lowest level of communalization between me, the
primordial monad, and the monad constituted in me as existing for
itself and only appresentationally accessible to me. The only conceivable manner in which others can have for me the sense of being
others that are thus and so determined consists in their being constituted in me as others. And if they get such a meaning from
sources that yield a continuous confirmation, then they are indeed
real beings that, however, exclusively have the meaning with which
they are constituted; they appear as monads, being for themselves
precisely as I am being for myself, yet being also in communion and
therefore in connection with me as concrete ego. To be sure, they are
actually separate from my monad insofar as no real connection leads
from their lived experiences to mine. On the other hand, however,

the original communion mentioned is not just nothing. Although each monad really is an absolutely separate unity, the unreal intentional reaching of the other into my primordial sphere is not unreal in the sense of being dreamt only. A being is in intentional communion with another being. This is an essentially unique connectedness and is precisely the one that makes transcendentally possible the being of a world of people and things.

After the first level of communalization and the first constitution of an objective world starting from my primordial world have been sufficiently explained, the higher levels offer relatively minor difficulties. First we must explain the community of human beings in which we find a mutual being-for-one-another, which already implies an objectifying equalization of my existence with that of all others, and in which we discover that everyone—that is, I and anyone else—appears as a human being among other human beings, because we find that the others experience me and everybody else as an "other" for them. If this community is clarified, then endlessly open nature itself becomes a nature that includes an open plurality of human beings as subjects of possible intercommunion. A similarly open *community* of monads, which we designate as *transcendental intersubjectivity,* naturally corresponds to this community.

It will be clear that for me this transcendental intersubjectivity is constituted purely within me, the meditating ego, purely by virtue of sources belonging to my intentional life; nevertheless, it is constituted then *as* a community that is also constituted in every other monad as the *same* community and as necessarily bearing within itself the *same* objective world. We need hardly remark again that every other monad is to be taken as a monad constituted by me with the modification "other."

Every analysis and theory of transcendental phenomenology, including the theory of the transcendental constitution of the objective world, can be repeated in the realm of the natural attitude, but then we first have to put the transcendental reduction out of action. Within the realm of our naive natural life, it becomes a theory belonging to psychology. In this way, it becomes clear that on the eidetic and empirical levels, a pure psychology corresponds to a transcendental phenomenology (*Cart. Med.* 128–31 [156–59]).

What has been said up to now evidently does not suffice to explain the constitution of the community that belongs to the full essence of humanity. On the basis, however, of our explanation of this community, it is not too difficult to understand the possibility of specifically personal acts of the ego that have the character of social acts by means of which all human personal communication is established. Starting from there, it must be possible to explain in a transcendental way the various types of social communities with their possible hierarchical order, among them the preeminent types that have the character of personalities of a higher level.

Once this is accomplished, one has to focus on the problem of the constitution of the specifically human surrounding world as a surrounding world of culture for each human being and for each human community, and the problem of the kind of objectivity belonging to each of them. The problem of the difference and the relation between nature and culture is also of great importance in this context.

A very important point in all these descriptions is that the constitution of worlds of any kind whatever—beginning with one's own stream of lived experiences, with its open and endless multiplicities, and continuing up through the objective world, with its various levels of objectivation—is subject to *the law of oriented constitution,* according to which every constitution at various levels presupposes something primordially and something secondarily constituted. At each of these levels, the primordially constituted world enters, with a new stratum of meaning, into the secondarily constituted world in such a way that the primordial occupies the central place because of its oriented modes of givenness. The secondarily constituted world is, as a world, necessarily given as a horizon of being that is accessible only from the primordially constituted world.

Applying this law to the constitution of the cultural world, we find that it, too, as a world of culture, is given finally on the underlying basis of nature common to all and on the basis of its spatiotemporal form. We see that in this way the cultural world is furthermore given first in relation to a "zero member," a "zero personality"; on this level, I and my culture are primordial, over against every alien culture. To me and to those who share in my culture, an alien culture is accessible only by an experiencing of someone else, a kind of empathy, by which we project ourselves into the alien cultural community and its culture. We must abandon here a more precise exploration of the layer of meaning that gives to the world of culture as such its specific meaning and makes it a world endowed with specifically spiritual predicates. For the present, it must suffice to indicate these problems of a higher level as problems of constitution and thereby to make it understandable that, with the systematic transcendental phenomenological explication of the apodictic ego, the transcendental meaning of the world must also become disclosed ultimately in the full concreteness with which it is necessarily the life-world for us all. That applies likewise to all the particular formations of the surrounding world. All these matters conform to an essential style that derives its necessity from the transcendental ego first, and then from the transcendental intersubjectivity that discloses itself in that ego. We want to conclude these considerations with one final remark. The problems of psychophysical, physiological, and psychological genesis, and especially the problems of the child's psychic development, have not yet been touched. They belong to a higher dimension and presuppose that the immense explication of the lower sphere is already realized (*Cart. Med.,* 131–36 [159–63]).

I NOTES

1. For the term "ontology" in the sense of "mundane," eidetic, descriptive sciences, see the commentary to Chapter Two above.

2. *Opuscules et fragments inédits de Leibniz,* ed. Louis Couturat (Paris: Alcan, 1903), 511–12.

3. Ibid., 524–29.

4. For what follows, see Cornelis van Peursen, "La notion de temps de l'ego transcendental chez Husserl," in *Husserl,* Cahiers de Royaumont: Philosophie, no. 3 (Paris: Minuit, 1959), 196–207; Bernet et al., *Edmund Husserl,* 190–98; Eduard Marbach, *Das Problem des Ich in der Phänomenologie Husserls* (The Hague: Nijhoff, 1974); Jan Broekman, *Phänomenologie und Egologie: Faktisches und transzendentales Ego bei Edmund Husserl* (The Hague: Nijhoff, 1963); Klaus Held, *Lebendige Gegenwart: Die Frage nach der Seinsweise des transzendentalen Ich bei Edmund Husserl, entwickelt am Leitfaden der Zeitproblematik* (The Hague: Nijhoff, 1966); Maurice Natanson, "The Empirical and Transcendental Ego," in *For Roman Ingarden: Nine Essays in Phenomenology and Literature, Philosophy, and the Social Sciences* (The Hague: Nijhoff, 1962), 44–54; Joseph J. Kockelmans, "Husserl and Kant on the Pure Ego," in *Husserl: Expositions and Appraisals,* 269–85.

5. For what follows here, see Husserl, *On the Phenomenology of the Consciousness of Internal Time (1893–1917),* trans. John Barnett Brough (Dordrecht: Kluwer Academic Publishers, 1991), and particularly the introduction, xi–lvii; "Einleitung des Herausgebers," in Husserl, *Zur Phänomenologie des inneren Zeitbewusstseins (1893–1917),* ed. Rudolf Boehm (The Hague: Nijhoff, 1966), xiii–xliv; Klaus Held, *Lebendige Gegenwart;* Gerd Brand, *Welt, Ich und Zeit* (The Hague: Nijhoff, 1955); Bernet et al., *Edmund Husserl,* 96–107; Enzo Paci, *Il problema del tempo nella fenomenologia di Husserl* (Milan: La Goliardica, 1960); John Brough, "The Emergence of an Absolute Consciousness in Husserl's Early Writings on Time-Consciousness," *Man and World* 5 (1972): 298–326.

6. Husserl, "Vorlesungen zur Phänomenologie des inneren Zeitbewusstseins," ed. Martin Heidegger, in *Jahrbuch für Philosophie und phänomenologische Forschung,* vol. 9. (Halle, Niemeyer, 1928).

7. Husserl, *Texte zur Phänomenologie des inneren Zeitbewusstseins* (1893–1917), ed. Rudolf Bernet (Hamburg: Meiner, 1985).

8. Cf. *Logical Investigations,* vol. 2, Investigation 5, chapter 3.

9. Cf. *On the Phenomenology of the Consciousness of Internal Time,* 186 [180–81].

298 | CHAPTER TEN

10. Brough, "Translator's Introduction," in *On the Phenomenology of the Consciousness of Internal Time,* xix.
11. Bernet et al., *Edmund Husserl,* 96–100. Brough, "Translator's Introduction," xix.
12. Brough, "Translator's Introduction," xxvii.
13. Ibid., xxvi–xxix.
14. *On the Phenomenology of the Consciousness of Internal Time,* 345 [332–33].
15. Brough, "Translator's Introduction," li–liii. Cf. Bernet et al., *Edmund Husserl,* 103–7.
16. For what follows, see Paul Ricoeur, *Husserl: An Analysis of His Phenomenology* (Evanston, Ill.: Northwestern University Press, 1967), 115–42; Bernet et al., *Edmund Husserl,* 143–53; Jean Hyppolite, "L'intersubjectivité chez Husserl," in *Figures de la pensée philosophique: Écrits, 1938–1968* (Paris: Presses Universitaires de France, 1968), 1:499–512; Klaus Held, "Das Problem der Intersubjektivität und die Idee einer phänomenologischen Transzendentalphilosophie," in *Perspektiven transzendentalphänomenologischer Forschung* (The Hague: Nijhoff, 1972), 3–61; Gerd Brand, "Edmund Husserl: Zur Phänomenologie der Intersubjektivität," *Philosophische Rundschau* 25 (1978): 54–80; Alfred Schütz, "Das Problem der transzendentalen Intersubjektivität bei Husserl," *Philosophische Rundschau* 5 (1957): 82–107.
17. Husserl, *Cart. Med.,* 91–92 [123–24]. Cf. *Ideas,* 2:170–80 [162–72], 181–210 [172–200], 346–47 [334–36], where he approached the basic issues from the perspective of phenomenological reflections on empathy.
18. Spiegelberg, *The Phenomenological Movement,* 1:158; Lauer, *The Triumph of Subjectivity,* 150.
19. Lauer, *The Triumph of Subjectivity,* 151.
20. Husserl, *Ideas,* 2:181–211 [172–200].

Phenomenology as the All-embracing Philosophy and the Science of the Ultimate and Highest Problems

Text

14. Die vollständige Phänomenologie als universale Philosophie

Eben damit restituiert sich der ursprünglichste Begriff der Philosophie als universaler Wissenschaft aus radikaler Selbstrechtfertigung—die im alten platonischen und wiederum im cartesianischen Sinn allein Wissenschaft ist. Die streng systematisch durchgeführte Phänomenologie des vorhin erweiterten Sinnes ist identisch mit dieser *alle* echte Erkenntnis umspannenden Philosophie. Sie zerfällt in die eidetische Phänomenologie (oder universale Ontologie) als *Erste Philosophie* und in die *Zweite Philosophie,* die Wissenschaft vom Universum der Fakta oder der sie alle synthetisch beschließenden transzendentalen Intersubjektivität. Die Erste Philosophie [299] ist das Universum der Methode für die Zweite und ist auf sich selbst zurückbezogen in ihrer methodischen Begründung.

15. Die "höchsten und letzten" Probleme als phänomenologische

In der Phänomenologie haben alle vernünftigen Probleme ihre Stelle, also auch die traditionell sich als in irgend einem besonderen Sinn als philosophisch bezeichnenden; aus den absoluten Quellen transzendentaler Erfahrung bzw. eidetischer Anschauung erhalten sie erst in der Phänomenologie ihre echte Formulierung und die gangbaren Wege ihrer Lösung. In ihrer universalen Selbstbezogenheit erkennt die Phänomenologie ihre eigene Funktion in einem möglichen transzendentalen Menschheitsleben. Sie erkennt die aus ihm herauszuschauenden absoluten Normen, aber auch seine ursprüngliche teleologisch-tendenziöse Struktur in Richtung auf die Enthüllung dieser Normen und ihre praktische bewußte Auswirkung. Sie erkennt sich dann als Funktion der universalen Selbstbesinnung der (transzendentalen) Menschheit

14. Complete Phenomenology as All-embracing Philosophy

Precisely through this {process} is restored the most primordial concept of philosophy—as all-embracing science based on radical self-justification, which is alone [truly] science in the ancient Platonic and again in the Cartesian sense. Phenomenology rigorously and systematically carried out, phenomenology in the broadened sense [which we have explained] above, is identical with this philosophy which encompasses all genuine knowledge. It is divided into eidetic phenomenology (or all-embracing ontology) as *first philosophy,* and as *second philosophy,* [it is] the science of the universe of *facta*, or of the transcendental intersubjectivity that synthetically comprises all *facta*. First philosophy is the universe of methods for the second, and is related back into itself for its methodological grounding.

15. The "Ultimate and Highest" Problems as Phenomenological

In phenomenology all rational problems have their place, and thus also those that traditionally are in some special sense or other philosophically significant. For out of the absolute sources of transcendental experience, or eidetic intuiting, they first [are able to] obtain their genuine formulation and feasible means for their solution. In its universal relatedness-back-to-itself, phenomenology recognizes its particular function within a possible life of mankind [*Menschheitsleben*] at the transcendental level. It recognizes the absolute norms which are to be picked out intuitively from it [life of mankind], and also its primordial teleological-tendential structure in a directedness towards disclosure of these norms and their conscious practical operation. It recognizes itself as a function of the all-embracing reflective meditation of (transcendental) humanity, [a self-examination] in the service of an all-inclusive praxis of reason; that

im Dienste einer universalen Vernunftpraxis, das ist im Dienste des durch die Enthüllung frei werdenden Strebens in Richtung auf die im Unendlichen liegende universale Idee absoluter Vollkommenheit oder, was dasselbe, in Richtung auf die—im Unendlichen liegende—Idee einer Menschheit, die in der Tat und durchaus in Wahrheit und Echtheit sein und leben würde. Sie erkennt ihre selbstbesinnliche Funktion für die relative Verwirklichung der korrelativen praktischen Idee eines im zweiten Sinne echten Menschheitslebens (dessen Wesensgestalten und praktische Normen sie zu erforschen hat), nämlich als eines bewußt und willentlich auf jene absolute Idee gerichteten. Kurzum die metaphysisch teleologischen, die ethischen, die geschichtsphilosophischen Probleme nicht minder wie selbstverständlich die Probleme der urteilenden Vernunft liegen in ihrem Rahmen, nicht anders wie alle sinnvollen Probleme überhaupt und alle in ihrer innersten synthetischen Einheit und ihrer Ordnung als solche der transzendentalen Geistigkeit.

is, in the service of striving towards the universal ideal of absolute perfection which lies in infinity, [a striving] which becomes free through [the process of] disclosure. Or, in different words it is a striving in the direction of the idea (lying in infinity) of a humanness which in action and throughout would live and move [be, exist] in truth and genuineness. It recognizes its self-reflective function [of self-examination] for the relative realization of the correlative practical idea of a genuine human life [*Menschheitsleben*] in the second sense (whose structural forms of being and whose practical norms it is to investigate), namely as one [that is] consciously and purposively directed towards this absolute idea. In short, the metaphysically teleological, the ethical, and the problems of philosophy of history, no less than, obviously, the problems of judging reason, lie within its boundary, no differently from all significant problems whatever, and all [of them] in their inmost synthetic unity and order as [being] of transcendental spirituality [*Geistigkeit*].

| Synopsis

In section 14, Husserl states that in the manner indicated one can restore the most primordial concept of philosophy as the all-embracing science based on a radical self-justification, whose idea was anticipated by both Plato and Descartes. If phenomenology were developed rigorously, systematically, and completely, it would be identical with this philosophy.

Phenomenology so understood is divided into eidetic phenomenology, the all-embracing ontology taken as *first philosophy;* and the science of the universe of all facts, or the transcendental intersubjectivity that concretely and synthetically comprises all facts, as *second philosophy.* First philosophy provides all methods for second philosophy and refers back to itself for its own methodical foundation.

In section 15, Husserl explains that in phenomenology all problems of reason have their proper place, including the problems of our philosophical tradition. These problems, too, receive their proper formulation as well as the proper means for their solution from the absolute sources of transcendental experience or, as the case may be, from the sources of eidetic reduction. Although phenomenology is universally related back to itself and its own foundation, it nonetheless recognizes its particular function within the possible life of humanity to lie at the transcendental level. It understands not only the absolute norms that are to be derived by means of intuition from that life itself but also the primordial, teleological structure through which this life must strive toward the disclosure of these norms and their conscious, practical consequences.

In this way it recognizes itself as a function of the all-encompassing self-reflection of transcendental humanity, which stands in the service of an all-encompassing praxis of reason—that is to say, in the service of a striving toward the universal idea of absolute perfection, which lies in infinity; and this striving becomes free only through the disclosure provided by phenomenology. Or, put otherwise, it is a striving toward the idea of a humane humankind that would live and act effectively and throughout in truth and authenticity. It also understands its self-reflective function in regard to the *imperfect* realization of the practical idea of a genuine life of humanity, namely, one that is consciously and purposely directed toward this absolute idea and whose structural, eidetic forms and practical norms have to be investigated by phenomenology.

In short, the metaphysically teleological problems, the ethical questions, and the problems of philosophy of history—no less than the problems of judging and evaluating reason—lie within the boundaries of phenomenology. And the same holds good for all other significant problems. All of these problems are to be considered by phenomenology in their inmost synthetic unity and order as problems of a transcendental spirituality.

In the commentary, I shall focus on three topics: the meaning of the expression "first and second philosophy," Husserl's conception of metaphysics, and the function of transcendental phenomenology for the life of humanity.

Commentary

First and Second Philosophy

In section 14, Husserl uses a terminology and introduces a basic distinction that is not used in this way in any of his major publications that appeared during his lifetime. The identification of philosophy with the science that "encompasses all genuine knowledge," as well as the subdivision in *first* and *second* philosophy are puzzling in that they run contrary to what is stated in *Ideas, Cartesian Meditations,* and *Crisis.* Also the term "all-embracing ontology" for eidetic (transcendental) phenomenology is strange, as we just saw in the commentary of the preceding chapter (see 254–61).

In what follows, I shall discuss Husserl's distinction between first and second philosophy in its historical origin.[1]

First and Second Philosophy in Plato and Aristotle — Although the *terminology* is found first in Aristotle, the *distinction* between first and second philosophy is already found in the dialogues of Plato. In addition to the dialectic of the eternal and unchangeable Ideas, Plato also developed disciplines that are concerned with changeable things, human beings, and the material world. A good example of what Plato could have called second philosophy is the *Timaeus,* in which Plato describes how the Demiurge created the world by taking the Ideas, studied in first philosophy, as his example.

The expressions "first philosophy" and "second philosophy" occur for the first time in Aristotle. The subject matter of first philosophy is what is eternal, separated from all matter, and unchangeable, whereas second philosophy is concerned with nature. Yet for Aristotle first philosophy is no longer the first science in his philosophy as a whole, but rather its crowning point.[2]

In a very controversial statement at the end of *Metaphysics* E, 1, Aristotle writes that

> if there were no substances other than those formed by nature, physics would be the first science; but if there is an immovable substance, this would be prior, and the science of it would be first philosophy and would be universal in this manner, in view

of the fact that it is first. And it would be the concern of this science, too, to investigate being qua being, both what being is and what belongs to it qua being.[3]

This statement has been debated over the centuries insofar as, at first sight, it seems to suggest that the so-called ontology[4] is merely a part of first philosophy that is concerned with the immovable substance, God.

First and Second Philosophy in Kant, Schelling, and Husserl — In all likelihood inspired by the ancient tradition, Kant, too, introduces a distinction between first and second philosophy and accordingly speaks of pure, transcendental philosophy, including the whole system of metaphysics, on the one hand, and applied philosophy on the other.[5] Anthropology and psychology belong to applied philosophy. In Schelling we find a distinction between negative or rational philosophy, which construes in an aprioric manner the content of reason as the necessary condition for the things of the world; and a positive philosophy, which, as a second philosophy, interprets the empirical history of mythology and revelation on the basis of the principles discovered in first philosophy.

Almost from the beginning, Husserl, too, made a clear distinction between phenomenology, a pure science of essences, and the sciences of facts of the natural attitude. This does not mean that there could not also be sciences of essences that remain within the realm of the natural attitude; manifestly there are a great number of such disciplines, all called ontologies. But this does not mean that transcendental phenomenology would be identical with philosophy as such for Husserl after 1909. In a letter to Karl Joel of 11 May 1914, quoted by Kern, Husserl makes it clear that, just as in Kant, the critical part of philosophy must be combined with the entire system of metaphysics, so in Husserl's phenomenology, too, a metaphysics is to be included in philosophy, in addition to transcendental phenomenology. Transcendental phenomenology is the eidetic science of the transcendentally pure consciousness and its intentional correlates; in a certain sense, this eidetic science encompasses all eidetic sciences (i.e., the system of all formal and material ontologies), yet it does not include them in itself, since they are sciences of the natural attitude. The complete and systematic development of the ontologies and the systematic presentation of transcendental phenomenology, which corresponds to them and brings them to a unity, are the basic condition of the possibility of a truly scientific philosophy, insofar as this development constitutes its complete eidetic foundation. This foundation makes possible a scientific metaphysics that—contrary to transcendental phenomenology, which is concerned only with ideal possibilities—is concerned only with *real* things.

Here Husserl thus claims that this scientific metaphysics has its foundation in part in pure, transcendental phenomenology, and in part in the eidetic ontologies. This is in complete harmony with his basic claim that everything that is a posteriori is to be founded in what is a priori. Thus he can write in *Ideas:* "The old ontological doctrine that the cognition of 'possibilities' must precede the cognition of actualities is, in my opinion, insofar as it is correctly understood and made useful in the right way, a great truth" (*Ideas,* 1:190 [159]). In *Cartesian Meditations,* he adds: "All the rationality of the facts lies, after all, in the Apriori. Apriori science is the science of radical universalities and necessities, to which the science of matters of fact must have recourse, precisely in order that it may ultimately become grounded on such radical principles" (*Cart. Med.,* 155 [181]). After the transcendental reduction, my true interest may be directed to the pure ego, to the uncovering of this de facto ego. "But the uncovering can become genuinely scientific, only if I go back to the apodictic principles that pertain to this ego as exemplifying the *eidos* ego: the essential universalities and necessities by means of which the fact is to be related to its rational grounds (those of its pure possibility) and thus must be made scientific (logical)" (*Cart. Med.,* 72 [106]). Thus the science of pure possibilities necessarily precedes the sciences of the real world and makes them precisely possible as sciences.

In *Cartesian Meditations,* Husserl also explains in what sense the formal and material ontologies belong to, but are not included in, transcendental phenomenology. There, as we have seen, he also introduces the term "ontology" in a radically new meaning. He says that all a priori sciences originate and receive their ground from the a priori transcendental phenomenology; taken with this origin they belong within an all-embracing, a priori phenomenology, *as its systematically differentiated branches.*

> This system of the all-embracing a priori is therefore to be designated also as the systematic *unfolding of the all-embracing a priori* innate in the essence of transcendental subjectivity (and consequently in that of a transcendental intersubjectivity)—or as the systematic unfolding of the *universal logos of all conceivable being.* In other words: As developed systematically and fully, transcendental phenomenology would be ipso facto the true and genuine universal ontology.

This science, however, would not be an emptily formal ontology but one that would include all material regional ontologies as well. "This universal *concrete* ontology (or universal and concrete *theory of science*—this concrete logic of being) would therefore be the intrinsically first universe of science grounded on an absolute foundation" (*Cart. Med.,* 155 [181]).

In opposition to this first philosophy stands the second philosophy, which Husserl describes as the empirical philosophy of factual, real entities. Second philosophy, also called *metaphysics,* appears then to be identical with the totality of all empirical sciences taken as sciences that receive their ultimate foundation in first philosophy.

When a number of formerly unpublished works were edited and published after Husserl's death, several enigmatic statements made in the *Encyclopaedia Britannica* article became understandable. Particularly the lecture series published as *First Philosophy* must be mentioned in this connection. The book begins with the following statement: "'First Philosophy' is, as we all know, an expression that Aristotle introduced for a certain philosophical discipline, but which later was replaced by the term 'metaphysics.'" Husserl explains that he selected the term because it fits the content of his lectures, in which transcendental phenomenology is described as the genuine and true first philosophy, and because the term is very seldom used, so that we can focus on what the expression literally says and suggests, instead of on the many sediments of our historical tradition (*E. Phil.,* 1:3). One should note that the term is used by Husserl not to refer to metaphysics or rational theology but rather to transcendental phenomenology, in which every other science, including metaphysics and rational theology, is to be founded. These sciences are to be preceded by a universal theory of knowing, valuing, and practical reason (ibid., 1:6). Husserl observes that what he wants to achieve in the lecture series brings him closer to Descartes, and yet even Descartes's *Meditations* were still metaphysical meditations, as the French title of the work explicitly states: *Les Méditations Métaphysiques . . . Touchant la Première Philosophie.* Husserl had obviously no intention to reject every form of metaphysics, but he was convinced that every metaphysics must be grounded in a transcendental and pure science and that Descartes was therefore wrong when he incorporated metaphysical ideas in his founding discipline and thus continued to make use of a "dogmatic" metaphysics.[6]

Husserl's first philosophy is a transcendental theory of knowledge; it must precede every metaphysics as the condition of its possibility. If metaphysics is to be a genuine and true science, then it must receive its foundation from a transcendental and pure theory of knowledge (*E. Phil.,* 1:369). From this characterization of the relationship between theory of knowledge and metaphysics, it is clear that Husserl is really trying to rethink the critical philosophy of Kant.

Husserl defines what he means by first philosophy explicitly as "a science of the totality of pure (aprioric) principles of all possible forms of knowledge and of the totality of all apriori truths that are systematically contained in it and thus purely can be deduced from it" (*E. Phil.*, 1:13–14). In contrast to this first philosophy stands the totality of the real, explaining sciences of fact, which proceed with a rational method; this totality has the form of a rational system, and its sciences are the disciplines of *one* "second philosophy," whose correlate and subject domain consist in the unity of actual reality (ibid., 1:14). Husserl stresses that facticity is the domain not of phenomenology and logic but rather of metaphysics (ibid., 1:394). Since this metaphysics focuses on the irrationality of the transcendental fact, which manifests itself in the constitution of the factical world and the factical life of the spirit, it is a metaphysics in a new sense (ibid., 1:187–88n).

> The spirit in a nature and the adaptation of the spirit to its nature, the development of knowing spirits, the development of the sciences and of cultural activities of mankind as such— all of this has also its philosophical sides; but these sides are not "epistemological" ones, not ones that belong to *First Philosophy;* they do not belong to first, but, as I should say, to the "last philosophy." (ibid., 1:385)

Boehm, too, suggests that in the final analysis, the manner in which Husserl here distinguishes between first and second philosophy reminds us of the manner in which Schelling distinguishes between negative and positive philosophy.[7]

Yet in Boehm's view, this reference to Schelling must be understood in view of the fact that little is known about Husserl's relationship to Schelling. Furthermore, it was Eduard von Hartmann who, in the context of reflections on the theory of knowledge, used the expression "first philosophy" to refer to Schelling's distinction between negative and positive philosophy. We know that only little contact can have existed between Husserl and Hartmann. Finally, Husserl was rather close to Natorp, with whom he corresponded regularly and who, in his review of the first volume of *Logical Investigations,* wrote:

> Anyone who takes it to be possible that one purely theoretically, and in an independent manner, can ground a logic of objective truth, is not likely next to this endeavor still to give validity to a metaphysics; rather he will in all likelihood claim that metaphysics precisely in this manner is resolved in logic, in the old "ontology", as Kant already called it, in the "analytic of pure understanding"; not to mention the fact here that critique of knowledge, taken as the philosophically basic science, legitimately can lay claim to the title *"prote philosophia."*

Boehm is of the opinion that the idea to present his transcendental phenomenology as first philosophy may very well have been suggested to Husserl by these observations of Natorp.[8]

We must now turn to the question of why Husserl thought it important to introduce his transcendental phenomenology under this rubric. The answer can perhaps be found through a brief reflection on the content of the lecture course published as *First Philosophy* and on the circumstances under which it developed.

We have seen that Husserl did not at first make a clear distinction between descriptive, or phenomenological, psychology and transcendental phenomenology. This distinction was made explicitly some time close to 1909, when Husserl mentions it for the first time. A first systematic description of his mature philosophy was then given in *Ideas,* of which only the first volume was published during Husserl's lifetime. The idea to present phenomenology as first philosophy came to him when he fully understood the basic reason behind Kant's critical philosophy and made it his own. This reason made it clear to him that a special transcendental reduction would be necessary to realize a genuine first philosophy. In 1912–13, he intended to divide the material for *Ideas* over three volumes. The third volume was meant to present Husserl's definitive view on the idea of philosophy. In the preface to the work of 1913, Husserl wrote:

> A *Third* and concluding Book is devoted to the idea of philosophy. The insight will be awakened that genuine philosophy, the idea of which is the actualizing of absolute cognition, is rooted in pure phenomenology; and rooted in it in a sense so important that the systematically strict grounding and working out of this first of all genuine philosophies is the incessant precondition for every metaphysics and other philosophy "that will be able to make its appearance as a *science*." (*Ideas,* 1:xxii [8])[9]

After the first volume was published, Husserl abandoned his original plan. When he decided to make the second and third volumes ready for publication in 1924–25, he decided against the idea of publishing volume 3 altogether and divided the material of the original second volume into two volumes, which posthumously appeared as volumes 2 and 3.

Yet the idea of presenting transcendental phenomenology as a first philosophy was never given up. In 1923–24, he gave a series of lectures in which this idea was taken up with the intention of eventually preparing his final view on the matter in *First Philosophy*. This two-volume work, which was published posthumously, contains a text with which Husserl was not yet fully satisfied. Yet the texts we actually have make abundantly clear how Husserl hoped with his new phenomenological method to realize the goal that Kant had set himself in his critical philosophy, namely, laying the foundations for a genuine and true metaphysics.[10]

I On Husserl's Conception of Metaphysics

The term "metaphysics" is very seldom used in Husserl's earlier works. This is understandable, since Husserl came from an empiricist tradition and moved to his own transcendental phenomenology under the influence of the critical philosophy of Kant. Husserl uses the term in *The Idea of Phenomenology* (1907) and writes that philosophical reflections on the nature of knowledge show that the sciences of the natural attitude are not yet the ultimate science of being. "This science, which we call metaphysics, grows out of a 'critique' of natural cognition in the individual sciences" (*The Idea,* 18 [22–23]). The context in which this statement is found suggests that at that time Husserl wanted to defend the view with Kant that a critique of pure reason, or phenomenology, must lay the foundation for any future meaningful metaphysics. Later Husserl distanced himself more and more from Kant and began to avoid the term "metaphysics." In the first volume of *Ideas,* for instance, metaphysics plays no part. The term appears again in *First Philosophy.* Reflecting critically on the history of philosophy, he defines metaphysics in agreement with the modern tradition since Descartes, Leibniz, and Kant as the universal doctrine of being (*Seienden*) in its absolute actuality (*Wirklichkeit*). According to this tradition, metaphysics must receive its foundation from an epistemological discipline—for instance, Kant's critical philosophy. In that context, Husserl does not explicitly state what he himself thinks about metaphysics from the perspective of transcendental phenomenology. He merely limits himself to the observation that metaphysics, understood in this manner, is to be distinguished from the various ontologies discussed in the context of Husserl's own phenomenology; thus metaphysics must be distinguished from regional ontologies, such as the ontologies of nature, space, and time, as well as from the general ontology of all possible reality as such. Husserl explicitly stipulates again that the ontologies mentioned are all sciences of the natural attitude and thus are not at all concerned with the basic problems discussed in the critical theory of knowledge. In passing, he observes that what he calls ontology of nature was called metaphysics of nature by Kant (*E. Phil.,* 1:192–93).

Husserl was always convinced, with Kant, that a radical theory of knowledge will show that metaphysics in the traditional sense is impossible because classical metaphysics forces reason to venture beyond the limits of human knowledge. In *Cartesian Meditations,* he even explicitly states this: "I would like to point out that, as already stated [namely, in section 60, to which I shall return shortly], phenomenology indeed *excludes every naïve metaphysics* that operates with absurd things in themselves, but *does not exclude metaphysics as such*" (*Cart. Med.,* 156 [182]). Phenomenology does not deny the importance of the problems with which traditional metaphysics concerned itself; yet in dealing with these problems, one used the wrong methods, and the investigations were consequently driven in the wrong direction. Phenomenology by no means stops short of the supreme and ultimate questions. This claim repeats another one made earlier in section 60, mentioned above, where Husserl wrote: "Our monadological results are metaphysical, if it be true that ultimate questions of Being should be called metaphysical" (ibid., 139 [166]).

Husserl continues by saying that the metaphysics proposed by transcendental phenomenology is anything but metaphysics in the customary sense of the tradition because, in his view, traditional metaphysics was degenerate and "by no means conforms to the sense with which metaphysics, as 'first philosophy', was instituted originally" (*Cart. Med.,* 139 [166]). Phenomenology's method, which is purely intuitive, concrete, and apodictic, excludes all "metaphysical adventures and speculative excesses."

Husserl then mentions some of the metaphysical results he has come to in his *Meditations*. (1) It is an a priori truth that my ego, as given to me apodictically, can be a world-experiencing ego only by being in communion with other egos, as members of a community of egos or monads. (2) I cannot conceive of a plurality of monads otherwise than as being in communion with each other, either explicitly or implicitly. The plurality of monads actually in communion constitutes the objective world and spatializes, temporalizes, and realizes *itself* in that world. Finally, it is essentially necessary that the togetherness of the monads be a temporal coexistence, temporalized in the form "real temporality." (3) It is impossible that two or more separate pluralities of monads sharing one world, but not in communion, would coexist. It is equally impossible for there to be two independent worlds and two independent spaces and space times. There can be different environments, but they are always subworlds of the common objective world shared by all. (4) There is only one space, one time, one objective world, and one objective nature. Moreover, this one nature *must* exist if there are any structures in me that imply the coexistence of other monads. (5) One can conceive of many monads and groups of monads, but they are not always compossible. Infinitely many worlds might have been created, but it is impossible that there are two or more at one and the same time.

Many other such examples could be given. From what has been said, it is apparent that in *Cartesian Meditations* Husserl understands by metaphysics the science of the ultimate and highest questions. He concludes section 60 with the observation that transcendental phenomenology together with the metaphysical results of its explanation of intersubjectivity enables us to understand how problems that for traditional philosophy had to lie beyond the limits of scientific reason can acquire meaning, regardless of how they may be resolved (*Cart. Med.,* 141 [167–68]).

Before moving on to the next section, one final observation is in order. In the concluding section of *Cartesian Meditations,* where Husserl again states that transcendental phenomenology is capable of dealing with supreme and ultimate questions, he says that one should not forget that for transcendental phenomenology the intrinsically first being, which precedes and bears every worldly object, is transcendental intersubjectivity. Yet it is within the de facto sphere of the individual monad, and ideally in the sphere of every conceivable monad, that all the problems of accidental factualness occur, that is, problems connected with death, fate, and destiny and the possibility of a genuine human life that is meaningful in a very particular sense; among these problems, that of the meaning of history and all still-higher problems, such as the ethical-religious problems, also belong. Husserl also states that the ethical-religious problems are to be formulated in such a manner that they remain within the realm in which every claim that can have a possible meaning for us must be stated (*Cart. Med.,* 155–56 [181–82]).

❚ The Function of
❚ Transcendental Phenomenology
❚ for the Life of Humanity

After he explains that phenomenology leaves room for metaphysics as the science of the highest and ultimate problems, Husserl goes on to say that this claim is not limited to typical theoretical and scientific issues. Transcendental phenomenology as philosophy can obviously also present the foundations for all reflections on practical and aesthetic problems. As a matter of fact, transcendental phenomenology wants to make possible that humanity eventually will be able to live a life of reason in every domain of its life. This implies that transcendental phenomenology must present the foundations to humanity's theoretical, practical, and evaluating reason.

This task suggests first that transcendental phenomenology must bring to light the absolute norms that can be derived from this

314 I CHAPTER ELEVEN

life by means of eidetic reduction; it must also be able to show the teleological and tendential structures of this life in its orientation toward the relevation and practical, conscious realization of these norms.

Here it appears that the ultimate goal of transcendental phenomenology consists in the realization of the universal self-reflection of transcendentally living humanity. This self-reflection will then lead humanity to a universal practice guided by reason; and when this practice, in turn, has been made possible, it will guide humanity on its road toward a realization of the idea of absolute perfection. While this ideal obviously lies in infinity and cannot be more than an ideal, it would indeed truly and genuinely come to life in the life of the community. One thus sees that transcendental phenomenology, by laying the foundations for theoretical, practical, and evaluating reason, will be capable of achieving the goal that phenomenology was supposed to serve almost from the beginning.

In the introduction to *Crisis,* Husserl speaks about the crisis of modern science and that of European humanity, which, in his view, was the consequence of the former. He is particularly concerned with the task that phenomenology has in this regard. For Husserl, the root of the crisis in which modern science finds itself consists in the conception of the nature of science that originated in the sixteenth century in connection with the origin of modern science. At that time, modern science of nature began to make extensive use of mathematical methods. Because of the success of modern science, the idea arose that it should be possible to apply the method of modern science, namely, mathematics, to all other sciences. It would also become possible in this way, so it was hoped, to unify all sciences together with philosophy to form one all-encompassing science. Thus one thought that the infinite totality of all that is and can be constitutes in itself a rational all-encompassing unity that can correlatively be governed completely by one universal science. According to Husserl, Descartes was the first thinker who was able to develop this conception into a consistent whole (*Crisis,* 7–10 [5–8]).

This project soon led to a crisis that concerned not the scientific character of the sciences but rather what they, or what science in general, had meant and could mean for the life of human beings. The exclusiveness with which the entire worldview of modern humanity in the nineteenth century became determined by the positive sciences and let itself be blinded by the prosperity that they produced led to indifference toward the questions that are decisive for a genuine humanity: "Merely fact-minded sciences make merely fact-minded people" (*Crisis,* 6 [4]).

All efforts on the part of the great thinkers of the modern era to deal with basic issues have failed because they were unable to discover the proper method to treat transcendental problems. The resulting crisis in philosophy brought with it a crisis in all positive sciences insofar as they are all members or branches of philosophy, and finally also led to a crisis of European humanity in regard to the meaningfulness of its cultural life, its total *Existenz* (*Crisis*, 12 [10]). Skepticism about the possibility of metaphysics and about its ability to deal with the basic questions of reason (ibid., 9 [6–7]) and the collapse of the belief in a universal philosophy as the guide for modern humanity actually represent the collapse of the belief in reason. It is reason that ultimately gives meaning to everything that is thought to be, to beings, values, ends. Along with this collapse of reason and truth, there is also the collapse of the faith in absolute reason, through which the entire world has its meaning, including faith in the meaning of history and of humanity, faith in humanity's freedom, and faith in one's capacity to secure rational meaning for one's individual and social existence. If human beings lose this faith, it means nothing less than the loss of faith in themselves, in their own true being. This true being is not something we possess with the self-evidence of the "I am" but something we only have and can have in the form of the struggle for the truth for us, the struggle to make ourselves be true. True being is everywhere an ideal goal, a task of reason and of *episteme* (ibid., 12–13 [10–11]).

Throughout the modern era, great thinkers have tried to defend the view that to be human at all is essentially to be a human being in a community that has a united civilization; since human beings are rational beings, their civilization must be a rational civilization, one with a latent or explicit orientation toward reason and the great ideals that reason can project. Husserl felt that we as philosophers of the present age cannot possibly give up the possibility of philosophy and our faith in reason. We must turn to philosophy in the full awareness that in our philosophizing we are the "functionaries of humanity": "The quite personal responsibility of our own true being as philosophers, our inner personal vocation, bears within itself at the same time the responsibility for the true being of mankind" (*Crisis*, 17 [15]). Husserl was convinced that his phenomenology was capable of restoring our faith in reason and in the meaning of human life (ibid., 17–18 [15–16]).

I NOTES

1. For what follows here, see Iso Kern, *Idee und Methode der Philosophie: Leitgedanken für eine Theorie der Vernunft* (Berlin: de Gruyter, 1975), 320–65; Bernet et al., *Edmund Husserl*, 109–213.
2. Aristotle, *Metaphysics*, E, 1, 1026a15–16; Z, 11, 1037a14–16.
3. Ibid., E, 1, 1026a27–32.

4. This "ontology" is contained in *Metaphysics,* books 7 through 9, chapter 9.

5. Kern, *Idee und Methode der Philosophie,* 333–37.

6. "Einleitung des Herausgebers," in Husserl, *Erste Philosophie (1923–1924),* 1:xvi–xvii.

7. Ibid., xvii.

8. Ibid., xvii–xx. For Natorp's criticisms, see *Kantstudien* 6 (1901): 270ff.

9. Note that later in Copy D of his own *Ideas,* vol. 1, Husserl made the marginal note: "Phenomenology as first philosophy." See: *Ideas,* 1:xxiin.

10. Ibid., xx–xxiii.

The Phenomenological Resolution of All Philosophical Antitheses

Text

16. Die phänomenologische Auflösung aller philosophischen Gegensätze

In der systematischen, von den anschaulichen Gegebenheiten zu den abstrakten Höhen fortschreitenden Arbeit der Phänomenologie lösen sich von selbst und ohne Künste einer argumentierenden [300] Dialektik und ohne schwächliche Bemühung und Kompromisse die altüberlieferten vieldeutigen Gegensätze philosophischer Standpunkte auf, Gegensätze wie die zwischen Rationalismus (Platonismus) und Empirismus, Relativismus und Absolutismus, Subjektivismus und Objektivismus, Ontologismus und Transzendentalismus, Psychologismus und Antipsychologismus, Positivismus und Metaphysik, teleologischer und kausalistischer Weltauffassung. Überall berechtigte Motive, überall aber Halbheiten oder unzulässige Verabsolutierungen von nur relativ und abstraktiv berechtigten Einseitigkeiten. Der *Subjektivismus* kann nur durch den universalsten und konsequentesten Subjektivismus (den transzendentalen) überwunden werden. In dieser Gestalt ist er zugleich Objektivismus, sofern er das Recht jedweder durch einstimmige Erfahrung auszuweisenden Objektivität vertritt, aber freilich auch ihren vollen und echten Sinn zur Geltung bringt, an dem sich der vermeinte realistische Objektivismus in seinem Unverständnis der transzendentalen Konstitution versündigt. Der *Relativismus* kann nur durch den universalsten Relativismus überwunden werden, den der transzendentalen Phänomenologie, die die Relativität alles "objektiven" Seins als transzendental konstituierten verständlich macht, aber in eins damit auch die radikalste Relativität, die der transzendentalen Subjektivität auf sich selbst. Eben dies weist sich aber als der einzig mögliche Sinn des "absoluten" Seins aus—gegenüber allem zu ihm relativen "objektiven" Sein—nämlich als "Für-sich-selbst"-Sein der transzendentalen Subjektivität. Wieder: der *Empirismus* kann nur

16. The Phenomenological Resolution of All Philosophical Antitheses

In the systematic work of phenomenology, which progresses from intuitively given [concrete] data to heights of abstraction, the old traditional ambiguous antitheses of the philosophical standpoint are resolved—by themselves and without the arts of an argumentative dialectic, and without weak efforts and compromises: oppositions such as between rationalism (Platonism) and empiricism, relativism and absolutism, subjectivism and objectivism, ontologism and transcendentalism, psychologism and anti-psychologism, positivism and metaphysics, or the teleological versus the causal interpretation of the world. Throughout all of these, [one finds] justified motives, but throughout also half-truths or impermissible absolutizing of only relatively and abstractively legitimate one-sidednesses.

Subjectivism can only be overcome by the most all-embracing and consistent subjectivism (the transcendental). In this [latter] form it is at the same time objectivism [of a deeper sort], in that it represents the claims of whatever objectivity is to be demonstrated through concordant experience, but admittedly [this is an objectivism which] also brings out its full and genuine sense, against which [sense] the supposedly realistic objectivism sins by its failure to understand transcendental constitution. *Relativism* can only be overcome through the most all-embracing relativism, that of transcendental phenomenology, which makes intelligible the relativity of all "objective" being [or existence] as transcendentally constituted; but at one with this [it makes intelligible] the most radical relativity, the relatedness of the transcendental subjectivity to itself. But just this [relatedness, subjectivity] proves its identity to be the only possible sense of [the term] "absolute" being—over against all "objective" being that is relative to it—namely, as the "for-itself"—

durch den universalsten und konsequentesten Empirismus überwunden werden, der für die beschränkte "Erfahrung" der Empiristen den notwendig erweiterten Erfahrungsbegriff der originär gebenden Anschauung setzt, die in allen ihren Gestalten (Anschauung vom Eidos, apodiktische Evidenz, phänomenologische Wesensanschauung usw.) durch phänomenologische Klärung Art und Form ihrer Rechtgebung erweist. Die Phänomenologie als Eidetik ist andererseits rationalistisch; sie überwindet aber den beschränkten dogmatischen *Rationalismus* durch den universalsten der auf die transzendentale Subjektivität, auf Ich, Bewußtsein und bewußte Gegenständlichkeit einheitlich bezogenen Wesensforschung. Ebenso hinsichtlich der anderen [301] mitverflochtenen Gegensätze. Die Zurückführung alles Seins auf die transzendentale Subjektivität und ihre konstitutiven intentionalen Leistungen läßt, um noch eins zu erwähnen, keine andere als eine *teleologische* Weltbetrachtung offen. Und doch erkennt die Phänomenologie auch einen Kern der Wahrheit dem *Naturalismus* (bzw. Sensualismus) zu. Indem sie nämlich die Assoziationen als ein intentionales Phänomen sichtlich macht, ja als eine ganze Typik von Gestalten passiver intentionaler Synthesis mit einer Wesensgesetzmäßigkeit transzendentaler und rein passiver Genesis, weist sie im *Hume*schen Fiktionalismus, insbesondere in seiner Lehre vom Ursprung der Fiktionen Ding, verharrende Existenz, Kausalität Vorentdeckungen nach, verhüllt in absurden Theorien.

Die phänomenologische Philosophie sieht sich in ihrer ganzen Methode als reine Auswirkung der methodischen Intentionen an, die schon die griechische Philosophie seit ihren Anfängen bewegen; vor allem aber der noch lebendigen Intentionen, die von *Descartes* in den beiden Linien des Rationalismus und Empirismus über *Kant* und den deutschen Idealismus in unsere verworrene Gegenwart hineinreichen. Reine Auswirkung methodischer Intentionen besagt wirkliche Methode, die die Probleme in die Bahnen konkret handanlegender und erledigender Arbeit bringt. Diese Bahn ist in der Weise echter Wissenschaft eine unendliche. Demnach fordert die Phänomenologie vom Phänomenologen, für sich dem Ideal eines philosophischen Systems zu entsagen und doch als bescheidener Arbeiter in Gemeinschaft mit anderen für eine *philosophia perennis* zu leben.

being of transcendental subjectivity. Likewise: *Empiricism* can only be overcome by the most universal and consistent empiricism, which puts in place of the restricted [term] "experience" of the empiricists the necessarily broadened concept of experience [inclusive] of intuition which offers original data, an intuition which in all its forms (intuition of *eidos,* apodictic self-evidence, phenomenological intuition of essence, etc.) shows the manner and form of its legitimation through phenomenological clarification. Phenomenology as eidetic is, on the other hand, rationalistic: it overcomes restrictive and dogmatic rationalism, however, through the most universal rationalism of inquiry into essences, which is related uniformly to transcendental subjectivity, to the I, consciousness, and conscious objectivity. And it is the same in reference to the other antitheses bound up with them. The tracing back of all being to the transcendental subjectivity and its constitutive intentional functions leaves open, to mention one more thing, no other way of contemplating the world than the *teleological.* And yet phenomenology also acknowledges a kernel of truth in naturalism (or rather sensationism). That is, by revealing associations as intentional phenomena, indeed as a whole basic typology of forms of passive intentional synthesis with transcendental and purely passive genesis based on essential laws, phenomenology shows Humean fictionalism to contain anticipatory discoveries; particularly in his doctrine of the origin of such fictions as thing, persisting existence, causality—anticipatory discoveries all shrouded in absurd theories.

Phenomenological philosophy regards itself in its whole method as a pure outcome of methodical intentions which already animated Greek philosophy from its beginnings; above all, however, [it continues] the still vital intentions which reach, in the two lines of rationalism and empiricism, from Descartes through Kant and German idealism into our confused present day. A pure outcome of methodical intentions means real method which allows the problems to be taken in hand and completed. In the way of true science this path is endless. Accordingly, phenomenology demands that the phenomenologist foreswear the ideal of a philosophic system and yet as a humble worker in community with others, live for a perennial philosophy [*philosophia perennis*].

| Synopsis

In the systematic work of phenomenology, which progresses from intuitively given data to heights of abstraction, the old, ambiguous antitheses of traditional philosophy can be resolved by themselves, without the tricks of argumentative dialectic and without compromises. Husserl mentions here as examples rationalism-empiricism, relativism-absolutism, and subjectivism-objectivism. In all of these positions, one can find justified motives, but also half-truths, or an impermissible absolutizing of theses that are legitimate only relatively speaking or taken in abstraction.

Husserl next explains how these oppositions can be overcome by phenomenology. *Subjectivism* can be overcome only by the most consistent and all-encompassing subjectivism, namely, the transcendental. Transcendental subjectivism is at the same time an objectivism of a deeper sort, insofar as it defends the validity of any objectivity that can be shown in and through concordant experience. *Relativism* can be overcome only through the all-encompassing relativism of transcendental phenomenology, which explains the relativity of all objective being as transcendentally constituted; and, at one with this, it also makes intelligible the most radical relativity of all, the relatedness of transcendental subjectivity to itself. This subjectivity even proves to be the only possible meaning of absolute being over against all objective being, which is relative to it; absolute being is the "being-for-itself" of transcendental subjectivity. *Empiricism* can be overcome only by the most universal and consistent form of empiricism, which puts in the place of the restricted experience of the empiricists (sense perception) the necessarily broadened concept of experience of the originally giving intuition, which in all its concrete forms (such as eidetic intuition, apodictic evidence, phenomenological intuition of essences) shows the manner and form of its legitimacy through the clarification of phenomenology. But, on the other hand, phenomenology, insofar as it is eidetic, is also rationalistic, since it overcomes the restrictive and dogmatic rationalism of our tradition through the most universal and consistent rationalism of its inquiry into essences. This rational inquiry is related uniformly to transcendental subjectivity and its intentional correlates.

The tracing back of all being to transcendental subjectivity and its constitutive intentional functions leaves no other way open of contemplating the world than the teleological, to mention just one more opposition. Yet phenomenology also acknowledges a kernel of truth in naturalism, or rather causal sensationism. By showing that associations are intentional phenomena and indeed constitute an entire typology of forms of passive, intentional synthesis that has an essential lawfulness characteristic of transcendental and purely passive genesis, phenomenology is able to show that Hume's fictionalism contains the anticipation of insights that only later would be fully discovered.

Phenomenology thus regards itself in its entire method as a pure realization of the methodical intentions that animated Greek philosophy from its beginning; and at the same time phenomenology also realizes the vital intentions that reach, in the conceptions known as rationalism and empiricism, from Descartes and Locke through Hume and Kant and German idealism into our confused present world. The pure realization of these methodical intentions requires a genuine method that allows all problems to be concretely formulated and solved. If this path is followed in the spirit of genuine science, it is endless. Thus phenomenology demands that the phenomenologist give up the ideal of a philosophical system; as a humble worker, in a community with others, he or she is asked to live for a perennial philosophy.

Commentary

Toward the Resolution of All Philosophical Antitheses: Husserl's Transcendental Idealism

In Chapter Ten we saw that Husserl characterizes transcendental phenomenology as "transcendental idealism." When he introduces this term, he immediately explains that it should not be taken in the sense given to it by Kant; nor should it be interpreted to mean a merely psychological idealism that tries to derive the meaning of the world from meaningless sense-data. Instead, the term should be taken to refer to a consistently executed self-explication in the form of a systematic egological science (*Cart. Med.*, 81–88 [114–21]).

By selecting this term to characterize his own position, Husserl nevertheless places himself within the general perspective of Kant and neo-Kantianism, and Husserl is, although perhaps somewhat reluctantly, well aware of the implications of this relationship. From the context in which Husserl uses the expression, as well as from his phenomenological philosophy as a whole, it becomes clear that he never intended to identify transcendental phenomenology with the philosophy of Kant, or even to state that transcendental phenomenology and Kant's critical philosophy completely agree on the basic philosophical question concerning realism or idealism. It seems that Husserl uses the term to refer to a general philosophical *climate* in which he thinks his philosophy belongs, the basic conception of which he nonetheless tries to reinterpret. This claim is to be examined and clarified here in greater detail.

It is well known that Husserl felt that Descartes as well as Kant greatly influenced the origin of the idea of his phenomenology. In the preceding pages, we have seen that whereas Husserl's interest in Descartes gradually decreased, his interest in Kant continuously increased. Not only did Husserl study Kant more and more carefully and extensively, but he also found himself approaching Kant's basic conceptions in many important aspects of his own philosophy. In many instances, his study of Kant and neo-Kantian philosophers seems to have been the major source of inspiration as far as particular topics of his phenomenology are concerned. While Husserl repeated time and again that there is a great difference between Kant's critical philosophy and his phenomenology, this difference does not so much consist in a different conception of philosophy or in a different metaphysical position in regard to the world, as it does almost exclusively in a difference of approach or method. Describing his own development in letters to Rickert, Natorp, and Ernst Cassirer, Husserl makes it quite clear that he came to his philosophy independently from the Kantian philosophy but that, using different methods and going along different roads, he gradually finds himself closer and closer to the metaphysical position defended by German idealism in general and Kant's transcendental idealism in particular.[1] Later he adds that his view on constitution and synthesis was deeply influenced by Kant and Natorp as far as its genetic conception of them is concerned. But then, he adds immediately that the goal Kant hoped, but was never able, to reach can be realized by his phenomenological philosophy: "[T]ranscendental phenomenology is an attempt to realize the deepest meaning of Kant's philosophizing" (*E. Phil.,* 1:287). "Phenomenology finds itself in harmony with Kant's philosophy as far as the final results it is able to come to are concerned" (ibid., 1:235).

In an important study of Kant's and Husserl's philosophies, Kern comes to the conclusion that the relationship between critique and phenomenology can perhaps best be described in the following way. First of all, one must realize that Husserl's conception of phenomenology, after its basic idea was discovered, gradually developed in dialogue with, and under the continuous influence of, Kantian and neo-Kantian philosophy. In addition to this general influence, one must secondly point to several basic topics and conceptions in Husserl's phenomenology whose origin may be found in Kantian philosophy. One could mention here, among other topics, Husserl's idea of objective logic; his conception of ontology and of the analytic and synthetic a priori; the distinction between the natural and the philosophical attitudes; the doctrines of constitution, synthesis, and active and passive genesis; Husserl's final conception of the reduction; and, finally, Husserl's idealistic interpretation of world.[2] Kern concludes that, all of this notwithstanding, Husserl's phenomenology cannot be characterized as neo-Kantianism, mainly because of essential differences concerning philosophy's method. Husserl claims that the methods used by Kant and the neo-Kantians have not been able to realize philosophy's main goal; he also claims that this goal, which he shares with Kant and his successors, has been (or at least can be in principle) realized by his phenomenology.[3]

We have mentioned several times that there is a close relationship between Kant's and Husserl's transcendental idealism. In order to be able later to refer to points of agreement and disagreement, we must first try precisely to determine what the term "transcendental idealism" signifies. We have seen in the foregoing discussion that Husserl conceives of the process of synthesis in and through which the world becomes constituted for the transcendental subject as an "achieving activity" (*Leistung*) or productivity (*Produktivität*). Husserl believed that this conception of synthesis indeed had its origin in Kant's conception of synthesis, but, on the other hand, that it is certainly also reinterpreted from the viewpoint of his own genetic phenomenology; Husserl explicitly eliminates, among other things, Kant's doctrine of the "thing in-itself" and his conception of the function of the "intellectus archetypus." Finally, Husserl thought that phenomenology and critical philosophy are in agreement concerning Kant's theory of the constitution of the phenomenal world through the transcendental functions of transcendental subjectivity, and that this basic conception can be characterized as transcendental idealism.[4]

Thus, according to Kant and Husserl, the experienced real world is a product (*Produkt, Gebilde*) of the constituting subjectivity. Neither Kant nor Husserl interprets this conception in a solipsistic way. Kant avoids solipsism by his doctrine of the "thing-in-itself," whereas Husserl avoids solipsism by claiming that although transcendental subjectivity constitutes the world in and through an intentional genesis, the being that is intended in this achievement is nonetheless not constituted by consciousness. In other words, the genetic constitution of what as in-itself is foreign to consciousness is indeed production, but what is produced here is not the in-itself but the in-itself's being-for-me. Insofar as that which as in-itself is foreign to consciousness and possesses a being-for-itself, it is obviously not the product of my constituting activities but rather something that is absolute in regard to my consciousness. Since now the world

326 I CHAPTER TWELVE

does not have any for-itself but merely is a being-for-us—since, in other words, the being of the world is its being-for-us—the world itself is, considered from the viewpoint of genetic constitution, nothing but a product of constituting subjectivity (*E. Phil.*, 1:270–80).

Kern rightly points out that Husserl's conception of the ideality of the world therefore fundamentally rests upon two different grounds: (1) the being of the world obviously consists in a being-for-the-experiencing-subjectivity, and, from a static point of view, the world is thus essentially relative to consciousness (*Ideas*, 1:94–104 [80–87]); whereas (2) from a genetic point of view, it is the product of the achieving activities of transcendental subjectivity (*E. Phil.*, 1:274–76); in other words, the second ground of Husserl's idealism is the fact that constitution must be conceived of as essentially genetic.[5]

In briefly elaborating these two different points, we must first ask why Husserl is convinced that the real world does not have a being-for-itself but merely a being-for-us. Husserl is clearly unable to justify this claim by pointing to the thesis that there is a strict correlation between consciousness and being, since it does not follow that the fundamental intelligibility of being entails that the corresponding being does not have any being-for-itself. In other words, it is not the transcendental reduction, which does indeed show the basic correlation of being and consciousness, that permits Husserl to conclude a fundamental relativity of the world. The reason for Husserl's claim is to be found in what we have said above about the experience of real things. There we noted that in Husserl's view, the *perception* of things—which is the primordial, giving act (*Ideas*, 1:6 [8])—is necessarily perspectivistic, and that this infinitely open perceptual process is subject to the condition that appearances to be actualized at later phases of the process will agree and conform both with one another and with those appearances actualized at earlier stages of the process. Since the fact that this condition has been fulfilled in the past with respect to a certain material thing does not lead to any unchangeable certainty that this condition will be fulfilled throughout the future course of the perceptual process as a whole, Husserl therefore concludes that what we call this material thing is no more than an idea in the Kantian sense, the very idea of an infinite system of appearances that can be realized in actual experiences (*Ideas*, 1:342–43 [297–98], 355–62 [309–16]). Husserl further believes that what is true for this particular thing is obviously true for the world at large.[6]

In order to avoid all possible misunderstandings, we must explicitly remark here that Husserl does not intend to deny the reality of the things of the world. Husserl repeatedly warned of this possible misunderstanding (*Ideas*, 1:57–60 [53–56]). Anyone who attacks

Husserl's view on this ground demonstrates a misunderstanding of the meaning of the reduction and still is in the realm of the naive and natural attitude. Husserl is not trying to reduce one being (for example, this chair, the totality of things) to another being (God, for instance, or to transcendental subjectivity conceived of as mundane being); he does not intend, in other words, to give a foundation to beings but he tries to found their "being and meaning."[7] Gaston Berger has formulated Husserl's view in this regard with great clarity: "Phenomenological idealism does not deny the true existence of the world. The only task consists in elucidating the meaning (=being, *Sein*) of this world. There is no doubt that the world exists, but one has to try to understand this indubitability."[8]

In trying to establish this indubitability, Husserl is of the opinion that, in contradistinction to the real world, transcendental subjectivity is something absolute. "Only subjectivity can be 'for-itself' in a genuine and absolute way. For being-for-itself is appearing-to-itself . . ." (*E. Phil.*, 2:189). Absolute being is being in the form of an intentional life that, whatever it may be concretely conscious of, is at the same time consciousness of itself (*Ideas*, 1:110 [92]; *Cart. Med.*, 21 [61]). Transcendental subjectivity does not depend upon a process by which meaning is given to it (this is characteristic of the world) and which is to be given by another subjectivity.[9]

But all of this does not yet necessarily mean that in Husserl's view transcendental subjectivity is the only and last ground of the world's being.[10] In order to explain this, it is necessary to compare more carefully Kant's and Husserl's conceptions of the relationship between subjectivity and world.

It is a well-known fact that Husserl's conception of the ego underwent a long and perhaps even never ending development. Generally speaking, one may say that Husserl originally thought that only one ego is to be admitted—an empirical, bodily-spiritual ego that, from a phenomenological point of view, manifests itself as the complex whole of all phenomena. At that time, he explicitly rejected Natorp's conception of the ego as the pole and reference center of all contents of consciousness, whereas Kant's transcendental ego, the ego of transcendental apperception, was not mentioned at all. Between 1900 and 1916, Husserl first added a pure ego as the individual ego-pole of all acts of consciousness (*Ideas*, 1:132–33 [109–10]) and then the ego that in its individuality is constituted by its "habitualities" (*Ideas*, 2:103–27 [97–120]). Finally, in 1916, Husserl developed this idea further, in that the ego and particularly its identity are not so much connected with the ego's habitual convictions concerning concrete contents of consciousness but are mainly conceived of as the consequence of the positing (*Setzung*) of the world as universal horizon (*E. Phil.*, 1:345–400). It is also known that Husserl's study of Natorp's works and Kant's conceptions deeply influenced this development in his thought.[11]

Husserl thus finally came to the conclusion that the pure ego is constituted in such a way that it can maintain itself as this identical ego only when it is able to maintain the objectivity-thought-of as identical with itself in all its thoughts. In other words, the ego constitutes its own concrete identity by means of its harmonizing and continuously maintained positions in regard to the world. The convictions of the ego in regard to concrete mundane objects may obviously change, but the identity of the ego requires that, in all these changes, it be determined by the idea of coherence and harmony in all its convictions, which as idea is founded in the always remaining conviction concerning the harmonious world itself.[12]

In summary, Husserl gradually became aware of the necessity of admitting that the constitution of the world as a harmonious cosmos (*einstimmiger Kosmos*) is a necessary condition for the unity and identity of the pure ego: the self-identity of the ego requires that, notwithstanding all changes of opinion in regard to concrete objects, the ego maintains its basic conviction concerning the harmonious world.[13] This ego, however, is not a pure ego-pole of ego acts but rather an ego that is convinced of its own transcendence in regard to the acts as well as in regard to their objects.[14]

Although Husserl thus gradually developed in the direction of Kant's conception of the ego, there are nonetheless many important differences between these views. The most important of these differences is that in Kant's conception, the original and *necessary* consciousness of the ego's self-identity is, at the same time, a consciousness of an *equally necessary* unity of the syntheses of all appearances *according to concepts,* that is, the ground of the unity of all objectivity. Husserl, on the other hand, was convinced that the ego of the transcendental apperception, which constitutes itself through its constitution of the world, as well as that which it so constitutes, is no more than a *mere fact* as soon as it is considered from the viewpoint of transcendental subjectivity. It is and remains always possible that the world be dissolved in a mere *"Gewühl,"* which would obviously entail a dissolution of the ego (*E. Phil.*, 2:44–58; *Ideas,* 1:109–12 [91–93]).

Husserl's relatively complicated position concerning the relationship between ego and world thus seems to involve the following seemingly conflicting theses:

1. The constitution of the world by the transcendental subjectivity in transcendental consciousness is a mere contingent fact.

2. The contingence of this fact not only relates to the fact *that* there is a world for consciousness but also to the *manner* in which the world is for consciousness.
3. It is nonetheless possible to develop an ontology of the world that describes the necessary and essential structures that determine the world's *So-Sein*.
4. The contingence of the constitution of the world does not put the world on the same level as contingent mundane things, in that the world (regardless of my fluctuating opinions about concrete mundane things) is and remains the ideal and always presumed horizon on the basis of which conflicting opinions about concrete mundane things can be brought into harmony with one another.[15]

This view is obviously different from those of Kant, Fichte, and Natorp, and Husserl was deeply aware of these differences. Husserl agrees with German idealism that the transcendental subjectivity productively brings about the world in and through its own life in genetic constitutions. However, Husserl claims, this constitution does not take place in such a way that it necessarily follows from the very essence and through the sole power of the transcendental subjectivity. That the subjectivity can and does constitute *such a world* as it in fact constitutes is not because of its own creative possibilities but depends upon a certain "gift" or "grace"; the subjectivity can withdraw from this "grace," and thus the world can always dissolve into a mere chaos of impressions. In other words, the subjectivity is indeed the ground of the being of the world, but it is not the *sufficient* ground of its being; the constitution of the world is not genuinely the work of the finite subjectivity. It seems that Husserl has taken this insight as the starting point for a metaphysics in the Kantian sense, explaining the constitution of the world as the product of a real and genuine Absolute, God.[16]

The Concern of Transcendental Phenomenology with the Life-world

The World as an Important Theme for Phenomenological Analysis

The World in the *Encyclopaedia* Article — The term "world" is very seldom used in the article for the *Encyclopaedia Britannica*. Furthermore, most references to the world are indirect. The world as a theme for phenomenological investigation is hinted at where Husserl speaks about reduction; it is also mentioned where he speaks about intersubjectivity as a community of monadic subjects that are at the root of the constitution of the world valid for everyone.

Obviously, the term has been used more frequently in my own commentary, but usually only in the two contexts just mentioned.

When Husserl mentions the theme of the world in the *Encyclopaedia* article, he never really dwells on the relevant issues; nor does he explain that the world, taken in its various connotations, is indeed a very rich theme for phenomenological analysis and description, and that the world, particularly taken as life-world, was beginning to occupy a central position in transcendental phenomenology during the last ten or fifteen years of his life.

In the pages to come, I shall make a few observations on the place of phenomenological investigations concerning the life-world in transcendental phenomenology in order then to dwell more systematically on Husserl's conception of the life-world.[17]

Confusion Surrounding the Role of the Life-world in Phenomenology — Many contemporary phenomenologists think that the life-world is one of the most important ideas to have come to light through the publication of Husserl's unpublished manuscripts. Although this idea had occupied him in one form or another at least since 1923, Husserl intended to communicate his insights concerning the life-world for the first time only about 1936, when he prepared the first part of his last book, *Crisis*. This conception, however, did not become generally known until Landgrebe and especially Merleau-Ponty had introduced it in their publications on the basis of their knowledge and studies of unpublished manuscripts.[18]

These publications created the impression that Husserl intended during his last years of life to replace his original studies of the transcendental subjectivity with these new investigations concerning the life-world. Some interpreters of Husserl's philosophy have even suggested this. Nothing, however, is further from the truth. On the contrary, the investigations about the life-world form only one of the four different ways in which the constituting activity of the transcendental subjectivity can be brought to the fore. The world of our daily lived experience is not the last level uncoverable by our phenomenological analyses, but it itself is also constituted, and the clarification of its constitution must precisely discover the anonymous achievements of the transcendental ego.[19] This is already evident from the fact that the title of the section of *Crisis* in which Husserl deals with the life-world speaks of the road to phenomenological transcendental philosophy starting from the life-world (*Crisis*, 103–89 [105–93]; 103–4 [105–6]). Thus the interest that this idea has for its own sake must not make us forget that it also has a very definite place and function within the context of Husserl's transcendental phenomenology as a whole.[20]

Furthermore, one must not forget that Husserl's conception of the life-world as it is found in *Crisis* is only the logical fruit of earlier investigations concerning the world in general. In the foregoing, we have seen that already between 1900 and 1913, Husserl undertook investigations with respect to the problem of the world as such, although at that time the world itself was not yet considered as a theme in its own right. Originally these investigations were oriented in two different directions: in connection with the problem of the phenomenological reduction, and in the course of inquiries attempting to clarify the very essence of human perception.[21] Later, by trying to lay the foundations of a general theory of science and thus delineating the subject matter of psychology in particular, Husserl focused on the world just as it is given to us in immediate experience (*Phen. Psych.*, 40–53 [55–72]). Only in the latter context do we find the motives that, in the period beginning about 1920, led Husserl to the problem of the life-world as it is explained in *Crisis*. Seen from this point of view, Husserl's doctrine of the life-world as it is presented in *Crisis* appears as a harmonious synthesis of his view on the phenomenological reduction found in *First Philosophy* and *Cartesian Meditations* and his mundane phenomenology of the world, which was briefly outlined for the first time in *Phenomenological Psychology*.

Although I shall pay special attention to the most important insights in regard to the life-world as Husserl has described them in *Crisis,* a brief introduction explaining the most significant results of Husserl's investigations concerning the world in general and the world of our immediate experiences in particular seems to be of some importance in this context.

The World and the Phenomenological *Epoche* — We have seen that Husserl generally describes the phenomenological *epoche* as a disconnection of the general thesis of our natural attitude. This thesis can be briefly characterized as follows: I find continuously present to me and standing over against me the one spatiotemporal fact-world to which I myself belong, as do all other human beings found in it and related to it in the same way as I am. I find this fact-world to be out there; and I also take it always just as it gives itself to me as something that exists out there. Any doubt, negation, or rejection of certain data of the natural world does not affect the general thesis of the natural standpoint. The world is, as a fact-world, always there, even if it sometimes appears to be other than I originally supposed. In order to know this fact-world more truly and comprehensively than our everyday experience is able to do, and to solve all the problems that manifest themselves on its basis, we have to build up different sciences, which, however, all remain sciences of the natural attitude.

Taken as a whole, therefore, our world, as the world in which we always find ourselves consciously living, remains certain, no matter how many details become doubtful. Only particular parts of it ever undergo the correction "not so but otherwise." This means that every positing or negation presupposes as a universal basis our belief in the reality of the world. Every positing is a positing, and every canceling is a canceling on this basis, which, within the realm of the natural attitude, we can never shake. Therefore, if the *epoche* is really meant to make us transcend the domain of the natural attitude, it has to be universal and not limited to particular acts and their meant objects as meant. In other words, by the phenomenological reduction, the general thesis of the natural attitude must be put out of action (*Ideas,* 1:51–57 [48–50]).

In this way, while developing the doctrine of the phenomenological *epoche,* Husserl acquired a first definition of the world as the all-encompassing doxic basis that as a total horizon includes every particular positing. While Husserl in these analyses was primarily concerned with acts of perceiving, since he was convinced that perception is the primordial existence-positing act and therefore constitutes the fundament of acts of every other kind, we may conclude that the world is the horizon of our total human attitude, that is, our intentional directedness in all our diverse acts.

Thus the general thesis as the universal fundamental doxic positing of the world does not consist in a determinate act that, at some time or other, is to be explicitly performed; rather, it is the foundation for every concrete act whatsoever. It is nothing but the elemental fact that, from the very start, the ego lives in the world, is intentionally directed toward beings that are always tacitly understood as intramundane beings.

The World as Appearing in the Phenomenological Analysis of Perception — Within the context of his investigations concerning the meaning of the phenomenological reduction, Husserl concluded that the world is to be understood as the all-embracing doxic basis that, as a total horizon, includes every particular positing. This view was in fact not more than a further clarification of the world as the horizon of every perception. As we have seen in the foregoing, analysis of the syntheses in which the perception of a material thing comes into being shows that we cannot restrict ourselves to the thing-perception as an isolated phenomenon if we intend to uncover the concrete and full meaning of this material thing. The perceived thing always manifests itself in a certain horizon, a background of things that are consciously and more or less explicitly meant along with the thing in question. Every material thing manifests itself in perception as having its outer horizon, which is not only spatially but also temporally extended (*Ideas,* 1:69–73 [61–64]).

We may thus conclude that Husserl's earlier analyses of the perception of a concrete thing uncovered to him a structure that he eventually understood as a first characterization of the world: first of all as the horizon of all our perceiving acts, then as the horizon to which every human activity finally points.

The Essential Structures of the World of Our Immediate Experience — These ideas, only very briefly indicated here, occupied Husserl more and more after *Ideas* appeared, and especially in the twenties, when he was looking for a deeper insight into the relationship between phenomenology and psychology and into the problem of the reduction. During that period, the concept of the world, which was at first defined generally as the all-embracing horizon of any experience, received a more differentiated content. According to Husserl, however, those analyses concerning the world, as analyses belonging to a mundane phenomenology that remains within the domain of the natural attitude, have only a preliminary character; on this level, the problem of the world can thus never find its final solution. A real understanding of the world can be obtained only by means of a radical explanation of its constitution by transcendental subjectivity, and, after the reduction has been performed, such an explanation can be given only with the help of detailed constitutional analyses, as was explained in the foregoing chapters.

But before returning to this point, let us first try to describe a few leading traits of Husserl's mundane-phenomenological analyses concerning the world of our immediate experience, especially as we find them in *Phenomenological Psychology.* In the series of lectures that formed this study, Husserl wished to delineate the subject matter, method, and function of a new eidetic science, which he called phenomenological psychology. According to him, however, it is impossible to define the pure psychical as the subject matter of phenomenological psychology if one does not take one's starting point in a general ontology of the world of our immediate experience (*Phen. Psych.,* 40–47 [55–64]).

In his brief outline of such a general ontology of the world of our immediate experience, Husserl deals first with the crucial problem created by the fact that many philosophers, influenced by Kant, explicitly deny that the world could ever be an object of any possible experience. Husserl admits that obviously only real, individual beings are immediately experienced, but it is his conviction that in these experiences, the world is coperceived as their necessary horizon. If it is true that the world is experienced as the necessary horizon in which individual beings can manifest themselves, it will be clear why every intersubjectively experienced being is conceivable only as being *in* the world and why space and time are the necessary a priori forms in which each concrete being is to be ordered. Originally, the world manifests itself only as a spatiotemporal horizon, as concretely filled space and concretely filled time (*Phen. Psych.*, 70–73 [93–97]).

Furthermore, from this conception of the world as the necessary horizon of every perceived thing it follows also, insofar as method is concerned, that the descriptive and eidetic analyses of the most general structures of the world must take their starting point in the consideration of exemplary, real, individual things taken in their essential relatedness to the horizon that in fact is the world (*Phen. Psych.*, 73–75 [98–99]).

When we, while studying those phenomena, use the eidetic reduction to focus attention on the essential structure of experienced being as such, it becomes clear that this being manifests itself as concretely being there, and that—within the realm of our natural attitude—we self-evidently conceive it as being real in the real world. This world, however, to which our whole natural life necessarily is referred, manifests itself as not only changing in itself but also as being subject to our always changing concepts and ideas. This means that what we normally call "the" world is not the world as it is immediately experienced but rather this world as always being already covered with layers of meaning that have their origin in our conceptions and opinions, which themselves are the result of our practical and theoretical activities.

On closer investigation, it becomes manifest that our view of "the" world is *especially* influenced by two factors. First, our way of apprehending the world is determined by the fact that the sciences have explained the world with the help of categories that, although they undergo continuous development and correction, claim to define the world objectively as a set of given objects and relationships, existing in themselves and capable of being grasped by exact methods. Our conception of the world therefore involves, quite as a matter of course, the belief that this is an objective, exactly determined and determinable world. However, the broadening of our historical, ethnological, and sociological knowledge has added the awareness that the view of the world determined by the sciences cannot be considered as the only one. Today, as in earlier times, we find human communities whose understanding of the world has in no way been affected by the sciences. The necessary consequence of this fact is that the scientific view of the world is itself only one among many and, like all the others, has been produced by a certain society under definite conditions. Thus, the conviction of many scientists that their view of the world is the only true one, the only one that is objectively valid, is unacceptable. We must admit a plurality and historical relativity of views of the world, none of which may claim for itself an absolute truth about "the" world.

Accordingly, when Husserl struggled with the problem of the world, it was evident to him from the very start that the determinations about the world accomplished by the sciences cannot be considered as essential structures that belong necessarily to the world as such. On the contrary, we must turn from the *world* as it always is already there for us, with its sense as explicated by the sciences, and go back to the world as it is prior to science, the immediately lived world with its original givenness, which is the underlying basis for every scientific determination. Correlatively, we must go back from our *scientific view* of the world to our prescientific experiences (*Phen. Psych.*, 38–42 [52–57]).

When we perform such a reduction, which obviously is to be distinguished from the transcendental reduction, "the" world begins to manifest itself as consisting of concrete substances, all of which have their characteristic "modes," such as size, shape, and color. Each individual, concrete substance manifests itself as a causal unity that is causally related to its surroundings and, within the context of the changing causal relations, manifests itself as a substratum of fixed and causally determined properties. To the general structure that necessarily belongs to the very essence of this and every conceivable world belongs, too, the distinction between different regions of being, of which the regions of living and nonliving beings are the most striking examples. The region of consciously living subjects appears to occupy a privileged and central place in the world of our immediate experience. Although every concrete substance in the world possesses necessarily and essentially spatial, temporal, and causal aspects, consciously living subjects also manifest themselves as having certain psychical characteristics (*Phen. Psych.*, 75–76 [99–100]).[22]

I The Life-world in *Crisis*

As was mentioned above, Husserl introduces the question of the life-world in *Crisis* as one of the four roads to transcendental phenomenology.[23] The life-world can give us a particularly interesting and revealing clue for the study of the universal and transcendental constitution of the transcendental ego. It is not, however, my intention to describe this new road to transcendental phenomenology in detail but rather to explain the most important insights regarding the nature and meaning of the life-world itself and its function within phenomenological philosophy as a whole. Therefore I shall confine myself here to a brief summary of some sections of Husserl's *Crisis* and some other important manuscripts written in 1936 and 1937. First I shall try to describe more accurately what is meant by the term *"Lebenswelt,"* then indicate the relation between the life-world and the scientific worlds. Ultimately I hope to explain the possibility of an ontology of the life-world and its significance for transcendental phenomenology. In so doing, I shall be guided by relevant sections of Aron Gurwitsch's study on *Crisis,* which will be quoted below.

Description of the Life-world — Under the influence of modern science since Galileo, the life-world—the world of our common lived experience—has been replaced by the objectively true world of science, which, as modern Western scientists would have it, passes for reality in the strict sense of the word. However, it can be shown quite easily that such a view is completely unacceptable. For one thing, no objective entity of science is available to direct and immediate experience, whereas the life-world does offer itself, actually or virtually, in every perceptual experience and all its possible derivatives. Furthermore, the universe of science proves to be a network of ideal constructs, a theoretical-logical superstructure; and its apprehension and conception are therefore of the same nature as those of any idea of the mathematical sciences. The construction of the world of science implies, as a mental accomplishment, certain definite procedures in which idealization plays an integral role. Idealization, however, obviously implies something to be idealized. Therefore, because of its intrinsic sense as a superstructure, the world of science must have a firm basis upon which it can rest. This foundational basis cannot be anything other than the life-world and the immediate evidence of our lived experiences—the term "evidence" referring to the immediate self-presentation of the objects involved. All theoretical truth, whether logical, mathematical, or scientific, thus has its final justification and roots in evidences that concern events and happenings in the life-world.

If Husserl therefore gives the evidences of the life-world a privileged status over those of scientific, objective theory, it is attributable to the latter's being based upon the former. The operations and procedures whose outgrowths and constituted correlates are objective theory and, generally speaking, the objective world of science always imply those acts of consciousness in and through which the life-world appears as always present and pregiven, as existing in its own right prior to all scientific endeavor. Therefore, for a really fundamental understanding of the world of science, we must return to the life-world and elucidate the role it plays in several respects in the constitution and development of science (*Crisis,* 48–53 [48–54], 111–14 [114–16], 127–35 [130–38]).

Radical philosophical reflection, then, must begin by clarifying the universal presupposition that is at the root of our life and all our engagements. This presupposition is the doxically accepted and even naive self-evidence of the world in which we live and with which we are always on familiar terms. Each minute of our life, we are somehow or other concerned with things, animals, and other people, which manifest themselves as intramundane beings; and we, too, see ourselves as part of this world. None of the beings appears in isolation; each refers to a certain framework into which it is inserted and manifests itself within an all-encompassing and ever extended horizon: the world-horizon. Unlike certain mundane beings, which may occasionally show themselves and then fade away, the world itself is continuously present to us as the universal field of all actual and possible activities of any conceivable kind. If the world is always there as pregiven, if to live is to be taken as living in the world, it is because the world proclaims itself simultaneously with the appearance of every particular mundane being with which we might be involved. The implicit and vague awareness of the world permeates all our comings and goings and becomes part of them as their most fundamental, though never explicitly formulated, presupposition. Correspondingly, the world, which is tacitly taken for granted, proves to be the ground for all our endeavors, regardless of their proper orientation (*Crisis,* 142–43 [145–46]).

The world indeed includes nature. However, nature is to be understood here as it is given in immediate experience, and not the idealized nature of the physical sciences. But the world comprises more than *mere* nature; there is also "culture." Among the beings in the midst of which we find ourselves, there are not only natural beings—objects which may be described exhaustively by pointing to their color, shape, size, or weight—but also tools, instruments, books, buildings, art objects—that is, objects that have human meaning, serve human aims and needs, and satisfy human desires. Because the world has such objects at all and therefore provides the framework within which we live our human life, we refer to it as our life-world (*Crisis,* 127–29 [130–32]).

Within the life-world, we encounter other human beings and assume without question that they not only live in the world but also are aware of it, that they are faced with those things and objects which confront us, although to each one of us, determined by his or her point of view, the objects and the world in general may appear under varying perspectives. Each of us nonetheless takes it for granted that the world is one and the same for all of us, a common intersubjective world, the world of our common experience (*Crisis,* 135–37 [138–40]).

As we encounter each other in the common world, each of us may adopt toward the other a disinterested attitude, or we may become involved with one another and engage in the myriad relationships of mutual enterprise and cooperation. We then not only live in the same world but work and actualize our potentialities in it together; we enmesh our intentions, plans, and activities with others' in full reciprocal interaction. If, because of its reference to human life, the world takes on the character of a life-world, the reference is not only to individual persons but also, and even principally, to a historical society whose social life consists in the interrelatedness of thought and action in different modalities. The term "life-world" has essentially a historical-social implication: a life-world is relative to a given society at a certain moment of its history. It must therefore be taken as it is thought of by the historical society whose world it is, as is, for instance, explained by Lucien Lévy-Bruhl in his interpretation of the mythical and magical world of primitive society.[24] Whether we act on our own or in cooperation with other people and engage in mutual endeavors, the things with which we are confronted, our own plans and projects, and finally the world in its entirety appear to us in the light of convictions, opinions, beliefs, and conceptions that are prevalent in the society of which we are part. The term "society" may be taken here in the broadest sense denoting the whole historical civilization to which we belong, or in the narrower sense of a special group within a larger community. The life-world provides the ground of our life, a basis always taken for granted, always taken as already given and existing independently of, and prior to, all our individual and collective activities. We meet one another as mundane beings among intramundane beings on this ground that we all share (*Crisis,* 137–44 [140–46]; *Phen. Psych.,* 38–42 [52–57]).

Besides being objects in the life-world, we are simultaneously subjects in relation to the life-world insofar as it derives its meaning from our collective human life. These collective accomplishments become a part of the life-world, which not only is as it is taken to be by the respective society but also comprises all its innovations. In and through the life of the society in question, its life-world undergoes changes and transformations and consequently is subject to always new reinterpretations.[25]

The Life-world and the World of Science — Reflecting upon the life-world as it immediately manifests itself to us, we have pointed to its historical character and its essential relativity to a certain living society. Now we want to focus on the fact that in the collective endeavors that have been referred to, our scientific activities play an important role. When, for instance, Einstein refers to the investigations and results of Hendrik Lorentz, the reference is obviously not to a physical or psychophysical construction of Lorentz that would show him as he really and objectively is in himself, although both Einstein and Lorentz—as well as their laboratories, the equipment involved, and the books used—could be investigated as physical objects with the help of physical methods. But to the working physicist Einstein, Lorentz appears as a colleague who lives in the same world, has certain interests in common with him, and is engaged in analogous endeavors. Meeting Lorentz in the same life-world and finding himself in contact and harmony with him, because of their shared aims and common knowledge, Einstein tries to understand Lorentz's ideas; he uses them as they are or changes them; he uses Lorentz's results as bases for further investigation and as premises for further conclusions or employs them in some other way in his own work, which he then presents to his scientific colleagues for further consideration and critique.

Science arises from, and develops in, such an interaction of the activities of the members of the scientific community. This community, of course, is made up not only of contemporary scientists but also of those who worked before them and upon whose achievements present-day scientists are building. It is, moreover, an open community, in that whatever is achieved now will be carried further by future scientists. This interaction is characterized by general discussion, constructive critique, agreement, and eventually any necessary alterations, all in order to come to a justifiable and satisfactory conclusion. Science taken in this light manifests itself as a collective cultural achievement, basically not too different from the results of other cultural accomplishments. In regard to scientific activities, Husserl significantly refers to a special type of praxis, namely, theorizing (*Crisis,* 129–32 [132–34]).

For a better understanding of what is involved in science, one has to investigate and analyze the mental functions and operations involved in scientific pursuits and the different modes in which mental activities come to be intersubjectively interrelated. Insofar as the human sciences deal with human psychical life and with the creations arising from that life, natural science as it developed since Galileo—being also a creation of the human mind—belongs within the domain of investigation of the human sciences. Objective nature, that is, nature as it really is in itself, should not be thought of as referring to a reality underlying the appearances in the life-world, a hidden reality that may be uncovered by means of certain methods and techniques. Rather, it implies the idea of an unlimited intersubjective achievement, an idea toward which the members of the community of scientists direct their work and which is approximated by the results of their complementary activities. These results are actually the scientific theories that also serve to delineate the successive phases of the historical advance of science.

As for all cultural activities, the search for scientific knowledge takes place in the life-world. Scientific questions and problems come up within the life-world and refer to certain aspects of it isolated in abstraction, like, for instance, the spatiotemporal or corporeal aspect. Over and over scientists make use of events and happenings in the life-world, in which they carry out their experimentation, find their equipment, and take their readings. To make use of those events and happenings in scientific theories is, however, not the same as to conceptualize and interpret them in scientific terminology. As far as scientists are concerned, the laboratory is for them a place of study and research. They see it in its relation to the specific human pursuits it serves and do not consider it in reference to what, taken in the context of a fully developed, universal scientific explanation of all phenomena, it would prove objectively to be in itself, no more so than they consider their colleagues as physical-chemical systems.

The aim of scientific pursuits refers to human existence in the life-world, too; it is but one of several ends that underlie collective scientific practice and other such intersubjectively concatenated endeavors. If the goals of science are of a specific nature, so are all other goals that determine our cultural life. The specific aim under consideration is to develop to the fullest extent in scope and accuracy the possibilities of prediction and induction going beyond those immediately relevant to prescientific common experience. As Husserl explains it, this aim is to replace knowledge, in the sense of the familiarity that we have of the life-world in our everyday life and that suffices for our practical needs and our orientation in the life-world, by knowledge in the strict sense of the term, understood in relationship to the ideas of objective truth and being-in-itself.

Again, as is true for all cultural endeavors, the concrete contributions and results of our scientific projects accrue to the life-world. The existence of science and scientific theories makes up an integral part of the historical-cultural reality of modern Western humanity, that is, of the life-world. Yet this is not to be construed as meaning, in the traditional sense, that the universe built up by science is the true reality that is to take the place of the life-world. It does, however, imply that, for Western humanity, nature, as given in common experience, seems to have the character of being available for possible scientific interpretation and explanation.

The life-world appears to be the base upon which the world of science is built as a superstructure; the specific logical-mathematical evidence refers, in its very essence, to evidences involving common experience. This does not mean that the life-world is to be seen solely as a point of departure for moving to another realm of being. Such a position could give rise to the idea of a double truth: subjective and relative truth pertaining to practical situations in the life-world; and objective and scientific truth, which, notwithstanding its relation to the first, is not fundamentally affected by this relation. However, as Husserl insists, the life-world does intervene in the implementations of science; the life-world is given to us, and we experience ourselves as existing in it, regardless of whether or not we are engaged in scientific projects. Over the centuries, people have lived in many life-worlds before the rise of science in the modern sense of this term. Finally, science is an integral part of the specific life-world of Western humanity. Insofar as the ideas of objective truth and being-in-itself—through which the subjectivity and relativity of common experience is to be transcended—serve to guide and give direction to the particular human activity that Husserl calls theoretical praxis, they are themselves related to the domain of the psychical, the subjective, and thus the relative.

Perhaps initially it seemed that the question of the life-world was considered for the sake of the philosophical elucidation of science only. Now it becomes evident that the philosophy of science, whatever its value and significance may be, deals only with a particular and partial theme. The life-world appears here not only as an autonomous theme but also as the more universal and therefore the principal theme.[26]

Ontology of the Life-world — A science of the life-world that recognizes this world's specific character and accepts it as it offers itself in immediate experience of prescientific life obviously cannot be a science in the sense of Galileo, that is, one in which a theoretical, logical-mathematical superstructure assumes preeminence over the life-world. In the first place, we must perform a reduction concerning objective science. This does not mean refusing to recognize that objective science really exists and pretending to live in a world devoid of objective science, or denying or even questioning its validity. Objective science with its conclusions and achievements continues to be what it always has been: a cultural fact related to our life-world. There is no idea of giving up interest in objective science. However, under the reduction, we refrain from following through on certain interests; we suspend them and take them out of action. We do not allow ourselves to be involved in the procedures of objective science; we assume a disinterested attitude in regard to them. Such an attitude involves not only an absence of consent to theories of objective science but also a refraining from assuming any critical position in regard to the truth or untruth of such theories; this automatically cancels out denial and doubt as specific critical attitudes. Valid theories of objective science remain valid for us. However, under the reduction we do not proceed on the basis of their accepted validity, which we wish neither to challenge nor to avail ourselves of. No theory, no finding, no statement of objective science will be allowed to enter into our consideration as a founded truth, starting point, premise, or argument. To be sure, the reduction not only deals with specific theories and outcomes but also concerns the very idea of objective science as such. While continuing to recognize this idea as playing an important role in our cultural life, we keep ourselves from being motivated and determined by it (*Crisis*, 135–37 [138–40]).

This reduction enables us to take the life-world for what it is, just as we experience it as our historical-cultural reality, without referring it to or considering it as supplanted by being as it really is in itself. Yet the whole notion of a general science of the life-world seems plagued by an insurmountable difficulty. Such a science, though not Galilean in nature, must have a certain objectivity and validity, too; it must develop methods that will enable it to make true and founded statements, that is, assertions which appear conclusive and convincing to everybody who employs the same methods. This, however, seems inconsistent with what has been explained concerning the essential relativity of the life-world to a certain society and even to a specific phase in the history of that society. Does not each life-world require a science for itself? Can there be such a thing as a general science of the life-world as such? (*Crisis*, 137–41 [140–45]).

Despite its relativity, the life-world shows itself to possess an invariant structure, an unchanging structural framework to which the relative and variable belong. Prior to, and completely separate from, objective science, the life-world manifests itself as extended in space and time. The space referred to is that which we experience, our lived space, and not a geometrical space; it does not contain any ideal mathematical entities, is not divisible ad infinitum, and does not constitute an infinitesimal continuum. This is true also for time. In the life-world, we meet corporeal beings, but they are not bodies in the sense of geometry or physics. Finally, the life-world exhibits causality, conceived not as laws of nature formulated in equations of functional dependency but rather as a certain regularity and typical uniformity. As Husserl expresses it, things have their habits of behaving in similar ways under typically similar conditions.

It should be mentioned that the categories belonging to the life-world and denoting its invariable structures are designated by the same terms as the objective categories that are developed in the a priori sciences, such as logic and the different mathematical disciplines. The identical terminology must not mask the distinction between the a priori belonging to the life-world and the objective a priori. What the identical terminology does indicate is the essential reference of the objective a priori to the a priori of the life-world: founded on the a priori of the life-world, the objective a priori is produced through idealization. Posing the issue of the origin of geometry, Husserl accordingly insists upon the historical-intentional investigations that have their point of departure in the invariable structure of perceptual space and spatiality as lived in pregeometrical experience, and not in the passing apperceptions of a specific historical period, such as the mythical-magical conceptions that, as a matter of recorded history, were involved in, and to some extent certainly had an influence upon, the rise of early geometry (*Crisis*, 140–41 [143–44]).

The general science of the life-world as conceived by Husserl has as its subject matter the invariable general style and the unchanging formal structure of the life-world. This science does not have to restrict itself to the life-world of Western humanity, or even to actual life-worlds of societies that exist or existed in past history. By moving from one actual life-world to another and determining the difference between them, we may free ourselves of all considerations of actuality. Starting from any actual life-world, we may in complete freedom vary and alter it in imagination and in this way fabricate varieties of possible life-worlds merely as possible, for which the problem of their historical actuality has no importance. The goal of free variation in this concrete case is to bring to light what essentially and necessarily belongs to a life-world as such (*Crisis*, 142–47 [145–51]).

In this way, Husserl arrives at the notion of an ontology of the life-world as such, understood as a possible world of intersubjective experience. The structures uncovered by this ontology are present in every factual life-world, whatever its historical and accidental content may be. An ontology of the life-world, however, differs fundamentally from the ontologies of the modern tradition, which have been strongly influenced by the notion of being-in-itself. In other words, traditional ontologies have had their roots in the objective a priori, whereas the ontology that Husserl has in mind is concerned with the a priori of the life-world. In bringing to the fore the idea of an ontology of the life-world, even in *Crisis* Husserl does not do much more than formulate this idea. His principal interest lies in another direction.[27]

Ontology of the Life-world and Transcendental Phenomenology — In the natural attitude, we are interested in the things themselves, their qualities and properties; we are concerned with what the objects are, whether as objects of the immediately lived world or as seen within the horizon of a specific scientific orientation interested in "being as it really is in itself." We are absorbed in our mundane projects and plans, so we do not focus on the modes in which intramundane beings and the world itself manifest themselves. The acts of consciousness through which the world and whatever is in it become accessible to us are lived but not explicitly thematized; they remain more or less hidden. We are, however, able to sever connections with our naive and natural attitude and to manifest a new *theoretical* interest in things—not as they are in themselves but as they manifest themselves—an interest in their appearances and the systematic concatenations of these appearances. At this point, our topic is no longer the world but the fabric of our conscious life, the syntheses of acts of consciousness that result in a permanent awareness of the world as always being there. Moving steadfastly in this direction, we near the threshold of phenomenology, whose general intention may be formulated as the endeavor to account for the world at large, the intramundane beings in particular, and, as a matter of fact, all objective entities whatsoever in terms of experiences, acts, and achievements of consciousness. Doing so is tantamount to disclosing the world and the objective entities referred to as products and correlates of systematically concatenated and synthesized multiplicities of conscious acts, through which the former find the basis for their validity and existence (*Crisis,* 148–51 [151–54]).

To implement such a program, we must perform a second reduction, this time in regard to the life-world itself. Here again, reduction means rendering inactive, and purposely laying aside, not denial or doubt. The whole of conscious life, in and through which beings of every conceivable kind and the life-world as such appear, remains untouched by the transcendental reduction, which is the second *epoche*. While living all these acts in their interwovenness, we do not permit ourselves, under the phenomenological reduction, to live *in* these acts; we no longer allow ourselves to be engaged in them. Our attitude is that of a disinterested onlooker who, rather than participating in it, just looks at the stream of conscious life—which flows on independently of the attitude we adopt—as a field of descriptive and analytical investigations. Acts that are just lived in our naive and natural attitude are now thematized and made subjects of reflexive analysis. In this way, all mundane entities and the life-world itself are transformed into phenomena referring to the acts of consciousness in and through which they are given.[28]

Conclusion — The life-world, it can be seen, is by no means immediately accessible as such, since everyone undergoes the influence of the culture of the "world" in which he or she is living, and Western culture particularly is somehow seduced by the scientific interpretation of the world. A particular reduction, a temporary suspension of culture and science, is therefore indispensable for uncovering the life-world and its essential structures. Once we have performed this reduction, we are in a position to study the life-world in an ontology of the life-world that is already a kind of phenomenology; Husserl calls this phenomenology a mundane phenomenology. Near the end of his life, Husserl believed this mundane phenomenology to be a necessary condition for a transcendental phenomenology. On the one hand, it is evident that the analyses of mundane phenomenology itself have no final meaning if they are not completed by analyses in the transcendental sphere toward which the transcendental reduction is the proper approach. But on the other hand, Husserl saw also that only after the inquiries of the mundane phenomenology have been effected does the transcendental reduction have a sound basis and proper guide. Thus we must first return from the world of culture to the original life-world by means of a first reduction; then the transcendental reduction must lead us further back from the structures of the life-world to the hidden achievements of a "functioning intentionality." The discovery of these achievements then allows us to describe the original constitution of the characteristic features of the life-world and all the objectivities later based upon them.[29]

| N O T E S

1.   Iso Kern, *Husserl und Kant.* See also Arion Kelkel's critical analysis of this book in *Revue de métaphysique et de morale* 71 (1966): 154–98. The passage referred to in the text is to be found in Kern, *Husserl und Kant,* 28–29.

2.   Ibid., 421–22.

3.   Ibid., 422–23.

4.   Ibid., 276–77; cf. *Cart. Med.,* 85–86 [117–19], 149–50 [175–76].

5.   Kern, *Husserl und Kant,* 279–80.

6.   *F. tr. L.,* 282 [288]; *E. Phil.,* 2:47; Kern, *Husserl und Kant,* 280–83.

7.   Diemer, *Edmund Husserl,* 16–17.

8.   Gaston Berger, *Le cogito dans la philosophie de Husserl* (Paris: Aubier, 1941), 95.

346 I CHAPTER TWELVE

9. Kern, *Husserl und Kant,* 284.
10. Ibid., 285.
11. Ibid., 286–88.
12. MS. A VI 30, 34b–44a, quoted by Kern, *Husserl und Kant,* 289–90.
13. Kern, *Husserl und Kant,* 290–91.
14. Ibid., 291–93.
15. Ibid., 295–96.
16. Ibid., 297–303. Cf. *E. Phil.,* 1:381–95; 187–88n.l; 2:254–55.
17. For what follows, see Paul Janssen, *Geschichte und Lebenswelt: Ein Beitrag zur Diskussion von Husserls Spätwerk* (The Hague: Nijhoff, 1970); Gerd Brand, "The Structure of the Life-world according to Husserl," *Man and World* 6 (1973): 143–62; idem, "Horizont, Welt, Geschichte," *Phänomenologische Forschungen* 5 (1977): 14–89; idem, *Welt, Ich und Zeit* (The Hague: Nijhoff, 1955); Walter Biemel, "Réflexions à propos des recherches husserliennes de la Lebenswelt," *Tijdschrift voor filosofie* 33 (1971): 659–83; Ulrich Claesges, "Zweideutigkeiten in Husserls Lebenswelt-Begriff," in *Perspektiven transzendentalphänomenologischer Forschung,* ed. Ulrich Claesges and K. Held (The Hague: Nijhoff, 1972); Aron Gurwitsch, "The Last Work of Edmund Husserl. II: The *Lebenswelt,*" in *Studies in Phenomenology and Psychology,* ed. Lester E. Embree (Evanston, Ill.: Northwestern University Press, 1966), 397–448; Fred Kersten, "The Life-world Revisited," *Research in Phenomenology* 1 (1971): 33–62; H. Hohl, *Lebenswelt und Geschichte* (Munich: Alber, 1962); Bernet et al., *Edmund Husserl,* 199–208.
18. Spiegelberg, *The Phenomenological Movement,* 1:159.
19. Biemel, "Les phases décisives," 32–71.
20. Spiegelberg, *The Phenomenological Movement,* 1:160.
21. Husserl, *Ideas,* 1:51–62 [51–57], 69–73 [61–64], 105–12 [87–93], 213–16 [180–83].
22. For the preceding pages, see also Ludwig Landgrebe, "The World as Phenomenological Problem," *Philosophy and Phenomenological Research* 1 (1940–41): 38–58, particularly 38–45.
23. See Boehm's introduction to Husserl's *Erste Philosophie,* 2:xxx–xxxvii.
24. Spiegelberg, *The Phenomenological Movement,* 1:161. Husserl's letter in which he speaks about Lévy-Bruhl's work is discussed by Merleau-Ponty in "Le philosophe et la sociologie," *Cahiers internationaux de sociologie* 10 (1951): 62–63.
25. Aron Gurwitsch, "The Last Work of Edmund Husserl," *Philosophy and Phenomenological Research* 16 (1955–56): 370–99, particularly 370–73.
26. Gurwitsch, "The Last Work of Edmund Husserl," 373–75. Cf. *Crisis,* 48–53 [48–54], 123–35 [126–38]; *Krisis,* 463–67.
27. Gurwitsch, "The Last Work of Edmund Husserl," 375–78. Cf. *Crisis,* 173–74 [176–77].
28. Gurwitsch, "The Last Work of Edmund Husserl," 378–80. Cf. *Crisis,* 151–53 [154–56].
29. Spiegelberg, *The Phenomenological Movement,* 1:160–62.

EPILOGUE

During his lifetime and especially after his death, Husserl's ideas have had an enormous influence on twentieth-century thought. Husserl may very well have been the most influential philosopher of the century. Toward the end of his life he was often discouraged. In addition to the almost unbearable political situation in which he had come to find himself, there was the full realization that there really was nobody willing and able to continue the work he had started. He had hoped that Heidegger would have been this person; yet Heidegger preferred to go his own way. In Husserl's view, the task of transcendental phenomenology is quasi-infinite and can be brought to completion only by a community of like-minded scholars. Yet he realized that he had failed to inspire such a community of scholars. Husserl also realized that he had very few genuine "followers." By a follower, Husserl would not have understood someone who merely would repeat what he had already said; a follower, in his view, would rather be the one who would turn to a task in the enormous domain of phenomenology still to be realized and who would deal with the issues at hand in the spirit of transcendental phenomenology.

On the other hand, there are very few continental European philosophers who were not influenced by Husserl. This is true for the most important ones, such as Jaspers, Hartmann, Heidegger, Sartre, Merleau-Ponty, Gadamer, Ricoeur, and others. But this is true also for numerous lesser-known ones.

And yet there are indeed very few, if any, important thinkers who have followed Husserl in his most basic claims. Almost everyone objected to his transcendental idealism, his methodical solipsism, his demand for presuppositionlessness, his "Cartesianism," and his demand that basic insights must be such that they can be presented with apodictic evidence. Yet very few have not been deeply impressed by many other ideas, such as intentionality, synthesis and constitution, intentional analysis, ideation, and his conceptions of the a priori and the transcendental.

It is too early to come to a more definitive evaluation of his genuinely impressive work. There are still manuscripts he left behind to be published. Various aspects of his work have not yet been fully unearthed and understood. Yet we can say that his work has generated a number of great philosophical works in which the seeds planted by the father of the modern phenomenological movement have come to fruition, even though they may have produced fruits of a different kind.

There are a number of bibliographies of works by Husserl and of publications on his thought. The most extensive one known to me is that prepared by François M. Lapointe, *Edmund Husserl and His Critics: An International Bibliography (1894–1979)* (Bowling Green, Ohio: Philosophy Documentation Center, 1980). There is another outstanding bibliography in Peter McCormick and Frederick Elliston, eds., *Husserl: Shorter Works* (Notre Dame, Ind.: University of Notre Dame Press, 1981), 377–430.

In the list to follow I shall limit myself to all the works by Husserl and to those publications on his thought which I have used in composing this book.

Works by Husserl with English Translations

"Amsterdamer Vorträge: Phänomenologische Psychologie" (Amsterdam Lectures). In *Phänomenologische Psychologie,* 302–49.

Analysen zur passiven Synthesis. Edited by M. Fleischer. The Hague: Nijhoff, 1966.

Cartesianische Meditationen und Pariser Vorträge. Edited by S. Strasser. The Hague: Nijhoff, 1950. *Cartesian Meditations: An Introduction to Phenomenology.* Translated by Dorion Cairns. The Hague: Nijhoff, 1960. *The Paris Lectures.* Translated by Peter Koestenbaum. The Hague: Nijhoff, 1964.

Ding und Raum. Vorlesungen 1907. Edited by Ulrich Claesges. The Hague: Nijhoff, 1973.

Erfahrung und Urteil: Untersuchungen zur Genealogie der Logik. Edited by Ludwig Landgrebe. Hamburg: Claassen, 1954. *Experience and Judgment: Investigations in a Genealogy of Logic.* Translated by James S. Churchill and Karl Ameriks. Evanston, Ill.: Northwestern University Press, 1973.

Erste Philosophie. Part 1: *Kritische Ideengeschichte* (1923–24). Edited by Rudolf Boehm. The Hague: Nijhoff, 1956.

Erste Philosophie. Part 2: *Theorie der phänomenologischen Reduktion.* Edited by Rudolf Boehm. The Hague: Nijhoff, 1959.

Formale und Transzendentale Logik: Versuch einer Kritik der logischen Vernunft (1929). Edited by Paul Janssen. The Hague: Nijhoff, 1974. *Formal and Transcendental Logic.* Translated by Dorion Cairns. The Hague: Nijhoff, 1969.

Husserl: Shorter Works. Edited by Peter McCormick and Frederick Elliston. Notre Dame, Ind.: University of Notre Dame Press, 1981.

Die Idee der Phänomenologie: Fünf Vorlesungen. Edited by Walter Biemel. The Hague: Nijhoff, 1950. *The Idea of Phenomenology.* Translated by William P. Alston and George Nakhnikian. The Hague: Nijhoff, 1964.

Ideen zu einer reinen Phänomenologie und phänomenologischen Philosophie. Book 1: *Allgemeine Einführung in die reine Phänomenologie* (1913). 2 vols. Edited by Karl Schuhmann. The Hague: Nijhoff, 1976. *Ideas Pertaining to a Pure Phenomenology and to a Phenomenological Philosophy.* Book 1: *General Introduction to a Pure Phenomenology.* Translated by F. Kersten. The Hague: Nijhoff, 1982.

Ideen zu einer reinen Phänomenologie und phänomenologischen Philosophie. Book 2: *Phänomenologische Untersuchungen zur Konstitution.* Edited by Marly Biemel. The Hague: Nijhoff, 1952. *Ideas Pertaining to a Pure Phenomenology and to a Phenomenological Philosophy.* Book 2: *Studies in the Phenomenology of Constitution.* Translated by R. Rojcewicz and A. Schuwer. Dordrecht: Kluwer Academic Publishers, 1989.

Ideen zu einer reinen Phänomenologie und phänomenologischen Philosophie. Book 3: *Die Phänomenologie und die Fundamente der Wissenschaften.* Edited by Marly Biemel. The Hague: Nijhoff, 1953. *Ideas Pertaining to a Pure Phenomenology and to a Phenomenological Philosophy.* Book 3: *Phenomenology and the Foundations of the Sciences.* Translated by Ted E. Klein and William E. Pohl. The Hague: Nijhoff, 1980.

Die Krisis der europäischen Wissenschaften und die transzendentale Phänomenologie: Eine Einleitung in die phänomenologische Philosophie. Edited by Walter Biemel. The Hague: Nijhoff, 1954. *The Crisis of European Sciences and Transcendental Phenomenology: An Introduction to Phenomenological Philosophy.* Translated by David Carr. Evanston, Ill.: Northwestern University Press, 1970.

Logische Untersuchungen. 2 vols. Halle: Niemeyer, 1900–1901. Second edition in 3 vols. Halle: Niemeyer, 1913–21. *Logical Investigations.* Translated by J. M. Findlay. 2 vols. New York: Humanities Press, 1970.

Phänomenologische Psychologie (1925). Edited by Walter Biemel. The Hague: Nijhoff, 1962. *Phenomenological Psychology: Lectures, Summer Semester, 1925.* Translated by John Scanlon. The Hague: Nijhoff, 1977.

Phantasie, Bildbewusstsein, Erinnerung: Zur Phänomenologie der anschaulichen Vergegenwärtigungen. Texte aus dem Nachlass (1898–1925). Edited by E. Marbach. The Hague: Nijhoff, 1980.

"Philosophie als strenge Wissenschaft." *Logos* 1 (1910–11): 289–341. "Philosophy as Rigorous Science." In Quentin Lauer, *Edmund Husserl: Phenomenology and the Crisis of Philosophy,* 69–147. New York: Harper & Row, 1965.

Philosophie der Arithmetik: Psychologische und logische Untersuchungen. Vol. 1. Halle a.S.: Pfeffer, 1891.

Texte zur Phänomenologie des inneren Zeitbewusstseins (1893–1917). Edited by Rudolf Bernet. Hamburg: Meiner, 1985.

Über den Begriff der Zahl. Halle: F. Beyer, 1887. "On the Concept of Number. Psychological Analysis." Translated by Dallas Willard. *Philosophia Mathematica* 9 (1972): 44–52; 10 (1973): 37–87.

"Vienna Lecture." In *Crisis,* 269–99.

Zur Phänomenologie der Intersubjektivität. Texte aus dem Nachlass. Edited by Iso Kern. Vols. 1–3. The Hague: Nijhoff, 1973.

Zur Phänomenologie des inneren Zeitbewusstseins (1893–1917). Edited by Rudolf Boehm. The Hague: Nijhoff, 1966. *On the Phenomenology of the Consciousness of Internal Time (1893–1917).* Translated by John Barnett Brough. Dordrecht: Kluwer Academic Publishers, 1991.

| Books and Articles on
| Husserl's Phenomenology

Bachelard, Gaston. *Recherches sur les conditions de la connaissance.* Paris: Aubier, 1942.

Bachelard, Suzanne. *La logique de Husserl: Etude sur logique formelle et logique transcendentale.* Paris: Presses Universitaires de France, 1957.

Becker, O. "Die Philosophie Edmund Husserls." *Kantstudien* 35 (1929): 119–50.

Bera, M.-A., ed. *Husserl. Actes du troisième colloque internationale de phénoménologie, Royaumont, 23 au 29 avril 1957.* Cahiers de Royaumont: Philosophie, no. 3. Paris: Minuit, 1959.

Berger, Gaston. *Le cogito dans la philosophie de Husserl.* Paris: Aubier, 1941.

Bernet, Rudolf, et al. *Edmund Husserl: Darstellung seines Denkens.* Hamburg: Meiner, 1989.

Biemel, Walter. "Husserls Encyclopaedia Britannica Artikel und Heideggers Anmerkungen dazu." *Tijdschrift voor filosofie* 12 (1950): 246–80.

———. "Les phases décisives dans le développement de la philosophie de Husserl." In *Husserl,* ed. M.-A. Bera, 32–71.

———. "Réflexions à propos des recherches husserliennes de la Lebenswelt." *Tijdschrift voor filosofie* 33 (1971): 659–83.

Boehm, Rudolf. "Basic Reflections on Husserl's Phenomenological Reduction." *International Philosophical Quarterly* 5 (1965): 183–202.

———. Introduction to Husserl's *Erste Philosophie,* 2:xxx–xxxvii.

———. *Vom Gesichtspunkt der Phänomenologie.* The Hague: Nijhoff, 1968.

Brand, Gerd. "Edmund Husserl: Zur Phänomenologie der Intersubjektivität." *Philosophische Rundschau* 25 (1978): 54–80.

———. "Horizont, Welt, Geschichte." *Phänomenologische Forschungen* 5 (1977): 14–89.

———. "The Structure of the Life-world according to Husserl." *Man and World* 6 (1973): 143–62.

———. *Welt, Ich und Zeit.* The Hague: Nijhoff, 1955.

Brentano, Franz. *Psychologie vom empirischen Standpunkt.* Edited by Oskar Kraus. Leipzig: Felix Meiner, 1924.

Broekman, Jan. *Phänomenologie und Egologie: Faktisches und transzendentales Ego bei Edmund Husserl*. The Hague: Nijhoff, 1963.

Brough, John. "The Emergence of an Absolute Consciousness in Husserl's Early Writings on Time-Consciousness." *Man and World* 5 (1972): 298–326.

Claesges, Ulrich. "Zweideutigkeiten in Husserls Lebenswelt-Begriff." In *Perspektiven transzendentalphänomenologischer Forschung*, ed. Ulrich Claesges and K. Held, 85–101. The Hague: Nijhoff, 1972.

Couturat, Louis, ed. *Opuscules et fragments inédits de Leibniz*. Paris: Alcan, 1903.

Diemer, Alwin. *Edmund Husserl: Versuch einer systematischen Darstellung seiner Phänomenologie*. Meisenheim am Glan: Hain, 1956.

Drüe, Max. *Edmund Husserls System der phänomenologischen Psychologie*. Berlin: de Gruyter, 1963.

Dupré, Louis. "The Concept of Truth in Husserl's 'Logical Investigations.'" *Philosophy and Phenomenological Research* 24 (1963–64): 345–54.

Eley, Lothar. "Logik und Sprache." *Kantstudien* 63 (1972): 247–60.

Elliston, Frederick, and Peter McCormick, eds. *Husserl: Expositions and Appraisals*. Notre Dame, Ind.: University of Notre Dame Press, 1977.

Elveton, R. O., ed. *The Phenomenology of Edmund Husserl*. Chicago, Ill.: Quadrangle Books, 1970.

Farber, Marvin. *The Foundation of Phenomenology: Edmund Husserl and the Quest for a Rigorous Science of Philosophy*. Cambridge, Mass.: Harvard University Press, 1940.

Fink, Eugen. "Operative Begriffe in Husserls Phänomenologie." *Zeitschrift für philosophische Forschung* 11 (1957): 321–37.

———. "Die phänomenologische Philosophie Edmund Husserls in der gegenwärtigen Kritik." *Kantstudien* 38 (1933): 319–83.

———. "Das Problem der Phänomenologie Edmund Husserls." *Revue internationale de philosophie* 1 (1938): 226–70.

———. "Reflexionen zu Husserls phänomenologischer Reduktion." *Tijdschrift voor filosofie* 33 (1971): 540–58.

Gurwitsch, Aron. *The Field of Consciousness*. Pittsburgh, Pa.: Duquesne University Press, 1964.

———. "The Last Work of Edmund Husserl." *Philosophy and Phenomenological Research* 16 (1955–56): 370–99.

———. "The Last Work of Edmund Husserl. II: The *Lebenswelt*." In *Studies in Phenomenology and Psychology*, ed. Lester E. Embree, 397–448. Evanston, Ill.: Northwestern University Press, 1966.

———. "Présuppositions philosophiques de la logique." *Revue de métaphysique et de morale* 56 (1951): 395–405.

Heidegger, Martin. *Being and Time*. Trans. John Macquarrie and Edward Robinson. London: S.C.M. Press, 1962.

———. *Identität und Differenz*. Tübingen: Niemeyer, 1957.

Heimsoeth, Heinz. "Christian Wolffs Ontologie und die Prinzipienforschung Immanuel Kants." In *Studien zur Philosophie Immanuel Kants,* 1:1–92. Cologne: Kölner Universitäts Verlag, 1956–71.

Held, Klaus. *Lebendige Gegenwart: Die Frage nach der Seinsweise des transzendentalen Ich bei Edmund Husserl, entwickelt am Leitfaden der Zeitproblematik*. The Hague: Nijhoff, 1966.

Hohl, H. *Lebenswelt und Geschichte.* Munich: Alber, 1962.

Ingarden, Roman. "Le problème de la constitution et le sens de la réflexion constitutive chez Husserl." In *Husserl,* ed. M.-A. Bera, 242–64.

Janssen, Paul. *Geschichte und Lebenswelt: Ein Beitrag zur Diskussion von Husserls Spätwerk.* The Hague: Nijhoff, 1970.

Kelkel, Arion L. "Husserl et Kant: Réflexions à propos d'une thèse rècente." *Revue de métaphysique et de morale* 71 (1966): 154–98.

———. "Le problème de l'autre dans la phénoménologie transcendentale de Husserl." *Revue de métaphysique et de morale* 61 (1956): 40–52.

Kelkel, Arion Lothar, and René Schérer. *Husserl: Sa vie, son œuvre, avec un exposé de sa philosophie.* Paris: Presses Universitaires de France, 1964.

Kern, Iso. *Husserl und Kant: Eine Untersuchung über Husserls Verhältnis zu Kant und zum Neukantianismus.* The Hague: Nijhoff, 1964.

———. *Idee und Methode der Philosophie: Leitgedanken für eine Theorie der Vernunft.* Berlin: de Gruyter, 1975.

———. "The Three Ways to the Transcendental Phenomenological Reduction in the Philosophy of Edmund Husserl." In *Husserl: Expositions and Appraisals,* ed. F. Elliston and P. McCormick, 126–49. Notre Dame, Ind.: University of Notre Dame Press, 1977.

Kersten, Fred. "The Life-world Revisited." *Research in Phenomenology* 1 (1971): 33–62.

Kockelmans, Joseph J. *Edmund Husserl's Phenomenological Psychology.* Pittsburgh, Pa.: Duquesne University Press, 1967.

———. *A First Introduction to Husserl's Phenomenology.* Pittsburgh, Pa.: Duquesne University Press, 1967.

———. "Husserl and Kant on the Pure Ego." In *Husserl: Expositions and Appraisals,* ed. F. Elliston and P. McCormick, 69–285. Notre Dame, Ind.: University of Notre Dame Press, 1977.

———. "On the Meaning and Function of Experience in Husserl's Phenomenology." In *Der Idealismus und seine Gegenwart,* ed. Ute Guzzoni et al., 297–317. Hamburg: Meiner, 1976.

———. "Phenomenologico-Psychological and Transcendental Reductions in Husserl's *Crisis.*" *Analecta Husserliana* 2 (1972): 78–89.

———. "World-Constitution: Reflections on Husserl's Transcendental Idealism." *Analecta Husserliana* 1 (1971): 11–35.

Kockelmans, Joseph J., ed. *Phenomenology: The Philosophy of Edmund Husserl and Its Interpretation.* Garden City, N.Y.: Doubleday, 1967.

Kolakowski, Lezek. *Husserl and the Search for Certitude.* New Haven, Conn.: Yale University Press, 1975.

Landgrebe, Ludwig. "Husserls Phänomenologie und die Motive zu ihrer Umbildung." *Revue internationale de philosophie* 1 (1938): 277–316.

———. *Phänomenologie und Metaphysik.* Hamburg: Schröder, 1949.

———. "Reflexionen zu Husserls Konstitutionslehre." *Tijdschrift voor filosofie* 36 (1974): 466–82.

———. "Seinsregionen und regionale Ontologien in Husserl's Phänomenologie." *Studium Generale* 9 (1956): 313–24.

———. *Der Weg der Phänomenologie.* Gütersloh: Gerd Mohn, 1963.

———. "The World as Phenomenological Problem." *Philosophy and Phenomenological Research* 1 (1940–41): 38–58.

Lauer, Quentin. *Phénoménologie de Husserl: Essai sur la genèse de l'intentionnalité.* Paris: Presses Universitaires de France, 1955.
———. *The Triumph of Subjectivity.* New York: Fordham University Press, 1958.
Levinas, Emmanuel. "L'œuvre d'Edmond Husserl." *Revue philosophique de France et de l'Étranger* 65 (1950): 33–85.
———. *Théorie de l'intuition dans la phénoménologie de Husserl.* Paris: Vrin, 1963.
Linschoten, Jan. "On Falling Asleep." In *Phenomenological Psychology: The Dutch School,* ed. Joseph J. Kockelmans, 79–117. The Hague: Nijhoff, 1987.
Marbach, Eduard. *Das Problem des Ich in der Phänomenologie Husserls.* The Hague: Nijhoff, 1974.
Merleau-Ponty, Maurice. *Phenomenology of Perception.* Trans. Colin Smith. London: Routledge & Kegan Paul, 1962.
Mohanty, J. N. *The Concept of Intentionality.* St. Louis, Mo.: W. H. Green, 1972.
———. *Edmund Husserl's Theory of Meaning.* The Hague: Nijhoff, 1964.
———. *Readings on Edmund Husserl's "Logical Investigations."* The Hague: Nijhoff, 1977.
Natanson, Maurice. *Edmund Husserl: Philosopher of Infinite Tasks.* Evanston, Ill.: Northwestern University Press, 1973.
———. "The Empirical and Transcendental Ego." In *For Roman Ingarden: Nine Essays in Phenomenology and Literature, Philosophy, and the Social Sciences,* edited by A.-T. Tymieniecka, 44–54. The Hague: Nijhoff, 1962.
Osborn, Andrew D. *The Philosophy of Edmund Husserl in Its Development from His Mathematical Interests to His First Conception of Phenomenology in "Logical Investigations."* New York: International Press, 1934.
Paci, Enzo. *Il problema del tempo nella fenomenologia di Husserl.* Milan: La Goliardica, 1960.
Ricoeur, Paul. "Analyses et problèmes dans 'Ideen II' de Husserl." In *Phénoménologie—Existence,* ed. H. Birault et al., 23–76. Paris: Gallimard, 1953.
———. "Étude sur les 'Méditations Cartésiennes' de Husserl." *Revue philosophique de Louvain* 52 (1954): 75–109.
———. *Husserl: An Analysis of His Phenomenology.* Trans. E. G. Ballard and L. E. Embree. Evanston, Ill.: Northwestern University Press, 1967.
———. "Kant et Husserl." *Kantstudien* 46 (1954): 44–67.
Schuhmann, Karl. *Die Fundamentalbetrachtung der Phänomenologie: Zum Weltproblem in der Philosophie Edmund Husserls.* The Hague: Nijhoff, 1971.
Seebohm, Thomas. *Die Bedingungen der Möglichkeit der Transzendental-Philosophie: Edmund Husserls transzendental-phänomenologischer Ansatz, dargestellt im Anschluss an seine Kant-Kritik.* Bonn: Bouvier, 1962.
Sepp, Hans Rainer, ed. *Edmund Husserl und die phänomenologische Bewegung: Zeugnisse in Text und Bild.* Freiburg: Alber, 1988.
Sokolowski, Robert. *The Formation of Husserl's Concept of Constitution.* The Hague: Nijhoff, 1964.

355 | B I B L I O G R A P H Y

————. "The Husserl Archives and the Editions of Husserl's Works." *The New Scholasticism* 38 (1964): 473–82.

————. "Immanent Constitution in Husserl's Lectures on Time." *Philosophy and Phenomenological Research* 24 (1963–64): 530–51.

————. "The Logic of Parts and Wholes in Husserl's *Logical Investigations*." *Philosophy and Phenomenological Research* 28 (1967–68): 537–53.

————. "The Structure and Content of Husserl's *Logical Investigations*." *Inquiry* 14 (1971): 318–47.

Spiegelberg, Herbert. *The Phenomenological Movement: A Historical Introduction*. 2 vols. The Hague: Nijhoff, 1960.

Strasser, Stephen. "Beschouwingen over het vraagstuk van de apodicticiteit en de critische verantwoording van de phaenomenologie." *Tijdschrift voor filosofie* 8 (1946): 226–70.

Ströker, Elisabeth. *Husserls transzendentale Phänomenologie*. Frankfurt: Klostermann, 1987.

Thévenaz, Pierre. *What is Phenomenology?* Trans. James M. Edie. Chicago, Ill.: Quadrangle Books, 1962.

Tugendhat, Ernst. *Der Wahrheitsbegriff bei Husserl und Heidegger*. Berlin: de Gruyter, 1970.

Van Breda, H. L. "Le sauvetage de l'héritage husserlien et la fondation des Archives-Husserl." In *Husserl et la pensée moderne: Actes du deuxième colloque international de phénoménologie,* Krefeld, 1–3 novembre, 1956, ed. H. L. Van Breda and J. Taminiaux, 1–77. The Hague: Nijhoff, 1959.

Van Breda, Herman L. "La réduction phénoménologique." In *Husserl,* ed. M.-A. Bera, 307–18.

Van Breda, Herman L., ed. *Problèmes actuels de la phénoménologie*. Paris: Desclée de Brouwer, 1952.

Van Breda, Herman L., and J. Taminiaux, eds. *Edmund Husserl: 1859–1959. Recueil commémoratif publié à l'occasion du centenaire de la naissance du Philosophe*. The Hague: Nijhoff, 1959.

Van Peursen, Cornelis. "La notion du temps de l'ego transcendental chez Husserl." In *Husserl,* ed. M.-A. Bera, 196–207.

Wahl, Jean. *Husserl*. 2 vols. Paris: Centre de Documentation Universitaire, 1958.

————. "Notes sur la première partie de *Erfahrung und Urteil* de Husserl." *Revue de métaphysique et de morale* 56 (1951): 6–34.

————. "Notes sur quelques aspects empiristes de la pensée de Husserl." *Revue de métaphysique et de morale* 57 (1952): 17–45.

————. *L'ouvrage posthume de Husserl: La "Krisis."* Paris: Centre de Documentation Universitaire, 1961.

Welch, E. Parl. *The Philosophy of Edmund Husserl: The Origin and Development of His Phenomenology*. New York: Octagon Books, 1965.

Willard, Dallas. *Logic and the Objectivity of Knowledge: A Study in Husserl's Early Philosophy*. Athens: Ohio University Press, 1984.

I N D E X

I Index of Names

Aristotle, 66, 67, 133, 199, 305

Bacon, Francis, 259
Baumgarten, Alexander, 192, 259
Berger, Gaston, 327
Berkeley, George, 33, 174, 175, 193, 194, 195
Bernet, Rudolf, 7, 271
Biemel, Marly, 6
Biemel, Walter, 6, 9, 32
Boehm, Rudolf, 6, 200, 225, 271, 309
Bolzano, Bernhard, 2, 4, 134
Brand, Gerd, 158
Brentano, Franz, 2, 31, 32, 33, 40, 42, 53, 54, 89, 90, 92, 93, 110, 111, 158, 271, 273

Cassirer, Ernst, 324
Claesges, Ulrich, 7

Descartes, René, 5, 11, 12, 16, 55, 90, 118, 123, 124, 133, 173, 174, 175, 176, 177, 184, 188, 189, 190, 191, 192, 193, 195, 196, 199, 204, 205, 215, 216, 219, 220, 225, 227, 256, 258, 277, 304, 308, 311, 314, 320, 321, 323, 324
Diemer, Alwin, 158
Dilthey, Wilhelm, 12, 53
Drüe, Max, 234, 238, 239, 240

Einstein, Albert, 339
Eley, Lothar, 7
Erdmann, Johann, 35

Fechner, Gustav Theodor, 55
Fichte, Johann, 4, 329
Fink, Eugen, 6, 7, 155, 234, 240
Fleischer, Margot, 7
Frege, Gottlob, 3, 35, 36

Gadamer, Hans-Georg, 347
Galileo, 189, 256, 336, 339, 341
Goclenius, 66

Hartmann, Eduard von, 309
Hartmann, Nicolai, 347
Hegel, Georg, 30
Heidegger, Martin, 4, 6, 271, 347
Helmholtz, Hermann von, 55
Hering, Ewald, 30, 31
Herz, Marcus, 200
Hobbes, Thomas, 90
Hume, David, 2, 4, 12, 33, 90, 146, 147, 174, 175, 193, 194, 195, 197, 198, 269, 321, 323

IJsseling, Samuel, 7

James, William, 53
Jansen, Paul, 7
Jaspers, Karl, 347
Joel, Karl, 306

Kant, Immanuel, 4, 10, 11, 12, 30, 67, 133, 166, 167, 188, 192, 193, 195, 197, 198, 199, 200, 201, 202, 203, 204, 205, 227, 260, 277, 306, 309, 310, 311, 320, 321, 323, 324, 325, 327, 328, 329
Kern, Iso, 7, 306, 325, 326
Königsberger, Leo, 2
Kronecker, Leopold, 1, 32
Kummer, Ernst, 1, 32

Landgrebe, Ludwig, 6, 63, 330
Lauer, Quentin, 226, 278
Leibniz, Georg, 4, 11, 66, 133, 192, 196, 245, 246, 247, 252, 254, 257, 258, 259, 260, 263, 311
Lévy-Bruhl, Lucien, 338
Linschoten, Jan, 167
Lipps, Theodor, 35, 36, 54, 279

▌Index of Subjects